Introduction to
Discrete Mathematics

The Prindle, Weber & Schmidt Series in Mathematics

Althoen and Bumcrot, *Introduction to Discrete Mathematics*
Brown and Sherbert, *Introductory Linear Algebra with Applications*
Buchthal and Cameron, *Modern Abstract Algebra*
Burden and Faires, *Numerical Analysis*, Third Edition
Cullen, *Linear Algebra and Differential Equations*
Cullen, *Mathematics for the Biosciences*
Dobyns, Steinbach, and Lunsford, *The Electronic Study Guide for Precalculus Algebra*
Eves, *In Mathematical Circles*
Eves, *Mathematical Circles Adieu*
Eves, *Mathematical Circles Revisited*
Eves, *Mathematical Circles Squared*
Eves, *Return to Mathematical Circles*
Fletcher and Patty, *Foundations of Higher Mathematics*
Geltner and Peterson, *Geometry for College Students*
Gilbert and Gilbert, *Elements of Modern Algebra*, Second Edition
Gobran, *Beginning Algebra*, Fourth Edition
Gobran, *College Algebra*
Gobran, *Intermediate Algebra*, Fourth Edition
Gordon, *Calculus and the Computer*
Hall, *Algebra for College Students*
Hall and Bennett, *College Algebra with Applications*
Hartfiel and Hobbs, *Elementary Linear Algebra*
Hunkins and Mugridge, *Applied Finite Mathematics*, Second Edition
Kaufmann, *Algebra for College Students*, Second Edition
Kaufmann, *Algebra with Trigonometry for College Students*
Kaufmann, *College Algebra*
Kaufmann, *College Algebra and Trigonometry*
Kaufmann, *Elementary Algebra for College Students*, Second Edition
Kaufmann, *Intermediate Algebra for College Students*, Second Edition
Kaufmann, *Precalculus*
Kaufmann, *Trigonometry*
Keisler, *Elementary Calculus: An Infinitesimal Approach*, Second Edition
Konvisser, *Elementary Linear Algebra with Applications*
Laufer, *Discrete Mathematics and Applied Modern Algebra*
Nicholson, *Linear Algebra with Applications*
Pasahow, *Mathematics for Electronics*
Powers, *Elementary Differential Equations*

Powers, *Elementary Differential Equations with Boundary Value Problems*
Powers, *Elementary Differential Equations with Linear Algebra*
Proga, *Arithmetic and Algebra*
Proga, *Basic Mathematics*, Second Edition
Radford, Vavra, and Rychlicki, *Introduction to Technical Mathematics*
Radford, Vavra, and Rychlicki, *Technical Mathematics with Calculus*
Rice and Strange, *Calculus and Analytic Geometry for Engineering Technology*
Rice and Strange, *College Algebra*, Third Edition
Rice and Strange, *Plane Trigonometry*, Fourth Edition
Rice and Strange, *Technical Mathematics*
Rice and Strange, *Technical Mathematics and Calculus*
Schelin and Bange, *Mathematical Analysis for Business and Economics*, Second Edition
Steinbach and Lunsford, *The Electronic Study Guide for Trigonometry*
Strnad, *Introductory Algebra*
Swokowski, *Algebra and Trigonometry with Analytic Geometry*, Sixth Edition
Swokowski, *Calculus with Analytic Geometry*, Second Alternate Edition
Swokowski, *Calculus with Analytic Geometry*, Fourth Edition
Swokowski, *Fundamentals of Algebra and Trigonometry*, Sixth Edition
Swokowski, *Fundamentals of College Algebra*, Sixth Edition
Swokowski, *Fundamentals of Trigonometry*, Sixth Edition
Swokowski, *Precalculus: Functions and Graphs*, Fifth Edition
Tan, *Applied Calculus*
Tan, *Applied Finite Mathematics*, Second Edition
Tan, *Calculus for the Managerial, Life, and Social Sciences*
Tan, *College Mathematics*, Second Edition
Venit and Bishop, *Elementary Linear Algebra*, Second Edition
Venit and Bishop, *Elementary Linear Algebra*, Alternate Second Edition
Willard, *Calculus and Its Applications*, Second Edition
Willerding, *A First Course in College Mathematics*, Fourth Edition
Wood and Capell, *Arithmetic*
Wood, Capell, and Hall, *Developmental Mathematics*, Third Edition
Wood, Capell, and Hall, *Intermediate Algebra*
Wood, Capell, and Hall, *Introductory Algebra*
Zill, *A First Course in Differential Equations with Applications*, Third Edition
Zill, *Calculus with Analytic Geometry*, Second Edition
Zill, *Differential Equations with Boundary-Value Problems*

Introduction to
Discrete Mathematics

Steven C. Althoen
University of Michigan–Flint

Robert J. Bumcrot
Hofstra University

PWS-KENT Publishing Company
Boston

PWS-KENT
Publishing Company

20 Park Plaza
Boston, Massachusetts 02116

Copyright © 1988 by PWS-KENT Publishing Company.

PWS-KENT Publishing Company is a division of Wadsworth, Inc.

Library of Congress Cataloging-in-Publication Data

Althoen, Steven C.
    Introduction to discrete mathematics/Steven C. Althoen, Robert
J. Bumcrot.
        p.   cm.
    Includes index.
    ISBN 0-534-91504-3
    1. Mathematics—1961–   . 2. Electronic data processing—Mathematics.
I. Bumcrot, Robert J., 1936–   . II. Title.
QA39.2.A49   1988   87-19831
510—dc19   CIP

Printed in the United States of America.
88 89 90 91 92 — 10 9 8 7 6 5 4 3 2 1

Sponsoring Editor   *Tom Stone*
Production Coordinator   *Elise Kaiser*
Production   *Greg Hubit Bookworks*
Composition   *H. Charlesworth & Co., Ltd.*
Interior/Cover Design   *Elise Kaiser*
Interior Illustration   *Carl Brown*
Cover Printer   *Algen Press Corp.*
Text Printer/Binder   *Halliday Lithograph*

Cover graphic by Sue Mabry. Copyright © 1987 by
Unique Photo Arts, Inc., Atlanta, Georgia.

To Hamilton

Preface

Computer science is a voracious consumer of mathematics. In order to get beyond the level of manipulating friendly packaged programs, the student of computer science must become familiar with a wide range of mathematical topics. The computer scientist's understanding of mathematics must not be superficial, but rather a deep comprehension of mathematical thinking itself. In order to create new and valuable products in computer science, one must be able to think abstractly, just like—or almost like—a pure mathematician. Consider the following off-hand remark from the 1940s attributed to John von Neumann (1903–1957), one of the great mathematicians of the twentieth century, and a founder of computer science: *"Instead of just storing data, why not store instructions?"* The transition from the mechanical process of storing data to the abstract concept of storing instructions is very significant for computer scientists.

Introduction to Discrete Mathematics is designed as an introduction to those mathematical topics necessary for the future computer scientist. This book was written for the freshman/sophomore level introduction to discrete mathematics course currently offered at most colleges and universities and at an increasing number of two-year schools. The text assumes a familiarity with mathematics consistent with a standard high school level education. No knowledge of programming languages is assumed, and therefore the text is not tied to any specific language.

Many fields of mathematics contribute to computer science: logic, combinatorics (in a wide sense), linear algebra, algebraic structures, mathematical machines and languages, and the calculus, to name the more significant. Our selection of topics for this course was based on three criteria:

1. Topics should be suitable for **first-year** college students with a reasonable, but not extraordinary, background in high school level mathematics.

2. Topics included in the text are those generally accepted as important and recommended by most (if not all) teachers of computer science and their professional societies.

3. Study of these topics will aid in the development of the student's skill in abstract reasoning.

A great number of mathematical topics fall under the general label "discrete."

The topics in this text are those that will provide the beginning computer science student with a solid and appropriate mathematical basis upon which to build. It is not our goal to offer a concrete definition of discrete mathematics in this preface. Rather, the definition will become clear as the student works through the book.

This text is unified by the use of **algorithms**. In order to design, run, and analyze computer programs (major activities of computer scientists), students must be comfortable with the construction and analysis of algorithms. We present algorithms for a wide variety of tasks, such as graph coloring, graph planarity, and minimization of machine states. Theoretical topics are presented in an intuitive manner and are immediately followed by detailed examples. To facilitate student understanding of these topics, we avoid the technicalities and limitations of "real" computer languages while still presenting the programming process. Examples are presented with the use of a powerful and friendly IMaginary COMputer (IMCOM). This will ensure that students with varied backgrounds will be able to truly participate in the combination of mathematical topics and the activities of computer science. We hope these features will contribute to students' ability to think abstractly while introducing them to the mathematical topics that will become increasingly important as their education continues.

ACKNOWLEDGMENTS

We would like to thank all two hundred forty-eight students who over the last few years studied from various versions of this material in courses at Hofstra and the University of Michigan–Flint. Special thanks to Paul Garlick, Ken Bartunek, and Nancy Anderson for their valuable comments. Inge Garlick and Wayne Brillhart taught from portions of the text and provided many valuable suggestions. Ken Shilling taught from almost the entire manuscript, and his specific suggestions and corrections were extremely helpful during the completion of this text. We would also like to thank Karen Anway, who solved every exercise in the book to ensure an accurate presentation.

The following mathematicians who reviewed various versions of the text provided a detailed critical basis that guided us in the development of this book. Their comments made this a substantially better text: V. K. Balakrishnan, University of Maine; Michael Ecker, Pennsylvania State University; Kent Harris, Western Illinois University; Seth Hochwald, Irvine Valley College; John Konvalina, University of Nebraska–Omaha; and George Schultz, St. Petersburg Junior College.

SUPPLEMENTS

An *Instructor's Manual* is available for this text. The manual contains answers to the even-numbered exercises; in addition, there is a special commentary and a test bank for each section.

We would greatly appreciate any comments on the text and the manual, including misprints and (heaven forbid) wrong answers.

Contents

CHAPTER ONE | ALGORITHMS AND DATA STRUCTURES | **1**

   1.1 Description of Algorithms **2**
   1.2 Arrays **7**
   1.3 Sets **18**
   1.4 Matrices **28**

CHAPTER TWO | COMBINATORICS | **45**

   2.1 Enumeration **47**
   2.2 Induction **55**
   2.3 Recursion **62**
   2.4 Algorithm Efficiency **68**

CHAPTER THREE | LOGIC AND CIRCUITS | **77**

   3.1 Switches and Gates **78**
   3.2 Circuits and Propositions **83**
   3.3 Boolean Algebra **89**
   3.4 Minimal Forms **99**

CHAPTER FOUR | GRAPHS | **109**

   4.1 Introduction **110**
   4.2 Trees and Searching **123**
   4.3 Eulerian Graphs and Hamiltonian Circuits **144**
   4.4 Minimal Paths and Circuits **158**
   4.5 Spanning Trees **167**

CHAPTER FIVE   GRAPH ALGORITHMS   183

                      5.1 Planarity   184
                      5.2 Graph Coloring   199
                      5.3 Networks   206
                      5.4 Error Propagation   228

CHAPTER SIX   RELATIONS, ALGEBRAIC SYSTEMS, AND MACHINES   247

                      6.1 Relational Closures and Equivalence Relations   248
                      6.2 Posets, Lattices, and Boolean Algebras   258
                      6.3 Monoids and Groups   264
                      6.4 Symmetries, Permutations, Rings, and Fields   277
                      6.5 Machines   283

                      ANSWERS TO ODD-NUMBERED EXERCISES   300

                      SYMBOL INDEX   337

                      SUBJECT INDEX   339

Introduction to Discrete Mathematics

CHAPTER

ONE

Algorithms and Data Structures

■ **1.1 Description of Algorithms**

□ **1.2 Arrays**

■ **1.3 Sets**

□ **1.4 Matrices**

1.1
Description of Algorithms

An **algorithm** is a list of instructions that will always produce the answer to any problem of a specified type. A recipe for oatmeal cookies is a sort of algorithm, as is a road map. The word *algorithm* stems from the name of the ancient Central Asian country Khorezm, which is now the Soviet Socialist Republics of the Kazakh, Turkmen, and Uzbek. In about A.D. 825 a major work on algebra and the Indian system of numerical notation was written by Mohammed, son of Musa, from Khorezm; that is, by *Mohammed ibn Musa al-Khowarizmi*. An 1857 Latin translation of this text begins, in English translation, "Spoken has Algoritmi, ..." Incidentally, from the title of al-Khowarizmi's text, *Hisab al-jabr w'al-muqabalah*, we get our word *algebra*. The first algorithm concerned the use of Hindu-Arabic numerals. We shall present a related algorithm (on binary notation) later in this section. The construction and analysis of algorithms is a major theme of this book.

We are interested in algorithms for problems in mathematics and data processing. For the first example, consider the equation

$$ax = b \tag{1}$$

where a and b are given numbers. We seek a solution algorithm that, given a and b, will return all numbers x for which Equation (1) is true. The simple formula $x = b/a$ gives the answer, *unless* $a = 0$. Since an algorithm must *always* work, we must also consider the special case $a = 0$; that is, the equation $0x = b$. If $b \neq 0$, then there are no numbers x such that $0x = b$. But if $b = 0$, then every number is a solution, because $0x = 0$ for any number x. The algorithm can now be described.

ALGORITHM 1.1

To solve $ax = b$.

If $a \neq 0$, then the answer is b/a.

If $a = 0$ and $b \neq 0$, then there is no answer.

If $a = 0$ and $b = 0$, then every number is an answer.

Algorithms will often be presented as programs for a computer. In this book we work with IMCOM, an *IM*aginary *COM*puter with great capabilities. IMCOM reads all data needed for a problem, no matter how it is presented, without having to be so instructed. IMCOM can do all arithmetic and analytic operations in ordinary mathematical notation; for instance, it understands $3x$ and x^2, so there is no need to use the BASIC formats: $3*x$ and $x \wedge 2$. IMCOM will write (that is, print out) anything that is enclosed in quotation marks, replacing variables by their current values. For instance, if $x = 78$ and $P = $ Carter, when the instruction

"In 19x, P was president."

is reached, then IMCOM will write

In 1978, Carter was president.

An IMCOM **program** is a list of instructions. IMCOM always begins with the first instruction and, *unless told otherwise*, proceeds to the next instruction and so on until told to stop. The imaginary nature of IMCOM, which frees us from worry about input–output formats and precise punctuation, implies that programs in this book are really what are often called pseudo-programs. If you know or are learning a programming language such as BASIC, PASCAL, or ALGOL, you should be able to turn IMCOM programs into programs that will run on a real machine.

Two useful types of instructions are the conditional instruction and the assignment instruction. A **conditional instruction** is of the form

<u>If</u> ... statement ... <u>then</u> ... action

When IMCOM reaches this instruction, if the statement is true, then it will execute the action; if the statement is false, it will go on to the next instruction. The next instruction can even be included in the conditional instruction as follows:

<u>If</u> ... statement ... <u>then</u> ... action; <u>otherwise</u> ... action ...

An **assignment instruction** is of the form

$$x \leftarrow y$$

(sometimes written $x := y$), which is read "assign y to x," or "replace x by y." Here y may be a complicated expression, perhaps involving x itself. For instance, if IMCOM executes the instruction $x \leftarrow 3$, then in later instructions x will be 3 until another assignment to x is made. If the next assignment is $x \leftarrow x + 4$, then x will be 7. If the next instruction is $x \leftarrow x^2$, then x will become 49.

IMCOM will accept any previously written program as a single instruction. For this reason, many programs are given names. Here is Algorithm 1.1 in program form.

■ PROGRAM 1.1   **Solve $ax = b$.**

1. If $a = 0$ then go to {instruction} 4
2. $c \leftarrow b/a$
3. "The answer is c." STOP
4. If $b = 0$ then go to 6
5. "There is no answer." STOP
6. "Every number is an answer." STOP ■

(Note that Instructions 2 and 3 could be replaced by the single instruction: "The answer is b/a." STOP.)

Each time an instruction is executed, a *step* is taken. To *run* a program, we write the sequence of steps taken and then the final output. It is often helpful to add some comments in a program or a run. Comments will always be made within {braces}, either above or next to the instruction or step. Here are three runs of Program 1.1.

Solve $7x = 14$.

$\{a = 7; b = 14\}$
$a = 0$. False. $\{7 \neq 0\}$
$c \leftarrow 2$. $\{b/a = 14/7 = 2\}$

The answer is 2.

Solve $0x = -5$.

$\{a = 0; b = -5\}$
$a = 0$. True.
$\{$Go to Step 4.$\}$
$b = 0$. False. $\{-5 \neq 0\}$

There is no answer.

Solve $0x = 0$.

$\{a = 0; b = 0\}$
$a = 0$. True.
$\{$Go to 4.$\}$
$b = 0$. True.
$\{$Go to 6.$\}$

Every number is an answer.

For a more interesting algorithm consider binary notation for positive integers. This is used in many ways in mathematics and computer science.

First let us review "ordinary" notation, that is, decimal notation. **Decimal notation** is based on the number *ten*. (*Decimus* is the Latin word for "one tenth.") It uses as **digits** the nonnegative integers less than ten: 0, 1, 2, 3, 4, 5, 6, 7, 8, 9 in combination with the **powers** of ten: $10^0 = 1$, $10^1 = 10$, $10^2 = 100$, $10^3 = 1000$, ... For example, the decimal notation 7043 signifies

$$7 \cdot 10^3 + 0 \cdot 10^2 + 4 \cdot 10^1 + 3 \cdot 10^0 = 7000 + 0 + 40 + 3$$

Binary notation is based on the number *two*. (*Bini* is the Latin word for "two by two.") The digits in binary notation are the nonnegative integers less than two: 0 and 1. The fact that only two digits are used accounts in large part for the importance of binary notation in computer science: in an electronic circuit, 1 may be represented by a current and 0 by no current. The digits 0 and 1 are used in combination with the powers of two: $2^0 = 1$, $2^1 = 2$, $2^2 = 4$, $2^3 = 8$, ... For example, the binary numeral 100101 signifies

$$1 \cdot 2^5 + 0 \cdot 2^4 + 0 \cdot 2^3 + 1 \cdot 2^2 + 0 \cdot 2^1 + 1 \cdot 2^0$$

which in decimal notation is

$$32 + 0 + 0 + 4 + 0 + 1 = 37$$

To write a positive integer n in binary notation, begin by finding the largest positive integer p such that $2^p \leqslant n$. Then the binary notation for n is $1 \_ \_ \_ \cdots \_$, where there are p digits to be filled in. Replace n by $n - 2^p$ and move one place to the right. If $2^{p-1} > n$ (the *new* n), enter 0 and move right; if $2^{p-1} \leqslant n$, enter 1, replace n by $n - 2^{p-1}$, and move right. Continue to the end. Here is the algorithm in program form.

PROGRAM 1.2   **Write n in binary notation.**

1. $p \leftarrow 0$
2. If $2^{p+1} > n$ then go to 5. {You have the largest $2^p \leqslant n$.}
3. $p \leftarrow p + 1$. Go to 2
4. If $2^p > n$ then go to 8
5. "1"
6. If $p = 0$ then STOP
7. $n \leftarrow n - 2^p$. $p \leftarrow p - 1$. Go to 4
8. "0"
9. If $p = 0$ then STOP
10. $p \leftarrow p - 1$. Go to 4   ■

Let's run the program for $n = 9$.

Write 9 in binary notation.
_____

$p \leftarrow 0$.
$2^{p+1} > 9$. False. $\{2^{0+1} = 2\}$
$p \leftarrow 1$.
$2^{p+1} > 9$. False. $\{2^{1+1} = 4\}$
$p \leftarrow 2$.
$2^{p+1} > 9$. False. $\{2^{2+1} = 8\}$
$p \leftarrow 3$.
$2^{p+1} > 9$. True. $\{2^{3+1} = 16\}$
"1"
$p = 0$. False. $\{p = 3\}$
$n \leftarrow 1$. $p \leftarrow 2$. $\{9 - 2^3 = 1, 3 - 1 = 2\}$
$2^p > 1$. True. $\{2^2 = 4\}$
"0"
$p = 0$. False. $\{p = 2\}$
$p \leftarrow 1$.

$2^p > 1$. True. $\{2^1 = 2\}$
"0"
$p = 0$. False. $\{p = 1\}$
$p \leftarrow 0$.
$2^p > 1$. False. $\{2^0 = 1\}$
"1"
$p = 0$. True.

_____
1001

CHECK $1001 = 1 \cdot 2^3 + 0 \cdot 2^2 + 0 \cdot 2^1 + 1 \cdot 2^0 = 8 + 0 + 0 + 1 = 9$.

EXERCISES

In Exercises 1–4 describe algorithms (not programs) to solve the equations for x, where a, b, c are given numbers.

1. $ax + b = 0$

2. $a/x = b$

3. $abx = c$

4. $ab/x = c$

In Exercises 5–8 write (IMCOM) programs for the given algorithms.

5. The algorithm for Exercise 1

6. The algorithm for Exercise 2

7. The algorithm for Exercise 3

8. The algorithm for Exercise 4

In Exercises 9–12 write the output of the given programs.

9. **1.** $a \leftarrow b$. **2.** $b \leftarrow a$. **3.** "ab" STOP.

10. **1.** $a \leftarrow b$. **2.** $b \leftarrow c$. **3.** $c \leftarrow d$. **4.** "$abcd$" STOP.

11. **1.** $c \leftarrow a$. **2.** $a \leftarrow b$. **3.** $b \leftarrow c$. **4.** "ab" STOP.

12. **1.** $d \leftarrow a$. **2.** $e \leftarrow b$. **3.** $a \leftarrow c$. **4.** $c \leftarrow e$. **5.** $b \leftarrow d$. **6.** "abc" STOP.

In Exercises 13–18 find how many steps IMCOM takes to do the program.

13. **1.** $n \leftarrow 0$. **2.** If $n = 4$ then STOP. **3.** $n \leftarrow n + 1$. Go to 2.

14. **1.** $n \leftarrow 0$. **2.** If $n = 4$ then STOP. **3.** $n \leftarrow n + 2$. Go to 2.

15. **1.** $n \leftarrow 0$. **2.** If $n = 4$ then STOP. **3.** $n \leftarrow n + 3$. Go to 2.

16. **1.** $n \leftarrow 1$. **2.** If $n = 64$ then STOP. **3.** $n \leftarrow 2n$. Go to 2.

17. **1.** $n \leftarrow 100$. **2.** If $n < 1$ then STOP. **3.** $n \leftarrow n/2$. Go to 2.

18. **1.** $n \leftarrow 1$. **2.** If $n \geqslant 1000$ then STOP. **3.** $n \leftarrow 3n$. Go to 2.

In Exercises 19 and 20 convert the binary numerals to decimal numerals.

19. 1101, 1011, 1001010

20. 10010, 11000, 10101010

In Exercises 21 and 22 run Program 1.2.

21. Write 38 in binary notation.

22. Write 29 in binary notation.

The **meet** and **join** of two binary numbers a, b, denoted $a \wedge b$ and $a \vee b$, respectively, are found as follows. First, if a and b do not have the same number of digits, then adjoin 0s on the left of the shorter number until they have the same length. For example, if $a = 10101$ and $b = 1100110$, write $a = 0010101$ so that a and b have seven digits each. Then the meet, $a \wedge b$, has 1 at each place where *both a and b* have 1 and has 0 at all other places. The join, $a \vee b$, has 1 at each place where *a or b* (or both) have 1 and has 0 at all other places (that is, at places where both a and b have 0). Thus,

$$
\begin{array}{rccccccc}
a = & 0 & 0 & 1 & 0 & 1 & 0 & 1 \\
b = & 1 & 1 & 0 & 0 & 1 & 1 & 0 \\
\hline
a \wedge b = & 0 & 0 & 0 & 0 & 1 & 0 & 0 \\
a \vee b = & 1 & 1 & 1 & 0 & 1 & 1 & 1
\end{array}
$$

23. Find $101101 \wedge 1110$ and $101101 \vee 1110$.

24. Convert 67 and 28 to binary, find their meet and join, and convert the answers back to base ten.

25. **Ternary notation** uses the digits 0, 1, 2 in combination with the powers of 3: 1, 3, 9, ... Write a program to convert any positive integer n from decimal to ternary notation. (*Terni* is Latin for "three each.")

26. Run the program of Exercise 25 for $n = 78$.

27. **Octal** (from the Latin *octo*, "eight") **notation**, which is used in computer design, uses the digits 0, 1, 2, 3, 4, 5, 6, 7 in combination with the powers of 8: 1, 8, 64, ... Describe a simple algorithm to write a binary number in octal notation. Use your algorithm to convert 101011110 and 110000001101 from binary to octal.

28. (See Exercise 27.) Describe a simple algorithm to write an octal numeral in binary notation. Use your algorithm to convert 347 and 2305 from octal to binary.

Binary notation is natural for computer circuits where 0 represents "no current" and 1 represents "current." However, it requires too much space to be convenient for output. While decimal notation is a familiar notation, it is much easier to convert from binary to base 8 or base 16. **Base 16 notation** is called **hexidecimal** (from the Greek εκκαιδεκα for "sixteen").

Hexidecimal notation is used for computer "dumps," which list the entire contents of the computer memory. It is also used to number the tracks on a floppy disk. It is even used to represent the characters in the word processor on which this text was originally typed. Hexidecimal uses the digits 0, 1, 2, 3, 4, 5, 6, 7, 8, 9, A, B, C, D, E, F in combination with the powers of 16: 1, 16, 256, 4096, ...

29. Write the following hexidecimal numerals in decimal notation: A1D, 2CE, BAD.

30. Write the following decimal numerals in hexidecimal notation: 27, 150, 37298.

31. (See Exercise 27.) Describe a simple algorithm to write a hexidecimal numeral in binary notation. Use your algorithm to convert A1D, 2CE, and BAD from hexidecimal to binary.

32. Describe a simple algorithm to write a binary numeral in hexidecimal notation. Use your algorithm to convert 101100010101 and 10011001011 from binary to hexidecimal.

Arrays

People and computers store data in many ways. A **data structure** is a mathematical model of a way to store information. Some of the important data structures in this book are called arrays, graphs, matrices, sequences, and sets. IMCOM stores all data in arrays. In fact, nearly all the data structures we consider can be viewed as arrays.

A **linear** (or one-dimensional) **array** may be viewed as a row of cells numbered 1, 2, 3, and so on:

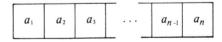

The number of a cell is called its **address**. In IMCOM any amount of data may be stored in a cell, and there are enough cells to store any number of pieces of data. In a real computer each of these capacities would be bounded.

Suppose that each of the first n cells of a linear array A contains one piece of data. Then the datum at address i, where $1 \leqslant i \leqslant n$, is denoted $A(i)$ in computer science and a_i in mathematics. In this case we may ignore all cells after the nth:

$$\boxed{a_1 \quad a_2 \quad a_3 \quad \cdots \quad a_{n-1} \quad a_n}$$

This arrangement of data is called a **(finite) sequence** of length n and is usually denoted

$$(a_1, a_2, \ldots, a_n) \tag{1}$$

Suppose the data in Sequence (1) consist of numbers. For example, the sequence $(3, 2, 4, 2)$ has $n = 4$ and $a_1 = 3$, $a_2 = 2$, $a_3 = 4$, and $a_4 = 2$. The smallest number in a numerical sequence is called its **minimum** and is denoted

$$\min(a_1, a_2, \ldots, a_n)$$

The largest number is the **maximum**, denoted

$$\max(a_1, a_2, \ldots, a_n)$$

Thus, $\min(3, 2, 4, 2) = 2$ and $\max(3, 2, 4, 2) = 4$. One algorithm to find $\min(a_1, a_2, \ldots, a_n)$ runs as follows.

1. Set m equal to a_1.
2. If $a_2 < m$, set m equal to a_2.
3. If $a_3 < m$, set m equal to a_3.
4. Continue until m has been compared and, if necessary, set equal to a_n.

As an IMCOM program we have the following.

■ PROGRAM 1.3   **To find $m = \min(a_1, a_2, \ldots, a_n)$.**

1. $i \leftarrow 1$
2. $m \leftarrow a_i$
3. If $i = n$ then go to 6
4. $i \leftarrow i + 1$
5. If $a_i < m$ then go to 2; otherwise go to 3
6. "The minimum is m." STOP   ■

In some applications it is not enough to know the value of

$$m = \min(a_1, a_2, \ldots, a_n);$$

one must also know the address at which m occurs. Say we want the first address of m. Proceed as in Program 1.3, but also note the address j at which the most recent revision $m \leftarrow a_j$ was made. Then the last value of j is the first address of the minimum.

■ PROGRAM 1.4   **To find $\min(a_1, a_2, \ldots, a_n)$ and the first address at which it occurs.**

1. $i \leftarrow 1$
2. $m \leftarrow a_i, j \leftarrow i$
3. If $i = n$ then go to 6
4. $i \leftarrow i + 1$
5. If $a_i < m$ then go to 2; otherwise go to 3
6. "The minimum is m, which first occurs at address j." STOP   ■

For the array (3, 2, 4, 2), Program 1.4 proceeds as follows.

$i \leftarrow 1.$
$m \leftarrow 3, j \leftarrow 1.$
$i = 4.$ False.
$i \leftarrow 2.$
$a_i < m\{2 < 3\}.$ True.
$m \leftarrow 2, j \leftarrow 2.$
$i = 4.$ False.
$i \leftarrow 3.$

$a_i < m\{4 < 2\}.$ False.
$i = 4.$ False.
$i \leftarrow 4.$
$a_i < m\{2 < 2\}.$ False.
$i = 4.$ True.

_____

The minimum is 2, which first occurs at address 2.

Occasionally, it may be required to find *every* address at which $\min(a_1, a_2, ..., a_n)$ occurs. To do this, use Program 1.4 to find m and j; then find each address beyond j at which the entry is equal to m.

_____

PROGRAM 1.5   **To find $\min(a_1, a_2, ..., a_n)$ and every address at which it occurs.**

1. $i \leftarrow 1$
2. $m \leftarrow a_i, j \leftarrow i$
3. If $i = n$ then go to 6
4. $i \leftarrow i + 1$
5. If $a_i < m$ then go to 2; otherwise go to 3
6. "The minimum is m, which occurs at address(es) j"
7. If $j = n$ then go to 11
8. $j \leftarrow j + 1$
9. If $a_j \neq m$ then go to 7
10. ", j", go to 7
11. "." STOP

Program 1.5 applied to (3, 2, 4, 2) proceeds as follows:

$i \leftarrow 1.$
$m \leftarrow 3, j \leftarrow 1.$
$i = 4.$ False.
$i \leftarrow 2.$
$a_i < m\{2 < 3\}.$ True.
$m \leftarrow 2, j \leftarrow 2.$
$i = 4.$ False.
$i \leftarrow 3.$
$a_i < m\{4 < 2\}.$ False.
$i = 4.$ False.
$i \leftarrow 4.$
$a_i < m\{2 < 2\}.$ False.
$i = 4.$ True.
"The minimum is 2, which occurs at address(es) 2"

$j = n\{2 = 4\}.$ False.
$j \leftarrow 3.$
$a_i \neq m\{4 \neq 2\}.$ True.
$j = n\{3 = 4\}.$ False.
$j \leftarrow 4.$
$a_j \neq m\{2 \neq 2\}.$ False.
", 4".
$j = n\{4 = 4\}.$ True.
"."

_____

The minimum is 2, which occurs at address(es) 2, 4.

It is often desirable to rewrite a numerical sequence $(a_1, a_2, \ldots, a_n)$ in nondecreasing order or in nonincreasing order. These are the most important ways to *sort* the sequence. For example, we sort $(3, 2, 4, 2)$ into nondecreasing order as $(2, 2, 3, 4)$ and into nonincreasing order as $(4, 3, 2, 2)$.

To sort a sequence, it will often be necessary to switch the order of two entries, say a_i and a_j. This action is denoted $a_i \leftrightarrow a_j$. For example, if $(a_1, a_2, a_3, a_4) = (3, 2, 4, 2)$, then $a_1 \leftrightarrow a_3$ gives $(4, 2, 3, 2)$. As you may have noticed in Exercise 9 of the previous section, the program

1. $a_i \leftarrow a_j$
2. $a_j \leftarrow a_i$. STOP

does not switch a_i and a_j. To switch entries, we must use a new variable, which we shall call "temporary."

■ PROGRAM 1.6 $a_i \leftrightarrow a_j$.

1. temporary $\leftarrow a_i$
2. $a_i \leftarrow a_j$
3. $a_j \leftarrow$ temporary. STOP   ■

The variable "temporary" can be pictured as the address of a cell not used for any of the data to which the switch program might be applied. For instance, in the switch $a_1 \leftrightarrow a_3$ of $(3, 2, 4, 2)$ described above, "temporary" could be at address 5:

	1	2	3	4	5	
given:	3	2	4	2	–	Irrelevant

temporary $\leftarrow a_1$:	3	2	4	2	3

$a_1 \leftarrow a_3$:	4	2	4	2	3

$a_3 \leftarrow$ temporary:	4	2	3	2	3	Irrelevant

An algorithm called **selection sort** uses Program 1.4 to sort $(a_1, a_2, ..., a_n)$ into nondecreasing order as follows:

ALGORITHM 1.2   **Selection Sort**

1. Find $\min(a_1, a_2, ..., a_n)$ at address j.
2. If $j \neq 1$, then switch a_1 and a_j.
3. Find $\min(a_2, ..., a_n) = a_j$.
4. If $j \neq 2$, then switch a_2 and a_j.
5. Continue until you find $\min(a_{n-1}, a_n) = a_j$.
6. If $j \neq n - 1$, then switch a_{n-1} and a_j.
7. Write the new $(a_1, a_2, ..., a_n)$. STOP.   □

Here is another sorting algorithm.

ALGORITHM 1.3   **Bubblesort**

1. If $a_1 > a_2$, then switch a_1 and a_2.
2. If now $a_2 > a_3$, then switch a_2 and a_3.
3. Continue until the next-to-last entry has been compared and, if necessary, switched with the last entry.
4. If no switches were performed, then the array is in nondecreasing order.
5. If switches were performed, let the last switch be

$$a_k \leftrightarrow a_{k+1}.$$

Since no switches were needed after $a_k \leftrightarrow a_{k+1}$, we must have $a_{k+1} \leqslant a_{k+2} \leqslant \cdots \leqslant a_n$. Moreover, since a_{k+1} got to where it now is after comparisons and switchings, when needed, with $a_1, a_2, ..., a_k$, we must have $a_1 \leqslant a_{k+1}$, $a_2 \leqslant a_{k+1}, ..., a_k \leqslant a_{k+1}$. The algorithm concludes:
6. apply the instructions above to the array $(a_1, ..., a_k)$.   □

For a moment, think of the array written vertically instead of horizontally, with a_1 at the bottom and a_n on top. The first run of the algorithm brings the largest entry to the top; the next run brings the next largest entry up to one position below the top, and so on. This suggests the popular name for this algorithm: **bubblesort**.

In the following program for bubblesort, we use i for the running index in the array and j for the index of the most recent switch $a_j \leftrightarrow a_{j+1}$ in a run; i and j

are reset to 1 at the start of each run. We use k for the index of the last switch in a run; that is, the last value of j. Initially, $k = n$. When $k = 1$, the sort is completed.

■ PROGRAM 1.7   **Bubblesort for** $(a_1, a_2, ..., a_n)$**.**

1. $k \leftarrow n$
2. $i \leftarrow 1, j \leftarrow 1$
3. If $i = k$ then go to 7
4. If $a_i \leqslant a_{i+1}$ then go to 6
5. $a_i \leftrightarrow a_{i+1}, j \leftarrow i$
6. $i \leftarrow i + 1$, go to 3
7. If $k = 1$ then go to 9
8. $k \leftarrow j$, go to 2
9. "$(a_1, a_2, ..., a_n)$" STOP   ■

Here are the steps of bubblesort for the sequence (3, 2, 4, 2).

$\{n = 4\}$
$\{(3, 2, 4, 2)\}$
$k \leftarrow 4$.
$\{$1st run$\}$
$i \leftarrow 1, j \leftarrow 1$.
$i = 4\{1 = 4\}$. False.
$a_i \leqslant a_{i+1}\{3 \leqslant 2\}$. False.
$a_i \leftrightarrow a_{i+1}, j \leftarrow 1$.
$\{(2, 3, 4, 2)\}$
$1 \leftarrow 2$.
$i = k\{2 = 4\}$. False.
$a_i \leqslant a_{i+1}$. True.
$i \leftarrow 3$.
$i = k\{3 = 4\}$. False.
$a_i \leqslant a_{i+1}\{4 \leqslant 2\}$. False.
$a_i \leftrightarrow a_{i+1}, j \leftarrow 3$.
$\{(2, 3, 2, 4)\}$
$i \leftarrow 4$.
$i = k$. True.
$k = 1\{4 = 1\}$. False.
$k \leftarrow 3$.
$\{$2nd run$\}$
$i \leftarrow 1, j \leftarrow 1$.
$i = k\{1 = 3\}$. False.

$a_i \leqslant a_{i+1}\{2 \leqslant 3\}$. True.
$i \leftarrow 2$.
$i = k\{2 = 3\}$. False.
$a_i \leqslant a_{i+1}\{3 \leqslant 2\}$. False.
$a_i \leftrightarrow a_{i+1}, j \leftarrow 2$.
$\{(2, 2, 3, 4)\}$
$i \leftarrow 3$.
$i = k$. True.
$k = 1\{3 = 1\}$. False.
$k \leftarrow 2$.
$\{$3rd run$\}$
$i \leftarrow 1, j \leftarrow 1$.
$i = k\{1 = 2\}$. False.
$a_i \leqslant a_{i+1}\{2 \leqslant 2\}$. True.
$i \leftarrow 2$.
$i = k$. True.
$k = 1\{2 = 1\}$. False.
$k \leftarrow 1$.
$\{$4th run$\}$
$i \leftarrow 1, j \leftarrow 1$.
$i = k$. True.
$k = 1$. True.

(2, 2, 3, 4)

For some sequences, selection sort makes fewer comparisons and switches than bubblesort; for other sequences, bubblesort is better than selection sort.

(See Exercises 11 and 12.) Comparison of various algorithms for solving a given problem is considered more fully in Section 2.4. Other sorting algorithms appear in the exercises and in subsequent sections.

Suppose a sequence of n terms has been sorted into nondecreasing order: $a_1 \leqslant a_2 \leqslant \cdots \leqslant a_n$. A new number b is to be placed in the proper order in the sequence to get the enlarged ordered sequence $a_1 \leqslant a_2 \leqslant \cdots \leqslant a_{n+1}$. There are two problems: (1) to find where b goes, and (2) to write the new sequence. A simple-minded solution to the first problem is the following program.

■ PROGRAM 1.8   **Given the nondecreasing sequence $a_1 \leqslant a_2 \leqslant \cdots \leqslant a_n$ and the number b, to find the address of a cell in the linear array containing the sequence, where b belongs in nondecreasing order.**

1. $i \leftarrow 1$

2. If $b > a_i$ then go to 4

3. b belongs in cell i. STOP

4. If $i = n$ then $i \leftarrow n + 1$ and go to 3

5. $i \leftarrow i + 1$. Go to 2   ■

This program is good if b is near the beginning of the sequence; but it is bad if b is near the end. If nothing is known about b, it might be better to start the comparisons at the middle of the sequence. We will say more about this in Section 2.2.

For the second problem, writing the new ordered sequence, the simple-minded approach is terrible. Suppose, for example, that b belongs at address 500 in the sequence $a_1 \leqslant a_2 \leqslant \cdots \leqslant a_{999}$. Then writing the new sequence $a_1 \leqslant a_2 \leqslant \cdots \leqslant a_{1000}$ in the simple-minded way requires 501 replacements: $a_{1000} \leftarrow a_{999}, a_{999} \leftarrow a_{998}, \ldots, a_{501} \leftarrow a_{500}, a_{500} \leftarrow b$. In practical applications the problem would be much worse. Consider the problem many phone companies face every day: place hundreds of new names in an alphabetized directory of several hundred thousand names.

A solution to this problem is provided by a **linked list**. This uses an array in which each cell contains a two-cell array.

A linked list is more conveniently pictured as a **two-column array**:

	1	2
1		a
2		
3	b	

The **address** of a cell in this array is an ordered pair (i, j), where i is the row address and j is the column address. Thus, in the array above, a is at address $(1, 2)$ and b is at $(3, 1)$. The entry at address (i, j) in a linked list L is denoted $L(i, j)$. To store the sequence $(a_1, a_2, ..., a_n)$ in a linked list L, place the word FIRST at $(1, 1)$ and the entries $a_1, a_2, ..., a_n$ *in any order* in the first column at addresses $(2, 1)$, $(3, 1)$, ..., $(n + 1, 1)$. In the cell next to FIRST—that is, at $(1, 2)$—place the address of the row containing a_1; in the cell next to a_1, place the address of the row containing a_2; and so on through a_{n-1}. These numbers (the row addresses) are called *pointers* and allow us to recover the sequence in order. Finally, in the cell next to a_n, place the word LAST, to indicate the end of the sequence. Here are two of the twenty-four ways to store the sequence (a_1, a_2, a_3, a_4) in a linked list.

	Data	Pointer
1	FIRST	4
2	a_3	3
3	a_4	LAST
4	a_1	5
5	a_2	2

(1)

	Data	Pointer
1	FIRST	5
2	a_2	3
3	a_3	4
4	a_4	LAST
5	a_1	2

(2)

Now suppose we wish to insert b in the sequence between a_2 and a_3, using linked list (1). Place b in the first empty cell of the data column, at address (6, 1). Since b is to follow a_2, change the pointer of a_2 to 6; since a_3 (in row 2) follows b, put the pointer 2 after b, at (6, 2). That does it:

1	FIRST	4
2	a_3	3
3	a_4	LAST
4	a_1	5
5	a_2	6
6	b	2

Similarly, to place b in linked list (2), which we now call L, make the replacements

$$L(6, 1) \leftarrow b, L(6, 2) \leftarrow 3, L(2, 2) \leftarrow 6$$

In general, to place any entry at any position in any linked list requires just three replacements.

The linked list idea of a linear array of two-cell arrays has a useful generalization to a linear array of general linear arrays:

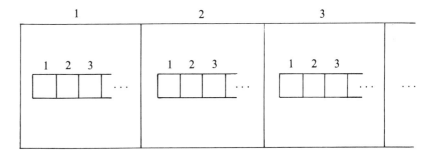

This is conveniently pictured as a **planar** (or **two-dimensional**) **array** of rows and columns:

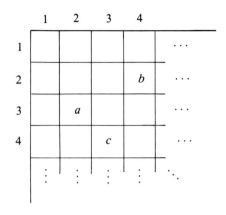

The **address** of the cell at row i and column j of the array is the ordered pair (i, j). Thus, in the planar array above, a is at $(3, 2)$, b at $(2, 4)$, and c at $(4, 3)$. Planar arrays will be studied in Section 1.4.

Although it is possible to make further generalizations to three-dimensional, four-dimensional, etc. arrays, these data structures are not used in practice as often as one- and two-dimensional arrays.

E X E R C I S E S

1. Write the sequence b with $b_5 = 3$, $b_2 - 4$, $b_1 = 7$, $b_3 = 0$, and $b_4 = 3$.

2. Write the sequence a with $a_2 = -1$, $a_1 = 6$, $a_4 = -1$, and $a_3 = -1$.

3. If a is the sequence $(2, 1, 2, 2, 3, 2, 2, 2)$, find a_5, a_2, and a_9.

4. If b is the sequence $(-1, -1, 0, 2, -3, 1, 2)$, find $b_4 - b_3 + b_5$.

5. Find the max and min of the sequence of Exercise 4.

6. Find the max and min of the sequence of Exercise 3.

7. Run Program 1.3 for the sequence of Exercise 3.

8. Run Program 1.4 for the sequence of Exercise 4.

9. Run Program 1.5 for the sequence of Exercise 3.

10. Run Program 1.5 for the sequence of Exercise 4.

11. Run Algorithms 1.2 and 1.3 for the sequence $(1, 2, 3, 4)$. How many comparisons and how many switches does each algorithm make?

12. Repeat Exercise 11 for the sequence $(4, 3, 2, 1)$.

13. Run bubblesort for $(4, 3, 4, 2, 1)$.

14. Run bubblesort for $(1, 4, 1, 3, 1)$.

15. Among all sequences of length n, for which ones does bubblesort make:

    a. the greatest number of switches?

    b. the least number of switches?

16. (*Hard*) What is the number of switches (in terms of n) in Exercise 15(a)?

17. Run Program 1.8 for $(1, 2, 3, 4, 5, 6)$, $b = 4.5$.

18. Run Program 1.8 for $(1, 1, 2, 2, 3, 3, 4, 4)$, $b = 3$.

19. Write the sequence in the linked list (a) on page 17. (Omit parentheses and commas.)

20. Write the sequence in the linked list (b) on page 17. (Omit parentheses and commas.)

21. Change pointers in the linked list (a) on page 17 to obtain the sequence KINDLE.

22. Change pointers in the linked list (b) on page 17 to obtain the sequence LINKED.

23. Change pointers in the linked list (a) on page 17 to get the letters in alphabetical order. Then adjust pointers to insert the letter G in alphabetical order.

	(a)			(b)	
1	FIRST	4		FIRST	7
2	I	1	2	N	6
3	D	LAST	3	L	4
4	L	2	4	E	LAST
5	K	6	5	I	2
6	E	3	6	D	3
7	N	5	7	K	5

24. In the list obtained in Exercise 23, insert C and P in alphabetical order.

25. Improve the English of Program 1.5 so that:

   a. if m occurs only once, it writes "address" instead of "address(es)";

   b. if m occurs exactly twice, say at addresses i and j, it writes "addresses i and j." instead of "i, j.";

   c. if m occurs more than twice and if the last address of m is k, it writes " , and k." instead of " , k.".

26. Write a program that will sort a sequence of positive integers into two sequences; the first sequence consisting of the even integers, if any, in nonincreasing order, and the second sequence consisting of the odd integers, if any, in nondecreasing order. Denote the sequence with no entries by ( ).

27. Write a program that will determine whether two or more entries in a sequence are equal and will write either "No two entries are equal." or "The entries at addresses __ and __ are equal."

28. Extend the program of Exercise 27 so that it will write either "No two entries are equal." or "No entry occurs more often than __, which is at addresses __, __, ..., __."

The concept of **lexicographic order**, that is, the order of words in a lexicon (or dictionary), can be used to order sequences of numbers. Let $a = (a_1, ..., a_m)$ and $b = (b_1, ..., b_n)$ be sequences of numbers. We say a *precedes* b in lexicographic order, written $a < b$, if one of the following is true:

1. $a_1 < b_1$.

2. There is an i such that $a_1 = b_1, ..., a_i = b_i$, and $a_{i+1} < b_{i+1}$.

3. $m < n$ and $a_1 = b_1, ..., a_m = b_m$.

Lexicographic order is easy for us because we are familiar with dictionaries. However, as Donald Knuth points out in his encyclopedic text *The Art of Computer Programming* (Volume 3, page 418), "... it has to be taught to children, and at some point in history it was necessary to teach it to adults!" He attributes the first description of the above rules of lexicographic order to Giovanni di Genoa, who in *Catholicon* (1286) remarks, "strenuous effort was required to derive these rules."

29. Write the sequences $A_1 = (4, 3, 4, 2)$, $A_2 = (2, 4, 5)$, $A_3 = (5)$, $A_4 = (4, 3, 2, 5)$, and $A_5 = (2, 4, 3, 7)$ in lexicographic order.

30. Consider a sequence of sequences $S = (A_1, ..., A_n)$, where $A_i = (a_{i1}, ..., a_{in_i})$. Write a program to do a switch $A_i \leftrightarrow A_j$ in S.

31. Write a program that will put S of Exercise 30 in lexicographic order.

Batcher's parallel sorting method (K. E. Batcher, 1964) uses the *meet* operation on binary numbers, which was described before Exercise 23 of Section 1.1, to select pairs of entries for comparison in such a way that in each step all necessary interchanges can be done simultaneously, that is, in parallel. In the following program, however, an interchange is made as soon as its necessity is found.

Batcher's Method to Sort a Sequence $(a_1, ..., a_n)$ into Nondecreasing Order.

1. $t \leftarrow 0$

2. If $2^t \geqslant n$ then go to 4

3. $t \leftarrow t + 1$, go to 2

4. $p \leftarrow 2^{t-1}$

5. $q \leftarrow 2^{t-1}$; $r \leftarrow 0$; $d \leftarrow p$

6. $i \leftarrow 0$

7. If $i \wedge p = r$ then go to 10

8. $i \leftarrow i + 1$

9. If $i = n - d$ then go to 11; otherwise go to 7

10. If $a_{i+1} > a_{i+d+1}$ then $a_{i+1} \leftrightarrow a_{i+d+1}$; go to 8

11. If $q = p$ then go to 13

12. $d \leftarrow q - p$; $q \leftarrow q/2$; $r \leftarrow p$; go to 6

13. If $p = 1$ then STOP

14. $p \leftarrow p/2$. Go to 5

32. Apply Batcher's Method to (4, 7, 3, 1, 0, 5, 2).

33. Apply Batcher's Method to (4, 1, 1, 5, 4).

Sets

Set theory provides a convenient and efficient way to work precisely with a number of important mathematical concepts. A **set** is any collection of things, called the **elements** of the set. If A is a set and x is an element of A, we write

$$x \in A \tag{1}$$

If x is not an element of A, we write

$$x \notin A \tag{2}$$

EXAMPLE 1.1   If T is the set of all positive integers less than four and P is the set of all last names of former U.S. presidents, then $2 \in T$, Taft $\in P$, Lincoln $\notin T$, and $2 \notin P$; $3 \in T$, Hayes $\in P$, Stassen $\notin P$, and $5 \notin T$.   ◻

Suppose that S is a statement about a variable x. The set whose elements are precisely those values of x for which the statement S is true is denoted

$$\{x : S\} \tag{3}$$

which is read, "the set of all x such that S." Thus, for Example 1,

$T = \{x : x \text{ is an integer and } 0 < x < 4\}$

$P = \{x : x \text{ is the last name of a former U.S. president}\}$

A set is **finite** if it has only a finite number of elements. Finite sets are sometimes written by listing all their elements between a pair of braces. Thus, the sets T and P of Example 1 are finite, and $T = \{1, 2, 3\}$.

PROBLEM 1.1   Let $F = \{x : x \text{ is a finite set of integers}\}$. Which of the following are elements of F?

a. The set T of Example 1.

b. The set E of all even integers.

c. The set A of ages (in years) of all persons living in the continental United States last Tuesday at noon.

d. The integer 7.

SOLUTION   a. T is a finite set of integers, so $T \in F$.

b. E is a set of integers, but it's not a finite set; so $E \notin F$.

c. The set A is a finite (although difficult to determine precisely) set of integers; so $A \in F$.

d. The number 7 is an integer, but it's not a set of integers; so $7 \notin F$. ■

You see from this problem that the elements of a set may themselves be sets. A set of sets is sometimes called a **collection** or *family* of sets.

Two sets are **equal** if they have precisely the same elements. Thus, $\{1, 2, 3\}$ $= \{2, 3, 1\}$ and $\{1, 2, 3\} = \{3, 2, 3, 1, 3, 2\}$, since each set has elements 1, 2, 3 and no others. Suppose $A = \{x : S\}$ and $B = \{x : T\}$. If $A = B$, then the statements S and T are true for precisely the same values of x. Conversely, if S and T are true for precisely the same values of x, then $A = B$. These statements may be summarized by saying that $A = B$ *if and only if* S and T are true for precisely the same values of x. For instance, the statements S: "x was a U.S. president whose last name begins with W" and T: "x was a U.S. president who died in the first half of December or the first half of February" are true for precisely the same values of x; so the sets $A = \{x : S\}$ and $B = \{x : T\}$ are equal.

IMCOM stores a finite set $A = \{a_1, \ldots, a_n\}$ in a linear array as a sequence $(a_1, \ldots, a_n)$. Since order matters in the sequence, a set can be listed as many different sequences. Thus, the set $\{1, 2, 3\}$ is stored as $(1, 2, 3)$. But if we rewrite $\{1, 2, 3\}$ as $\{2, 3, 1\}$, we store a *different* sequence $(2, 3, 1)$. Repetitions can also result in different sequences for the same set. Thus, if we rewrite $\{1, 2, 3\}$ as $\{3, 2, 3, 1, 3, 2\}$, we obtain yet a third sequence $(3, 2, 3, 1, 2, 3)$.

■ PROGRAM 1.9   **To evaluate the statement $b \in \{a_1, \ldots, a_n\}$ as true or false.**

1. $i \leftarrow 1$
2. If $b = a_i$ then "True." STOP
3. If $i = n$ then "False." STOP
4. $i \leftarrow i + 1$. Go to 2   ■

■ PROGRAM 1.10   **To remove repetitions from a set $A = \{a_1, \ldots, a_n\}$.**

1. $B \leftarrow \{a_1, i \leftarrow 1$
2. If $i = n$ then $A \leftarrow B\}$ and STOP
3. $i \leftarrow i + 1$

{Now use Program 1.9}

4. If $a_i \in B$ then go to 2
5. $B \leftarrow B, a_i$. Go to 2   ■

Set A is **contained in** set B if every element of A is an element of B. If A is contained in B, we write

$$A \subset B \tag{4}$$

which is read either "A is contained in B" or "A is a **subset** of B." Statement (4) is also written

$$B \supset A \tag{5}$$

which is read either "B **contains** A" or "B is a **superset** of A." (Some authors write $A \subseteq B$ and $A \supseteq B$, reserving $A \subset B$ and $A \supset B$ only for the case in which A does not equal B.) Thus, $\{1, 3\} \subset \{1, 2, 3\}$ and $\{1, 3\} \subset \{1, 3\}$, but $\{1, 2\} \not\subset \{1, 3\}$.

The set with no elements is called the **empty set** and is denoted

$$\varnothing \tag{6}$$

The empty set is, of course, a finite set. Since $\varnothing$ has no elements, the statement "every element of $\varnothing$ is an element of A" can not be false, and so must be true. Hence, $\varnothing \subset A$ for all sets A.

■ PROGRAM 1.11

To evaluate the statement $A \subset B$ as True or False, where A is empty or $A = \{a_i, \ldots a_m\}$ and B is empty or $B = \{b_i, \ldots b_n\}$.

1. If $A = \varnothing$ then "True" and STOP
2. If $B = \varnothing$ then "False" and STOP
3. $i \leftarrow 1$
4. If $a_i \in B$ is False then "False" and STOP
5. If $i = m$ then "True" and STOP
6. $i \leftarrow i + 1$. Go to 4   ■

Clearly, $A = B$ if and only if $A \subset B$ and $A \supset B$.

■ PROGRAM 1.12

To evaluate $A = B$ as True or False, where A and B are finite sets.

1. If $A \subset B$ is False then "False" and STOP
2. If $B \subset A$ is False then "False" and STOP
3. "True." STOP   ■

For two sets A, B, the **union** of A and B, denoted $A \cup B$ and read "A union B" is defined by

$$A \cup B = \{x : x \in A \text{ or } x \in B\} \tag{7}$$

The **intersection** of A and B, denoted $A \cap B$ and read "A intersection B" is defined by

$$A \cap B = \{x : x \in A \text{ and } x \in B\} \tag{8}$$

Thus, $\{1, 2, 3\} \cup \{2, 3, 4\} = \{1, 2, 3, 4\}$ and $\{1, 2, 3\} \cap \{2, 3, 4\} = \{2, 3\}$. Also, $\{1, 2, 3\} \cap \{4, 5, 6\} = \varnothing$, $\{1, 2, 3\} \cap \{2, 3\} = \{2, 3\}$, and $\{1, 2, 3\} \cup \{2, 3\} = \{1, 2, 3\}$.

The **complement** of a set A **relative to** a set B, denoted $B \sim A$, and read "B minus A," is defined by

$$B \sim A = \{x : x \in B \text{ and } x \notin A\} \tag{9}$$

Thus, $\{1, 2, 3\} \sim \{2, 3, 4\} = \{1\}$, $\{2, 3, 4\} \sim \{4, 5, 6\} = \{2, 3\}$, $\{2, 3\} \sim \{2, 3, 4\} = \varnothing$, and $\{1, 2, 3\} \sim \{4, 5, 6\} = \{1, 2, 3\}$. (Some authors write $B - A$ or $B \backslash A$ instead of $B \sim A$.) In many discussions, all sets are subsets of a given set, called the **universe** of that discussion, and often denoted by $\mathscr{U}$. When a universe $\mathscr{U}$ has been specified, the set $\{x : S\}$ is to be understood as $\{x : x \in \mathscr{U} \text{ and } S \text{ is true for } x\}$. Thus, if $\mathscr{U}$ is the set of all positive integers, then $\{x : x^2 < 17\} = \{1, 2, 3, 4\}$. For instance, although $(2.5)^2 < 17$, 2.5 is not in our set since 2.5 is not in $\mathscr{U}$. In such a discussion, the complement of a set A relative to $\mathscr{U}$ is called simply the **complement** of A, denoted A', and read "A complement." Thus,

$$A' = \mathscr{U} \sim A \tag{10}$$

(Some authors write A^c, $\bar{A}$, or $C(A)$ instead of A'.) For instance, if the universe $\mathscr{U}$ is the set of all positive integers and if $B = \{x : x > 2\}$, then $B' = \{1, 2\}$.

Results in set theory may also be depicted by **Venn* diagrams**, in which the sets are represented by regions in the plane. For example, the results

$$(A \cup B)' = A' \cap B' \tag{11}$$

and $$A \sim (B \sim C) = (A \sim B) \cup (A \cap C) \tag{12}$$

are shown in Figures 1.1 and 1.2. Other ways to establish results in set theory (truth tables and Boolean algebra) are described in Chapter 3.

The use of Venn diagrams to verify that two sets are equal is often called a "proof" that they are equal. Of course, you are familiar with proofs from high school geometry. For our purposes a "proof" is any convincing argument that a statement is correct. There are many ways in which the correctness of a mathematical assertion can be made clear. We will point out several of these "proof techniques" as we proceed. Logicians have a more precise definition of what it means to prove an assertion. This precise notion of proof is well beyond the scope of this text. The use of Venn diagrams might be called "proof by pictures." You probably learned in geometry that you cannot prove anything by simply drawing a picture. Nevertheless, proofs by Venn diagrams can be shown to be logically correct.

---

* Though named for the English mathematician John Venn (1834–1923), who used them in his fundamental work on probability, these diagrams were first introduced by the Swiss supermathematician Leonhard Euler (pronounced "oiler") (1707–1783). Charles L. Dodgson (1832–1898), another English mathematician, devised a much better though largely forgotten method for depicting sets. Today he is remembered as Lewis Carroll, author of *Alice in Wonderland* and *Through the Looking Glass*.

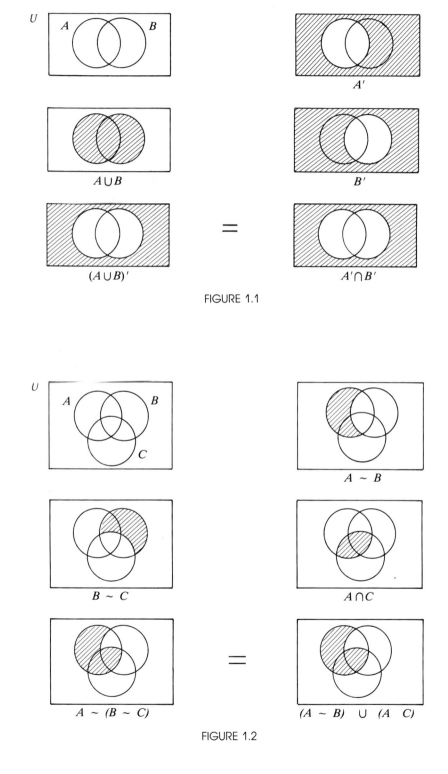

FIGURE 1.1

FIGURE 1.2

> The **Cartesian* product** of two sets A and B, which is denoted $A \times B$ and read "A cross B," is defined by
>
> $$A \times B = \{(x, y) : x \in A \text{ and } y \in B\} \qquad (13)$$

Thus,

$$\{1, 2\} \times \{1, 3, 4\} = \{(1, 1), (1, 3), (1, 4), (2, 1), (2, 3), (2, 4)\}$$

Cartesian products can be used to define relationships between two sets. Consider again the sets $A = \{1, 2\}$ and $B = \{1, 3, 4\}$. One of many possible relationships between elements of A and elements of B is "less than." To determine if an element of A is less than an element of B, we simply compare them. For example, $1 \in A$ and $3 \in B$ and $1 < 3$. So 1 and 3 are related by less than. On the other hand, $2 \in A$ and $1 \in B$, but $2 \not< 1$. That is, 2 and 1 are not related by less than. Another way, admittedly more cumbersome, to tell whether a number in A is less than a number in B is to have a complete list of all pairs that are so related. In our case the list would include $(1, 3), (1, 4), (2, 3)$, and $(2, 4)$ and no others. Now to tell if $a < b$, we need only check to see if the pair (a, b) is on the list. This is a bit silly in the case of the relation "less than" since it is so much easier to check directly without referring to a list. However, there are other ways to relate elements than "less than." For example, let's say that the element a is related to the element b if and only if the pair (a, b) is on the list $(1, 1), (2, 1),$ $(2, 4)$. Now the *only* way to check whether or not a is related to b is by referring to this list.

The precise mathematical formulation of these ideas goes as follows. If A and B are sets, a **relation from A to B** is any subset of $A \times B$. If R is a relation from A to B (that is, $R \subset A \times B$), and $(x, y) \in A \times B$, the statement $(x, y) \in R$ is written

$$x \, R \, y \qquad (14)$$

Thus, for the sets A and B given above, the relation "less than" is equal to the subset $\{(1, 2), (1, 3), (1, 4), (2, 3), (2, 4)\}$ of $A \times B$. Although it looks a bit peculiar, we may even write

$$< \; = \{(1, 2), (1, 3), (1, 4), (2, 3), (2, 4)\}$$

With this definition we have $R = \,<$ and put $x < y$ if $(x, y) \in \,<$.

---

* Named for the French philosopher René Descartes (1596–1650). He is properly credited with introducing the idea of analytic geometry to modern mathematics. In honor of this accomplishment, a plane with a rectangular coordinate system is often called a *cartesian plane*. Since points in a coordinate plane are labeled with ordered pairs, the more general notion in set theory also bears his name.

EXAMPLE 1.2   If H is the relation "is half of" from $\{2, 3, 7, 8\}$ to $\{1, 4, 6, 9\}$, then $H = \{(2, 4), (3, 6)\}$, and we have $2\,H\,4$ and $3\,H\,6$. The relation "equals" from the first set to the second is $\varnothing$. (Thus, in this case, $= = \varnothing$.)   ■

Let R be a relation from A to B. For some elements $x \in A$ there may be no element $y \in B$ such that $x\,R\,y$. For other elements $x \in A$ there may be many $y \in B$ such that $x\,R\,y$. (Consider, for instance, the relation "is the father of.") Suppose we have a relation R such that each x in A is related to *exactly one* $y \in B$. Then R is an "unambiguous" relation from A to B in this sense: given $x \in A$, there is a unique $y \in B$ such that $x\,R\,y$. Such a relation is called a **function from A to B**. (Consider, for instance, the relation "is the son of," from any set of males to the set of all males.) Functions can also be viewed as correspondences. To each $x \in A$ corresponds the unique y such that $x\,R\,y$. Functions are usually denoted by lowercase letters, such as f, g, or h. There is a special notation to express the relationship $x\,f\,y$ for a function f. If $x \in A$, then $f(x)$ (read "f of x") denotes the unique y such that $x\,f\,y$. That is, $x\,f\,f(x)$. There is also special terminology associated with functions. If f is a function from A to B, then the set A is called the **domain** and the set B is called the **range** of f. If $y = f(x)$, then y is called the **image** of x or the **value of f at** x. The set

$$\{y : y = f(x) \text{ for some } x \in A\}$$

is called the **image** of f.

EXAMPLE 1.3   Consider the following relations from $\{1, 2, 3\}$ to $\{3, 4, 5\}$:

a. $R = \{(1, 5), (2, 3), (1, 4), (3, 5)\}$

b. $f = \{(1, 4), (2, 4), (3, 3)\}$

c. $g = \{(1, 2), (3, 5)\}$

R is not a function since $1\,R\,5$ and $1\,R\,4$, but f is a function. Note that the element 4 in the range is related to two elements in the domain. That is fine; all that matters is that no element in the domain is related to two or more elements in the range. The relation g is not a function from $\{1, 2, 3\}$ to $\{3, 4, 5\}$ since g is not defined at 2; that is, 2 is not related by g to any element of $\{3, 4, 5\}$. However, g is a function from $\{1, 3\}$ to $\{3, 4, 5\}$.   ■

The statement "f is a function from A to B" is sometimes presented diagramatically as $f : A \rightarrow B$ or as $A \xrightarrow{f} B$.

A function f from A to B is **surjective** (from the French *sur*, which means "on") if the image of f equals the range B of f. A surjective function is called a **surjection**. A surjective function f from A to B is said to be **onto** B, because each element y of B is the image of at least one element x of A. If f is a surjection, then for every y in B, the equation $f(x) = y$ can be solved for x, with x in A.

EXAMPLE 1.4   The set of integers is usually denoted Z for the German word *zahlen*, for "numbers." Consider the functions f_1 and f_2, from Z to Z, described by the formulas $f_1(x) = x - 7$ and $f_2(x) = 7x$. Suppose $y \in Z$ and $f_1(x) = y$. Then $x - 7 = y$; so $x = y + 7$. Since $y + 7 \in Z$, f_1 is surjective. Suppose $y \in Z$ and $f_2(x) = y$. Then $7x = y$, $x = y/7$. But $y/7$ may not be in Z. For instance, the solution of $f(x) = 4$ is $x = 4/7$, which is not an integer. Thus, f_2 is not surjective.   □

To *prove* that f_1 was surjective, we proceeded directly. We assumed $y \in B$ and then found $x \in A$ (namely, $x = y + 7$) such that $f(x) = y$. To *disprove* that f_2 was surjective, we had only to give one example. (We saw that $f_2(x) = 4$ had no solution in A.) Such an example is called a **counterexample**. While you cannot prove a statement by giving a few examples (unless the statement is very simple), you can disprove a statement with just one counterexample.

A function f from A to B is **injective** if the images of distinct elements of A are always distinct elements of B. An injective function is called an **injection**. An injection f from A to B is said to be **one-to-one**, because each element y of the image of f is the image of *only one* element x of A.

Suppose f is an injection from A to B and x_1, x_2 are elements of A. By definition:

$$\text{for all } x_1, x_2 \text{ in } A, \text{ if } x_1 \neq x_2, \text{ then } f(x_1) \neq f(x_2) \qquad \textbf{(15)}$$

Now suppose that $f(x_1) = f(x_2)$. Could we have $x_1 \neq x_2$? No! Because if we had $x_1 \neq x_2$, then we would have $f(x_1) \neq f(x_2)$ rather than $f(x_1) = f(x_2)$. Thus, for an injection f:

$$\text{for all } x_1, x_2 \text{ in } A, \text{ if } f(x_1) = f(x_2), \text{ then } x_1 = x_2 \qquad \textbf{(16)}$$

If a function satisfies Statement (15), then it satisfies Statement (16); conversely, if it satisfies Statement (16), then it satisfies Statement (15). Statements (15) and (16) are said to be **logically equivalent**, and either of them may be used to prove that a function is injective.*

EXAMPLE 1.5   Consider the functions f_2 and f_3 from Z to Z defined by the formulas $f_2(x) = 7x$ and $f_3(x) = x^2$. If $f_2(x_1) = f_2(x_2)$, then $7x_1 = 7x_2$. Then $x_1 = x_2$; so by (2), f_2 is injective. We prove that f_3 is not injective by the following counterexample to (15): $2 \neq -2$, but $f_3(2) = 4$ and $f_3(-2) = 4$.   □

---

* In logic, the **contrapositive** of the statement "if A, then B" is the statement "if not B, then not A." These statements are always logically equivalent.

> A function is **bijective**, and is called a **bijection**, if it is both surjective and injective.

EXAMPLE 1.6   For any set A, the **identity function** on A, denoted i_A and defined for all x in A by

$$i_A(x) = x$$

is obviously a bijection. The function f_1 from Z to Z defined by the formula $f_1(x) = x - 7$ was shown in Example 1.4 to be surjective. Suppose $f_1(x_1) = f_1(x_2)$. Then $x_1 - 7 = x_2 - 7$; so $x_1 = x_2$. Thus, f_1 is also injective, and so f_1 is a bijection.   ■

Suppose f is a bijection from A to B. If $y \in B$, then, since f is surjective, there is *at least one* $x \in A$ such that $f(x) = y$. Since f is also injective, there is *at most one* $x \in A$ such that $f(x) = y$. Thus, for each $y \in B$ there is *exactly one* $x \in A$ such that $f(x) = y$. For this reason a bijection is often called a **one-to-one correspondence**. If f is a bijection from A to B, we can, in view of this result, define a function f^{-1}, read "f inverse," from B to A as follows: For $y \in B$, $f^{-1}(y)$ is the element x of A such that $f(x) = y$. The function f^{-1} is called the **inverse function** of the function f.

EXAMPLE 1.7   We have seen that $f_1(x) = x - 7$ is a bijection from Z to Z. Then from Example 1.4 it follows that the inverse function f_1^{-1} is given by $f_1^{-1}(y) = y + 7$.   ■

EXAMPLE 1.8   Let A be the set of all even integers and B be the set of all odd integers. The function f_4 from A to B, given by $f_4(x) = x + 1$, is a bijection for which $f_4^{-1}(y) = y - 1$. The function f_5 from A to B, given by $f_5(x) = x + 3$, is a bijection, and $f_5^{-1}(y) = y - 3$.   ■

Suppose f is a bijection from A to B. If $x \in A$ and $y = f(x)$, then by definition of f^{-1}, $f(x) = y$. Thus, $f(f^{-1}(y)) = y$ for all y in B. We may informally summarize these results by saying that the inverse of a bijective function undoes what the function does. Now we want to investigate the converse of this result. Suppose f is a function from A to B and suppose g is a function from B to A such that $g(f(x)) = x$ for all x in A and $f(g(y)) = y$ for all y in B. Does it follow that f must be a bijection and that $g = f^{-1}$? Yes! We conclude with a direct proof of this.

First, we will prove that f is surjective. Suppose $y \in B$. Let $x = g(y)$. Then $f(x) = f(g(y)) = y$.

Second, we will prove that f is injective. Suppose $f(x_1) = f(x_2)$. Then $g(f(x_1)) = g(f(x_2))$; that is, $x_1 = x_2$.

Now since f is a bijection, it has an inverse f^{-1}. If $y \in B$, then $x = f^{-1}(y) \in A$ and $f(x) = y$. Then $g(y) = g(f(x)) = x = f^{-1}(y)$; that is, $g(y) = f^{-1}(y)$ for all y in B. Then $g = f^{-1}$.

We shall make many uses of functions in later sections.

EXERCISES

In Exercises 1–8 list the elements of the given sets.

1. The even integers between 3 and 11

2. The odd integers between 6 and 16

3. The prime numbers between 20 and 30

4. The composite numbers between 23 and 31

5. The last names of 18th century U.S. presidents

6. The last names of former U.S. presidents who were alive in 1920

7. The prime numbers between 89 and 97

8. The set of last names of current U.S. vice-presidents

In Exercises 9–14 write the given sets in Notation (3). Various answers may be correct.

9. $\{2, 4, 6, 8\}$

10. $\{3, 7, 11, 13\}$

11. $\{$Kennedy, Johnson, Nixon$\}$

12. $\{$Alaska, Hawaii$\}$

13. $\varnothing$

14. $\{$one, two, six, ten$\}$

Let $A = \{a, b\}$, $B = \{a, \{b, c\}\}$, $C = \{\{a, b\}, c\}$. In Exercises 15–20 answer true or false and give reasons why your answer is correct.

15. $A \subset B$

16. $B = C$

17. $A \cap B = \{a\}$

18. $A \cap C = \varnothing$

19. $c \in A \cup B$

20. $\{c\} \subset B \cup C$

Let $P = \{1, 3\}$, $Q = \{2, 3, 4\}$, $R = \{1, 4\}$, and the universe $\mathcal{U} = \{1, 2, 3, 4\}$. In Exercises 21–24 list the elements of the given sets.

21. $P \sim Q$

22. $(Q \sim R) \cup (R \sim Q)$

23. $P' \cap R'$

24. $Q' \sim (P \cup R)'$

In Exercises 25–28 use Venn diagrams, as in Figures 1.1 and 1.2, to prove the statements for all sets A, B, C.

25. $A \cap (B \cup C) = (A \cap B) \cup (A \cap C)$

26. $A \cup (B \cap C) = (A \cup B) \cap (A \cup C)$

27. $A \cup (A \cap B) = A$

28. $A \cap (A \cup B) = A$

29. Write an IMCOM program to find $A \cap B$, where A and B are finite sets.

30. Write an IMCOM program to find $A \sim B$, where A and B are finite sets.

31. (*Hard*) The set-theoretic definition of the **ordered pair** (x, y) is

$$(x, y) = \{\{x\}, \{x, y\}\}$$

Prove from this definition and the definition of set equality that $(x, y) = (u, v)$ if and only if $x = u$ and $y = v$.

32. The **ordered triple** (x, y, z) is defined as

$$(x, y, z) = ((x, y), z)$$

Prove that $(x, y, z) = (u, v, w)$ if and only if $x = u$, $y = v$, and $z = w$.

33. List the elements of $\{a, b, c\} \times \{a, b\}$.

34. List the elements of $\{a, b\} \times \{a, b, c\}$.

Let $A = \{1, 2, 3\}$ and $B = \{3, 4, 5\}$. In Exercises 35–38 list the elements of the given relations from A to B.

35. "Equals"

36. "Is greater than"

37. "Is divisible by"

38. "Is a divisor of"

39. Which of the relations of Exercises 35 and 37 are functions from A to B?

40. Which of the relations of Exercises 36 and 38 are functions from A to B?

In Exercises 41–44 let $A = \{1, 2, 3, 4\}$ and let Z denote the set of integers. List the given function from A to Z as a set of ordered pairs.

41. $f(x) = x^2$

42. $f(x) = 2x + 3$

43. $f(x) =$ the number of letters in the English word for x

44. $f(x) =$ the number of elements in A less than x

In Exercises 45–54 decide whether the functions f from A to B are bijections, injections but not surjections, surjections but not injections, or neither surjections nor injections. For the functions that are bijections, find f^{-1}.

45. $A = B = Z,\ f(x) = 2x + 3$

46. $A = B = Z,\ f(x) = 4 - 5x$

47. $A = B = Z,\ f(x) = \begin{cases} x - 1, & \text{if } x \geqslant 0 \\ x + 1, & \text{if } x < 0 \end{cases}$

48. $A = B = Z,\ f(x) = \begin{cases} x/2, & \text{if } x \text{ is even} \\ x^2, & \text{if } x \text{ is odd} \end{cases}$

49. $A = B = Z,\ f(x) = 3 - x$

50. $A = B = Z,\ f(x) = -x$

51. $A =$ the set of all students, $B = Z,\ f(x) =$ age of x in years

52. $A =$ the set of all positive integers, $B = \{0, 1\}$, $f(x) = x/x$

53. (*Hard*) $A = B = f = \varnothing$

54. $A = B =$ the set of all negative integers, $f(x) = x^3$

Matrices

A **matrix** of **size** (or dimension) $m \times n$ (read "m by n") is an arrangement of elements in m rows and n columns. The elements, called **entries** of the matrix, are often numbers, but they may be other mathematical objects, such as sets or functions. For example,

$$P = \begin{bmatrix} 1 & 2 & 3 & 4 \\ 4 & 3 & 2 & 1 \end{bmatrix} \tag{1}$$

is a matrix of size 2×4. Matrices are stored in planar arrays. Thus, the entry in matrix P at address $(2, 3)$—that is, at row 2, column 3 of the array—is 2. The entry at address (i, j) of a matrix A is written in **double subscript notation** as a_{ij}. Thus, for the matrix P above $p_{23} = 2$ and $p_{14} = 4$. A matrix A of size $m \times n$ is sometimes written $[a_{ij}]_{m \times n}$, or simply as $[a_{ij}]$ if the size has been prescribed.

Two matrices are **equal** if they have the same size and equal entries at each address. For example, if

$$Q = \begin{bmatrix} 1 & x & 3 & y \\ z & 3 & 2 & w \end{bmatrix} \quad \text{and} \quad R = \begin{bmatrix} 1 & 2 & 3 \\ 4 & 3 & 2 \end{bmatrix}$$

then $P = Q$ if and only if $x = 2$ and $y = 4$ and $z = 4$ and $w = 1$; but $P \neq R$, since R has size 2×3, which is not the size of P.

Matrices have many uses in applied mathematics and computer science, some of which will be discussed in this and later chapters. Many of these uses involve various operations of **matrix arithmetic**, which we are now going to describe for matrices of numbers.

Multiplication of a Matrix by a Number.   To multiply a matrix A by a number k, multiply each entry of A by k. The result kA is a matrix of the same size as A. Thus,

$$k[a_{ij}]_{m \times n} = [b_{ij}]_{m \times n}, \text{ where } b_{ij} = ka_{ij} \tag{2}$$

For example,

$$3\begin{bmatrix} 1 & 2 & 4 \\ 3 & 4 & 5 \end{bmatrix} = \begin{bmatrix} 3 & 6 & 12 \\ 9 & 12 & 15 \end{bmatrix}$$

Addition and Subtraction of Matrices.   To add or subtract two matrices A and B of the same size, add or subtract entries at corresponding addresses. The results $A + B$ and $A - B$ have the same size as A and B. Thus,

$$[a_{ij}]_{m \times n} + [b_{ij}]_{m \times n} = [c_{ij}]_{m \times n} \tag{3}$$

where $c_{ij} = a_{ij} + b_{ij}$, and

$$[a_{ij}]_{m \times n} - [b_{ij}]_{m \times n} = [d_{ij}]_{m \times n} \tag{4}$$

where $d_{ij} = a_{ij} - b_{ij}$. If A and B do not have the same size, then $A + B$ and $A - B$ are not defined. For example,

$$\begin{bmatrix} 1 & 2 & 4 \\ 3 & 4 & 5 \end{bmatrix} + \begin{bmatrix} 3 & 2 & 1 \\ 4 & 3 & 6 \end{bmatrix} = \begin{bmatrix} 4 & 4 & 5 \\ 7 & 7 & 11 \end{bmatrix}$$

$$\begin{bmatrix} 1 & 2 & 4 \\ 3 & 4 & 5 \end{bmatrix} - \begin{bmatrix} 3 & 2 & 1 \\ 4 & 3 & 6 \end{bmatrix} = \begin{bmatrix} -2 & 0 & 3 \\ -1 & 1 & -1 \end{bmatrix}$$

and $\begin{bmatrix} 1 & 2 & 4 \\ 3 & 4 & 5 \end{bmatrix} + \begin{bmatrix} 3 & 2 \\ 4 & 3 \end{bmatrix}$ is not defined

A **row matrix** is a matrix with only one row, such as

$$[3 \quad 4 \quad 2 \quad 7]$$

A **column matrix** is a matrix with only one column, such as

$$\begin{bmatrix} 3 \\ 4 \\ 2 \\ 7 \end{bmatrix}$$

Column and row matrices can be stored in linear arrays; for both of our examples the array is (3, 4, 2, 7). If A is an $m \times n$ matrix, then row i of A is the row matrix

$$R_i = [a_{i1} \quad a_{i2} \quad \cdots \quad a_{in}], \text{ for } i = 1, 2, \ldots, m;$$ and column j of A is

$$C_j = \begin{bmatrix} a_{1j} \\ a_{2j} \\ \vdots \\ a_{mj} \end{bmatrix}, \text{ for } j = 1, 2, \ldots, n$$

For example, matrix P of Equation (1) has

$$R_1 = [1 \quad 2 \quad 3 \quad 4], R_2 = [4 \quad 3 \quad 2 \quad 1]$$

$$C_1 = \begin{bmatrix} 1 \\ 4 \end{bmatrix}, C_2 = \begin{bmatrix} 2 \\ 3 \end{bmatrix}, C_3 = \begin{bmatrix} 3 \\ 2 \end{bmatrix}, C_4 = \begin{bmatrix} 4 \\ 1 \end{bmatrix}$$

Multiplication of a Row Matrix by a Column Matrix. Let R be a row matrix and C be a column matrix that has the same number of entries as R. The product *RC in that order* (*CR* is something different) is a 1×1 matrix, that is, a matrix with just one entry. To find this entry, multiply each entry of R by the corresponding entry of C, and add the results. For example,

$$[2 \quad 3 \quad 5] \begin{bmatrix} 4 \\ 6 \\ 2 \end{bmatrix} = [36] \qquad \begin{array}{l} 2 \cdot 4 \text{ (1st entry} \times \text{1st entry)} \\ 3 \cdot 6 \text{ (2nd entry} \times \text{2nd entry)} \\ 5 \cdot 2 \text{ (3rd entry} \times \text{3rd entry)} \\ \hline 36 \end{array}$$

Thus,

$$[a_1 \quad a_2 \quad \cdots \quad a_n] \begin{bmatrix} b_1 \\ b_2 \\ \vdots \\ b_n \end{bmatrix} = [c]$$

where

$$c = a_1 b_1 + a_2 b_2 + \cdots + a_n b_n \tag{5}$$

If R and C do not have the same number of entries, then the product *RC in that order* is not defined. Thus,

$$[2 \quad 3] \begin{bmatrix} 4 \\ 6 \\ 2 \end{bmatrix} \text{ is not defined}$$

Multiplication of a Matrix by a Matrix. Let A be an $m \times n$ matrix and B be a $p \times q$ matrix. The product AB, in that order, is found by multiplying each row R_i of A by each column C_j of B. More specifically, the entry at address (i, j) of AB is found by multiplying R_i of A by C_j of B. Now R_i has size $1 \times n$ and C_j has size $q \times 1$; so in order for R_iC_j to be defined, we must have $n = q$. In other words, AB *is defined only if the number of columns* of A *equals the number of rows* of B. Suppose now that A has size $m \times n$ and B has size $n \times q$. Then

$$AB = [c_{ij}]_{m \times q}, \text{ where } R_iC_j = [c_{ij}] \tag{6}$$

Here is Definition (6) as an IMCOM program.

PROGRAM 1.13   **Given $A = [a_{ij}]_{m \times n}$ and $B = [b_{ij}]_{p \times q}$, to find AB.**

1. If $n \neq p$ then "Not defined." and STOP
2. $i \leftarrow 1$
3. $j \leftarrow 1$
4. $k \leftarrow 1, c_{ij} \leftarrow 0$
5. $c_{ij} \leftarrow c_{ij} + a_{ik}b_{kj}$
6. If $k \neq n$ then $k \leftarrow k + 1$ and go to 5
7. Store c_{ij} at address (i, j)
8. If $j \neq q$ then $j \leftarrow j + 1$ and go to 4
9. If $i \neq m$ then $i \leftarrow i + 1$ and go to 3
10. "$[c_{ij}]$" STOP

For example, suppose

$$A = \begin{bmatrix} 2 & 3 & 4 \\ 5 & 2 & 3 \end{bmatrix} \quad \text{and} \quad B = \begin{bmatrix} 5 & 4 \\ 3 & 6 \\ 4 & 2 \end{bmatrix}$$

Since A is 2×3 and B is 3×2, AB exists and is 2×2. As a computational aid we can write the factors and the product in the following display:

$$\begin{bmatrix} 5 & 4 \\ 3 & 6 \\ 4 & 2 \end{bmatrix} = B$$

$$A = \begin{bmatrix} 2 & 3 & 4 \\ 5 & 2 & 3 \end{bmatrix}\begin{bmatrix} 35 & 34 \\ 43 & 38 \end{bmatrix} = AB$$

The entries in the product are obtained by multiplying the row to its left by the column above it:

$$[2 \quad 3 \quad 4] \begin{bmatrix} 5 \\ 3 \\ 4 \end{bmatrix} = 2 \cdot 5 + 3 \cdot 3 + 4 \cdot 4 = 35$$

$$[2 \quad 3 \quad 4] \begin{bmatrix} 4 \\ 6 \\ 2 \end{bmatrix} = 2 \cdot 4 + 3 \cdot 6 + 4 \cdot 2 = 34$$

$$[5 \quad 2 \quad 3] \begin{bmatrix} 5 \\ 3 \\ 4 \end{bmatrix} = 5 \cdot 5 + 2 \cdot 3 + 3 \cdot 4 = 43$$

$$[5 \quad 2 \quad 3] \begin{bmatrix} 4 \\ 6 \\ 2 \end{bmatrix} = 5 \cdot 4 + 2 \cdot 6 + 3 \cdot 2 = 38$$

We will illustrate Program 1.13 as it computes the $(1, 1)$ entry in this product.

$\{m = 2, n = 3, p = 3, q = 2, a_{11} = 2, ..., b_{32} = 2\}$
$n \neq p$. False.
$i \leftarrow 1$.
$j \leftarrow 1$.
$k \leftarrow 1, c_{ij} \leftarrow 0$.
$c_{ij} \leftarrow 10\{0 + 2 \cdot 5\}$.
$k \neq n$. True, $k \leftarrow 2$.
$c_{ij} \leftarrow 19\{10 + 3 \cdot 3\}$
$k \neq n$. True, $k \leftarrow 3$.
$c_{ij} \leftarrow 35\{19 + 4 \cdot 4\}$
$k \neq n$. False.
Store c_{ij} {at address $(1, 1)$}

The reader should verify that for matrices A and B above, the product in the opposite order is

$$BA = \begin{bmatrix} 30 & 27 & 32 \\ 36 & 21 & 30 \\ 18 & 16 & 22 \end{bmatrix}$$

Thus, $AB \neq BA$. This explains our concern about the order in which two matrices are to be multiplied.

A matrix is **square** if it has the same number of rows as columns. The **main diagonal** of a matrix consists of all addresses (i, i). For matrices A and B above, neither A nor B is square, but both AB and BA are square. The main diagonal of A has entries 2, 2; of B has entries 5, 6; of AB has entries 35, 38; of BA has entries 30, 21, 22. An **identity matrix** is a square matrix with 1 for all entries on the main diagonal and 0 for all other entries. For example, the 2×2 and 3×3 identity matrices are

$$\begin{bmatrix} 1 & 0 \\ 0 & 1 \end{bmatrix} \quad \text{and} \quad \begin{bmatrix} 1 & 0 & 0 \\ 0 & 1 & 0 \\ 0 & 0 & 1 \end{bmatrix}$$

It is easy to see that if I is an identity matrix and IA is defined, then $IA = A$; and if BI is defined, then $BI = B$. For instance:

$$\begin{bmatrix} 1 & 0 \\ 0 & 1 \end{bmatrix} \begin{bmatrix} 2 & 3 & 4 \\ 5 & 2 & 3 \end{bmatrix} = \begin{bmatrix} 2 & 3 & 4 \\ 5 & 2 & 3 \end{bmatrix}$$

and

$$\begin{bmatrix} 1 & 0 & 0 \\ 0 & 1 & 0 \\ 0 & 0 & 1 \end{bmatrix} \begin{bmatrix} 5 & 4 \\ 3 & 6 \\ 4 & 2 \end{bmatrix} = \begin{bmatrix} 5 & 4 \\ 3 & 6 \\ 4 & 2 \end{bmatrix}$$

Elementary Row Operations.   Three types of row operations with the rows of a matrix are used in various applications:

I.   Replace a row by a nonzero number times that row. For example, if

$$T = \begin{bmatrix} 2 & 1 & 3 & 4 \\ 3 & 2 & 1 & 3 \\ 4 & 2 & 3 & 4 \end{bmatrix} \tag{7}$$

then the row operation $R_2 \leftarrow -3R_2$ changes T to

$$T = \begin{bmatrix} 2 & 1 & 3 & 4 \\ -9 & -6 & -3 & -9 \\ 4 & 2 & 3 & 4 \end{bmatrix}$$

II.   Replace a row by the sum of that row and some number times another row. For example, the operation $R_3 \leftarrow -2R_1 + R_3$ on T replaces $R_3 = [4 \quad 2 \quad 3 \quad 4]$ by

$$-2[2 \quad 1 \quad 3 \quad 4] + [4 \quad 2 \quad 3 \quad 4] = [-4 \quad -2 \quad -6 \quad -8] + [4 \quad 2 \quad 3 \quad 4]$$
$$= [0 \quad 0 \quad -3 \quad -4]$$

and thus changes T to

$$\begin{bmatrix} 2 & 1 & 3 & 4 \\ 3 & 2 & 1 & 3 \\ 0 & 0 & -3 & -4 \end{bmatrix}$$

III. Switch two rows. For example, the operation $R_2 \leftrightarrow R_3$ changes T to

$$\begin{bmatrix} 2 & 1 & 3 & 4 \\ 4 & 2 & 3 & 4 \\ 3 & 2 & 1 & 3 \end{bmatrix}$$

Clearing a Column.   Let R_i be a row and C_j be a column of a matrix A. If the entry a_{ij} at the intersection of R_i and C_j is not zero, we may use elementary row operations I and II to replace C_j by a column with 1 in R_i and 0's everywhere else. This operation is called **clearing C_j with R_j**. To do this, first replace R_i by $(1/a_{ij})R_i$ to get a 1 at address (i, j). Then for each $k \neq i$, we replace R_k with $-a_{kj}R_i + R_k$ to get a 0 at address (k, j). Let us, for example, clear C_1 of matrix T above with R_1. First, we divide R_1 by the $(1, 1)$ entry: $R_1 \leftarrow (\frac{1}{2})R_1$:

$$\begin{bmatrix} 1 & \frac{1}{2} & \frac{3}{2} & 2 \\ 3 & 2 & 1 & 3 \\ 4 & 2 & 3 & 4 \end{bmatrix}$$

Next: $R_2 \leftarrow -3R_1 + R_2$:

$$\begin{bmatrix} 1 & \frac{1}{2} & \frac{3}{2} & 2 \\ 0 & \frac{1}{2} & -\frac{7}{2} & -3 \\ 4 & 2 & 3 & 4 \end{bmatrix}$$

Finally, $R_3 \leftarrow -4R_1 + R_3$:

$$\begin{bmatrix} 1 & \frac{1}{2} & \frac{3}{2} & 2 \\ 0 & \frac{1}{2} & -\frac{7}{2} & -3 \\ 0 & 0 & -3 & -4 \end{bmatrix} \tag{8}$$

Note that to save writing, we could have written Matrix (8) without the intermediate steps. Instead of writing the old R_3, we simply enter the new one.

You can not always use a row to clear a column; for example, in Matrix (8) we could not clear C_2 with R_3 because there is a 0 at address $(3, 2)$.

We leave it to the reader to write IMCOM programs for the elementary row operations and for clearing a column. We assume that the instruction

$$\text{Clear } C_j \text{ with } R_i$$

is now accepted by IMCOM for any $m \times n$ matrix A with

$$1 \leqslant i \leqslant m,\ 1 \leqslant j \leqslant n,\ \text{and } a_{ij} \neq 0$$

For our first application of matrix operations, consider the following **system of linear equations**.

$$\left.\begin{array}{r} 2x + y + 3z = 4 \\ 3x + 2y + z = 3 \\ 4x + 2y + 3z = 4 \end{array}\right\} \tag{9}$$

Note that this system can be written as a matrix equation as follows:

$$\begin{bmatrix} 2 & 1 & 3 \\ 3 & 2 & 1 \\ 4 & 2 & 3 \end{bmatrix} \begin{bmatrix} x \\ y \\ z \end{bmatrix} = \begin{bmatrix} 4 \\ 3 \\ 4 \end{bmatrix} \tag{10}$$

We seek an efficient algorithm that will find all solutions of System (9) and any other system. Erasing the variables, + (or −) signs, and = signs in System (9), we are left with matrix T of Equation (7). This matrix, called the **matrix of the system**, contains all the information of System (9). (Some authors would call T the **augmented matrix** of System (9) and would insert a vertical line to the left of the rightmost column.) Notice that elementary row operations on this matrix correspond to operations with the equations of the system. These operations on the equations neither create nor destroy solutions of the system. With an operation of Type I, we multiply both sides of an equation (a row of the matrix) by the same nonzero number. With an operation of Type II, we add the left and right sides of one equation to the left and right sides of another equation. A Type III operation simply lists the equations in a different order. We may therefore clear columns of T so as to obtain a simpler matrix from which the solution may be apparent. We have already cleared C_1 with R_1 to obtain Matrix (8). In this matrix, clear C_2 with R_2 as follows: $R_2 \leftarrow 2R_2$:

$$\begin{bmatrix} 1 & \frac{1}{2} & \frac{3}{2} & 2 \\ 0 & 1 & -7 & -6 \\ 0 & 0 & -3 & -4 \end{bmatrix}$$

$R_1 \leftarrow -\frac{1}{2}R_2 + R_1$:

$$\begin{bmatrix} 1 & 0 & 5 & 5 \\ 0 & 1 & -7 & -6 \\ 0 & 0 & -3 & -4 \end{bmatrix}$$

Now clear C_3 with R_3: $R_3 \leftarrow (-\frac{1}{3})R_3$:

$$\begin{bmatrix} 1 & 0 & 5 & 5 \\ 0 & 1 & -7 & -6 \\ 0 & 0 & 1 & \frac{4}{3} \end{bmatrix}$$

$R_1 \leftarrow -5R_3 + R_1$ and $R_2 \leftarrow 7R_3 + R_2$:

$$\begin{bmatrix} 1 & 0 & 0 & -\frac{5}{3} \\ 0 & 1 & 0 & \frac{10}{3} \\ 0 & 0 & 1 & \frac{4}{3} \end{bmatrix} \tag{11}$$

Matrix (11) corresponds to the following system:

$$\left. \begin{array}{l} 1x + 0y + 0z = -\frac{5}{3} \\ 0x + 1y + 0z = \frac{10}{3} \\ 0x + 0y + 1z = \frac{4}{3} \end{array} \right\}$$

That is, the **solution** of System (9) is

$$x = -\frac{5}{3}, \; y = \frac{10}{3}, \; z = \frac{4}{3}$$

We may check this solution by substitution, either in the original System (9) or in the matrix Equation (10). Substitution in (10) means multiplying

$$\begin{bmatrix} 2 & 1 & 3 \\ 3 & 2 & 1 \\ 4 & 2 & 3 \end{bmatrix} \text{ by } \begin{bmatrix} -\frac{5}{3} \\ \frac{10}{3} \\ \frac{4}{3} \end{bmatrix}, \text{ which gives } \begin{bmatrix} 4 \\ 3 \\ 4 \end{bmatrix}$$

as it should.

The idea of this solution algorithm is to successively clear columns *without unclearing previously cleared columns.* Thus, once a row has been used to clear a column, it must not be used to clear another column. It may become impossible to clear a column, in which case we simply skip that column. Finally, it would be of no help to clear the last column (which contains the numbers on the right of the = signs); so when the next-to-last column has been cleared (or skipped), we are ready to read the answer. This algorithm is called **Gauss-Jordan reduction***.

---

* The algorithm is named in honor of the mathematician and scientist Carl Gauss (1777–1855) and the geodecist Wilhelm Jordan (1842–1899). In 1888 Jordan published his modification of an algorithm first presented by Gauss in 1810. For a detailed historical account of Gauss-Jordan reduction see *The American Mathematical Monthly*, Volume 94(1987), pages 130–142.

□ ALGORITHM 1.4   **To solve a system of linear equations in n unknowns.**

1. Write the matrix of the system.
2. $i \leftarrow 1$.
3. If C_i can be cleared with an unused row, then pick such a row and use it to clear C_i.
4. If $i \neq n$, then $i \leftarrow i + 1$ and go to 3.
5. Write the system with the reduced matrix.
6. If there is an equation of the form $0 = a$, where $a \neq 0$, then there is no solution. STOP.
7. Each variable in an uncleared column (if any) is **free**; that is, it may be assigned any value.
8. Each variable in a cleared column will occur in just one equation. Solve that equation for that variable (in terms of free variables, if any are present in that equation). This is the solution.
9. Check your answer, either by substitution or matrix multiplication. STOP.

□

The solution of System (9), as described above, is an example of this algorithm; here are two more examples.

EXAMPLE 1.9   Solve

$$x + 2y + 3z = 1$$
$$4x + 5y + 6z = 1$$
$$7x + 8y + 9z = 3$$

$$\begin{bmatrix} 1 & 2 & 3 & 1 \\ 4 & 5 & 6 & 1 \\ 7 & 8 & 9 & 3 \end{bmatrix}$$

$R_2 \leftarrow -4R_1 + R_2$ and $R_3 \leftarrow -7R_1 + R_3$:

$$\begin{bmatrix} 1 & 2 & 3 & 1 \\ 0 & -3 & -6 & -3 \\ 0 & -6 & -12 & -4 \end{bmatrix}$$

$R_2 \leftarrow (-\frac{1}{3})R_2$:

$$\begin{bmatrix} 1 & 2 & 3 & 1 \\ 0 & 1 & 2 & 1 \\ 0 & -6 & -12 & -4 \end{bmatrix}$$

$R_1 \leftarrow -2R_2 + R_1$ and $R_3 \leftarrow 6R_2 + R_3$:

$$\begin{bmatrix} 1 & 0 & -1 & -1 \\ 0 & 1 & 2 & 1 \\ 0 & 0 & 0 & 2 \end{bmatrix}$$

(Skip C_3.)

$$\left. \begin{array}{rcl} x \quad - z &=& -1 \\ y + 2z &=& 1 \\ 0 &=& 2 \end{array} \right\} \leftarrow \text{No solution} \qquad \blacksquare$$

Since the third equation of this system has no solution, the system itself has no solution. Then the original system must have no solution. Such a system of linear equations is said to be **inconsistent**. If at any point in Gauss-Jordan reduction you obtain a matrix row of the form $|0 \quad 0 \quad 0 \quad \cdots \quad 0 \quad k|$, where $k \neq 0$, then you may stop at once; the system is inconsistent.

EXAMPLE 1.10   Solve

$$\left. \begin{array}{rcl} x + 2y + 3z &=& 1 \\ 4x + 5y + 6z &=& 1 \\ 7x + 8y + 9z &=& 1 \end{array} \right\}$$

SOLUTION   The same steps as in Example 1.9 lead to

$$\begin{bmatrix} 1 & 0 & -1 & -1 \\ 0 & 1 & 2 & 1 \\ 0 & 0 & 0 & 0 \end{bmatrix}$$

$$\left. \begin{array}{rcl} x \quad - z &=& -1 \\ y + 2z &=& 1 \\ 0 &=& 0 \end{array} \right\} \leftarrow \text{Nothing wrong with this; we can ignore it}$$

Thus, the information conveyed by the three equations of the original system can be conveyed by only two equations. Such a system of linear equations is said to be **redundant**. In this system, z is free, $x = -1 + z$, and $y = 1 - 2z$. There are an infinite number of solutions, one for each value of z. For instance, for $z = 3$, the solution is $x = 2$, $y = -5$, $z = 3$; for $z = 0$, the solution is $x = -1$, $y = 1$, $z = 0$.

CHECK   For all z,

$$\begin{bmatrix} 1 & 2 & 3 \\ 4 & 5 & 6 \\ 7 & 8 & 9 \end{bmatrix} \begin{bmatrix} -1 + z \\ 1 - 2z \\ z \end{bmatrix} = \begin{bmatrix} 1 \\ 1 \\ 1 \end{bmatrix}$$

$\blacksquare$

Matrix Inversion. The **inverse** of a matrix A is a matrix A^{-1} (read "A inverse") such that both AA^{-1} and $A^{-1}A$ are identity matrices. For example, the inverse of

$$U = \begin{bmatrix} 1 & 2 & 2 \\ -2 & 3 & 4 \\ 3 & 5 & 5 \end{bmatrix} \text{ is } U^{-1} = \begin{bmatrix} -5 & 0 & 2 \\ 22 & -1 & -8 \\ -19 & 1 & 7 \end{bmatrix}$$

because, as the reader should check,

$$UU^{-1} = U^{-1}U = \begin{bmatrix} 1 & 0 & 0 \\ 0 & 1 & 0 \\ 0 & 0 & 1 \end{bmatrix}$$

The following useful facts about the inverses of matrices are established in linear algebra texts. We list them without proof; however, the reader is urged to pursue the study of linear algebra in subsequent courses.

1. If A is not a square matrix, then A does not have an inverse.

2. A square matrix has at most one inverse. (There are square matrices without inverses.)

3. If A and B are square matrices of the same size and if at least one of the products AB or BA is an identity matrix, then both products are the same identity matrix and $B = A^{-1}$.

We present an algorithm that uses Gauss-Jordan reduction to find the inverse of a matrix, if it exists. If A is a matrix, denote by $[A|I]$ the matrix consisting of A followed by the identity matrix with the same number of rows as A. For example, if U is the matrix defined above, then

$$[U|I] = \begin{bmatrix} 1 & 2 & 2 & 1 & 0 & 0 \\ -2 & 3 & 4 & 0 & 1 & 0 \\ 3 & 5 & 5 & 0 & 0 & 1 \end{bmatrix}$$

The notation $[I|B]$ is defined similarly.

☐ ALGORITHM 1.5   **To find the inverse of an $m \times n$ matrix A.**

1. If $m \neq n$, then "Inverse does not exist." and STOP.

2. Write $[A|I]$.

3. $i \leftarrow 1$.

4. If C_i cannot be cleared with an unused row, then "Inverse does not exist." and STOP.

5. Clear C_i with a row R_j. The row R_j is now used.

6. If $i \neq j$, then $R_i \leftrightarrow R_j$.

7. If $i \neq n$, then $i \leftarrow i + 1$ and go to (4).

8. You now have $[I | A^{-1}]$.

9. Check either $AA^{-1} = I$ or $A^{-1}A = I$.   □

In Step (5) we say "row R_j is now used." In Step (6) we might change the location of this row. Thus, if we use R_3 to clear C_5, then R_3 is used. We would then switch $R_3 \leftrightarrow R_5$. Now the row that is five rows down in the matrix is the one that is used. That is, in the new matrix R_5 is used. It is the row itself and not its particular location that matters. In Exercise 53 you will be asked to explain why this algorithm works.

EXAMPLE 1.11   Find the inverse of matrix U above.

SOLUTION   We wrote $[U | I]$ above. Use R_1 to clear C_1:

$$
\begin{array}{c}
 \\
R_2 \leftarrow 2R_1 + R_2 \\
R_3 \leftarrow -3R_1 + R_3
\end{array}
\left[
\begin{array}{cccccc}
1 & 2 & 2 & 1 & 0 & 0 \\
0 & 7 & 8 & 2 & 1 & 0 \\
0 & -1 & -1 & -3 & 0 & 1
\end{array}
\right]
$$

To make the arithmetic easier, now use R_3 to clear C_2:

$$
\begin{array}{c}
R_1 \leftarrow 2R_3 + R_1 \\
R_2 \leftarrow 7R_3 + R_2 \\
R_3 \leftarrow -R_3
\end{array}
\left[
\begin{array}{cccccc}
1 & 0 & 0 & -5 & 0 & 2 \\
0 & 0 & 1 & -19 & 1 & 7 \\
0 & 1 & 1 & 3 & 0 & -1
\end{array}
\right]
$$

Now we switch rows, $R_2 \leftrightarrow R_3$:

$$
\left[
\begin{array}{cccccc}
1 & 0 & 0 & -5 & 0 & 2 \\
0 & 1 & 1 & 3 & 0 & -1 \\
0 & 0 & 1 & -19 & 1 & 7
\end{array}
\right]
$$

Now R_1 and R_2 (formerly R_3) are used. Finally, we use R_3 to clear C_3:

$$
\begin{array}{c}
 \\
R_2 \leftarrow -R_3 + R_2 \\
 \\
\end{array}
\left[
\begin{array}{ccc|ccc}
1 & 0 & 0 & -5 & 0 & 2 \\
0 & 1 & 0 & 22 & -1 & -8 \\
0 & 0 & 1 & -19 & 1 & 7
\end{array}
\right]
$$

U^{-1}

Note that you have already checked that the square matrix on the right is U^{-1}.   ■

EXAMPLE 1.12   Find

$$
\begin{bmatrix} 1 & 2 & 3 \\ 4 & 5 & 6 \\ 7 & 8 & 9 \end{bmatrix}^{-1}
$$

SOLUTION

$$
\begin{bmatrix} 1 & 2 & 3 & 1 & 0 & 0 \\ 4 & 5 & 6 & 0 & 1 & 0 \\ 7 & 8 & 9 & 0 & 0 & 1 \end{bmatrix}
$$

$$
\begin{array}{c} R_2 \leftarrow -4R_1 + R_2 \\ R_3 \leftarrow -7R_1 + R_3 \end{array}
\begin{bmatrix} 1 & 2 & 3 & 1 & 0 & 0 \\ 0 & -3 & -6 & -4 & 1 & 0 \\ 0 & -6 & -12 & -7 & 0 & 1 \end{bmatrix}
$$

$$
\begin{array}{c} R_1 \leftarrow (\tfrac{2}{3})R_2 + R_1 \\ R_2 \leftarrow (-\tfrac{1}{3})R_2 \\ R_3 \leftarrow -2R_2 + R_3 \end{array}
\begin{bmatrix} 1 & 0 & -1 & -\tfrac{5}{3} & \tfrac{2}{3} & 0 \\ 0 & 1 & 2 & \tfrac{4}{3} & -\tfrac{1}{3} & 0 \\ 0 & 0 & 0 & 1 & -2 & 1 \end{bmatrix}
$$

C_3 cannot be cleared with the only unused row, R_3; so the given matrix has no inverse.   ∎

E X E R C I S E S

Let $A = \begin{bmatrix} 6 & -1 & -5 \\ -7 & 1 & 5 \\ -10 & 2 & 11 \end{bmatrix}$ and $B = \begin{bmatrix} 2 & -2 & 3 \\ 3 & 1 & 4 \\ 7 & -3 & 10 \end{bmatrix}$ for this entire set of exercises.

1. Find a_{12}, a_{31}, and a_{22}.
2. Find b_{21}, b_{13}, and b_{11}.
3. Find the addresses in A of the entries -5, 1, and -7.
4. Find the addresses in B of the entries 3, 4, and 10.
5. Solve

$$
A = \begin{bmatrix} 6 & x & y \\ -7 & 1 & z \\ w & 2 & u \end{bmatrix}
$$

6. Solve

$$
B = \begin{bmatrix} x & -2 & y \\ 3 & z & u \\ v & -3 & w \end{bmatrix}
$$

7. Solve

$$
A = \begin{bmatrix} 6 & -1 & x \\ y & 1 & 5 \end{bmatrix}
$$

8. Solve

$$
B = \begin{bmatrix} 2 & -2 \\ 3 & 1 \\ 7 & -3 \end{bmatrix}
$$

9. Find $4A$.

10. Find $-2B$.

11. Find a number k and a matrix C with all integer entries such that

$$\begin{bmatrix} \frac{1}{2} & -\frac{2}{3} \\ -\frac{3}{4} & \frac{5}{8} \end{bmatrix} = kC$$

12. Find a number k and a matrix C with all integer entries such that

$$\begin{bmatrix} 1 & \frac{3}{4} & -\frac{2}{5} \\ \frac{7}{10} & -2 & \frac{1}{3} \end{bmatrix} = kC$$

13. Find $A + B$.

14. Find $2A + 3B$.

15. Find $A - B$.

16. Find $2A - 3B$.

17. Given k and $C = [c_{ij}]_{m \times n}$, write an IMCOM program to find kC.

18. Given $C = [c_{ij}]_{m \times n}$ and $D = [d_{ij}]_{p \times q}$ write an IMCOM program to find $C + D$.

19. Write the row matrices of A.

20. Write the column matrices of B.

21. Find

$$[2 \quad -3 \quad 4 \quad -5] \begin{bmatrix} -3 \\ -4 \\ -2 \\ 2 \end{bmatrix}$$

22. Find

$$[3 \quad -4 \quad 5 \quad -6] \begin{bmatrix} 1 \\ -2 \\ -3 \end{bmatrix}$$

23. Find AB.

24. Find $AB - BA$.

25. Write the first twenty steps of Program 1.13 for AB.

26. For BA in Program 1.13, set $i \leftarrow 3$ and $j \leftarrow 2$. Run the program to the end.

27. If R is a row matrix with n entries and C is a column matrix with m entries, then what size is CR?

28. Find

$$\begin{bmatrix} 3 \\ 4 \end{bmatrix} [5 \quad 6 \quad 2]$$

29. Multiply $\begin{bmatrix} 4 & 5 & 6 & 5 & 4 \\ 7 & 8 & 9 & 8 & 7 \end{bmatrix}$ on the right by the appropriate-size identity matrix.

30. Repeat Exercise 29 with right $\leftarrow$ left.

31. Perform $R_2 \leftarrow 3R_2$ on A.

32. Perform $R_3 \leftarrow -2R_3$ on B.

33. Perform $R_3 \leftarrow -2R_1 + R_3$ on A.

34. Perform $R_2 \leftarrow 4R_3 + R_2$ on A.

35. Perform $R_1 \leftrightarrow R_3$ on A.

36. Perform $R_3 \leftrightarrow R_2$ on B.

37. Write a program to do $R_i \leftarrow kR_i$.

38. Write a program to do $R_i \leftarrow kR_j + R_i$, where $i \neq j$.

39. Write a program to do $R_i \leftrightarrow R_j$ where $i \neq j$.

40. Write a program using the programs above to do $R_k \leftarrow pR_i + qR_j$.

41. In A, use R_2 to clear C_2.

42. In B, use R_1 to clear C_1.

43. Write a program to use R_i to clear C_j in a matrix M.

44. In A, use R_3 to clear C_1.

45. Solve

$$A \begin{bmatrix} x \\ y \\ z \end{bmatrix} = \begin{bmatrix} 1 \\ -2 \\ 1 \end{bmatrix}$$

46. Solve

$$A \begin{bmatrix} x_1 \\ x_2 \\ x_3 \end{bmatrix} = \begin{bmatrix} 1 \\ 52 \\ 7 \end{bmatrix}$$

47. Solve

$$B \begin{bmatrix} x \\ y \\ z \end{bmatrix} = \begin{bmatrix} -2 \\ 3 \\ -1 \end{bmatrix}$$

48. Solve

$$\left. \begin{array}{l} x_1 - x_2 + x_3 - x_4 = 0 \\ x_1 + x_2 + x_3 - x_4 = 1 \end{array} \right\}$$

49. Find A^{-1}.

50. Find B^{-1}.

51. Which row matrices have inverses?

52. Which column matrices have inverses?

53. Algorithm 1.5 works by finding A^{-1} one column at a time "all at once." Let x_1, x_2, x_3 be the entries in the first column of A^{-1}. Write the system that must be satisfied if the equation

$$\begin{bmatrix} 6 & -1 & -5 \\ -7 & 1 & -5 \\ -10 & 2 & 11 \end{bmatrix} \begin{bmatrix} x_1 \\ x_2 \\ x_3 \end{bmatrix} = \begin{bmatrix} 1 & 0 & 0 \\ 0 & 1 & 0 \\ 0 & 0 & 1 \end{bmatrix}$$

is true. Now let x_1, x_2, x_3 be the entries in the second column of A^{-1}. Write the system that must be satisfied if the equation

$$\begin{bmatrix} 6 & -1 & -5 \\ -7 & 1 & -5 \\ -10 & 2 & 11 \end{bmatrix} \begin{bmatrix} x_1 \\ x_2 \\ x_2 \end{bmatrix} = \begin{bmatrix} 1 & 0 & 0 \\ 0 & 1 & 0 \\ 0 & 0 & 1 \end{bmatrix}$$

is true. Finally, let x_1, x_2, x_3 be the entries in the third column of A^{-1}. Write the system that must be satisfied if the equation

$$\begin{bmatrix} 6 & -1 & -5 \\ -7 & 1 & -5 \\ -10 & 2 & 11 \end{bmatrix} \begin{bmatrix} x_1 \\ x_2 \\ x_3 \end{bmatrix} = \begin{bmatrix} 1 & 0 & 0 \\ 0 & 1 & 0 \\ 0 & 0 & 1 \end{bmatrix}$$

is true. Now explain how Algorithm 1.5 works.

CHAPTER

TWO

Combinatorics

2.1 Enumeration

2.2 Induction

2.3 Recursion

2.4 Algorithm Efficiency

THE ESSENTIAL POINT about a discrete set is that its elements can, at least in theory, be listed. Obviously, any finite set can be listed. To list a finite nonempty set A, pick any element of A and write it first. Then pick another element of A, if there is one, and write it next. Continue until A is listed. Of course, some ways of listing A may be more useful than others.

There are some infinite sets that can be listed. The **natural** numbers can be listed in increasing order: 1, 2, …. While the entire list cannot be actually written, it is clear that every natural number will eventually appear in the list. For a more interesting example, consider the set B of all **rational** numbers from 0 to 1; that is, the set of all numbers of the form m/n, where m and n are natural numbers and $m \leqslant n$. B cannot be listed in increasing order. (If you think that m/n is the first element of B, then what will you do with $m/(2n)$?) But B *can* be listed in other ways, such as the following:

1 (that is, $\frac{1}{1}$)

$\frac{1}{2}$ ($\frac{2}{2} = 1$ is already listed)

$\frac{1}{3}, \frac{2}{3}$ ($\frac{3}{3}$ is already listed)

$\frac{1}{4}, \frac{3}{4}$ ($\frac{2}{4} = \frac{1}{2}$ and $\frac{4}{4} = 1$ are already listed)

$\frac{1}{5}, \frac{2}{5}, \frac{3}{5}, \frac{4}{5}$

$\frac{1}{6}, \frac{5}{6}$

$\vdots$

Clearly, each element of B will eventually be listed.

Can the set C of all **real** numbers from 0 to 1 be listed? C can be described as the set of all numbers with decimal expressions of the form 0.⋯. (Note that $1 = 0.9999\cdots$ is in C.) In the 1870s Georg Cantor (1845–1918) proved that it is impossible to list all the elements of C as a sequence $(c_1, c_2, \ldots)$. Thus, while B and C are both infinite sets, B can be written as a discrete set but C cannot.

> **Combinatorics** (or combinatorial mathematics) may be defined as the study of ways to list or arrange discrete sets.

This chapter contains introductions to several of the most important ideas and techniques of combinatorics, as well as an application of some of these ideas to the study of algorithm efficiency.

Students of computer science or mathematics are urged to pursue the study of combinatorics as they gain in mathematical maturity. One excellent book is *Applied Combinatorics* by Fred Roberts (Prentice-Hall Inc., Englewood Cliffs, New Jersey, 1984).

Enumeration

This section is concerned with various techniques for counting the elements of a finite set. The simplest technique is the **Principle of Addition**:

> Suppose each element to be counted is of one and only one of two types. If there are N_1 elements of type 1 and N_2 elements of type 2, then the total number of elements is
>
> $$N_1 + N_2 \qquad\qquad (1)$$

EXAMPLE 2.1   Suppose Hillsdale College now has 460 male students and 480 female students. Then the number of students is $460 + 480 = 940$.   □

The Principle of Addition extends to more than two types, of course. If each element is of one and only one of n types, with N_i elements of type i, then the number of elements is

$$N_1 + N_2 + \cdots + N_n \qquad\qquad (2)$$

EXAMPLE 2.2   Last year Hillsdale had 320 freshmen, 210 sophomores, 230 juniors, 150 seniors, and 85 graduate students. Then the number of students was $320 + 210 + 230 + 150 + 85 = 995$.   □

These ideas also suggest a **Principle of Subtraction**, which need not be written out precisely. Here is an example.

EXAMPLE 2.3   Two years ago, 990 students attended Hillsdale, of whom 280 were sophomores, 200 were juniors, 180 were seniors, and 215 were graduate students. How many were freshmen?

SOLUTION   Let x be the number of freshmen. Then

$$x + 280 + 200 + 180 + 215 = 990$$
$$x + 875 = 990$$
$$x = 115 \text{ freshmen} \qquad □$$

The next example introduces an important extension of the Principles of Addition and Subtraction.

EXAMPLE 2.4   Every Hillsdale athlete is fast or strong (or both). One hundred athletes are fast, 80 are strong, and 50 are both fast and strong. How many athletes are there?

SOLUTION   The sum $100 + 80$ is too large, because it counts the 50 fast and strong athletes twice. There are $100 + 80 - 50 = 130$ athletes.   ∎

In terms of enumeration we have the following principle:

> If N_1 elements have property 1, N_2 have property 2, and N_{12} (read "N sub one two") have properties 1 and 2, then the number of elements that have at least one property is
>
> $$N_1 + N_2 - N_{12} \qquad (3)$$

What if there are three properties, 1, 2, and 3? Let P_i be the set of elements with property i. See Figure 2.1. The sum $N_1 + N_2 + N_3$, shown in (2), counts all

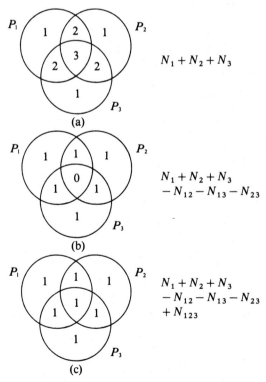

FIGURE 2.1

elements, but it counts elements that are in exactly two sets twice and it counts the elements in all three sets—that is, in $P_1 \cap P_2 \cap P_3$—three times. Subtracting N_{12} and N_{13} and N_{23}, we have counted each element exactly once, except for the elements with all three properties, which are now not counted at all, as shown in (b). Let N_{123} be the number of elements with all three properties. Then the number of elements with at least one property is

$$\begin{aligned} &N_1 + N_2 + N_3 \\ &- N_{12} - N_{13} - N_{23} \\ &+ N_{123} \end{aligned} \tag{4}$$

This is shown in Figure 2.1(c).

For four properties, the number of elements with at least one property is

$$\begin{aligned} &N_1 + N_2 + N_3 + N_4 \\ &- N_{12} - N_{13} - N_{14} - N_{23} - N_{24} - N_{34} \\ &+ N_{123} + N_{124} + N_{134} + N_{234} \\ &- N_{1234} \end{aligned} \tag{5}$$

The generalization of (3), (4), and (5) to n properties is called the **Principle of Inclusion-Exclusion**:

To count the elements with at least one of n properties, include the properties one at a time (that is, add the N_i), then exclude the properties two at a time (that is, subtract the N_{ij}, $i < j$), then include three at a time, and so on. The last term $N_{12...n}$ is included if n is odd (as in (4)) and excluded if n is even (as in (3) and (5)).

EXAMPLE 2.5 A computer store has 400 machines. Three hundred have two disk drives, 250 have a color monitor, and 200 have extended memory. Two hundred and ten have two disk drives and a color monitor, 120 have two disk drives and extended memory, 80 have a color monitor and extended memory, and 40 have all three features. How many computers have none of these features?

SOLUTION Let property 1 be "two disk drives," property 2 be "color monitor," and property 3 be "extended memory." Then by (4), the number of computers with at least one property is

$$300 + 250 + 200 - 210 - 120 - 80 + 40 = 380$$

Then by the Principle of Subtraction, the number of computers with none of these properties is $400 - 380 = 20$. □

We turn next to the **Principle of Multiplication:**

> Suppose that each element to be counted is the result of one and only one sequence of two actions. If the first action has N_1 outcomes and if, no matter what that outcome is, the second action has N_2 outcomes, then the number of elements is
>
> $$N_1 N_2 \qquad\qquad (6)$$

EXAMPLE 2.6   One dormitory at Hillsdale has seven stories, and there are nine rooms on each floor. Then the number of rooms is $7 \cdot 9 = 63$. (You may think of the two actions as: (1) go to a floor, (2) go to a room on that floor.)   ◻

The Principle of Multiplication is actually a consequence of the Principle of Addition. Here is a "direct proof" of this fact. Let the outcomes of the first action be $1, 2, \ldots, N_1$. There are N_2 elements for which the first choice had outcome 1; another N_2 elements for which the first choice had outcome 2; $\ldots$; and finally another N_2 elements for which the first choice had outcome N_1. Then the total number of elements equals $N_2 + N_2 + \cdots + N_2$, where there are N_1 of these N_2's; that is, the number of elements is $N_1 N_2$.

The Principle of Multiplication extends to any number of actions. Suppose we are given n actions. If action i has N_i outcomes, no matter what the outcomes of the previous actions, then the number of elements is

$$N_1 N_2 \cdots N_n \qquad\qquad (7)$$

EXAMPLE 2.7   There are seven floppy disks, each containing different data. In how many ways can the disks be placed in drives A and B of computers I and II?

SOLUTION   Here's one way to proceed.

Action 1: Load Drive A of Computer I: 7 outcomes (Use any one of the disks.)

Action 2: Load Drive B of Computer I: 6 outcomes (One disk is already loaded.)

Action 3: Load Drive A of Computer II: 5 outcomes

Action 4: Load Drive B of Computer II: 4 outcomes

ANSWER $7 \cdot 6 \cdot 5 \cdot 4 = 840$ ways.   ◻

Sometimes the Principles of Addition and Multiplication must both be used in an enumeration.

EXAMPLE 2.8   Consider Example 2.7, but suppose computer II has a third disk drive, C. In how many ways can exactly one of the computers be fully loaded?

SOLUTION   Computer I can be loaded in $7 \cdot 6 = 42$ ways. Computer II can be loaded in $7 \cdot 6 \cdot 5 = 210$ ways. Then one computer can be loaded in $42 + 210 = 252$ ways. ∎

The next example introduces the **Principle of Division**.

EXAMPLE 2.9   How many different samples of two microcomputers can be selected for testing from a store containing 50 computers?

SOLUTION   The first computer can be chosen from 50, and the second computer can be chosen from the remaining 49; so there are $50 \cdot 49$ choices. But this enumeration counts each sample twice. For instance, the sample consisting of computers numbered 42 and 17 is counted once when 42 is chosen first and 17 is chosen second, and again when 17 is first and 42 second. Thus, the total number of two-computer samples is $50 \cdot 49/2 = 1225$. ∎

Perhaps the most important application of the Principle of Division is to the enumeration of all j-element subsets of an n-element set, where j and n are nonnegative integers and $j \leqslant n$. An easy case is $j = 0$: there is only one 0-element subset of an n-element set, namely $\varnothing$. Now suppose $j \geqslant 1$. The first element of a j-element subset can be chosen in n ways, the second element in $n - 1$ ways, ..., and the jth element in $n - j + 1$ ways. Thus, there are $n(n - 1) \cdots (n - j + 1)$ choices. But each j-element subset has been counted $j(j - 1) \cdots (1)$ times, since the first element could be any of the j elements of that subset, the second could be any of the remaining $j - 1$ elements, and so on. Then the number of j-element subsets, where $j \geqslant 1$, is

$$\frac{n(n - 1) \cdots (n - j + 1)}{j(j - 1) \cdots (1)} \tag{8}$$

EXAMPLE 2.10   The 5-element set $A = \{a, b, c, d, e\}$ has ten 3-element subsets: $\dfrac{5 \cdot 4 \cdot 3}{3 \cdot 2 \cdot 1} = 10$. The subset $\{b, d, e\}$, for instance, can be obtained as a sequence of choices from A in $3 \cdot 2 \cdot 1 = 6$ ways: (b, d, e), (b, e, d), (d, b, e), (d, e, b), (e, b, d), and (e, d, b). These are the ways to fill out the "order form" ☐☐☐ that will produce the subset $\{b, d, e\}$. Altogether there are $5 \cdot 4 \cdot 3 = 60$ ways to fill out this "order form." The hard-working reader may wish to fill out the "order form" in all 60 ways and show the ten 3-element subsets that result. ∎

EXAMPLE 2.11   The number of possible hands in straight poker is the number of 5-element subsets (hands) of a 52-element set (the deck), which by (8) is

$$\frac{52 \cdot 51 \cdot 50 \cdot 49 \cdot 48}{5 \cdot 4 \cdot 3 \cdot 2 \cdot 1} = 13 \cdot 17 \cdot 5 \cdot 49 \cdot 48 = 2{,}598{,}960$$

□

In enumeration a j-element subset of an n-element set is often called a **combination** of j elements chosen from n, and the number of combinations of j elements chosen from n is denoted $\binom{n}{j}$ and read "n choose j." Formula (8) for $\binom{n}{j}$, where $1 \leqslant j \leqslant n - 1$, can be neatly written with factorial notation. If m is a positive integer, then m **factorial**, written $m!$, is

$$m! = m(m-1)(m-2) \cdots 3 \cdot 2 \cdot 1 \tag{9}$$

For instance, $6! = 6 \cdot 5 \cdot 4 \cdot 3 \cdot 2 \cdot 1 = 720$. Now,

$$n(n-1) \cdots (n-j+1) = \frac{n(n-1) \cdots (n-j+1)(n-j)(n-j-1) \cdots 1}{(n-j)(n-j-1) \cdots 1}$$

$$= \frac{n!}{(n-j)!}$$

Then by (8),

$$\binom{n}{j} = \frac{n!}{j!(n-j)!} \tag{10}$$

for $1 \leqslant j \leqslant n - 1$. It is traditional (and, for reasons beyond the scope of this text, rigorously correct) to define the factorial of zero to be one:

$$0! = 1 \tag{11}$$

With this definition, Formula (10) is also correct for $j = 0$ and $j = n$:

$$\binom{n}{0} = \frac{n!}{0!(n-0)!} = \frac{n!}{1 \cdot n!} = 1$$

$$\binom{n}{n} = \frac{n!}{n!(n-n)!} = \frac{n!}{n! \cdot 1} = 1$$

As a final example of enumeration, consider the celebrated *hatcheck problem*. Suppose n men check their hats before entering a club. Someone yells "fire!" and the men all run out, each grabbing a hat at random. What are the chances that no man grabs his own hat? The first man has a choice of n hats, the next of $n - 1$, etc.; so there are $n(n-1) \cdots \cdot 3 \cdot 2 \cdot 1 = n!$ ways in which the hats may be distributed. How many of these are **derangements**, in which no one has his own hat? Call the men $1, \ldots, n$ and say that a distribution of hats has property i if man i has his own hat. Then the number of derangements is $n! - M$, where M is the number of distributions with at least one of the properties 1, 2, ..., n. We shall find M by Inclusion-Exclusion:

$$M = N_1 + \cdots + N_n - N_{12} - \cdots + N_{123} + \cdots$$

Consider a typical term $N_{i_1 \cdots i_j}$. This is the number of distributions in which men $i_1, \ldots, i_j$ have their own hats. Of the remaining men, the first can have any of the $n - j$ remaining hats (even perhaps his own), the next can have any of $n - j - 1$ hats, etc. Then

$$N_{i_1 \cdots i_j} = (n - j)(n - j - 1) \cdots \cdot 3 \cdot 2 \cdot 1 = (n - j)!$$

Now for a given j, how many terms $N_{i_1 \cdots i_j}$ are there? This is the same as asking how many j-element subsets the set $\{1, \ldots, n\}$ has; so the answer is $\binom{n}{j}$. Then since $N_{i_1 \cdots i_j} = (n - j)!$, the sum of all $N_{i_1 \cdots i_j}$ for fixed j is

$$\binom{n}{j}(n - j)! = \frac{n!}{j!(n - j)!}(n - j)! = \frac{n!}{j!}$$

Then $M = \dfrac{n!}{1!} - \dfrac{n!}{2!} + \dfrac{n!}{3!} - \cdots + (-1)^{n-1}\dfrac{n!}{n!}$, and so the number of derangements is

$$D_n = n! - M = n!\left(1 - \frac{1}{1!} + \frac{1}{2!} - \cdots + \frac{(-1)^n}{n!}\right) \tag{12}$$

Thus, in D_n out of $n!$ cases, no man grabs his own hat. Then the probability (or "the chances") that no man grabs his own hat is

$$\frac{D_n}{n!} = \frac{1}{0!} - \frac{1}{1!} + \frac{1}{2!} - \cdots + \frac{(-1)^n}{n!} \tag{13}$$

where we have written 1 as $1/0!$ so as to better show the symmetry of this answer. (In fact, the first two terms of (13) are both equal to 1 and so they cancel.)

Let us check Formula (12) for $n = 4$:

$$D_4 = 4!\left(1 - \frac{1}{1!} + \frac{1}{2!} - \frac{1}{3!} + \frac{1}{4!}\right)$$

$$= 24\left(1 - 1 + \frac{1}{2} - \frac{1}{6} + \frac{1}{24}\right)$$

$$= 9$$

Here are the $4! = 24$ arrangements (called **permutations**) of 1, 2, 3, 4 with the 9 derangements marked D:

```
1 2 3 4     2 1 3 4     3 1 2 4     4 1 2 3 D
1 2 4 3     2 1 4 3 D   3 1 4 2 D   4 1 3 2
1 3 2 4     2 3 1 4     3 2 1 4     4 2 1 3
1 3 4 2     2 3 4 1 D   3 2 4 1     4 2 3 1
1 4 2 3     2 4 1 3 D   3 4 1 2 D   4 3 1 2 D
1 4 3 2     2 4 3 1     3 4 2 1 D   4 3 2 1 D
```

It can be shown (using calculus) that for all $n \geqslant 7$, the probability given by (13) is always within 0.001 of 0.368.

EXERCISES

1. In its first year of operation, Hillsdale College had 172 undergraduates, of which 90 were freshmen, 40 were female sophomores, and 22 were either juniors or seniors. How many male sophomores were there?

2. (See Exercise 1.) In its first year of operation, twelve male juniors and eight female seniors attended Hillsdale. How many female upperclasspersons (i.e., nonfreshmen) were there?

3. (See Exercises 1 and 2.) In its first year of operation, no class (freshmen, sophomore, junior, or senior) at Hillsdale was all of one sex. How many male seniors were there?

4. (See Exercises 1, 2, 3.) In its first year of operation, there were equally many males and females at Hillsdale. How many male freshmen were there?

5. An English class of 40 students includes 25 computer science majors, 15 athletes, and 5 computer science majors who are athletes. How many students in the class are neither computer science majors nor athletes?

6. A calculus class of 40 includes 17 students who are neither computer science majors nor athletes, 2 computer science majors who are athletes, and 8 computer science majors. How many athletes are in the class?

7. Yesterday the Sweete Shoppe sold 40 sundaes, of which 17 had nuts, 16 had cherries, 18 had fudge, 6 had nuts and cherries, 9 had cherries and fudge, 5 had nuts and fudge, and 2 had all three toppings. How many had no topping (at least, none of *these* toppings)?

8. Last week Sweete Shoppe sold 25 plain sundaes with cherries only, 70 with nuts, 70 with cherries, 70 with fudge, 30 with nuts and cherries, 30 with nuts and fudge, and 10 with everything. How many sundaes had exactly one topping?

9. An eight-element **bit string** is an ordered sequence of eight bits, where each bit is 0 or 1. Thus, 01101101 and 11100011 are eight-element bit strings. How many different symbols can be encoded by eight-element bit strings?

10. (See Exercise 9.) If we need to encode one thousand different symbols with bit strings of fixed length, how long would the strings have to be?

11. A **string** of length n is an ordered sequence of n letters (from the English alphabet). Thus, ABACC is a string of length 5.

  a. How many strings of length 5 are there?

  b. How many strings of length 5 are there in which no letter appears more than once?

12. (See Exercise 11.) How many strings of length 5 begin and end with a vowel (A, E, I, O, U)?

13. (See Exercises 11 and 12.) How many strings of length 5 have all letters different and exactly two vowels?

14. (*Hard*) (See Exercise 11.) How many strings of length 5 have all letters different and in alphabetical order?

15. (*Hard*) (See Exercise 11.) How many strings of length 5 have their letters in alphabetical order (such as PQQRS, AABCC, ADDDD)?

A **binomial** is the sum of two variables, such as $x + y$. The **binomial theorem**, which tells us how to expand $(x + y)^n$, where n is a natural number, is the subject of the next five exercises.

16. Expand $(x + y)^2$, $(x + y)^3$, and $(x + y)^4$.

17. To expand $(x + y)^n = (x + y)(x + y) \cdots (x + y)$, choose either x or y from each parentheses and multiply; then add the results. If you choose x from exactly k parentheses, where $0 \leqslant k \leqslant n$, and thus choose y from the other parentheses, and multiply together, what do you get?

18. In how many ways can you choose x from exactly k parentheses?

19. If you add all the terms obtained by choosing x from exactly k parentheses, what do you get?

20. Now show that the binomial theorem is true:

$(x + y)^n =$

$$\binom{n}{0}x^n y^0 + \binom{n}{1}x^{n-1}y + \cdots + \binom{n}{n}x^0 y^n \quad \text{(14)}$$

Recall that a^0 is defined as 1, provided $a \neq 0$.

21. One could obtain a subset of an n-element set $A = \{a_1, a_2, \ldots, a_n\}$ by filling out an "order form:"

a_1	a_2	$\cdots$	a_n

where the box below a_k is checked if a_k is to be included in the subset. Then the number of subsets of A equals the number of different ways this "order form" would be filled out. What is this number?

22. (See Exercise 21.) Count the number of subsets of A with 0 elements, 1 element, 2 elements, ..., n elements, and hence obtain another expression for the number of subsets of A.

23. If you did Exercises 21 and 22, you discovered that

$$\binom{n}{0} + \binom{n}{1} + \binom{n}{2} + \cdots + \binom{n}{n} = 2^n$$

Prove this directly from the binomial theorem (14).

24. Prove directly that for all natural numbers n,

$$\binom{n}{0} - \binom{n}{1} + \binom{n}{2} - \cdots + (-1)^n\binom{n}{n} = 0$$

25. Use Formula (12) to find the number of derangements of 1 2 3 4 5.

26. (See Exercise 25.) List the derangements of 1 2 3 4 5.

Induction

Let S be a set. Suppose

$$1 \in S \quad \text{(1)}$$

and for all integers n,

$$\text{if } n \in S, \text{ then } n + 1 \in S \quad \text{(2)}$$

By (1), $1 \in S$. Then by (2) (with $n = 1$), $2 \in S$. Then by (2) (with $n = 2$), $3 \in S$. Then $4 \in S$, $5 \in S$, ..., and, in fact, S contains *all* positive integers. This simple observation, called the **principle of mathematical induction**, is a powerful tool in discrete mathematics.

Induction is used to prove that a result involving a positive integer n is true for all n. As you might expect, this proof technique is called "proof by induction." A proof by induction has two steps. First show that the result holds for $n = 1$. Then assume that the result holds for an arbitrary positive integer n and deduce that it also holds for $n + 1$. This deduction, called the **inductive step**, is the main part of the proof. The inductive step may be easy or hard, depending on the result to be proved. Once the inductive step is established, it follows from the principle of induction that the result holds for all positive integers.

Induction proofs often work well for formulas involving **summation notation** or **product notation**. The sum of the entries in a sequence of numbers $(a_1, \ldots, a_n)$ is written $\sum_{k=1}^{n} a_k$ and read "the sum of a sub k as k goes from 1 to n."

Thus,

$$\sum_{k=1}^{n} a_k = a_1 + \cdots + a_n \qquad (3)$$

The product of these numbers is

$$\prod_{k=1}^{n} a_k = a_1 \cdot \cdots \cdot a_n \qquad (4)$$

read "the product of a sub k as k goes from 1 to n." In these notations k is called the **index** of summation or product. Letters other than k are often used. Here are a few examples:

$$\sum_{k=1}^{4} k^2 = 1^2 + 2^2 + 3^2 + 4^2 = 30$$

$$\prod_{k=1}^{4} k^2 = 1^2 \cdot 2^2 \cdot 3^2 \cdot 4^2 = 576$$

$$\sum_{j=1}^{5} (2j - 1) = (2 \cdot 1 - 1) + \cdots + (2 \cdot 5 - 1)$$
$$= 1 + 3 + 5 + 7 + 9 = 25$$

$$\sum_{i=1}^{3} \frac{i}{i+1} = \frac{1}{1+1} + \frac{2}{2+1} + \frac{3}{3+1} = \frac{23}{12}$$

$$\prod_{i=1}^{3} \frac{i}{i+1} = \frac{1}{2} \cdot \frac{2}{3} \cdot \frac{3}{4} = \frac{1}{4}$$

The sum of the first $n + 1$ entries of $(a_1, a_2, \ldots)$ equals the sum of the first n entries plus the $n + 1$st entry:

$$\sum_{k=1}^{n+1} a_k = \sum_{k=1}^{n} a_k + a_{n+1} \qquad (5)$$

This simple observation is the key to many induction proofs.

EXAMPLE 2.12   Show that the sum of the first n positive odd integers is the square of n.

SOLUTION   The truth of this result is apparent from Figure 2.2, but we wish to establish it by induction. The kth odd integer is $2k - 1$; so we are to prove that

$$\sum_{k=1}^{n} (2k - 1) = n^2 \qquad (6)$$

For $n = 1$:

$$\sum_{k=1}^{1} (2k - 1) = 2 \cdot 1 - 1 = 1, \text{ and } 1^2 = 1$$

Now assume that (6) holds for arbitrary n. We must deduce Result (6) with n

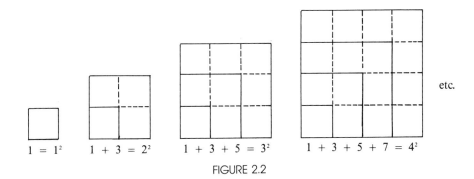

$$1 = 1^2 \qquad 1 + 3 = 2^2 \qquad 1 + 3 + 5 = 3^2 \qquad 1 + 3 + 5 + 7 = 4^2$$

FIGURE 2.2

replaced by $n + 1$; that is, $\sum_{k=1}^{n+1} (2k - 1) = (n + 1)^2$. Using (5) and then (6), we have

$$\sum_{k=1}^{n+1} (2k - 1) = \sum_{k=1}^{n} (2k - 1) + 2(n + 1) - 1$$
$$= n^2 + 2(n + 1) - 1 = n^2 + 2n + 1 = (n + 1)^2$$

Thus, $\sum_{k=1}^{n+1} (2k - 1) = (n + 1)^2$, that is, (6) holds for $n + 1$. This completes the proof that (6) holds for all n. ∎

EXAMPLE 2.13 Show that

$$\sum_{k=1}^{n} k^2 = n(n + 1)(2n + 1)/6 \qquad (7)$$

PROOF We use induction on n. For $n = 1$: $1^2 = 1$, and $1(1 + 1)(2 \cdot 1 + 1)/6 = 1$. Assume that (7) holds for n. Then $a_k = \sum_{k=1}^{n+1} k^2 = \sum_{k=1}^{n} k^2 + (n + 1)^2 = n(n + 1)(2n + 1)/6 + 6(n + 1)^2/6 = (n + 1)(2n^2 + n + 6n + 6)/6 = (n + 1)(n + 2)(2n + 3)/6$, which (as you should check) is (7) with n replaced by $n + 1$. This completes the proof. ∎

Not all inductions start at $n = 1$. If S contains an integer a and S satisfies (2) for every integer $n \geq a$, then S contains $a, a + 1, a + 2, \ldots$ and all integers beyond.

Not all results proved by induction are equalities, such as (6) and (7). Here is an example of another type of result that can be proved by induction.

EXAMPLE 2.14 For which positive integers n is 2^n greater than n^2?

SOLUTION $2^n > n^2$ is false for $n = 2, 3, 4$ and true for $n = 5$ and 6. We conjecture that $2^n > n^2$ for all $n \geq 5$, and we prove this conjecture by induction starting at 5. For $n = 5$:

$2^5 = 32 > 25 = 5^2$. Assume that $n \geqslant 5$ and $2^n > n^2$. Then

$$2^{n+1} = 2 \cdot 2^n > 2n^2$$
$$= n^2 + n^2 \geqslant n^2 + 5n$$
$$= n^2 + 2n + 3n > n^2 + 2n + 1$$
$$= (n+1)^2$$

Thus, $2^{n+1} > (n+1)^2$, and the proof is complete.   ■

Here is an enumeration result in set theory, proved by induction.

EXAMPLE 2.15   Prove that every n-element set has exactly 2^n subsets.

PROOF   (By induction on n.) Since the empty set has no elements, we begin at $n = 0$. The only subset of $\varnothing$ is $\varnothing$; so the number of subsets of $\varnothing$ is $1 = 2^0$. Now assume that every n-element set has 2^n subsets. Let A be an $(n+1)$-element set, where $n \geqslant 0$. We must deduce that A has exactly 2^{n+1} subsets. Since $A \neq \varnothing$, we may choose an element a of A. Partition the class of all subsets of A into two subclasses: (1) the subsets that do not contain a; (2) the subsets that do contain a. The subsets in subclass (1) are just the subsets of the n-element set $A \sim \{a\}$; by the assumption, there are 2^n of these. The subsets of subclass (2) are the subsets of the form $B \cup \{a\}$, where $B \subset A \sim \{a\}$. Again by the assumption, there are 2^n of these. Then the total number of subsets of A is $2^n + 2^n = 2 \cdot 2^n = 2^{n+1}$, and the result is proved.   ■

For an example of an induction application in computer science, we first introduce some useful definitions.

The **floor** of a number x, denoted $\lfloor x \rfloor$, is the largest integer that is less than or equal to x.   **(8)**

(Some texts and computers call the floor "the greatest integer in x," and denote it $[x]$ or INT x.)

The **ceiling** of a number x, denoted $\lceil x \rceil$, is the smallest integer that is greater than or equal to x.   **(9)**

For example, $\lfloor \pi \rfloor = 3$ and $\lceil \pi \rceil = 4$.

The **binary logarithm** of a positive number x, denoted lg x (or $\log_2 x$), is the number y such that $2^y = x$.   **(10)**

For instance, $\lg 8 = 3$, because $2^3 = 8$, and $\lg 0.25 = -2$, because $2^{-2} = 1/2^2$ $= 1/4 = 0.25$.

Your calculator probably does not have a lg key, but $\lg x$ can be found with the log key from the formula

$$\lg x = \frac{\log x}{\log 2} \tag{11}$$

For example, $\lg 747 = \log 747/\log 2 \doteq 2.873/0.301 \doteq 9.545*$; so $\lfloor \lg 747 \rfloor = 9$ and $\lceil \lg 747 \rceil = 10$. For a full explanation of logarithms see any precalculus text.

EXAMPLE 2.16   In Program 1.8 of Section 1.2 we presented an algorithm to find the position of a number b in an ordered sequence $a_1 \leqslant \cdots \leqslant a_n$. The algorithm used between 1 and n comparisons of b with various a_i, depending on the position of b. We now present an algorithm that will always find the position of b with at most $\lfloor \lg n \rfloor$ $+ 1$ comparisons. The idea is simple: first find in which half of the sequence b belongs; then find in which half of that half b belongs; continue until b is positioned.

In order to be able to divide the sequence into equal halves, the halves into equal halves, and so on, we first consider the case where the length of the sequence is a power of two; that is, $n = 2^m$, for some nonnegative integer m. Then $\lg n = m$ and $\lfloor \lg n \rfloor + 1 = m + 1$. We prove by induction on m that b can be positioned in $a_1 \leqslant \cdots \leqslant a_{2^m}$ with at most $m + 1$ comparisons. For $m = 0$: b can be positioned in one comparison. Now assume the result for arbitrary $m \geqslant 0$ and consider the sequence $a_1 \leqslant \cdots \leqslant a_{2^{m+1}}$. We must deduce that b can be positioned in this sequence with at most $m + 2$ comparisons. Compare b with a_{2^m} (one comparison). If $b \leqslant a_{2^m}$, then position b in $a_1 \leqslant \cdots \leqslant a_{2^m}$ (by assumption, this will require at most $m + 1$ comparisons). Otherwise, position b in $a_{2^m+1} \leqslant \cdots \leqslant a_{2^{m+1}}$ (this sequence also has 2^m members, so again by assumption this can be done in at most $m + 1$ comparisons). Then b has been positioned in $a_1 \leqslant \cdots \leqslant a_{2^{m+1}}$ in at most $1 + m + 1 = (m + 1) + 1$ comparisons, and the result is proved.

If it is known in advance that $b \leqslant a_{2^m}$, then, in fact, b can be positioned in $a_1 \leqslant \cdots \leqslant a_{2^m}$ in at most m (rather than $m + 1$) comparisons. We prove this by induction. For $m = 0$: If $b \leqslant a_1$, then b is first in the sequence a_1, with no comparisons needed. Now assume the result for m and consider the sequence $a_1 \leqslant \cdots \leqslant a_{2^{m+1}}$, with $b \leqslant a_{2^{m+1}}$. Compare b with a_{2^m}. If $b \leqslant a_{2^m}$, position b in $a_1 \leqslant \cdots \leqslant a_{2^m}$, with at most m comparisons. Otherwise, position b in a_{2^m+1} $\leqslant \cdots \leqslant a_{2^{m+1}}$, with at most m comparisons, since $b \leqslant a_{2^{m+1}}$. Then b can be positioned in $a_1 \leqslant \cdots \leqslant a_{2^{m+1}}$, with at most $m + 1$ comparisons, and the result is shown.

---

* The symbol $\doteq$ means "equal to within one digit in the last decimal place shown." For instance, $\frac{1}{7} \doteq 0.1$; $\frac{1}{7} \doteq 0.14$; $\frac{1}{7} \doteq 0.141$; and $\frac{1}{7} \doteq 0.142$.

Finally, suppose the length n of the sequence $a_1 \leqslant \cdots \leqslant a_n$ is not a power of 2. Let 2^m be the largest power of 2 (with m an integer) that is less than n. Then $2^m < n < 2^{m+1}$; so $m < \lg n < m + 1$ and $\lfloor \lg n \rfloor = m$. Choose a number c at least as large as a_n and b ($c = |a_n| + |b|$ will do) and define $a_{n+1} = \cdots = a_{2^m+1} = c$. Then $a_1 \leqslant \cdots \leqslant a_{2^m+1}$ and $b \leqslant a_{2^m+1}$; so by the result above, b can be positioned in the sequence $a_1 \leqslant \cdots \leqslant a_{2^m+1}$ with at most $m + 1$ comparisons. Moreover, since $b \leqslant a_{n+1}$, the position of b in the extended sequence $a_1 \leqslant \cdots \leqslant a_{2^m+1}$ will also be the position of b in the original sequence $a_1 \leqslant \cdots \leqslant a_n$. Thus, b can be positioned in $a_1 \leqslant \cdots \leqslant a_n$ with at most $m + 1 = \lfloor \lg n \rfloor + 1$ comparisons. This completes the example.   ◻

There is another form of mathematical induction called **strong induction** (or **complete induction**), which is easier to use for some results. Despite its name, strong induction is logically equivalent to, not stronger than, "ordinary" induction (which is sometimes called **weak induction**). To prove a result by strong induction beginning at an integer a, first obtain the result for a. Then for an arbitrary integer $n \geqslant a$, assume that the result holds for *all* integers from a to n *inclusive*; that is, for all integers k such that $a \leqslant k \leqslant n$, and deduce that the result holds for $n + 1$. It follows that the result holds for all integers greater than or equal to a.

For an example of a proof by strong induction, recall first that a **prime** is an integer greater than one that is not the product of two smaller positive integers. Thus, 11 is prime, but $12 = 3 \cdot 4$ is not.

EXAMPLE 2.17   Prove that every integer $n > 1$ is either a prime or the product of primes.

SOLUTION   We will use strong induction on n, beginning at 2. First, $n = 2$ is prime. Now assume that $n \geqslant 2$ and that every integer k with $2 \leqslant k \leqslant n$ is either prime or the product of primes. We must show that $n + 1$ is a prime or the product of primes. If $n + 1$ is a prime, we are done. Otherwise, $n + 1$ is the product of two smaller integers, say $n + 1 = k_1 k_2$. Then $2 \leqslant k_1 \leqslant n$ and $2 \leqslant k_2 \leqslant n$, so by assumption k_1 is a prime or the product of primes and k_2 is a prime or the product of primes. Then $k_1 k_2 = n + 1$ is the product of primes. This completes the proof.   ◻

The expression of an integer $n > 1$ as the product of primes is called its **prime decomposition**. It is economical to group repeated primes in a decomposition and write their product in exponent form. Thus, $360 = 2 \cdot 2 \cdot 2 \cdot 3 \cdot 3 \cdot 5 = 2^3 3^2 5$. By Example 2.17, every $n > 1$ may be written as

$$n = \prod_{i=1}^{m} p_i^{e_i} \tag{12}$$

where $p_1, \ldots, p_m$ are distinct primes and $e_1, \ldots, e_m$ are positive integers. Some algorithms connected with prime decomposition appear in the exercises.

EXERCISES

1. Prove that $\sum_{k=1}^{n} k^3 = n^2(n+1)^2/4$.

2. Prove that $\sum_{k=1}^{n} k^3 = \left(\sum_{k=1}^{n} k\right)^2$.

3. What's wrong with the following "proof by induction" that all students in any class have equal ability? Let n be the size of the class. If $n = 1$, then the result is trivially true. Suppose that all students in any class of size n have the same ability. Consider a class of $n + 1$ students. The first n students have the same ability, and the last n students have the same ability; so they *all* have the same ability. This concludes the proof.

4. (See Exercise 3.) How about this "proof by induction" that every class of n students contains one who can run a 3-minute mile? Consider a class of $n + 1$ students. Make one student leave. The remaining students are in a class of n, so one of them can run a 3-minute mile. Since that student was in the original class, we are done.

5. Prove that the sum of the first n positive even integers is $n^2 + n$.

6. Prove that $\sum_{k=0}^{n} \dfrac{k+1}{k+2} = 1/(n+2)$.

7. For which natural numbers n is $n! > 4^n$?

8. Prove by induction that the number of lines containing at least two of n given points is at most $n(n-1)/2$.

9. Prove that the sum of every other square: $1^2 + 3^2 + 5^2 + \cdots + (n-1)^2$ is $n(n^2-1)/6$.

10. (See Exercise 9.) Prove that the sum of every other square: $2^2 + 4^2 + 6^2 + \cdots + (n-1)^2$ is also $n(n^2-1)/6$.

In Exercises 11–14 graph the equations.

11. $y = \lfloor x \rfloor$.

12. $y = \lceil x \rceil$.

13. $y = x - \lfloor x \rfloor$.

14. $y = \lceil x \rceil - x$.

15. Find all solutions of $\lfloor x \rfloor = \lceil x \rceil$.

16. Find, either exactly or to within 0.001, the binary logarithms of 2, 5, 512, and 1000.

17. Establish Formula (11) as follows. Let $y = \lg x$. Explain why $x = 2^y$. Take log of both sides. Solve for y.

18. Find $\lg(\lg 256)$.

19. Use induction to deduce the general principle of multiplication (Result 2.1(7)) from the principle of multiplication (Result 2.1(6)).

20. Prove that every polygon can be divided into triangles. (Do not assume that the polygon is convex; it might be as shown.)

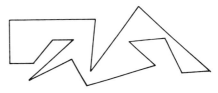

21. Let f be a function from the set $\mathbf{N}$ of natural numbers to $\mathbf{N}$ such that $f(0) = 1$ and, for all natural numbers m and n, $f(n+m) = f(m)f(n)$. Prove that, for all positive integers n, $f(n) = [f(1)]^n$.

22. Let m and n be natural numbers with $m \leqslant n$. Prove that

$$\sum_{k=m}^{n} \binom{k}{m} = \binom{n+1}{m+1}$$

2.3

Recursion

Consider an infinite sequence $(a_0, a_1, a_2, \ldots)$. Suppose that

$$a_0 = 0, \quad a_1 = 1 \qquad (1)$$

and for all integers $n \geqslant 2$,

$$a_n = a_{n-1} + a_{n-2} \qquad (2)$$

Then $a_2 = a_1 + a_0 = 1 + 0 = 1$. Then $a_3 = a_2 + a_1 = 1 + 1 = 2$. Then $a_4 = a_3 + a_2$ $= 2 + 1 = 3$; $a_5 = 3 + 2 = 5$; $a_6 = 5 + 3 = 8$; and so on. Thus, in this case the sequence begins: $(0, 1, 1, 2, 3, 5, 8, \ldots)$. Equation (2) is an example of a **recurrence relation**, in which a mathematical object (in this case the number a_n) is described in terms of previously described objects (a_{n-1} and a_{n-2}). Equations (1) are the **initial conditions**, which enable us to start using the recurrence relation to obtain the rest of the sequence. Although the fact seems obvious, we will use strong induction on n to prove that (1) and (2) really do define a_n for all nonnegative integers n. First, (1) defines a_0 and a_1. Now assume that $n \geqslant 2$ and that a_k has been defined for $0 \leqslant k \leqslant n - 1$. Then by (2) a_n is defined. This completes the proof. Even though (1) and (2) define a_n for all $n \geqslant 0$, we have not been given a simple formula for a_n in terms of n. For instance, it would take a number of applications of (2) to find a_{15}. (Show that $a_{15} = 610$.)* Sometimes a simple formula can be found.

EXAMPLE 2.18   Suppose $a_1 = 1$ and for $n \geqslant 2$, $a_n = 3a_{n-1}$. Find a simple formula for a_n.

FIRST SOLUTION $a_1 = 1$; $a_2 = 3$; $a_3 = 3^2$; $a_4 = 3^3$. We conjecture that $a_n = 3^{n-1}$. This conjecture can easily be proved by induction.

SECOND SOLUTION $a_n = 3a_{n-1} = 3^2 a_{n-2} = 3^3 a_{n-3} = \cdots = 3^{n-1} a_1 = 3^{n-1}$.   ∎

A **general recurrence relation** for a sequence $(a_0, a_1, \ldots)$ is an equation of the form

$$a_n = f(n, a_{n-1}, a_{n-2}, \ldots, a_{n-k}), \text{ for } n \geqslant k \qquad (3)$$

where f is a function of $k + 1$ variables and k is a fixed positive integer. To use (3) to obtain the sequence, the values of $a_0, a_1, \ldots, a_{k-1}$ must be given. Thus, the

---

* The sequence defined by (1) and (2) is called the **Fibonacci sequence**. Fibonacci (meaning "son of Bonaccio") was the nickname of Leonardo of Pisa (circa 1180–1250), who was the greatest medieval mathematician. Fibonacci completed the classic *Liber Abaci* in 1202. This text helped introduce the Hindu-Arabic notation for numbers in use today. The book also contains the problem:

> How many pairs of rabbits will be produced in a year, beginning with a single pair, if in every month each pair bears a new pair which becomes productive from the second month on?

This problem gives rise to the Fibonacci sequence. (See *A History of Mathematics* by Carl B. Boyer, Wiley, New York, 1968, page 281.)

initial conditions are of the form

$$a_0 = b_0, \ a_1 = b_1, \ \ldots, \ a_{k-1} = b_{k-1} \tag{4}$$

where $b_0, \ldots, b_{k-1}$ are given numbers.

EXAMPLE 2.19 Find a_5 for the sequence given by the initial conditions $a_0 = 1$, $a_1 = -1$, $a_2 = 2$, and recurrence relation $a_n = 2a_{n-1}a_{n-3} - a_{n-2}$, $n \geq 3$.

SOLUTION $a_3 = 2a_2a_0 - a_1 = 2 \cdot 2 \cdot 1 - (-1) = 5$; $\quad a_4 = 2a_3a_1 - a_2 = 2 \cdot 5(-1) - 2 = -12$; $a_5 = 2a_4a_2 - a_3 = 2(-12) \cdot 2 - 5 = -53$. □

Much work has been done on recurrence relations. In particular, there is a method for solving any **linear** recurrence relation of **order** k; that is, any relation of the form*

$$a_n = c_1 a_{n-1} + c_2 a_{n-2} + \cdots + c_k a_{n-k}, \ n \geq k \tag{5}$$

where $c_1, \ldots, c_k$ are constants and $c_k \neq 0$. The idea is to first seek solutions of the form $a_i = x^i$. Substituting this into (5) gives

$$x^n = c_1 x^{n-1} + c_2 x^{n-2} + \cdots + c_k x^{n-k}$$

Divide through by x^{n-k} to obtain

$$x^k = c_1 x^{k-1} + c_2 x^{k-2} + \cdots + c_k$$

and hence

$$x^k - c_1 x^{k-1} - c_2 x^{k-2} - \cdots - c_{k-1}x - c_k = 0 \tag{6}$$

Equation (6) is called the **characteristic equation** of Relation (5). The solutions of (6) are the **characteristic roots** of (5). Thus, $a_n = x^n$ is a solution of (5) if and only if x is a characteristic root.

At this point we restrict ourselves to linear recurrences of order $k = 2$ and leave higher orders to the exercises. Then the characteristic equation is a quadratic, which can be solved by the following well-known formula:

The **roots** of $ax^2 + bx + c$, $a \neq 0$, are

$$r_1 = \frac{-b + \sqrt{b^2 - 4ac}}{2a} \quad \text{and} \quad r_2 = \frac{-b - \sqrt{b^2 - 4ac}}{2a} \tag{7}$$

Note that if $b^2 - 4ac = 0$, then $r_1 = r_2$ and the equation has only one root.

---

* Actually, (5) is a special kind of linear recurrence relation, the full name of which is **linear homogeneous constant-coefficient** recurrence relation.

Let r_1 and r_2 be the characteristic roots of a second-order linear recurrence relation. Then r_1^n and r_2^n are solutions. In fact, it is easy to see that $p_1 r_1^n + p_2 r_2^n$ is a solution for all constants p_1, p_2. If $r_1 \neq r_2$, it can be shown that *every* solution is of this form, so $p_1 r_1^n + p_2 r_2^n$ is the **general solution** of the relation. If $r_1 = r_2$, it can be shown that nr_1^n is also a solution and that the general solution is $p_1 r_1^n + p_2 n r_2^n$ where p_1, p_2 are constants. These solutions are general solutions for the recurrence relation only. A particular problem will also have initial conditions. In a particular problem, the initial conditions will determine particular values of p_1 and p_2.

☐ ALGORITHM 2.1

To solve the recurrence $a_n = c_1 a_{n-1} + c_2 a_{n-2}$, $n \geqslant 2$, with initial conditions $a_0 = b_0$, $a_1 = b_1$.

1. Write the characteristic equation ($x^2 - c_1 x - c_2 = 0$) and find the characteristic roots r_1 and r_2.
2. If $r_1 \neq r_2$, let $g_n = p_1 r_1^n + p_2 r_2^n$. If $r_1 = r_2$, let $g_n = p_1 r_1^n + p_2 n r_2^n$.
3. Solve the system $g_0 = b_0$, $g_1 = b_1$, for p_1 and p_2.
4. Using the values of p_1 and p_2 found in Step 3, the solution is $a_n = g_n$. ☐

EXAMPLE 2.20

SOLUTION

Solve the recurrence relation (2) with initial conditions (1).

The characteristic equation is $x^2 - x - 1 = 0$. By (7) with $a = 1$, $b = -1$, and $c = -1$, the characteristic roots are $r_1 = (1 + \sqrt{5})/2)$ and $(1 - \sqrt{5})/2)$. Since $r_1 \neq r_2$, let $g_n = p_1 r_1^n + p_2 r_2^n$. We must solve the system $g_0 = 0$, $g_1 = 1$; that is,

$$\begin{bmatrix} p_1 + p_2 = 0 \\ p_1(1 + \sqrt{5})/2 + p_2(1 - \sqrt{5})/2 = 1 \end{bmatrix}$$

This is easily done by Gauss-Jordan Reduction or other means. The reader should obtain the solution, which is $p_1 = \sqrt{5}/5$, $p_2 = -\sqrt{5}/5$. Then

$$a_n = \frac{\sqrt{5}}{5}\left[\left(\frac{1+\sqrt{5}}{2}\right)^n - \left(\frac{1-\sqrt{5}}{2}\right)^n\right] \tag{8*}$$

Earlier we found directly that $a_2 = 1$ and $a_{15} = 610$. It is easy to use (8) to check the first result:

$$a_2 = (\sqrt{5}/5)[((1 + \sqrt{5})/2)^2 - ((1 - \sqrt{5})/2)^2]$$
$$= (\sqrt{5}/5)[(1 + 2\sqrt{5} + 5)/4 - (1 - 2\sqrt{5} + 5)/4]$$
$$= (\sqrt{5}/5)(4\sqrt{5}/4) = 1$$

---

* Equation (8) is often called **Binet's formula** after J. P. M. Binet, who discovered it in 1843.

For the second result, our calculator gives

$$a_{15} = (\sqrt{5}/5)[((1+\sqrt{5})/2)^{15} - ((1-\sqrt{5})/2)^{15}] \doteq 609.9999995$$

Since a_{15} must obviously be an integer, the result is verified.   ■

EXAMPLE 2.21   Solve $a_0 = 2$, $a_1 = -3$, $a_n = -6a_{n-1} - 9a_{n-2}$.

SOLUTION   The characteristic equation is $x^2 + 6x + 9 = 0$, so the roots are $r_1 = r_2 = -3$. Let $g_n = p_1(-3)^n + p_2 n(-3)^n$ and solve $g_0 = 2$, $g_1 = -3$; that is,

$$\begin{bmatrix} p_1 & = & 2 \\ -3p_1 - 3p_2 & = & -3 \end{bmatrix}$$

to get $p_1 = 2$, $p_2 = -1$. Then $a_n = 2(-3)^n - n(-3)^n = (2-n)(-3)^n$. We can check by substitution into the relation:

$$\begin{aligned}
-6a_{n-1} - 9a_{n-2} &= -6[2-(n-1)](-3)^{n-1} - 9[2-(n-2)](-3)^{n-2} \\
&= (-3)^{n-2}[-6(3-n)(-3) - 9(4-n)] \\
&= (-3)^{n-2}(18-9n) \\
&= (-3)^{n-2}9(2-n) \\
&= (2-n)(-3)^n \\
&= a_n \checkmark
\end{aligned}$$
■

Recursion is used in many ways besides recurrence relations. Here, for example, is a recursive description of an algorithm called MAX to find the maximum M of a sequence $(a_i, \ldots, a_{i+n-1})$ of length n. For $n = 1$, the program is

1. $M \leftarrow a_i$. STOP

Now assume that $n > 1$ and that the program has been described for all sequences of length k, where $1 \leqslant k \leqslant n-1$. To obtain the program for $(a_i, \ldots, a_{i+n-1})$, note that the sequences $(a_i, \ldots, a_{i+\lfloor n/2 \rfloor - 1})$ and $(a_{i+\lfloor n/2 \rfloor}, \ldots, a_{i+n-1})$ have lengths $\lfloor n/2 \rfloor$ and $n - \lfloor n/2 \rfloor$, which are between 1 and $n-1$, inclusive. Then by assumption, MAX may be applied to these sequences. Here is MAX for $(a_i, \ldots, a_{i+n-1})$.

1. $M_1 \leftarrow \text{MAX}(a_i, \ldots, a_{i+\lfloor n/2 \rfloor - 1})$
2. $M_2 \leftarrow \text{MAX}(a_{i+\lfloor n/2 \rfloor}, \ldots, a_{i+n-1})$
3. If $M_1 \leqslant M_2$ then $M \leftarrow M_2$; otherwise $M \leftarrow M_1$. STOP

Figure 2.3 shows schematically the operation of MAX on the sequence $(2, 4, 1, 5, 3)$.

Many sorting algorithms are easy to describe recursively. One called MERGESORT works like this: (1) split the sequence in half; (2) sort each half; (3) merge the halves. We first describe Step 3.

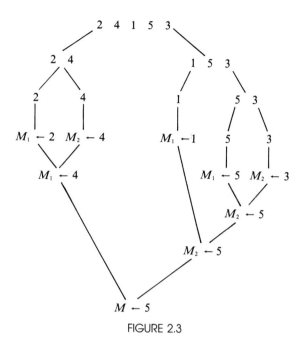

FIGURE 2.3

■ PROGRAM 2.1 **MERGE $(a_1, \ldots, a_m)$ and $(a_{m+1}, \ldots, a_n)$. This program merges two nondecreasing sequences $a_1 \leqslant \cdots \leqslant a_m$ and $a_{m+1} \leqslant \cdots \leqslant a_n$ into a nondecreasing sequence, renamed $a_1 \leqslant \cdots \leqslant a_n$.**

1. {Label positions in the sequences.} $i \leftarrow 1$.
   {position in first sequence}; $j \leftarrow m + 1$ {position in second sequence};
   $k \leftarrow 1$ {position in merged sequence}

2. If $i = m + 1$ or $j = n + 1$ then go to 5

3. {Temporarily store the merged sequence in array b.} If $a_i \leqslant a_j$ then $b_k \leftarrow a_i$
   and $i \leftarrow i + 1$; otherwise $b_k \leftarrow a_j$ and $j \leftarrow j + 1$

4. $k \leftarrow k + 1$ and go to 2

5. If $i = m + 1$ then go to 7

6. {The second sequence is merged; copy the rest of the first sequence.} $b_k \leftarrow a_i$;
   $i \leftarrow i + 1$; $k \leftarrow k + 1$; and go to 5

7. If $j = n + 1$ then go to 9

8. {The first sequence is merged; copy the rest of the second sequence.} $b_k \leftarrow a_j$;
   $j \leftarrow j + 1$; $k \leftarrow k + 1$; and go to 7

9. {Transfer array b to array a.} $k \leftarrow 1$

10. $a_k \leftarrow b_k$

11. If $k = n$ then STOP; otherwise $k \leftarrow k + 1$ and go to 10.   ■

We can now recursively describe MERGESORT for $(a_1, \ldots, a_n)$. For $n = 1$, the program is

1. STOP

Assume that $n > 1$ and that the program has been described for all programs of length k, where $1 \leqslant k \leqslant n - 1$. Then the program for $(a_1, \ldots, a_n)$ is

1. MERGESORT $(a_1, \ldots, a_{\lfloor n/2 \rfloor})$
2. MERGESORT $(a_{\lfloor n/2 \rfloor + 1}, \ldots, a_n)$
3. MERGE $(a_1, \ldots, a_{\lfloor n/2 \rfloor})$ and $(a_{\lfloor n/2 \rfloor + 1}, \ldots, a_n)$. STOP

Another sorting program is described in the exercises.

EXERCISES

1. If $a_0 = 2$, $a_1 = 0$, and $a_n = a_{n-1}^2 - a_{n-2}^2$, for $n \geqslant 2$, find a_7.

2. If $a_0 = 0$, $a_1 = 2$, and $a_n = a_{n-1}^2 - a_{n-2}^2$, for $n \geqslant 2$, find a_7.

3. If $a_1 = a_2 = a_3 = a_4 = 1$ and

$$a_n = (a_{n-1} + a_{n-2})a_{n-3}/a_{n-4}$$

for $n \geqslant 5$, find a_7.

4. If $a_{-2} = a_0 = 0$, $a_{-1} = a_1 = 1$, and $a_n = a_{n-1}^2 + a_{n-2}^2 + a_{n-3}^2 + a_{n-4}^2$, for $n \geqslant -2$, find a_7.

5. Solve $a_n = 5a_{n-1} - 6a_{n-2}$, $a_0 = -1$, $a_1 = 0$.

6. Solve $a_n = a_{n-2}/4$, $a_0 = 6$, $a_1 = -1$.

7. Solve $a_n = 10a_{n-1} - 25a_{n-2}$, $a_0 = 1$, $a_1 = 0$.

8. Solve $a_n = a_{n-2}$, $a_0 = 2$, $a_1 = 0$.

9. Solve $a_n = 17a_{n-1}/4 - a_{n-2}$, $a_0 = \frac{17}{4}$, $a_1 = 2$.

10. Solve $9a_n = 12a_{n-1} - 4a_{n-2}$, $a_0 = 1$, $a_1 = \frac{5}{3}$.

If Equation (6) has distinct roots $r_1, r_2, \ldots, r_k$, then the general solution of (5) is $a_n = p_1 r_1^n + p_2 r_2^n + \cdots + p_k r_k^n$. The constants $p_1, p_2, \ldots, p_k$ may be found from the initial conditions $a_0 = b_0$, $a_1 = b_1, \ldots, a_{k-1} = b_{k-1}$. Use this formula to solve Exercises 11–14. In each exercise the roots are integers.

11. Solve $a_n = 9a_{n-1} - 26a_{n-2} + 24a_{n-3}$, $n \geqslant 3$; $a_0 = 1$, $a_1 = 3$, $a_2 = 11$.

12. Solve $a_n = 5a_{n-1} + a_{n-2} - 5a_{n-3}$, $n \geqslant 3$; $a_0 = 2$, $a_1 = -6$, $a_2 = -22$.

13. Solve $a_n = 5a_{n-2} - 4a_{n-4}$, $n \geqslant 4$; $a_0 = 5$, $a_1 = -1$, $a_2 = 15$, $a_3 = -7$.

14. Solve $a_n = 15a_{n-2} + 10a_{n-3} - 24a_{n-4}$, $n \geqslant 4$; $a_0 = 4$, $a_1 = 8$, $a_2 = 14$, $a_3 = 86$.

15. Solve $a_n = na_{n-1}$, $n \geqslant 1$; $a_0 = 1$.

16. Solve $a_n = 2na_{n-1}$, $n \geqslant 1$; $a_0 = 1$.

In Exercises 17 and 18 run the MAX algorithm for the given sequences by drawing a figure like Figure 2.3.

17. $(2, 4, 3, 5, 4, 5, 2)$

18. $(1, 7, 4, 2, 4, 3, 2, 4, 1)$

In Exercises 19 and 20 run the MERGE algorithm for the given sequences.

19. MERGE $(4, 5, 8)$ and $(2, 4, 6, 9)$.

20. MERGE $(1, 3, 5, 7)$ and $(3, 5, 6, 8)$.

In Exercises 21 and 22 run MERGESORT for the given sequences by drawing a figure. For example, splitting $(4, 5, 2, 1, 3, 9, 7)$ at $\lfloor n/2 \rfloor = 3$ is shown as

$$(4, 5, 2, 1, 3, 9, 7)$$

$$(4, 5, 2) \qquad (1, 3, 9, 7)$$

and merging $(2, 4, 5)$ with $(1, 3, 7, 9)$ is shown as

$$(2, 4, 5) \qquad (1, 3, 7, 9)$$

$$(1, 2, 3, 4, 5, 7, 9)$$

21. MERGESORT (7, 6, 5, 4, 3, 2, 1).

22. MERGESORT (1, 2, 1, 3, 1, 2, 1, 2, 1).

23. Suppose we wish to LOCATE b in $(a_1, \ldots, a_n)$, that is, to find the smallest i, if any, such that $b = a_i$. One way to proceed is this: Locate b in the left half sequence. If b is not there then locate b in the right half. If b is not there, then report "not found." Give a recursive description of LOCATE.

The QUICKSORT algorithm to sort a sequence $(a_1, \ldots, a_n)$, where $n > 1$, may be recursively described as follows.

1. $i \leftarrow 1, j \leftarrow n$
2. If $a_1 < a_j$ then $j \leftarrow j - 1$ and go to 2

3. If $i = j$ then go to 5; otherwise $i \leftarrow i + 1$
4. If $a_i < a_1$ then go to 3; otherwise $a_i \leftrightarrow a_j$ and go to 2
5. $a_i \leftrightarrow a_1$
6. If $i = 1$ then go to 8
7. QUICKSORT $(a_1, \ldots, a_{i-1})$
8. If $i = n$ then STOP
9. QUICKSORT $(a_{i+1}, \ldots, a_n)$

24. What is the QUICKSORT algorithm for $n = 1$?

25. After instruction 5 has been executed, what is the relation between a_i and the other entries of the sequence?

26. Run QUICKSORT for (4, 3, 1, 6, 7, 2, 8, 5).

2.4
Algorithm Efficiency

The **efficiency** of an algorithm in solving a given problem may be measured by the amount of storage space required by the algorithm during its operation or by the time required for the answer to be obtained. In this section we concentrate on the time measure. The time required to solve a problem is determined by the number and types of steps taken by the algorithm. In practice some types of steps take much more time than others, so that only these types of steps need be enumerated to get a reasonable measure of efficiency. For IMCOM programs we shall enumerate only arithmetic operations with data $(+, -, \times, \div)$, and comparisons of data (If $a = b$, then ...; If $a \leqslant b$, then ...; etc.), and replacements of data $(a \leftarrow b)$.

The efficiency of an algorithm depends on the size of the problem, as measured by the amount of data it contains. But two problems of the same size may have very different solution times. For problems of fixed size, we may consider the **best case**, consisting of a problem for which the solution requires the fewest number of steps, the **worst case**, consisting of a problem for which the solution requires the greatest number of steps, and the **average case**, which is the average of the numbers of steps required to solve all problems of that size.

For a simple example, consider the following program for finding the first address, if any, at which a datum b appears in a sequence of data $(a_1, a_2, \ldots, a_n)$.

■ PROGRAM 2.2

1. $i \leftarrow 1$
2. If $b = a_i$ then "Datum first appears at address i." and STOP
3. If $i = n$ then "Datum not found." and STOP
4. $i \leftarrow i + 1$ and go to 2.   ■

The size of a problem for Program 2.2 is the length n of the data sequence. For a given problem, we will not count the comparisons $i = n$ of Instruction 3 or the operations $i \leftarrow i + 1$ of Instruction 4, but only the comparisons $b = a_i$ of Instruction 2. The reason is that i and n are merely positive integers, while the data b and a_i are likely to be more complicated material, such as business addresses or titles of magazine articles, which will take more time to compare.

If b first appears at address j, then Program 2.2 executes j steps, namely, the comparisons $b = a_1$, ..., $b = a_j$, before stopping. If b does not appear in the sequence, then n steps are executed. Thus, the best case has efficiency 1 and the two worst cases have efficiency n. Since there are two worst cases, there are $n + 1$ cases in all. Then the average efficiency is

$$\frac{(1 + \cdots + n) + n}{n + 1}$$

Now the reader may easily show by induction (Section 2.2) that

$$\sum_{j=1}^{n} j = \frac{n(n + 1)}{2} \tag{1}$$

Then the average efficiency of Program 2.2 is

$$E(\text{Program 2.2}) = \frac{n(n + 1)/2 + n}{n + 1} = \frac{n^2 + 3n}{2n + 2} \tag{2}$$

To help understand the size and rate of growth of complicated expressions such as (2), a number of techniques and notations are used to approximate expressions by simpler expressions. By long division,

$$\frac{n^2 + 3n}{2n + 2} = \frac{n}{2} + 1 - \frac{1}{n + 1}$$

For large n, the term $1/(n + 1)$ is almost 0 and the constant term 1 is very small compared to the leading term $n/2$. We express this observation in two ways. First, two positive expressions $f(n)$ and $g(n)$ are said to be **asymptotic**, written $f(n) \sim g(n)$, if the quotient $f(n)/g(n)$ gets closer and closer to 1 as n gets larger and larger. To put this another way, $f(n) \sim g(n)$ if $f(n) = g(n)h(n)$, where $h(n)$ approaches 1 as n increases. We have

$$\frac{n}{2} + 1 - \frac{1}{n + 1} = \frac{n}{2}\left(1 + \frac{2}{n} - \frac{2}{n(n + 1)}\right)$$

and obviously $1 + \dfrac{2}{n} - \dfrac{2}{n(n + 1)}$ approaches 1 as n increases. Thus,

$$E(\text{Program 2.2}) \sim \frac{n}{2} \tag{3}$$

Second, $f(n)$ is said to be of **order of magnitude** $g(n)$, written $f(n) = O(g(n))$ and read "$f(n)$ is big oh $g(n)$," if there are constants N and k such that

$$\text{for all } n > N, \; f(n) \leqslant kg(n) \tag{4}$$

Now $n/2 + 1 - 1/(n+1) \leqslant n/2 + 1 \leqslant n/2 + n/2 = n$ for all $n > 1$; so

$$E(\text{Program } 2.2) = O(n) \tag{5}$$

An order-of-magnitude statement is less precise than an asymptotic statement. If $f(n) \sim g(n)$, then $f(n) = O(g(n))$, but not conversely. For example, $2n = O(n)$, but $2n$ is not asymptotic to n. We say $g_1(n)$ *has lower order of magnitude than* $g_2(n)$, written $O(g_1(n)) \ll O(g_2(n))$, if $g_1(n) = O(g_2(n))$ but $g_2(n) \neq O(g_1(n))$. For example, we claim that $O(n) \ll O(n^2)$. Clearly, $n = O(n^2)$ (take $k = N = 1$). Suppose that $n^2 = O(n)$. Then there are constants N and k such that $n^2 \leqslant kn$ for all $n > N$. But then $n \leqslant k$ for all $n > N$, which is absurd. Hence, $n^2 \neq O(n)$. Similarly, $O(n^2) \ll O(n^3) \ll O(n^4) \ll \cdots$. In the other direction it is not hard to see that $O(n) \gg O(\sqrt{n}) \gg O(\sqrt[3]{n}) \gg \cdots$. A very high order is the binary exponential order $O(2^n)$. It can be shown that $O(n^m) \ll O(2^n)$ for all integers m. A very low order is the binary logarithmic order $\lg n$. It can be shown that $O(\sqrt[m]{n}) \gg O(\lg n)$ for all integers m. The lowest order is 1. If $f(n) = O(1)$, then $f(n) \leqslant k \cdot 1 = k$ for all $n > N$. If $K = \max(f(1), \ldots, f(N), k)$, then $f(n) \leqslant K$ for all n. Thus, an expression of order 1 is bounded. An important order of magnitude for computer science is $n \lg n$. It can be shown that $O(n) \ll O(n \lg n) \ll O(n^2)$. For most calculations of algorithmic efficiency, it is enough to remember that

$$O(\lg n) \ll O(n) \ll O(n \lg n) \ll O(n^2) \ll \cdots \ll O(2^n) \tag{6}$$

Notice that only a few simple expressions $g(n)$ are used in the notation $O(g(n))$.

To get some feeling for these orders, suppose that a step requires $10^{-6} = 0.000001$ second to complete. (10^{-6} is one-millionth of a second, or a **microsecond**.) Consider a problem of size $n = 10^5 = 10,000$. If the algorithm has efficiency $\lg n$, then it will take $\lg 10^5 \doteq 17$ steps and will solve the problem in $17 \times 10^{-6} = 0.000017$ second. If the efficiency is n, it will take $10^5 \times 10^{-6} = 0.1$ second. If the efficiency is $n \lg n$, it will take $10^5 \lg 10^6 \times 10^{-6} \doteq 1.7$ seconds. If the efficiency is n^2, it will take $(10^5)^2 \times 10^{-6} = 10^4$ seconds, or about 4 hours 44 minutes. If the efficiency is 2^n, it will take $2^{10^5} \times 10^{-6}$ seconds, or about 10^{30000} years. Even if the problem size is only $n = 30$, an algorithm of efficiency 2^n would take over 30 years to obtain the solution.

EXAMPLE 2.22   In Example 2.16 of Section 2.2 we described an algorithm to find the position of an entry b in an ordered sequence $a_1 \leqslant \cdots \leqslant a_n$, with at most $\lfloor \lg n \rfloor + 1$ comparisons. Since $\lfloor \lg n \rfloor + 1 \leqslant \lg n + 1 \leqslant 2 \lg n$ for $n > 1$, the efficiency of this algorithm is $O(\lg n)$.   ∎

For another efficiency calculation, consider Gauss-Jordan Reduction of a system of linear equations (Section 1.4). Consider a system of n equations in n unknowns, $AX = B$. For the worst case, assume that no a_{ij} is 0 or 1 and that after each row operation no coefficients are 0 or 1 except for those that were deliberately made 0 or 1. First, clear C_1 with R_1. The first row operation is $R_1 \leftarrow a_{11}^{-1} R_1$, which involves $n+1$ divisions. The next $n-1$ row operations are $R_i \leftarrow -a_{i1} R_1 + R_i$, for $i = 2, 3, \ldots, n$. Each of these operations involves $n+1$ multiplications and $n+1$ additions. Then the number of arithmetic operations needed to clear C_1 with R_1 is $n+1+(n-1)(n+1+n+1) = (n+1)(2n-1)$. Since a_{21} is now 0, no arithmetic operations need be done with it. Then the number of arithmetic operations needed to clear C_2 with R_2 is $n + (n-1)(n+n) = n(2n-1)$. Similarly, the number of arithmetic operations needed to clear C_3 with R_3 is $(n-1)(2n-1)$, $\ldots$, and finally the number of arithmetic operations needed to clear C_n with R_n is $2(2n-1)$. At this point the answer may be read with no further operations. Then the efficiency of Gauss-Jordan Reduction of n equations in n unknowns, in the worst case, is

$$E(\text{Gauss-Jordan Reduction}) = (2n-1)[(n+1) + n + \cdots + 2]$$

We use Formula (1) to simplify the sum in brackets: $(n+1) + n + \cdots + 2 + 1$

$$= \sum_{j=1}^{n+1} j = (\tfrac{1}{2})(n+1)(n+2). \text{ Thus, } (n+1) + n + \cdots + 2 = (\tfrac{1}{2})(n+1)(n+2) - 1.$$

Then

$$\begin{aligned} E(\text{Gauss-Jordan Reduction}) &= (2n-1)[(\tfrac{1}{2})(n+1)(n+2) - 1] \\ &= n^3 + \tfrac{5}{2}n^2 - \tfrac{3}{2}n \end{aligned} \tag{7}$$

Another algorithm for solving a system of linear equations, known as **Gaussian Elimination,*** proceeds as follows. Instead of clearing all of C_k with R_k, clear only that part of C_k *below* R_k. For a system of n equations in n unknowns, in which no zeros appear before they are deliberately created, this will reduce the system to **triangular form**:

$$\begin{bmatrix} x_1 + b_{12}x_2 + b_{13}x_3 + \cdots + \quad b_{1n}x_n = c_1 \\ x_2 + b_{23}x_3 + \cdots + \quad b_{2n}x_n = c_2 \\ \cdots \\ x_{n-1} + b_{n-1,n}x_n = c_{n-1} \\ x_n = c_n \end{bmatrix} \tag{8}$$

---

* Carl Friedrich Gauss (1777–1855) is regarded by many as the greatest mathematician who ever lived. He became the first to systematically consider systems of equations when in 1810 he invented Gaussian Elimination as a mere computational aid to more accurately determine the orbit of the asteroid Pallas to help measure the mass of Jupiter.

The last equation gives $x_n = c_n$. Substituting this in the preceding equation gives

$$x_{n-1} + b_{n-1}c_n = c_{n-1} \text{ or } x_{n-1} = c_{n-1} - b_{n-1}c_n$$

Substituting the values of x_{n-1} and x_n in the next equation, we obtain x_{n-2}. Proceeding up, we eventually get the full solution. The reduction of the system to triangular form is called **triangularization**; the subsequent procedure to obtain the solution is called **back substitution**.

EXAMPLE 2.23   Solve

$$\begin{bmatrix} 4x_1 + 8x_2 + 8x_3 = 12 \\ -2x_1 - 7x_2 + 2x_3 = -15 \\ 3x_1 + 4x_2 + 12x_3 = -3 \end{bmatrix}$$

by Gaussian Elimination.

SOLUTION   First, triangularize:

$$\begin{bmatrix} 4 & 8 & 8 & 12 \\ -2 & -7 & 2 & -15 \\ 3 & 4 & 12 & -3 \end{bmatrix} \xrightarrow{R_1 \leftarrow (\frac{1}{4})R_1} \begin{bmatrix} 1 & 2 & 2 & 3 \\ -2 & -7 & 2 & -15 \\ 3 & 4 & 12 & -3 \end{bmatrix}$$

$$\begin{array}{c} R_2 \leftarrow 2R_1 + R_2 \\ R_3 \leftarrow -3R_1 + R_3 \end{array} \begin{bmatrix} 1 & 2 & 2 & 3 \\ 0 & -3 & 6 & -9 \\ 0 & -2 & 6 & -12 \end{bmatrix} \xrightarrow{R_2 \leftarrow (-\frac{1}{3})R_2} \begin{bmatrix} 1 & 2 & 2 & 3 \\ 0 & 1 & -2 & 3 \\ 0 & -2 & 6 & -12 \end{bmatrix}$$

$$R_3 \leftarrow 2R_2 + R_3 \begin{bmatrix} 1 & 2 & 2 & 3 \\ 0 & 1 & -2 & 3 \\ 0 & 0 & 2 & -6 \end{bmatrix} \xrightarrow{R_3 \leftarrow (\frac{1}{2})R_3} \begin{bmatrix} 1 & 2 & 2 & 3 \\ 0 & 1 & -2 & 3 \\ 0 & 0 & 1 & -3 \end{bmatrix}$$

Now back substitute:

$$x_3 = -3$$
$$x_2 - 2(-3) = 3, \; x_2 = -3$$
$$x_1 + 2(-3) + 2(-3) = 3, \; x_1 = 15$$

CHECK

$$\begin{bmatrix} 4(15) + 8(-3) + 8(-3) = 12 \\ -2(15) - 7(-3) + 2(-3) = -15 \\ 3(15) + 4(-3) + 12(-3) = -3 \end{bmatrix} \begin{array}{c} \checkmark \\ \checkmark \\ \checkmark \end{array}$$

■

The first step in triangularization of a system of n equations in n unknowns, clearing C_1 with R_1, is the same as in Gauss-Jordan Reduction. We saw above that the number of arithmetic operations needed for this step is $(n+1)(2n-1)$, which equals

$$2n^2 + n - 1 \tag{9}$$

The next step, using R_2 to clear C_2 below R_2, is the same as Gauss-Jordan Reduction *if* we ignore R_1 and C_1. In other words, this step is the same as the first step of Gauss-Jordan Reduction for a system of $n-1$ equations in $n-1$ unknowns. Thus, the number of arithmetic operations for this step is given by Formula (9) with n replaced by $n-1$:

$$2(n-1)^2 + (n-1) - 1$$

Proceeding in this way for every step, we find the total number of arithmetic operations needed for triangularization to be

$$
\begin{aligned}
[2n^2 + n - 1] &+ [2(n-1)^2 + (n-1) - 1] + \cdots + [2(1)^2 + (1) - 1] \\
&= 2[n^2 + (n-1)^2 + \cdots + 1^2] + [n + (n-1) + \cdots + 1] - [1 + 1 + \cdots + 1] \\
&= 2 \sum_{j=1}^{n} j^2 + \sum_{j=1}^{n} j - n \\
&= 2[n(n+1)(2n+1)/6] + n(n+1)/2 - n \\
&= \tfrac{2}{3}n^3 + \tfrac{3}{2}n^2 - \tfrac{1}{6}n \tag{10}
\end{aligned}
$$

where we have used Formula (7) of Section 2.2 and Formula (1) of this section.

It remains to count the number of arithmetic operations in the back substitution step. Consider the triangularized system (8). No arithmetic operations are required to find x_n. Two arithmetic operations are required to find x_{n-1} (one $\times$, one $-$). Four arithmetic operations are required to find x_{n-2} (two $\times$, two $-$; or, if you prefer, two $\times$, one $+$, one $-$). In general, $2(j-1)$ operations are required to find x_{n-j+1}. Then the total number of arithmetic operations required in back substituting is

$$
\begin{aligned}
0 + 2 \cdot 1 + 2 \cdot 2 + \cdots + 2(n-1) &= 2 \sum_{k=1}^{n-1} j \\
&= 2[(n-1)(n)/2] \\
&= n^2 - n \tag{11}
\end{aligned}
$$

Adding (10) and (11) gives the worst case efficiency for Gaussian Elimination for a system of n equations in n unknowns:

$$E(\text{Gaussian Elimination}) = \tfrac{2}{3}n^3 + \tfrac{5}{2}n^2 - \tfrac{7}{6}n \tag{12}$$

Comparison of (12) and (7) reveals that for all $n > 1$,

$$E(\text{Gaussian Elimination}) < E(\text{Gauss-Jordan Reduction})$$

that is, Gaussian Elimination is more efficient than Gauss-Jordan Reduction. In asymptotic terms, we have

$$E(\text{Gaussian Elimination}) \sim \tfrac{2}{3}n^3$$

and $E(\text{Gauss-Jordan Reduction}) \sim n^3$

Thus, for large n, Gaussian Elimination is one-third more efficient than Gauss-Jordan Reduction. In big oh notation, the efficiency of each algorithm is $O(n^3)$, and the actual advantage of Gaussian Elimination is obscured. In actual practice with small-size problems, most students have an easier time with Gauss-Jordan Reduction, especially for problems with multiple solutions. In the case of $n = 3$, $E(\text{Gaussian Elimination}) = 37$ and $E(\text{Gauss-Jordan Reduction}) = 45$. Thus, it doesn't matter too much which method is used. However, for $n = 100$, Gauss-Jordan Reduction requires 333,300 more steps than Gaussian Elimination, and the difference in efficiency is not only significant, it is somewhat surprising.

EXERCISES

1. How many comparisons are required to BUBBLESORT the following sequences?

   a. (1, 2, 3, 4, 5, 6)

   b. (6, 5, 4, 3, 2, 1)

   c. (6, 2, 3, 4, 5, 1)

   d. (1, 6, 2, 5, 3, 4)

   e. (6, 5, 4, 1, 2, 3)

2. How many comparisons are required to BUBBLESORT the following sequences?

   a. (1, 1, 2, 2, 3, 3)

   b. (3, 3, 2, 2, 1, 1)

   c. (3, 1, 3, 2, 2, 1)

   d. (1, 3, 1, 3, 2, 2)

   e. (1, 2, 3, 1, 2, 3)

3. What is the greatest number of comparisons needed to BUBBLESORT a sequence of length n?

4. What is the smallest number of comparisons needed to BUBBLESORT a sequence of length n?

5. How many comparisons are needed to MERGE the following pairs of sequences?

   a. (1, 2, 3) and (4, 5, 6)

   b. (4, 5, 6) and (1, 2, 3)

   c. (1, 3, 5) and (2, 4, 6)

   d. (2, 4, 6) and (1, 3, 5)

6. How many comparisons are needed to MERGE the following pairs of sequences?

   a. (1, 2, 3) and (1, 2, 3)

   b. (3, 3, 3) and (1, 2)

   c. (1, 3, 5, 7) and (2, 4, 6)

   d. (2, 4) and (1, 3, 5, 7)

7. What is the least number of comparisons needed to MERGE a nondecreasing sequence of length m with one of length n?

8. What is the greatest number of comparisons needed to MERGE a nondecreasing sequence of length m with one of length n?

9. How many comparisons are needed to MERGESORT each sequence of Exercise 1?

10. How many comparisons are needed to MERGESORT each sequence of Exercise 2?

11. How many comparisons are needed to MERGESORT the sequence $(2^n, 2^n - 1, \ldots, 1)$?

12. How many comparisons are needed to MERGESORT the sequence $(2, 2, \ldots, 2, 1, 1, \ldots, 1)$, where there are 2^m twos and 2^m ones?

13. Let A be an $m \times m$ matrix and B be an $n \times p$ matrix. How many arithmetic operations are needed to find AB?

14. Let T be an $n \times n$ matrix in which all entries below the main diagonal are zero. How many arithmetic operations are needed to find T^3?

15. Let A be an $m \times n$ matrix and B and C be $n \times p$ matrices. Compare the number of arithmetic operations needed to compute $A(B + C)$ and $AB + AC$.

16. Let A, B, and C be matrices of respective sizes $m \times n$, $n \times p$, and $p \times q$. Compare the number of arithmetic operations needed to compute $(AB)C$ and $A(BC)$.

17. The **transpose** of the $m \times n$ matrix $A = [a_{ij}]_{m \times n}$ is the $n \times m$ matrix $A^t = [a'_{ij}]_{n \times m}$, where $a'_{ij} = a_{ji}$. Find the transposes of

a. $\begin{bmatrix} 1 & 2 \\ 3 & 4 \end{bmatrix}$

b. $[1 \quad 2 \quad 3 \quad 4]$

c. $\begin{bmatrix} 1 & 2 & 3 \\ 4 & 5 & 6 \end{bmatrix}$

d. $\begin{bmatrix} 1 & 2 & 3 \\ 2 & 4 & 5 \\ 3 & 5 & 6 \end{bmatrix}$

18. Write a program that uses the interchange instruction $x \leftrightarrow y$ to transpose a square matrix.

19. How many interchanges does the program of Exercise 18 make?

The remaining exercises pertain to the important concept of the determinant of a square matrix.

20. Let n be a positive integer. A **permutation** of the set $I_n = \{1, 2, ..., n\}$ is a bijection from I_n to I_n. The **symmetric group** S_n is the set of all permutations of I_n. Find $|S_n|$, the number of elements of S_n.

21. Let n be a positive integer and x_1, x_2, ..., x_n be distinct variables. Let

$$p_n = \prod_{1 \leqslant i < j \leqslant n} (x_i - x_j)$$

a. Write p_3.

b. How many factors does p_n have?

22. For $f \in S_n$, define

$$f(p_n) = \prod_{1 \leqslant i < j \leqslant n} (x_{f(i)} - x_{f(j)})$$

a. Suppose $f \in S_3$, $f(1) = 2$, $f(2) = 3$, $f(3) = 1$. Find $f(p_3)$.

b. Show that for all f in S_n, $f(p_n)$ is either p_n or $-p_n$.

23. (See Exercise 21.) A permutation $f \in S_n$ is *even* if $f(p_n) = p_n$; *odd* if $f(p_n) = -p_n$. The set of all even permutations in S_n is called the **alternating group** of degree n and is denoted A_n. Find $|A_n|$.

24. The **sign** of $f \in S_n$, denoted sgn f, is defined to be $+1$ if f is even, -1 if f is odd. Write out all the permutations in S_3 and find their signs.

25. The **determinant** of an $n \times n$ matrix of numbers $A = [a_{ij}]_{n \times n}$, denoted det A (or sometimes $|A|$), is defined as

$$\det A = \sum_{f \in S_n} (\text{sgn } f) a_{1f(1)} a_{2f(2)} \cdots a_{nf(n)} \quad \textbf{(D.1)}$$

For example,

$$\det \begin{bmatrix} a_{11} & a_{12} \\ a_{21} & a_{22} \end{bmatrix} = a_{11}a_{22} - a_{12}a_{21}$$

Write out det A for $n = 1$ and $n = 3$.

26. How many arithmetic operations are needed to use Definition (D.1) for an $n \times n$ matrix? (Neglect operations needed to find sgn f and to attach the sign to the terms. Thus, for $n = 2$, only three operations are needed: two multiplications and one subtraction.)

27. Let A be an $n \times n$ matrix with $n > 1$ and i, j integers from 1 to n. Denote by A_{ij} the $(n-1) \times (n-1)$ matrix obtained from A by erasing row i and column j. It can be shown that for any i,

$$\det A = \sum_{j=1}^{n} (-1)^{i+j} a_{ij} \det A_{ij} \quad \textbf{(D.2)}$$

This formula is called the **expansion** of det A along row i. Verify the formula for $n = 3$, $i = 1$ and $n = 3$, $i = 2$.

28. Formula (D.2) can be applied recursively to evaluate the determinant of an $n \times n$ matrix. Let m_n be the number of arithmetic operations needed to do this.

a. Find a recursive relation and initial condition for m_n.

b. Calculate m_5 and compare it to the result of Exercise 26.

29. Suppose A is an $n \times n$ matrix in which all entries below the main diagonal are zero. Use (D.1) or (D.2) to quickly find det A.

30. Let R_i and R_j be rows of a square matrix A where $i \neq j$, and let c be any number. Let A' be the result of the elementary row operation $R_j \leftarrow R_j + cR_i$ on A. It can be shown that det $A' =$ det A. Verify this for

a. A an arbitrary 2×2 matrix, c arbitrary, $i = 1$, $j = 2$.

b. $A = \begin{bmatrix} 1 & 2 & -1 \\ 2 & -1 & 1 \\ 1 & 1 & 2 \end{bmatrix}$, $i = 2, j = 3$.

31. Let R_i and R_j be rows of a square matrix A, where $i \neq j$. Let A'' be the result of the elementary row operation $R_i \leftrightarrow R_j$ on A. It can be shown that det $A'' = -$ det A. Verify this for

a. A an arbitrary 2×2 matrix.

b. A an arbitrary 3×3 matrix, $i = 2, j = 3$.

32. A more efficient method to calculate det A is based on the previous three exercises: Use row operations $R_j \leftarrow R_j + cR_i$ and $R_i \leftrightarrow R_j$ (keeping track of sign changes) to change A to a matrix $A*$ in which all entries below the main diagonal are zero; then find det $A*$. This gives $\pm$ det A, depending on the sign changes. In the calculations, the arithmetic operations that change the entries below the main diagonal to zero do not have to be carried out. The result is the following program:

To find the determinant of $A = [a_{ij}]_{m \times n}$.

1. If $m \neq n$ then "det A is not defined." and STOP
2. $d \leftarrow 1$ and $i \leftarrow 1$
3. If $a_{ii} \neq 0$ then $d \leftarrow da_{ii}$ and go to 12
4. $k \leftarrow i$
5. If $k = n$ then $d \leftarrow 0$ and go to 12
6. $k \leftarrow k + 1$
7. If $a_{ki} = 0$ then go to 5
8. $j \leftarrow i$

9. $a_{ij} \leftrightarrow a_{kj}$
10. If $j \neq n$ then $j \leftarrow j + 1$ and go to 9
11. $d \leftarrow -da_{ii}$
12. If $d = 0$ or $i = n$ then "det $A = d$." and STOP
13. $k \leftarrow i + i$
14. If $a_{ki} = 0$ then go to 18
15. $c \leftarrow a_{ki}/a_{ii}$ and $j \leftarrow i + 1$
16. $a_{kj} \leftarrow a_{kj} - ca_{ij}$
17. If $j \neq n$ then $j \leftarrow j + 1$ and go to 16
18. If $k \neq n$ then $k \leftarrow k + 1$ and go to 14
19. $i \leftarrow i + 1$ and go to 3

Run this program for

a. $\begin{bmatrix} 1 & 2 & -1 \\ 2 & -1 & 1 \\ 1 & 1 & 2 \end{bmatrix}$

b. $\begin{bmatrix} 1 & 2 & 3 \\ 4 & 5 & 6 \\ 7 & 8 & 9 \end{bmatrix}$

c. $\begin{bmatrix} 1 & 2 & -1 \\ 2 & 4 & 1 \\ 3 & 4 & 1 \end{bmatrix}$

Each time Instruction 19 is reached, write the entire matrix.

33. Count the greatest number of arithmetic operations performed by the program above to find the determinant of an $n \times n$ matrix. Compute this number for $n = 5$ and compare it to the result of Exercise 28.

34. (See Exercise 17.) It can be shown that if A is a square matrix, then det $A^t =$ det A. Verify this for

a. A an arbitrary 3×3 matrix.

b. $A = \begin{bmatrix} 1 & 2 & 1 & 0 \\ 0 & 2 & 1 & 1 \\ 1 & 1 & 1 & 1 \\ 0 & 1 & 2 & 1 \end{bmatrix}$

C H A P T E R

T H R E E

Logic and Circuits

3.1 Switches and Gates

3.2 Circuits and Propositions

3.3 Boolean Algebra

3.4 Minimal Forms

COMPUTER HARDWARE DESIGN is an important application of the introduction to switches and circuits contained in this chapter. In fact, switching circuits are essential for any situation in which a machine must make a logical decision. For example, consider a buzzer wired into a car. Let's look at five statements:

1. The headlights are on.
2. The key is in the ignition.
3. The motor is running.
4. The door is open.
5. The seatbelt is fastened.

If 1 is true and 2 is false, then the buzzer should sound, since the driver has forgotten to turn off the lights. If 2, 3, and 4 are true, the buzzer should sound. If 2 is true, 4 is false, and 5 is false, the buzzer should sound to warn the driver to fasten the seatbelt. How do you design a circuit that will make the buzzer sound precisely when it should? For another example, consider a self-cleaning oven that must decide whether or not to let you open the oven door. The machine's decision is based on the temperature of the oven, the time on the clock, and whether or not the oven is in cleaning mode. Again, a logic circuit must be built into the latch mechanism to protect the consumer.

This chapter begins with a description of logic circuits and ends with an algorithm to simplify them. It is important to reduce the number of switches in a circuit to save current and space. Although there is no known general algorithm to minimize the number of switches that yield a desired circuit, the algorithm we present generally results in significant savings.

Switches and Gates

How does IMCOM work? The heart of a computer consists essentially of a huge collection of electronic switches that are connected in various patterns called **switching circuits**. Each switch may be turned on or off by an electric current, which we shall call the **switch current**. We assume that when a switch is closed, it transmits a current of 1 (the unit of measure is of no concern), and when it is open, it transmits 0 (Figure 3.1). Throughout this chapter the only values of

FIGURE 3.1

switch current transmitted will be 0 and 1. There are several patterns of switches called **gates** that are of fundamental importance. The basic gates are called NOT, AND, and OR.

The **NOT gate**, also called the **inversion gate**, has one input and one output. It consists of one switch that is closed when there is no switch current and open when there is a switch current (Figure 3.2). If the input (0 or 1) is denoted by a,

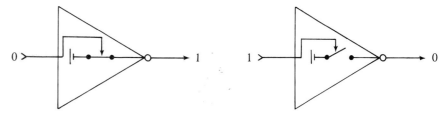

FIGURE 3.2

then the output is denoted by

$$a'$$

pronounced "not a" or "a prime." The operation of the inverter gate is fully described by Table 3.1. Suppose, for example, that the input is 1 for one second,

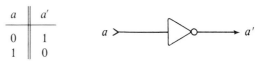

a	a'
0	1
1	0

TABLE 3.1

then 0 for two seconds, then 1 for two seconds. Then the output is 0 for the first second, 1 for the next two seconds, and 0 for the last two seconds (Figure 3.3).

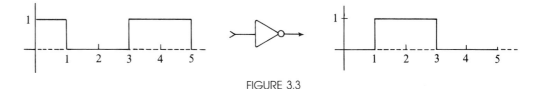

FIGURE 3.3

The number of inputs to AND and OR gates may be any integer greater than one. The gates have one output. The two-input **AND gate**, also called the two-input **conjunction gate**, consists of two switches connected **in series** (Figure 3.4).

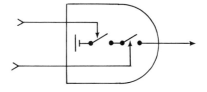

FIGURE 3.4

Each switch is open if there is no switch current and closed if there is switch current. If the inputs are denoted by a and b, then the output is written

$$a \wedge b$$

which is read "a and b" or "a cap b." It is clear from Figure 3.4 that the operation of the two-input conjunction gate is fully described by Table 3.2. The gate transmits 1 if and only if *both a and b* are 1.

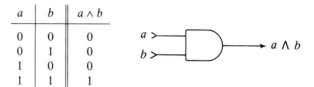

a	b	$a \wedge b$
0	0	0
0	1	0
1	0	0
1	1	1

TABLE 3.2

It is now easy to design an AND gate with n inputs $a_1, a_2, \ldots, a_n$, where $n \geq 2$. The output of this n-input conjunction gate is denoted

$$a_1 \wedge a_2 \wedge \cdots \wedge a_n$$

and is 1 if and only if each of $a_1, a_2, \ldots, a_n$ is 1. Figure 3.5 shows a three-input conjunction gate.

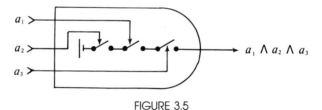

FIGURE 3.5

The two-input **OR gate**, also called the two-input **disjunction gate**, consists of two switches **in parallel** (Figure 3.6). Each switch is open if there is no switch

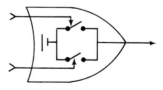

FIGURE 3.6

current and closed if there is switch current. If the inputs are denoted by a and b, then the output is written

$$a \vee b$$

which is read "a or b" or "a cup b." Thus, $\wedge$ stands for "and" and $\vee$ stands for "or." It is clear from Figure 3.6 that the operation of the two-input disjunction gate is fully described by Table 3.3. The gate transmits 1 if and only if a is 1 *or* b is

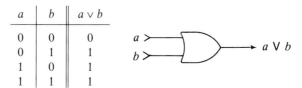

a	b	$a \vee b$
0	0	0
0	1	1
1	0	1
1	1	1

TABLE 3.3

1 *or both a and b* are 1. Thus, the OR gate represents the **inclusive** "or," rather than the **exclusive** "or."

It is now easy to design an OR gate with n inputs $a_1, a_2, \ldots, a_n$, where $n \geq 2$. The output of this n-input disjunction gate is denoted

$$a_1 \vee a_2 \vee \cdots \vee a_n$$

This output is 1 if one or more of $a_1, a_2, \ldots, a_n$ is 1; the output is 0 only if each of $a_1, a_2, \ldots, a_n$ is 0. Figure 3.7 shows a three-input disjunction gate. The operations of the three-input AND and OR gates are completely described by Table 3.4.

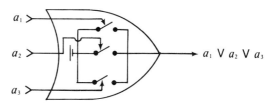

FIGURE 3.7

a_1	a_2	a_3	$a_1 \wedge a_2 \wedge a_3$	$a_1 \vee a_2 \vee a_3$
0	0	0	0	0
0	0	1	0	1
0	1	0	0	1
0	1	1	0	1
1	0	0	0	1
1	0	1	0	1
1	1	0	0	1
1	1	1	1	1

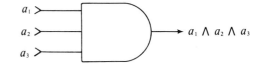

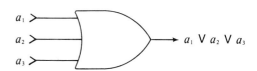

TABLE 3.4

From now on, all switching circuits will be constructed from AND gates and OR gates , with appropriate numbers of inputs, and NOT gates 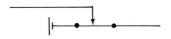 , with one input. No actual switches need be shown, except in some of the following exercises.

EXERCISES

Let the inputs a, b, c during the first five seconds be as shown in Figure 3.8.

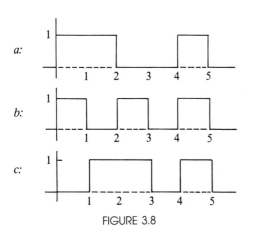

FIGURE 3.8

In Exercises 1–8 graph the given outputs.

1. c'

2. b'

3. $a \wedge b$

4. $b \wedge c$

5. $a \vee c$

6. $b \vee c$

7.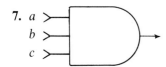

8.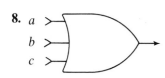

9. Design a circuit for $a_1 \wedge a_2 \wedge a_3 \wedge a_4$.

10. Design a circuit for $a_1 \vee a_2 \vee a_3 \vee a_4$.

11. Fill out the table that fully describes the operation of the four-input conjunction gate.

12. Add a column to the table of Exercise 11 for the output of the four-input disjunction gate.

In Exercises 13–24 design circuits with the following outputs. Use switches, not gates. Denote a switch that is closed when there is no switch current by

13. $a \wedge b'$

14. $a' \wedge b$

15. $(a \wedge b)'$

16. $(a \vee b)'$

17. $(a \wedge b')'$

18. $(a' \vee b)'$

19. $a' \vee b \vee c'$

20. $a \wedge b' \wedge c'$

21. $(a \wedge b) \vee c'$

22. $(a \vee b)' \wedge c$

23. $(a \vee b) \wedge (c \vee d)$

24. $(a \wedge b) \vee (c \wedge d)$

25. Fill out the table that fully describes the output of Exercise 13.

26. Add columns to the table of Exercise 25 to describe the outputs of Exercises 14, 15, 16, 17, and 18.

27. Fill out the table that fully describes the output of Exercise 19.

28. Add columns to the table of Exercise 27 to describe the outputs of Exercises 20, 21, and 22.

29. Fill out the table that fully describes the output of Exercise 23.

30. Add a column to the table of Exercise 29 to describe the output of Exercise 24.

By connecting NOT, AND, and OR gates in various patterns, many different switching circuits can be built. In this section we show how to build *every* switching circuit in this way. Algorithm 3.1 is a simple algorithm for designing a circuit with any prescribed operation. First, we discuss switching circuits (*circuits* for short) in general, and we introduce some useful new words.

Consider an unknown switching circuit, with n inputs $a_1, a_2, ..., a_n$, where $n \geqslant 1$, and one output f, as in Figure 3.9. The operation of this circuit is fully

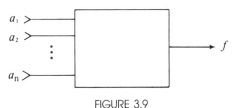

FIGURE 3.9

described by a table giving the value of f (0 or 1) for every possible assignment of 0's and 1's to $a_1, a_2, ..., a_n$. The principles of enumeration in Section 2.1 tell us that each such table has 2^n rows. In Section 3.1, Table 3.1 has $2^1 = 2$ rows; Tables 3.2 and 3.3 each have $2^2 = 4$ rows; and Table 3.4 has $2^3 = 8$ rows. The total number of different tables with n inputs is easily seen to be 2^{2^n}. So the total number of tables with two inputs is $2^{2^2} = 2^4 = 16$. Two circuits are **equivalent** if they have the same table of operation. If we could design 16 different two-input circuits, each with a different table, then every two-input circuit, no matter how complicated, would be equivalent to one of them.

We turn now to the outputs of circuits constructed entirely from AND, OR, and NOT gates. The inputs to such a circuit are called **variables**. The output of such a circuit is called a **proposition** (or **sentence**). Thus, a proposition in the variables $a_1, a_2, ..., a_n$ is any expression that can be built up from $a_1, a_2, ..., a_n$, where each variable may be used any number of times, through a finite number of **negations** (uses of NOT gates), **conjunctions** (AND gates), and **disjunctions** (OR gates). The following is an example of a proposition in a_1, a_2, a_3 with output f:

$$([(a_2' \vee a_3) \wedge (a_1' \wedge a_2 \wedge a_3)] \vee a_3')' = f \qquad (1)$$

Variables and their negations are called **literals**. A **term** is a literal or the disjunction or conjunction of a finite number of literals. Thus, in Proposition (1), the literals are

$$a_1', a_2, a_2', a_3, \text{ and } a_3'$$

and the terms are

$$a_2' \vee a_3, a_1' \wedge a_2 \wedge a_3, \text{ and } a_3'$$

It is easy to design a circuit for any given proposition; the proposition serves as a "wiring diagram." For Proposition (1): first, build the terms:

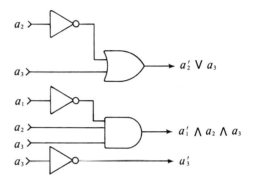

next, connect the first two with AND:

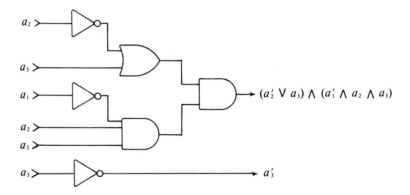

next, connect this and the last term with OR and run the output through NOT:

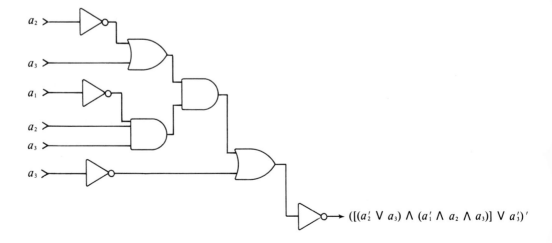

Then, finally, join the common inputs, as shown in Figure 3.10.

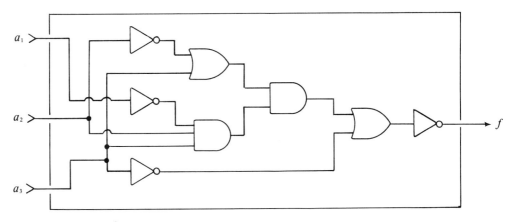

FIGURE 3.10

In our notation it is often necessary to use parentheses in propositions. In (1), for example, no parentheses or brackets can be removed except for those around the term $a'_1 \wedge a_2 \wedge a_3$. For notations in which no parentheses are used, see the exercises.

Our circuit-design problem is now reduced to this: given the table of operation of a circuit, write a proposition whose circuit has that table of operation. To do this, we now introduce a type of proposition called a **disjunctive form**, which is either one term or a disjunction of terms, where each term is either a literal or the conjunction of literals. Suppose, for example, that a circuit with output f has four inputs—a_1, a_2, a_3, a_4— and that $f = 1$ when $a_1 = 1$, $a_2 = 0$, $a_3 = 0$, $a_4 = 1$. Consider the term $a_1 \wedge a'_2 \wedge a'_3 \wedge a_4$. This term is 1 if and only if $a_1 = 1$, $a_2 = 0$, $a_3 = 0$, $a_4 = 1$. For all other variable values this term is 0. If we write such a term for each assignment of variable values that gives $f = 1$, then the disjunction of these terms will be the required proposition.

□ ALGORITHM 3.1 **To write the disjunctive form for a circuit with inputs $a_1, a_2, ..., a_n$ and output f.**

1. If $f = 0$ for all assignments, the form is $a_1 \wedge a'_1$; if $f = 1$ for all assignments, the form is $a_1 \vee a'_1$. Otherwise, proceed.

2. For each assignment with $f = 1$ write

$$a_1^{e_1} \wedge a_2^{e_2} \wedge \cdots a_n^{e_n}$$

where $a_i^{e_i}$ is a_i if $a_i = 1$ and $a_i^{e_i}$ is a'_i if $a_i = 0$.

3. If only one term has been written, it is the form. Otherwise, the form is the disjunction of all terms written.   □

PROBLEM 3.1   Design a circuit with three inputs that has output 1 if and only if at least two inputs are 1.

SOLUTION   Denote the output by f. Step one of Algorithm 3.1 does not apply; we write step two as follows:

a_1	a_2	a_3	corresponding term
	input array that gives $f = 1$		
0	1	1	$a_1' \wedge a_2 \wedge a_3$
1	0	1	$a_1 \wedge a_2' \wedge a_3$
1	1	0	$a_1 \wedge a_2 \wedge a_3'$
1	1	1	$a_1 \wedge a_2 \wedge a_3$

Then

$$f = (a_1' \wedge a_2 \wedge a_3) \vee (a_1 \wedge a_2' \wedge a_3) \vee (a_1 \wedge a_2 \wedge a_3') \vee (a_1 \wedge a_2 \wedge a_3)$$

The design is in Figure 3.11.

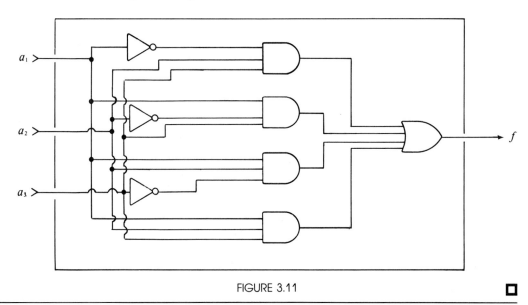

FIGURE 3.11   ◻

If a switching circuit with n inputs has output $f = 1$ for more than half the input arrays—that is, for more than 2^{n-1} arrays—then the following modification will give a circuit design with fewer gates:

1. Use Algorithm 3.1 to draw a circuit with output f'.
2. Run this output through a NOT gate to get f.

PROBLEM 3.2   Design a circuit with four inputs that has output 1 if and only if two or more inputs are 1.

SOLUTION   Denote the output by f. There are $2^4 = 16$ input arrays, all but five of which give $f = 1$. Thus, the original diagram would produce a design with eleven AND gates, four NOT gates, and one OR gate. Since $f = 1$ for $16 - 5 = 11$ arrays, we elect to use the modified algorithm just described. Consider those arrays for which $f' = 1$, that is, $f = 0$.

arrays for which $f = 0$				corresponding term
a_1	a_2	a_3	a_4	
0	0	0	0	$a_1' \wedge a_2' \wedge a_3' \wedge a_4'$
0	0	0	1	$a_1' \wedge a_2' \wedge a_3' \wedge a_4$
0	0	1	0	$a_1' \wedge a_2' \wedge a_3 \wedge a_4'$
0	1	0	0	$a_1' \wedge a_2 \wedge a_3' \wedge a_4'$
1	0	0	0	$a_1 \wedge a_2' \wedge a_3' \wedge a_4'$

Then

$$f = [(a_1' \wedge a_2' \wedge a_3' \wedge a_4') \vee (a_1' \wedge a_2' \wedge a_3' \wedge a_4) \vee (a_1' \wedge a_2' \wedge a_3 \wedge a_4') \\ \vee (a_1' \wedge a_2 \wedge a_3' \wedge a_4') \vee (a_1 \wedge a_2' \wedge a_3' \wedge a_4')]'$$

The design is in Figure 3.12.

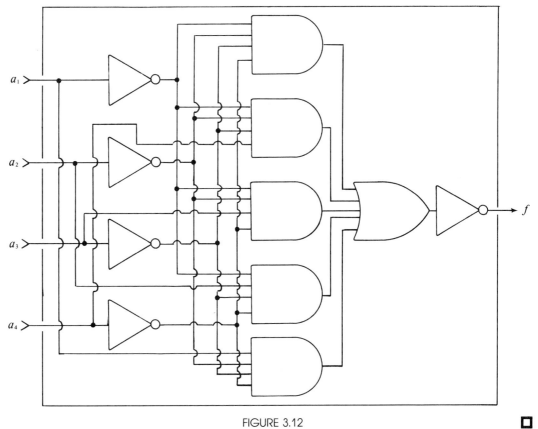

FIGURE 3.12

This circuit has five AND gates, five NOT gates, and one OR gate. Later (Exercise 15 of Section 3.3) we will obtain an equivalent diagram with one fewer gate.

EXERCISES

1. Design a circuit with two inputs that has output 1 if and only if exactly one input is 1. (This is the **exclusive OR** gate.)

2. Design a circuit with two inputs that has output 1 if and only if the inputs are not both 1. (This is the

NAND gate, symbolized by ⊐o . In logic, a

NAND gate is called a **Sheffer stroke**.)

3. Design a circuit with two inputs that has output 1 if and only if neither input is 1. (This is the **NOR gate**,

symbolized by ⊐o .)

4. Design a circuit with inputs a_1, a_2 that has output 1 if and only if $a_1 = 0$.

5. Design a circuit with three inputs that has output 1 if and only if exactly one input is 1.

6. Design a circuit with three inputs that has output 1 if and only if either no inputs are 1 or all inputs are 1.

7. Design a circuit with five inputs whose output is always 1.

8. Design a circuit with six inputs whose output is never 1.

In Exercises 9–16 you will show that any circuit can be built using only NOT gates and two-input AND gates, and that any circuit can be built using only NOT gates and two-input OR gates.

9. Show how to construct a 3-input AND gate from two 2-input AND gates.

10. Show how to construct a 3-input OR gate from two 2-input OR gates.

11. Show how to construct an n-input AND gate, where $n > 2$, from 2-input AND gates. How many 2-input gates are needed?

12. Do Exercise 11 for OR gates.

13. Construct a 2-input OR gate from a 2-input AND gate and three NOT gates.

14. Construct a 2-input AND gate from a 2-input OR gate and three NOT gates.

15. Using Exercises 11 and 13, explain how to replace any circuit by an equivalent circuit that employs only NOT gates and two-input AND gates.

16. Using Exercises 12 and 14, explain how to replace any circuit by an equivalent circuit that employs only NOT gates and two-input OR gates.

17. (See Exercise 2.) Explain how to replace any circuit by an equivalent circuit that employs only two-input NAND gates.

18. (See Exercise 3.) Explain how to replace any circuit by an equivalent circuit that employs only two-input NOR gates.

In Exercises 19–22 construct the table for the given circuit; then design an equivalent circuit having fewer gates.

19.

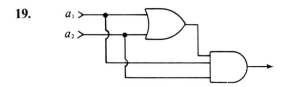

20.

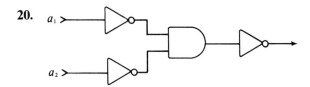

21.

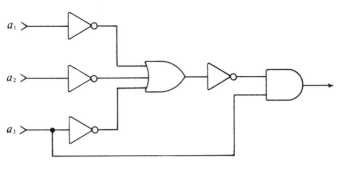

22.

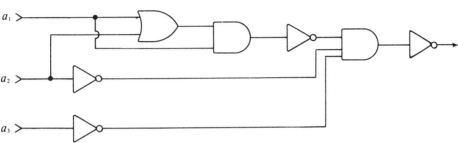

In **Polish notation** (so named after a school of Polish logicians), a' is written $\sim a$, $a \vee b$ is written $\vee ab$, and $a \wedge b$ is written $\wedge ab$. Thus, $(a \wedge b)'$ becomes $\sim \wedge ab$, $a \vee b'$ becomes $\vee a \sim b$, and $(a \vee b) \wedge (c \vee d)$ becomes $\wedge \vee ab \vee cd$. All propositions can be written in Polish notation without any use of parentheses. Unfortunately, $a \vee b \vee c$ must be written $\vee \vee abc$. [**Reverse Polish notation** is also used, in which a', $a \vee b$, $a \wedge b$ become $a\sim$, $ab\vee$, $ab\wedge$, respectively. This notation is especially useful on hand calculators and is, in fact, standard on one famous series of calculators.] In Exercises 23–34 translate the propositions into or from Polish notation as appropriate.

23. $(a \vee b) \wedge c$

24. $a \wedge (b \vee c)$

25. $a' \wedge b'$

26. $(a \wedge b)' \vee c'$

27. $(a' \vee b')'$

28. $([(a \wedge b') \vee c'] \wedge d')'$

29. $\wedge \vee abc$

30. $\wedge a \vee bc$

31. $\wedge \sim a \sim b$

32. $\vee \sim \wedge ab \sim c$

33. $\sim \vee \sim a \sim b$

34. $\sim \wedge \vee \wedge a \sim b \sim c \sim d$

 3.3

Boolean Algebra

Two propositions x and y are **equivalent**, written

$$x \equiv y$$

if they have the same table of operation. In other words, $x \equiv y$ if for every array of values of the variables involved x and y have the same value.

PROBLEM 3.3   Prove that the propositions $x = b \wedge a$ and $y = a \wedge (b \wedge a)$ are equivalent.

SOLUTION   The propositions involve the variables a and b.

a	b	$b \wedge a$	$a \wedge (b \wedge a)$
0	0	0	0
0	1	0	0
1	0	0	0
1	1	1	1

x y

same; therefore, $x \equiv y$ ■

To **rewrite** a proposition means to write a proposition equivalent to it. Thus, by Problem 3.3, $a \wedge (b \wedge a)$ may be rewritten as $b \wedge a$. A proposition may be rewritten again and again. We seek an algorithm for rewriting any given proposition into a form that is, in some sense, as simple as possible. Such an algorithm will be developed in the next section. In this section we first present a number of rules and principles needed in the algorithm. Then we discuss a new interpretation of propositions, which will also be needed in the algorithm.

The result of Problem 3.3 may be extended by replacing the variables a, b by arbitrary propositions x, y to obtain

$$x \wedge (y \wedge x) \equiv y \wedge x \qquad (1)$$

Whatever variables are involved in x and y, it is obvious that both sides of (1) involve the same variables. Each array of values of these variables will give some values to x and y; then by Problem 3.3 both sides of (1) will have the same value, no matter what these values of x and y are. Hence, Equivalence (1) holds. This illustrates the fundamental **Principle of Substitution**:

> In an equivalence any variable may be replaced by a proposition and any proposition may be replaced by an equivalent proposition.

PROBLEM 3.4   Prove that

$$(a \vee b') \wedge [(c' \vee d \vee e) \wedge (a \vee b')] \equiv (c' \vee d \vee e) \wedge (a \vee b')$$

SOLUTION   This follows from Equivalence (1) with $x = a \vee b'$ and $y = c' \vee d \vee e$.   ■

We are going to list a number of equivalences that are of great help in rewriting propositions. These are sometimes called the **laws of Boolean algebra**, after George Boole (1815–1864), an English logician who may be considered as one of the founders of computer science. When we use these laws to rewrite a proposition, we are "doing" Boolean algebra. We denote by 1 the proposition whose value is always 1, and by 0, the proposition whose value is always 0. In a switching circuit, 1 is a permanently closed switch and 0 is a permanently open switch. Here are some of the laws of Boolean algebra.

For all propositions x, y, and z:

Idempotent Laws

$$x \wedge x \equiv x \text{ and } x \vee x \equiv x$$

Commutative Laws

$$x \wedge y \equiv y \wedge x \text{ and } x \vee y \equiv y \vee x$$

Associative Laws

$$x \wedge (y \wedge z) \equiv (x \wedge y) \wedge z$$

and

$$x \vee (y \vee z) \equiv (x \vee y) \vee z$$

Distributive Laws

$$x \wedge (y \vee z) \equiv (x \wedge y) \vee (x \wedge z)$$

and

$$x \vee (y \wedge z) \equiv (x \vee y) \wedge (x \vee z)$$

Absorption Laws

$$x \wedge (x \vee y) \equiv x$$

and

$$x \vee (x \wedge y) \equiv x$$

Bound Laws

$$x \wedge 0 \equiv 0 \text{ and } x \vee 1 \equiv 1$$

also, $x \vee 0 \equiv x$ and $x \wedge 1 \equiv x$

Complement Laws

$$x \wedge x' \equiv 0 \text{ and } x \vee x' \equiv 1$$

Involution Law

$$(x')' \equiv x$$

DeMorgan's* Laws

$$(x \wedge y)' \equiv x' \vee y'$$

and

$$(x \vee y)' \equiv x' \wedge y'$$

Note that except for the involution law, the laws occur in pairs where one law is obtained from the other by switching $\vee$ and $\wedge$ and, in two cases, 0 and 1. This illustrates the labor-saving **Principle of Duality**:

Given any true statement of equivalence, the **dual** statement, obtained by switching $\vee$ and $\wedge$, and 0 and 1, is also true.

PROBLEM 3.5   Use Boolean algebra to prove Equivalence (1) and the equivalence $x \vee (y \vee x) \equiv y \vee x$.

SOLUTION   In the following, the reader should state which law is used in each step.

$$x \wedge (y \wedge x) \equiv x \wedge (x \wedge y)$$
$$\equiv (x \wedge x) \wedge y$$
$$\equiv x \wedge y$$
$$\equiv y \wedge x$$

The second equivalence follows from the Principle of Duality.   ◻

The laws of Boolean algebra are all easily proven by tables of operation and the Principle of Substitution. We prove the first DeMorgan law and the second distributive law. The remaining proofs are left as exercises.

x	y	$x \wedge y$	$(x \wedge y)'$	x'	y'	$x' \vee y'$
0	0	0	1	1	1	1
0	1	0	1	1	0	1
1	0	0	1	0	1	1
1	1	1	0	0	0	0

same

---

* Augustus DeMorgan (?–1871), an English contemporary of George Boole, once remarked that he was n years old in the year n^2. When was he born?

Therefore, $(x \wedge y)' \equiv x' \vee y'$.

x	y	z	$y \wedge z$	$x \vee (y \wedge z)$	$x \vee y$	$x \vee z$	$(x \vee y) \wedge (x \vee z)$
0	0	0	0	0	0	0	0
0	0	1	0	0	0	1	0
0	1	0	0	0	1	0	0
0	1	1	1	1	1	1	1
1	0	0	0	1	1	1	1
1	0	1	0	1	1	1	1
1	1	0	0	1	1	1	1
1	1	1	1	1	1	1	1

$$\underbrace{\qquad\qquad\qquad}_{\text{same}}$$

Therefore, $x \vee (y \wedge z) \equiv (x \vee y) \wedge (x \vee z)$.

The laws of Boolean algebra have useful generalizations to any number of propositions $x_1, x_2, \ldots, x_n$. We shall discuss only one form of each law, since the dual form will then be obvious.

According to the general associative law, all ways of inserting parentheses in the expression $x_1 \wedge x_2 \wedge \cdots \wedge x_n$ give equivalent propositions. Thus,

$$(x_1 \wedge x_2) \wedge (x_3 \wedge x_4) \equiv x_1 \wedge [x_2 \wedge (x_3 \wedge x_4)]$$
$$\equiv [x_1 \wedge (x_2 \wedge x_3)] \wedge x_4$$

and so forth. For this reason we may write $x_1 \wedge x_2 \wedge \cdots \wedge x_n$ without any parentheses, as we have, in fact, been doing all along.

By the general commutative law, any reordering of the propositions in $x_1 \wedge x_2 \wedge \cdots \wedge x_n$ gives an equivalent proposition. Thus, $x_1 \wedge x_2 \wedge x_3 \equiv x_3 \wedge x_2 \wedge x_1 \equiv x_2 \wedge x_1 \wedge x_3$, and so forth.

By the above laws and the general idempotent laws, all repetitions of propositions in $x_1 \wedge x_2 \wedge \cdots \wedge x_n$ may be deleted, leaving an equivalent proposition. Thus,

$$x_2 \wedge x_1 \wedge x_3 \wedge x_2 \wedge x_3 \wedge x_1 \equiv x_1 \wedge x_2 \wedge x_3$$

From the bound and complement laws, if the list $x_1, x_2, \ldots, x_n$ either contains 0 or contains a proposition and its negation, then $x_1 \wedge x_2 \wedge \cdots \wedge x_n \equiv 0$. Also, all 1's in $x_1 \wedge x_2 \wedge \cdots \wedge x_n$ may be dropped, unless the whole proposition is 1. Thus,

$$x_1 \wedge x_2 \wedge 0 \wedge x_3 \equiv 0$$

$$x_1 \wedge x_2' \wedge x_3 \wedge x_4 \wedge x_2 \equiv 0$$

$$1 \wedge x_3 \wedge 1 \wedge x_1 \wedge x_2 \wedge 1 \equiv x_1 \wedge x_2 \wedge x_3$$

Denote by $x^{[n]}$ the expression $(\cdots (x')' \cdots)'$, where there are n primes, $n \geq 2$. By the general involution law, $x^{[n]} \equiv x$ if n is even, and $x^{[n]} \equiv x'$ if n is odd. Thus,

$$(((((x')')')')' \equiv x' \text{ and } (((x')')')' \equiv x$$

Finally, the general distributive and DeMorgan's laws are, respectively,

$$x \wedge (x_1 \vee x_2 \vee \cdots \vee x_n) \equiv (x \wedge x_1) \vee (x \wedge x_2) \vee \cdots \vee (x \wedge x_n)$$

$$(x_1 \wedge x_2 \wedge \cdots \wedge x_n)' \equiv x_1' \vee x_2' \vee \cdots \vee x_n'$$

and their duals.

The second absorption law may sometimes be used to delete terms from a disjunctive form. Recall that a **term** in a disjunctive form is a literal or the conjunction of literals. A term u **contains** a term x if every literal in x is in u. For examples,

$$a_1 \wedge a_2 \wedge a_3 \text{ contains } a_1 \wedge a_2 \text{ and } a_3 \text{ (among others)}$$

$$a_1 \wedge a_2' \wedge a_3' \wedge a_4 \text{ contains } a_1 \wedge a_2' \wedge a_4 \text{ and } a_2' \wedge a_4 \text{ (among others)}$$

You should be able to show that a conjunction of n literals contains $2^n - 1$ different terms.

Suppose that u and x are terms in a disjunctive form $f = u \vee x \vee \cdots$ and that u contains x. We shall show that u may be deleted. Note that if u is not equal to x, then u will have *more* literals than x. It is the *longer* term that may be deleted. Here's why. By the idempotent law we may repeat every literal in u that occurs in x, and thus obtain $u \equiv u \wedge x$. Then $f \equiv (u \wedge x) \vee x \vee \cdots \equiv x \vee \cdots$ by the second absorption law.

PROBLEM 3.6   Delete as many terms as possible from the disjunctive form

$$(a_1 \wedge a_2' \wedge a_3 \wedge a_4) \vee (a_3 \wedge a_1 \wedge a_4) \vee (a_1' \wedge a_4) \vee (a_1 \wedge a_3) \vee (a_4 \wedge a_5 \wedge a_1')$$

SOLUTION   The first term contains the second, the second term contains the fourth, and the fifth term contains the third. Thus, the first, second, and fifth terms may be eliminated, leaving the equivalent form

$$(a_1' \wedge a_4) \vee (a_1 \wedge a_3) \qquad\qquad \blacksquare$$

By repeated use of the general laws of Boolean algebra, any proposition may be written in a **short disjunctive form** (abbreviated s.d.f.), that is, a disjunctive form in which no term contains another term. Here is an algorithm for doing this.

ALGORITHM 3.2   **To write a Boolean expression in short disjunctive form.**

1. Apply the DeMorgan and involution laws as many times as possible.

2. Apply the general first distributive law as many times as possible. The proposition is now in **disjunctive form** (d.f.).

3. Apply the idempotent, bound, and complement laws as many times as possible.

4. Apply the second absorption law as many times as possible. The proposition is now in short disjunctive form (s.d.f.).   □

PROBLEM 3.7   Rewrite Proposition (1) of Section 3.2 in s.d.f.

SOLUTION

$$([(a_2' \vee a_3) \wedge (a_1' \wedge a_2 \wedge a_3)] \vee a_3')' \equiv$$
$$[(a_2' \vee a_3) \wedge (a_1' \wedge a_2 \wedge a_3)]' \wedge a_3 \equiv$$
$$[(a_2' \vee a_3)' \vee (a_1' \wedge a_2 \wedge a_3)'] \wedge a_3 \equiv$$
$$[(a_2 \wedge a_3') \vee (a_1 \vee a_2' \vee a_3')] \wedge a_3 \equiv \text{ [end Step 1.]}$$
$$[(a_2 \wedge a_3') \wedge a_3)] \vee [(a_1 \vee a_2' \vee a_3') \wedge a_3] \equiv$$
$$(a_2 \wedge a_3' \wedge a_3) \vee (a_1 \wedge a_3) \vee (a_2' \wedge a_3) \vee (a_3' \wedge a_3) \equiv \quad \text{[d.f.]}$$
$$(a_1 \wedge a_3) \vee (a_2' \wedge a_3) \qquad \text{[s.d.f.]}$$
■

The switching circuit for this s.d.f., Figure 3.13, is obviously simpler than the circuit for the original form of the proposition, Figure 3.10.

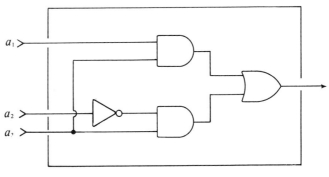

a_1
a_2
a_3

FIGURE 3.13

We note in passing that the s.d.f. does not always yield the simplest circuit. The s.d.f. for the proposition $a \wedge (b \vee c)$ is $(a \wedge b) \vee (a \wedge c)$, which requires three switches instead of two. Given a circuit, the general problem of finding an equivalent circuit with the fewest possible switches has not been solved. In the next section we will learn how to find the minimal s.d.f. for a given circuit. While not a perfect solution to the real problem, it is often minimal or nearly so.

Switching circuits have an equivalent interpretation in mathematical logic, in which each input variable stands for a statement that may be true or false. If the proposition denoted by the variable a is true, we set $a = 1$; if it is false, we set $a = 0$. The **truth value** (1 if true, 0 if false) of any proposition may be easily calculated when the truth values of the component statements are known.

PROBLEM 3.8   True or False: Four equals five, or three is half of six; and it is not the case that four does not equal five, and seven is half of fifteen.

SOLUTION   Let a be "$4 = 5$," b be "$3 = (\frac{1}{2})6$," and c be "$7 = (\frac{1}{2})15$." Then the proposition is $(a \lor b) \land (a' \land c)'$. Now $a = 0$, $b = 1$, and $c = 0$; so $a \lor b = 1$, $a' = 1$, $a' \land c = 0$, $(a' \land c)' = 1$, and $(a \lor b) \land (a' \land c)' = 1$: the proposition is true. These calculations may be written as follows:

$$(a \lor b) \land (a' \land c)' = (0 \lor 1) \land (0' \land 0)' = 1 \land 0' = 1 \land 1 = 1$$

Alternatively, we may first write the proposition in s.d.f.:

$$(a \lor b) \land (a' \land c)' \equiv (a \lor b) \land (a \lor c') \equiv a \lor (b \land c')$$

Then

$$a \lor (b \land c') = 0 \lor (1 \land 0') = 0 \lor (1 \land 1) = 0 \lor 1 = 1 \qquad ■$$

A **tautology** is a proposition that has truth value 1 for all values of its component statements; a **contradiction** is a proposition with truth value 0 for all values of its component statements. Thus, a proposition f is a tautology if $f \equiv 1$ and a contradiction if $f \equiv 0$.

PROBLEM 3.9   Prove that the proposition $f = [(a' \lor b) \land (c \lor a')] \lor (c \lor a)$ is a tautology.

SOLUTION   One way to prove this is to construct the table of operation of f, which in logic is called the **truth table** of f.

a	b	c	a'	$a' \lor b$	$c \lor a'$	$(a' \lor b) \land (c \lor a')$	$c \lor a$	f
0	0	0	1	1	1	1	0	1
0	0	1	1	1	1	1	1	1
0	1	0	1	1	1	1	0	1
0	1	1	1	1	1	1	1	1
1	0	0	0	0	0	0	1	1
1	0	1	0	0	1	0	1	1
1	1	0	0	1	0	0	1	1
1	1	1	0	1	1	1	1	1

$\uparrow$
tautology

This method of proof is a "proof by cases" in which each possible value of a, b, and c is checked. A direct proof proceeds by Boolean algebra:

$$\begin{aligned} [(a' \lor b) \land (c \lor a')] \lor (c \lor a) &\equiv a' \lor (b \land c') \lor c \lor a \\ &\equiv a' \lor a \lor (b \land c') \lor c \\ &\equiv 1 \lor (b \lor c') \lor c \\ &\equiv 1 \qquad\qquad ■ \end{aligned}$$

PROBLEM 3.10 Prove by use of a truth table and by Boolean algebra that the proposition $g = (a \lor b) \land (a' \land b')$ is a contradiction.

SOLUTION

a	b	$a \lor b$	a'	b'	$a' \land b'$	g
0	0	0	1	1	1	0
0	1	1	1	0	0	0
1	0	1	0	1	0	0
1	1	1	0	0	0	0

contradiction

$$(a \lor b) \land (a' \land b') \equiv (a \lor b) \land (a \lor b)' \equiv 0 \qquad \blacksquare$$

An important logical connective not mentioned in our work with switching circuits is **implication**. For propositions x and y the notation

$$x \Rightarrow y$$

is read "x implies y" or "if x, then y." Implication is defined by the following truth table:

x	y	$x \Rightarrow y$
0	0	1
0	1	1
1	0	0
1	1	1

In other words, the only way for $x \Rightarrow y$ to be false is for x to be true and y to be false. This distinguishes the "logical" implication defined here from the "material" implication of everyday life. For example, we might say "if you stand in the rain without an umbrella, then you will get wet." For this material implication it is understood that standing in the rain *causes* wetness. In a logical implication the aspect of cause and effect is irrelevant. For example, the statement "if $2 = 3$, then Frankfort is the capital of Kentucky" is logically true (since $0 \Rightarrow 1$ is true) even though it wouldn't make a whole lot of sense in a conversation.

Implication can be constructed from one NOT gate and one OR gate since we have

$$x \Rightarrow y \equiv x' \lor y \qquad \textbf{(2)}$$

It might seem reasonable that the statement "if x, then x or y" is always true; that is, that $x \Rightarrow (x \lor y)$ is a tautology. We prove this by Boolean algebra and Equivalence (2):

$$\begin{aligned} x \Rightarrow (x \lor y) &\equiv x' \lor (x \lor y) \\ &\equiv (x' \lor x) \lor y \\ &\equiv 1 \lor y \\ &\equiv 1 \end{aligned}$$

In general, if $f = x_1 \vee x_2 \vee \cdots \vee x_n$, then $x_1 \Rightarrow f$, $x_2 \Rightarrow f$, ..., and $x_n \Rightarrow f$ are tautologies. Thus, each term in a disjunctive form implies the form. For this reason the terms in a disjunctive form are sometimes called **implicants**. Similarly, the reader may show that $x \wedge y \Rightarrow x$ is a tautology. Suppose that u and x are terms in a d.f. and that u contains x. Then, as explained before, $u \equiv u \wedge x$ and so by the previous result, $u \Rightarrow x$. Thus, if u contains x, then u implies x.

The proposition $x \Rightarrow y$ could also be written $y \Leftarrow x$. The proposition $(x \Rightarrow y) \wedge (x \Leftarrow y)$ is usually written

$$x \Leftrightarrow y$$

and read "x if and only if y."

PROBLEM 3.11   Prove by truth tables and by Boolean algebra that

$$x \Leftrightarrow y \equiv (x \wedge y) \vee (x \vee y)'$$

SOLUTION   Let $f = (x \wedge y) \vee (x \vee y)'$.

x	y	$x \Rightarrow y$	$x \Leftarrow y$	$x \Leftrightarrow y$	$x \wedge y$	$x \vee y$	$(x \vee y)'$	f
0	0	1	1	1	0	0	1	1
0	1	1	0	0	0	1	0	0
1	0	0	1	0	0	1	0	0
1	1	1	1	1	1	1	0	1

└── same ──┘

Therefore $x \Leftrightarrow y \equiv f$.

$$
\begin{aligned}
x \Leftrightarrow y &\equiv (x' \vee y) \wedge (y' \vee x) \\
&\equiv [(x' \vee y) \wedge y'] \vee [(x' \vee y) \wedge x] \\
&\equiv [(x' \wedge y') \vee (y \wedge y')] \vee [(x' \wedge x) \vee (y \wedge x)] \\
&\equiv (x' \wedge y') \vee (y \wedge x) \\
&\equiv (x \wedge y) \vee (x' \wedge y') \\
&\equiv (x \wedge y) \vee (x \vee y)'
\end{aligned}
$$

■

Applications of logic are made in subsequent sections.

E X E R C I S E S

In Exercises 1–4 use tables of operation to prove the stated laws.

1. The idempotent and involution laws.

2. The bound and complement laws.

3. The commutative and absorption laws.

4. The associative and distributive laws.

In Exercises 5–8 use Boolean algebra to prove the given equivalences.

5. $(x \wedge y) \vee (z \wedge w)$
$\equiv (x \vee z) \wedge (x \vee w) \wedge (y \vee z) \wedge (y \vee w)$

6. $(x \vee y) \wedge (x' \vee y) \equiv y$

7. $x \Rightarrow y \equiv y' \Rightarrow x'$ [**Law of Contraposition**]

8. (*Hard*) $(x \Rightarrow y) \wedge (y \Rightarrow z) \wedge (z \Rightarrow x)$
$\equiv (y \Rightarrow x) \wedge (z \Rightarrow y) \wedge (x \Rightarrow z)$

In Exercises 9–12 rewrite the given proposition in short disjunctive form.

9. $[(a_1 \vee a_2') \wedge a_3'] \vee [a_2' \wedge (a_3 \vee a_1')]'$

10. $[(a_3' \wedge a_2) \vee (a_1' \wedge a_4')]' \vee [(a_1 \vee a_2' \vee a_3) \wedge a_4']$

11. $a_1 \vee ([(a_2 \wedge a_3) \vee (a_2 \wedge a_1')] \wedge (a_2' \vee a_3'))$

12. $(a_1 \wedge a_2' \wedge a_3 \wedge a_4' \wedge a_5) \vee (a_2 \wedge a_3' \wedge a_5)$
$\vee (a_1 \wedge a_5 \wedge a_3) \vee (a_3' \wedge a_4' \wedge a_5) \vee (a_5 \wedge a_2)$

13. If $a_1 = 0$, $a_2 = 0$, and $a_3 = 1$, find the truth value of the propositions of Exercises 9 and 11.

14. For which truth values of the variables is the proposition of Exercise 10 true?

15. Design a circuit equivalent to that of Figure 3.12 of Section 3.2 with only four NOT gates.

16. For which values of a_1, a_2, a_3, a_4 will the circuit of Exercise 15 transmit no current?

In Exercises 17–20 determine whether the statements are true or false.

17. If squares are round, then circles have corners.

18. If circles have corners, then squares have corners.

19. Squares are round or circles have no corners, and it is not the case that triangles aren't flat and rectangles have five sides.

20. If a square has four corners and a triangle is not round, then it is not the case that if a triangle is round, then a square has five corners.

In Exercises 21–28 determine whether each statement is a tautology, a contradiction, or neither.

21. $a \Rightarrow (a \Rightarrow b)$

22. $a \Rightarrow (b \Rightarrow a)$

23. $(a \Rightarrow b) \vee (b \Rightarrow a)$

24. $(a \Rightarrow b) \wedge (b \Rightarrow a')$

25. $(a \Rightarrow b) \wedge (a' \Rightarrow b')$

26. $(a' \Leftrightarrow b) \vee (a \Leftrightarrow b')$

27. $[(a \Rightarrow b) \wedge (b \Rightarrow c)] \Rightarrow (a \Rightarrow c)$ [**Law of Transitivity of Implication**]

28. $b' \wedge (a \Rightarrow b) \wedge a$

Minimal Forms

The "best" form in which to write a proposition depends to some extent upon the type of components to be used in building the switching circuit. Let us restrict our attention to disjunctive forms. Thus, for this section, a **term** is a literal or a conjunction of literals. For example,

$$a, \ b', \ a \wedge b' \wedge d, \text{ and } c' \wedge d'$$

are terms. A proposition f may have many different though equivalent disjunctive forms. Among these forms, consider only those with the smallest number of terms. For instance, if f has a disjunctive form with four terms but no disjunctive forms with one, two, or three terms, then we would consider all disjunctive forms of f with four terms. Finally, among these remaining forms of f, choose only those forms with the smallest total number of literals (counting repetitions). We regard these as the "best" forms of f, and we call them the minimal forms of f. Thus:

A **minimal form** of a proposition is a disjunctive form such that (1) no equivalent d.f. has fewer terms, and (2) no equivalent d.f. with the same number of terms has fewer literals (counting repetitions).

EXAMPLE 3.1   You can easily verify that

$$(a \wedge b') \vee (b' \wedge c) \vee (a \wedge c) \vee (a \wedge c') \qquad (1)$$

$$\equiv a \vee (a \wedge b' \wedge c) \vee (a' \wedge b' \wedge c) \qquad (2)$$

$$\equiv (a \wedge c) \vee (b' \wedge c) \vee (a \wedge c') \qquad (3)$$

Form (1) is not minimal because it has four terms, while Forms (2) and (3) have only three terms. Form (2) is not minimal because it has seven literals, while Form (3) has only six literals. In fact, you can also show that these forms are equivalent to

$$a \vee (b' \wedge c) \qquad (4)$$

Thus, Form (3) is also not minimal. Finally, it can be shown that no d.f. equivalent to Form (4) has only one term and that every d.f. equivalent to (4) that has two terms will have at least three literals. It follows that (4) is a minimal form. In fact, by using the algorithms to be presented in this section, it can be shown that (4) is the only minimal form of the propositions of Example 3.1. Some propositions, however, have several minimal forms.   ◻

It is the goal of this section to present an algorithm that will find all minimal forms of any given proposition. There are several such algorithms. For small propositions (usually defined as propositions involving at most six variables), diagrammatic devices known as **Karnaugh maps** are fairly effective, but not easily implemented on a computer. The **Quine-McClusky method** applies to general propositions, but it is not as easy to describe as the following method of **consensus expansion and selection**. This method finds all minimal forms of a proposition f in two phases. In Algorithm 3.3 we find all terms that could occur in any minimal form of f. In Algorithm 3.4 we find all subsets of the set of terms found in Algorithm 3.3 that give a minimal form of f. (It may happen that some of the terms found in Algorithm 3.3 are never selected by Algorithm 3.4.)

Algorithm 3.3 makes use of the following result of Boolean algebra, known as the **consensus law**. For all propositions x, y, z:

$$(x \wedge z) \vee (y \wedge z') \equiv (x \wedge z) \vee (y \wedge z') \vee (x \wedge y) \qquad (5)$$

We derive this fact from previous laws, asking the reader to state which laws are used in each step.

$$(x \wedge z) \vee (y \wedge z') \vee (x \wedge y)$$
$$\equiv (x \wedge z) \vee (y \wedge z') \vee [x \wedge (z \vee z') \wedge y]$$
$$\equiv (x \wedge z) \vee (y \wedge z') \vee (x \wedge z \wedge y) \vee (x \wedge z' \wedge y)$$
$$\equiv (x \wedge z) \vee (y \wedge z')$$

To understand how the consensus law is used, we must first explain what is meant by the expression, "the terms u and v have a consensus." The terms u and v **have a consensus** if there is exactly one literal in u whose negation is in v. Here are some examples.

EXAMPLE 3.2   a. The terms $a \wedge b \wedge c$ and $a' \wedge c \wedge d$ have a consensus. The literal a occurs in the first; its negation a' occurs in the second; and no other literal has this property.

b. The terms $a \wedge b'$ and $b \wedge c \wedge d$ have a consensus. The literal b' occurs in the first and its negation b occurs in the second and no other literal has this property.

c. The terms $a \wedge b'$ and $b' \wedge c \wedge d$ do not have a consensus. The literals a and b' are in the first, but their negations, a' and b, are not in the second.

d. The terms $a \wedge b'$ and $a' \wedge b \wedge c$ do not have a consensus because, although a is in the first and a' is in the second, we also have b in the second and b' in the first. To have a consensus, there must be *only one* literal with that property.

e. The terms $a \wedge b' \wedge d' \wedge e'$ and $b' \wedge e \wedge f$ have a consensus.   ■

If two terms have a consensus, we will use the words, "consensus literal" and "consensus term." The **consensus literal** is the literal that is the reason for the consensus. It occurs in one term and its negation occurs in the other term. The **consensus term** is the conjunction of the two terms without the consensus literal and its negation. The idempotent law allows us to omit repetitions of literals in the consensus term. Here is another look at the terms in Example 3.2:

EXAMPLE 3.3   a. The terms $a \wedge b \wedge c$ and $a' \wedge c \wedge d$ have a consensus. The consensus literal is a and the consensus term is $(b \wedge c) \wedge (c \wedge d) \equiv b \wedge c \wedge d$.

b. The terms $a \wedge b'$ and $b \wedge c \wedge d$ have a consensus. The consensus literal is b' and the consensus term is $a \wedge c \wedge d$.

c. The terms $a \wedge b'$ and $b' \wedge c \wedge d$ do not have a consensus.

d. The terms $a \wedge b'$ and $a' \wedge b \wedge c$ do not have a consensus.

e. The terms $a \wedge b' \wedge d' \wedge e'$ and $b' \wedge e \wedge f$ have a consensus, with consensus literal e and consensus term $a \wedge b' \wedge d' \wedge f$.   ■

Look again at the consensus law (5):

$$(x \wedge z) \vee (y \wedge z') \equiv (x \wedge z) \vee (y \wedge z') \vee (x \wedge y)$$

Note that on the left side are two terms with a consensus: $x \wedge z$ and $y \wedge z'$. The consensus literal is z and the consensus term is $x \wedge y$. The consensus law says that if two terms have a consensus, we can adjoin the consensus term and obtain an equivalent proposition. This strikes most people as a strange thing to do since the right side of (5) looks longer and more complicated than the left. It looks as if sticking on the consensus term makes things worse. It does, but only for a moment. The absorption law is the reason. Usually, the right side of (5) will simplify because some long term contains a shorter one and the longer one is absorbed, that is, erased. In the general statement in (5), no absorption takes place. But trust us, at least until we have a chance to present the algorithm and an example to illustrate how a momentary complication will often lead to a later simplification.

The idea of Algorithm 3.3 is simple. If two terms of f have a consensus with a consensus term X that does not contain any term already in f, then *add* X to f; that is, replace f by $f \vee X$. When this process cannot be continued, you are done.

☐ ALGORITHM 3.3   **To find the consensus expansion of a proposition f in short disjunctive form.**

1. If there are two terms that have a consensus term that does not contain a term already in the form, then choose two such terms and add their consensus term to the form. Otherwise, go to 3.

2. Delete every previous term that contains the term just added; then go to 1.

3. STOP. You have the **consensus expansion** of f, that is, the disjunction of all terms that could occur in a minimal form of f.   ☐

EXAMPLE 3.4   Let's find the consensus expansion of the proposition

$$\overset{1}{} \quad \overset{2}{} \quad \overset{3}{} \quad \overset{4}{} \quad \overset{5}{}$$
$$f = (a \wedge b \wedge c) \vee (a \wedge c') \vee (a \wedge b \wedge d') \vee (a' \wedge c) \vee (a' \wedge b' \wedge c' \wedge d')$$

The proposition is already in short disjunctive form. We've numbered the terms. Terms 1 and 2 have a consensus with consensus term $a \wedge b$. When we list the steps followed in applying the algorithm, the fact that 1 and 2 have been compared will be indicated by "1–2" and the fact that they have a consensus will be indicated by "1–2 $a \wedge b$." The term $a \wedge b$ does not contain any of the terms 1 through 5, so we add it and give it the next available number, 6: $\overset{6}{a \wedge b}$. If the new term does contain a term already present, we could add it, but it would be immediately absorbed. Now terms 1 and 3 contain term 6; so we delete them and return to instruction 1 of the algorithm. In hand work you would just cancel terms 1 and 3 and proceed; but to indicate our steps clearly, we will write "delete 1 and 3." Since 1 and 3 are gone, the next comparison is 2–4. Terms 2 and 4 have no consensus, so we just write "2–4" and go on. The first eight steps follow:

$$\overset{6}{}$$
1–2 $a \wedge b$

delete 1 and 3

2–4

$$\overset{7}{}$$
2–5 $b' \wedge c' \wedge d'$

delete 5

2–6

2–7

                8
4–6 $b \wedge c$

The next comparison is 2–8, not 4–7, since each time a new term is added we go back to the first comparison not yet made. Now 2–8 has consensus term $a \wedge b$, which contains (in fact equals) term 6. If you notice this before writing $a \wedge b$, fine. Otherwise, just don't give $a \wedge b$ a number, and go on. The steps conclude:

2–8 $a \wedge b$

                9
4–7 $a' \wedge b' \wedge d'$

2–9 $b' \wedge c' \wedge d'$

4–8

4–9

6–7 $a \wedge c' \wedge d'$ (contains 2)

6–8

6–9

7–8

7–9

8–9 $a' \wedge c \wedge d'$ (contains 4)

STOP. The consensus expansion is

$$
\begin{array}{cccccc}
A & B & C & D & E & F \\
\end{array}
$$
$$
f \equiv (a \wedge c') \vee (a' \wedge c) \vee (a \wedge b) \vee (b' \wedge c' \wedge d') \vee (b \wedge c) \vee (a' \wedge b' \wedge d')
$$

The use of the capital letters is explained below.   ◼

You might have noticed that the consensus expansion has six terms while the original proposition has only five. Each has 14 literals. Again, we must suffer a momentary complication to achieve our ultimate objective: all minimal forms.

When a proposition has been written in full prime form, we are ready for Algorithm 3.4: the determination of all minimal forms. First, we introduce two more definitions and a convenient coding technique.

A term in a disjunctive form of a proposition is a **minterm** if for each variable in the proposition, either that variable or its negation occurs in the term. Thus, if a proposition involves the variables a, b, c, d, then the terms $a' \wedge b' \wedge c \wedge d'$ and $a \wedge b \wedge c \wedge d$ are minterms, while $a' \wedge c \wedge d'$, $a \wedge d$, and b are not. To determine whether or not a term is a minterm requires having a list of all possible variables for the problem. If we switch the variable set to a, b, c, d, e, then none of the terms just written is a minterm. If the variable set is a, d, then $a \wedge d$ is a minterm and $a' \wedge c \wedge d'$ doesn't make any sense.

It can be shown that every term is equivalent to the disjunction of all minterms that contain it. This disjunction is called the **minterm expansion** of the term. Consider, for example, the term $x = a' \wedge c \wedge d'$ in a proposition with variables a, b, c, d. The only minterms that contain x are $a' \wedge b \wedge c \wedge d'$ and $a' \wedge b' \wedge c \wedge d'$; and we have

$$(a' \wedge b \wedge c \wedge d') \vee (a' \wedge b' \wedge c \wedge d')$$
$$\equiv a' \wedge (b \vee b') \wedge c \wedge d'$$
$$\equiv a' \wedge 1 \wedge c \wedge d'$$
$$\equiv a' \wedge c \wedge d'$$

This example suggests a way to obtain the minterm expansion of any term y:

1. For each variable v in the proposition such that neither v nor v' occurs in y, write the disjunction $v \vee v'$.

2. Form the conjunction of y and all the disjunctions written in Step 1.

3. Rewrite the result of Step 2 in disjunctive form. This is the minterm expansion of y.

As an illustration we find the minterm expansion of the term $A = a \wedge c'$ at the end of Example 3.4. Variables b, d and their negations are missing from A, so we write the disjunctions $b \vee b'$ and $d \vee d'$. Now form the conjunction $a \wedge (b \vee b') \wedge c' \wedge (d \vee d')$ and rewrite it to obtain the minterm expansion

$$A \equiv (a \wedge b' \wedge c' \wedge d') \vee (a \wedge b' \wedge c' \wedge d) \vee (a \wedge b \wedge c' \wedge d')$$
$$\vee (a \wedge b \wedge c' \wedge d)$$

It is easy to enumerate the number of possible minterms. If the proposition has n variables, then there are 2^n different possible minterms to be considered.

Again we must warn the reader that the minterm expansion of a term is generally much longer than the term. Algorithm 3.4 is a concise way to carry out an otherwise lengthy and cumbersome procedure. The idea is to take the consensus expansion, write the minterm expansion for each term, and then use this expansion to identify the redundant terms. In our example the complete expansion of f has six terms, and its minterm expansion has $4 + 4 + 4 + 2 + 4 + 2 = 20$ terms. These 20 terms are represented by X's in the forthcoming table. Before you get discouraged by all this complication, look ahead to the bottom line: there are many cancellations; the minimal forms for f have only 4 terms and 9 literals. To get to that answer requires a trip through an expression with 6 terms and 24 literals. Here we go.

To begin, we need a brief way to represent terms in the minterm expansion. First, be sure to write the literals in each term, whether they are negated or not, in the same order. (If the variables are a, b, c, ..., use alphabetical order; if the variables are a_1, a_2, ..., use numerical order.) Then encode each minterm as an **n-place binary number** by writing 1 for each variable in the term and 0 for each negated variable in the term. For example, the minterms $a \wedge b' \wedge c' \wedge d'$, $a \wedge b' \wedge c' \wedge d$, $a \wedge b \wedge c' \wedge d'$, and $a \wedge b \wedge c' \wedge d$ in the complete expansion of A obtained above are encoded, respectively, as 1 0 0 0, 1 0 0 1, 1 1 0 0, and 1 1 0 1. Finally, to further shorten the notation for minterms, convert their n-place binary code numbers to base ten. Thus, the 4-place binary code numbers for A of 1 0 0 0, 1 0 0 1, 1 1 0 0, and 1 1 0 1 become, respectively, 8, 9, 12, and 13. The possible minterms for a proposition with n variables are thus finally encoded by the base ten numbers 0, 1, ..., $2^n - 1$. Conversely, each of these numbers may be decoded to a minterm provided you know n, the number of variables. For example, consider the minterm with base ten code 22 in a proposition with five variables a, b, c, d, e. The 5-place binary expansion of 22 is 1 0 1 1 0, so the term is $a \wedge b' \wedge c \wedge d \wedge e'$. If the proposition has six variables a, b, c, d, e, f, then 22 is written 0 1 0 1 1 0, and the corresponding minterm is $a' \wedge b \wedge c' \wedge d \wedge e \wedge f'$.

With this notation it is easy to write the base ten codes of the minterm expansion of any term. We illustrate this with the term $A = a \wedge c'$ above. Encode A, writing dashes for missing literals: 1 _ 0 _. Now fill in the dashes with 0 and 1 in every possible way, and convert the resulting binary numbers to base ten: 8 (1 0 0 0), 9 (1 0 0 1), 12 (1 1 0 0), 13 (1 1 0 1).

□ ALGORITHM 3.4   **Selection of All Minimal Forms from the Consensus Expansion**

1. For each term in the consensus expansion, write the base ten codes of its minterm expansion.

2. Make a table with rows headed by the terms of the consensus expansion and columns headed by the base ten codes that appear in at least one minterm expansion. Place X's to indicate the minterm expansions of each term.

3. Circle each X that has no other X in its column. Then star each term in the consensus expansion that has a circle in its row. These are the **essential** terms of the original proposition. Then circle each column head that has an X in a starred row. If there are no uncircled column heads, then the only minimal form is the disjunction of the essential terms. Otherwise, proceed.

4. For each uncircled column head, write the disjunction of the terms heading rows with X in that column. Then write the conjunction of the terms you have written. This proposition is called the **Petrick proposition** of the original proposition.

5. Rewrite the Petrick proposition in short disjunctive form; call it Π.

6. Retain only those terms of Π that involve the smallest number of minterms.

7. For each retained term of Π, count the number of literals (including repetitions) that occur in the terms of the consensus expansion that appear in that term of Π. Omit all retained terms of Π except those for which this count is smallest.

8. For each term of Π that still remains, the terms of the consensus expansion that appear in that term of Π, together with all essential terms found in Step 3, are the terms of a minimal form of the original proposition. Moreover, every minimal form is obtained in this way. □

We illustrate Algorithm 3.4 for the proposition f of Example 3.4.

Step I.　Write the minterm expansion of each prime term in base ten code. For the proposition f:

term	binary form	terms in minterm expansion (base 10 code)
A	1 _ 0 _	8, 9, 12, 13
B	0 _ 1 _	2, 3, 6, 7
C	1 1 _ _	12, 13, 14, 15
D	_ 0 0 0	0, 8
E	_ 1 1 _	6, 7, 14, 15
F	0 0 _ 0	0, 2

Step II.　Make a table with rows headed by the terms and columns headed by the base ten codes that actually appear in at least one minterm expansion. Place X's to indicate the minterm expansion of each term.

In our example there are four variables, so the possible codes are 0, 1, ..., $2^4 - 1 = 15$. But the codes 1, 4, 5, 10, and 11 do not appear; so the table is as follows:

	0	2	3	6	7	8	9	12	13	14	15
A						X	X	X	X		
B		X	X	X	X						
C								X	X	X	X
D	X						X				
E				X	X					X	X
F	X	X									

Now any set of terms whose disjunction is equivalent to the proposition must include every minterm in the table. Note that the minterm with code 3 appears only in term B; so B is an **essential** term; that is, it must be included in every minimal form. Since B must be included, minterms 2, 6, and 7 are taken care of. Similarly, A is essential (because of 9), and so 8, 12, and 13 are taken care of. Step 3 is the general instruction:

Step III.　Circle each X that has no other X in its column. Then star each term in the consensus expansion that has a circle in its row. These starred terms are the essential terms. Then circle each minterm that has an X in a starred row.

For our example the table becomes as shown:

	0	(2)	(3)	(6)	(7)	(8)	(9)	(12)	(13)	14	15
*A						X	(X)	X	X		
*B		X	(X)	X	X						
C								X	X	X	X
D	X						X				
E				X	X					X	X
F	X	X									

In this table, minterms 0, 14, and 15 must still be picked up; so we are not done. Term 0 can be obtained from D or F; 14 from C or E; and 15 from C or E. Using the logical interpretation of $\wedge$ and $\vee$, then, we must have $(D \vee F) \wedge (C \vee E) \wedge (C \vee E)$. This is the Petrick proposition of the original proposition. Step 4 is the general instruction:

Step IV.   For each uncircled column head, write the disjunction of the terms heading rows with X in that column. Then write the conjunction of the terms you have written. (This is the Petrick proposition.)

The next instruction uses Algorithm 3.2.

Step V.   Rewrite the Petrick proposition in short disjunctive form.

For our example:

$$(D \vee F) \wedge (C \vee E) \wedge (C \vee E)$$
$$\equiv (D \vee F) \wedge (C \vee E)$$
$$\equiv (C \wedge D) \vee (C \wedge F) \vee (D \wedge E) \vee (E \wedge F) \equiv \Pi$$

Each term of Π, together with the essential terms, gives a set of terms whose disjunction is equivalent to the proposition. To get down to the minimal forms, we continue the algorithm as follows:

Step VI.   Retain only those terms of Π with the smallest number of minterms.

For our example each of the terms $C \wedge D$, $C \wedge F$, $D \wedge E$, and $E \wedge F$ is retained. If, say, the term $C \wedge D \wedge F$ had been present, then it would have been discarded.

Step VII.   The term $C \wedge D$ consists of the prime terms $C = a \wedge b$ and $D = b' \wedge c' \wedge d'$, which involve a total of five literals. In fact, each of the terms $C \wedge F$, $D \wedge E$, and $E \wedge F$ also involves exactly five literals; so none of these terms is omitted.

Step VIII.   Thus, the original proposition f has four minimal forms: the disjunction of A, B, C, D, or of A, B, C, F, or of A, B, D, E, or of A, B, E, F:

$$f \equiv (a \wedge c') \vee (a' \wedge c) \vee (a \wedge b) \vee (b' \wedge c' \wedge d')$$
$$\equiv (a \wedge c') \vee (a' \wedge c) \vee (a \wedge b) \vee (a' \wedge b' \wedge d')$$
$$\equiv (a \wedge c') \vee (a' \wedge c) \vee (b' \wedge c' \wedge d') \vee (b \wedge c)$$
$$\equiv (a \wedge c') \vee (a' \wedge c) \vee (b \wedge c) \vee (a' \wedge b' \wedge d')$$

and these are all the minimal forms of f.

Here is a summary of the entire method.

To Find All Minimal Forms of a Proposition

1. Write the proposition in short disjunctive form.

2. Use the consensus law to write the consensus expansion.

3. Find the minterm expansions in base ten code of each term.

4. Make a table to find the essential terms and the Petrick proposition. (If there is no Petrick proposition, then the conjunction of the essential terms is the only minimal form.)

5. Write the Petrick proposition in short disjunctive form. Retain only the terms with the fewest variables. Of these, retain only the terms for which the consensus expansion terms have the fewest total literals.

6. The disjunction of the consensus expansion terms of each retained term, together with the essential terms, constitutes a minimal form; and every minimal form is found in this way.

EXERCISES

In Exercises 1–4 decide whether or not the two terms have a consensus and, if they do, write the consensus term.

1. $a \wedge b' \wedge d$, $a' \wedge b \wedge c$

2. $a' \wedge b \wedge c$, $a \wedge c' \wedge d$

3. $b' \wedge c \wedge e$, $a \wedge c' \wedge e \wedge f$

4. $a' \wedge c' \wedge d'$, $a' \wedge d \wedge e' \wedge f'$

In Exercises 5–8 write the consensus expansion of the proposition.

5. $(a \wedge b') \vee (b' \wedge c) \vee (a \wedge c) \vee (a \wedge c')$ (See Example 3.1.)

6. $(a \wedge b' \wedge c) \vee (a \wedge b' \wedge c') \vee (a \wedge b \wedge c')$

7. $(a \wedge b \wedge c \wedge d) \vee (a' \wedge b \wedge c \wedge d) \vee (a' \wedge b' \wedge c \wedge d)$
   $\vee (a' \wedge b' \wedge c' \wedge d) \vee (a' \wedge b' \wedge c' \wedge d')$

8. $(a \wedge b \wedge d) \vee (a \wedge d') \vee (a \wedge b \wedge c') \vee (a' \wedge d)$
   $\vee (a' \wedge b' \wedge c' \wedge d')$

In Exercises 9 and 10 write the minterm expansions using the variables a, b, c, d of the given terms.

9. $a' \wedge b \wedge d'$, $c' \wedge d$

10. $a \wedge d$, b'

In Exercises 11 and 12 write the 5-place binary and the base ten codes for the given minterms.

11. $a \wedge b' \wedge c \wedge d' \wedge e$, $a' \wedge b \wedge c' \wedge d \wedge e'$

12. $a' \wedge b' \wedge c' \wedge d \wedge e$, $a' \wedge b \wedge c \wedge d \wedge e$

In Exercises 13 and 14 write, using the given variables, the minterms with the given base ten codes.

13. a, b, c, d: 14, 6, 2

14. a_1, a_2, a_3, a_4, a_5: 5, 18, 30

In Exercises 15–24 find all minimal forms of the given proposition.

15. The proposition of Exercise 5.

16. The proposition of Exercise 6.

17. The proposition of Exercise 7.

18. The proposition of Exercise 8.

19. $(a \wedge b \wedge c \wedge e) \vee (a \wedge c') \vee (a \wedge b \wedge d') \vee (a' \wedge c)$
    $\vee (a' \wedge b' \wedge c' \wedge d' \wedge e')$

20. $(a \wedge b) \vee (a' \wedge c) \vee (b' \wedge c) \vee (b' \wedge d) \vee (d' \wedge e)$
    $\vee (e' \wedge f)$

21. $[(a' \vee b \vee d') \wedge (b \wedge c' \wedge d)'] \vee (a' \wedge d)'$

22. $(a' \vee b \vee c) \wedge (a' \vee d') \wedge (b \vee c \vee d') \wedge (c' \vee d')$

23. $[(a \wedge b' \wedge d)' \wedge (c' \wedge d)'] \vee (a \wedge b' \wedge c')$

24. $(b' \vee c' \vee d') \wedge (a' \vee b' \vee c) \wedge (a' \wedge c' \wedge d')$

C H A P T E R

F O U R

Graphs

4.1 Introduction

4.2 Trees and Searching

4.3 Eulerian Graphs and Hamiltonian Circuits

4.4 Minimal Paths and Circuits

4.5 Spanning Trees

GRAPHS ARE IMPORTANT in computer science for at least two reasons. First, they are used in the design of computers and computer programs. They are used to organize the storage of data and to describe computer networks. They can also be an aid in complicated counting problems which arise in determining machine calculation times. Second, computers are used to solve graph theory problems, especially in the area of management decision making known as Operations Research. Of course, the purely mathematical theory of graphs is a growing and fascinating area in itself. In this chapter and the next we will investigate these and other aspects of graph theory.

4.1

Introduction

A **graph** is a set of **vertices*** and a set of **edges** such that each two distinct vertices are joined by at most one edge and each edge joins two distinct vertices. (This use of the term *graph* has little to do with the "graph of an equation" in analytic geometry.)

EXAMPLE 4.1   Here is a description of a graph G. The set of vertices is $V = \{a, b, c, d\}$, the set of edges is $E = \{e, f, g\}$; e joins a and b, f joins a and c, and g joins c and d.   ◻

A graph may be drawn in the plane by depicting vertices as dots (or sometimes by small circles) and edges by line segments (not necessarily straight) joining them. Figure 4.1 shows two drawings of the graph of Example 4.1.

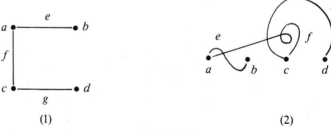

FIGURE 4.1

There is an important generalization of the concept of graph. A **pseudograph** is a set of vertices and a set of edges such that each edge joins a vertex to a vertex. In a pseudograph there are two possible situations that may occur that would not be allowed in a graph. First, there may be two vertices that are joined by more than one edge, as with vertices a and b in Figure 4.2. Such situations

---

* Pay attention to the singular and plural of vertex: it's one vertex, not one "vertice," and two vertices, not two "vertexes."

may be called **multiple connections**. Also, there may be edges that join a vertex to itself, as with c and d in Figure 4.2. Such edges are called **loops**. (There are two loops at d.) A graph is a pseudograph with no multiple connections and no loops.

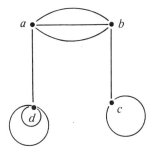

FIGURE 4.2

The true nature of a pseudograph as a mathematical abstraction is perhaps best understood by realizing that a pseudograph is completely described by its incidence matrix. Consider a pseudograph with only a finite number of vertices $v_1, \ldots, v_m$ and a finite number of edges $e_1, \ldots, e_n$. An edge is said to be **incident** with the vertex or vertices it connects. The **incidence matrix** of a pseudograph is an $m \times n$ matrix whose rows correspond to the vertices and whose columns correspond to the edges. The (i, j) entry is 1 if vertex v_i is on edge e_j; otherwise, the (i, j) entry is 0. Since each edge is incident with either one or two vertices, each column of the incidence matrix contains either one or two 1's, and the other entries are 0. The incidence matrix of a graph has precisely two 1's in each column, and no two columns are the same. For a pseudograph a column might contain just one 1 (if the corresponding edge is a loop at a vertex), and two or more columns might be identical (if two or more distinct edges connect the same pair of vertices). The incidence matrix of the pseudograph of Figure 4.3 is as shown:

$$
\begin{array}{c c c c c c c c c c}
 & e_1 & e_2 & e_3 & e_4 & e_5 & e_6 & e_7 & e_8 & e_9 \\
v_1 & \begin{bmatrix} 1 & 1 & 1 & 0 & 0 & 0 & 0 & 0 & 0 \\ \end{bmatrix} \\
v_2 & 0 & 1 & 0 & 1 & 1 & 0 & 0 & 0 & 0 \\
v_3 & 0 & 0 & 1 & 1 & 0 & 1 & 0 & 0 & 0 \\
v_4 & 0 & 0 & 0 & 0 & 1 & 0 & 1 & 1 & 0 \\
v_5 & 0 & 0 & 0 & 0 & 0 & 1 & 0 & 1 & 1 \\
\end{array}
$$

The fact that we obtain the same incidence matrix for each of the three pictures in Figure 4.3 tells us that they represent the same pseudograph.

Any matrix, all of whose entries are 0 or 1 and such that each column contains either one or two 1's, is the incidence matrix for a pseudograph. For

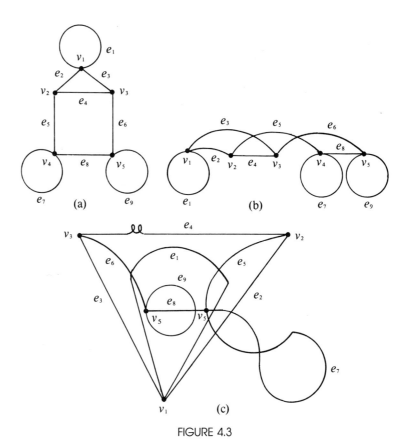

FIGURE 4.3

example, given the matrix

$$\begin{bmatrix} 1 & 1 & 0 & 1 & 1 & 0 & 0 \\ 0 & 1 & 0 & 0 & 1 & 0 & 1 \\ 0 & 0 & 1 & 0 & 0 & 1 & 0 \\ 0 & 0 & 0 & 1 & 0 & 1 & 0 \\ 0 & 0 & 1 & 0 & 0 & 0 & 0 \end{bmatrix}$$

we label the rows $v_1, \ldots, v_5$ and the columns $e_1, \ldots, e_7$;

$$\begin{array}{c c} & \begin{array}{c c c c c c c} e_1 & e_2 & e_3 & e_4 & e_5 & e_6 & e_7 \end{array} \\ \begin{array}{c} v_1 \\ v_2 \\ v_3 \\ v_4 \\ v_5 \end{array} & \begin{bmatrix} 1 & 1 & 0 & 1 & 1 & 0 & 0 \\ 0 & 1 & 0 & 0 & 1 & 0 & 1 \\ 0 & 0 & 1 & 0 & 0 & 1 & 0 \\ 0 & 0 & 0 & 1 & 0 & 1 & 0 \\ 0 & 0 & 1 & 0 & 0 & 0 & 0 \end{bmatrix} \end{array}$$

pick five points in the plane; label them $v_1, \ldots, v_5$; and connect them with edges according to the "instructions" in the matrix. One possible picture is shown in Figure 4.4.

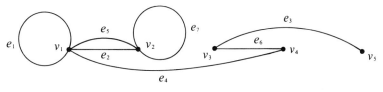

FIGURE 4.4

The **adjacency matrix** of a pseudograph is an $m \times m$ matrix whose rows and columns correspond to the vertices of the pseudograph. The entry at address (i, j) is the number of edges that join vertex v_i to vertex v_j. If this entry is not zero, we say that vertices v_i and v_j are **adjacent**. Of course, the entry at address (i, j) is the same as the entry at (j, i) for all pairs (i, j). A square matrix with the property that the entry at address (i, j) is the same as the entry at address (j, i) for all pairs (i, j) is said to be **symmetric**. In an adjacency matrix row i consists entirely of 0's if and only if vertex v_i is **isolated**. The adjacency matrix for the pseudograph shown in Figures 4.3(a), (b), and (c) is

$$
\begin{array}{c c}
& \begin{array}{c c c c c} v_1 & v_2 & v_3 & v_4 & v_5 \end{array} \\
\begin{array}{c} v_1 \\ v_2 \\ v_3 \\ v_4 \\ v_5 \end{array} &
\left[
\begin{array}{c c c c c}
1 & 1 & 1 & 0 & 0 \\
1 & 0 & 1 & 1 & 0 \\
1 & 1 & 0 & 0 & 1 \\
0 & 1 & 0 & 1 & 1 \\
0 & 0 & 1 & 1 & 1
\end{array}
\right]
\end{array}
$$

Note that the adjacency matrix of a *graph* has 0's on the diagonal (since there are no loops) and 0's and 1's off the diagonal. As with the incidence matrix, the adjacency matrix completely determines the pseudograph. Any symmetric matrix with nonnegative integer entries is the adjacency matrix for a pseudograph. For example, given the matrix

$$
\left[
\begin{array}{c c c c c c}
0 & 1 & 2 & 0 & 0 & 0 \\
1 & 2 & 0 & 0 & 0 & 1 \\
2 & 0 & 1 & 0 & 0 & 1 \\
0 & 0 & 0 & 0 & 0 & 0 \\
0 & 0 & 0 & 0 & 1 & 0 \\
0 & 1 & 1 & 0 & 0 & 0
\end{array}
\right]
$$

label the rows and columns $v_1, \ldots, v_6$; pick six corresponding points in the plane and connect them according to the "instructions" in the matrix. One possible picture is shown in Figure 4.5.

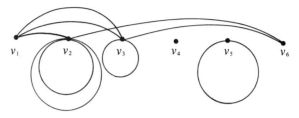

FIGURE 4.5

It can be very hard to tell whether or not two drawings of a pseudograph really depict the same pseudograph. The graphs in Figure 4.6(1) and (2) do not

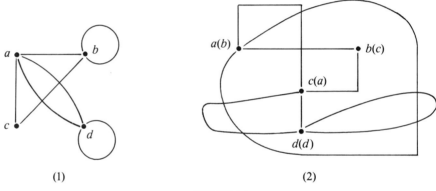

(1)   (2)

FIGURE 4.6

look the same. If the vertices are labeled a, b, c, d as shown, then the adjacency matrices of (1) and (2) are

$$A_1 = \begin{bmatrix} 0 & 1 & 1 & 2 \\ 1 & 1 & 1 & 0 \\ 1 & 1 & 0 & 0 \\ 2 & 0 & 0 & 1 \end{bmatrix} \text{ and } A_2 = \begin{bmatrix} 1 & 1 & 1 & 0 \\ 1 & 0 & 1 & 0 \\ 1 & 1 & 0 & 2 \\ 0 & 0 & 2 & 1 \end{bmatrix}$$

respectively, which are not the same. But if we relabel the vertices of graph (2) with the labels (a), (b), (c), (d) as shown, then its adjacency matrix is equal to A_1; so the pseudographs are actually the same.

One way to help tell whether two graphs are the same would be to redraw each graph as simply as possible. We shall pursue this idea in Section 5.1.

For positive integers m and n there are two particular graphs that will be of use later on. One is K_n, the **complete graph on n vertices**. It has n vertices and precisely one edge between each pair of distinct vertices. Thus, its adjacency matrix is an $n \times n$ matrix, all of whose entries are 1 except for the main diagonal entries, all of which are 0. A description of its incidence matrix is left as an exercise. The other graph we will need is denoted $K_{m,n}$ and is called the **complete bipartite graph on m and n points**. The graph itself has $m + n$ vertices in two "parts," one with m vertices and the other with n. Each vertex in one part is joined by an edge to each vertex in the other part, but no edges connect vertices in the same part. Figure 4.7 shows a graphical presentation of K_4, K_5, $K_{3,3}$, $K_{4,4}$, $K_{1,5}$, and $K_{2,4}$.

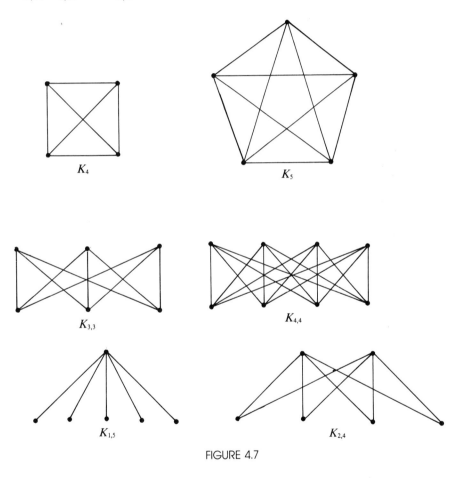

FIGURE 4.7

Given two vertices v and w in a pseudograph G, it may be possible to trace over edges of G beginning at v and ending at w without lifting your pen or pencil (that is, without ever leaving G). The sequence of edges of G that you choose to trace as you move from v to w comprises a **path** from v to w. You do not have to be efficient in getting from v to w. You can backtrack, go up and down "blind alleys," trace over edges more than once, etc. The important thing is that all the edges used are "connected" to one another. For example, in Figure 4.8, paths from vertex v to vertex w include

(i) e_{10}, e_2, e_4

(ii) e_8, e_5, e_4

(iii) $e_{10}, e_9, e_7, e_6, e_5, e_3, e_4$

(iv) $e_{10}, e_1, e_1, e_2, e_3, e_3, e_3, e_3, e_5, e_5, e_4, e_4, e_4$

among others.

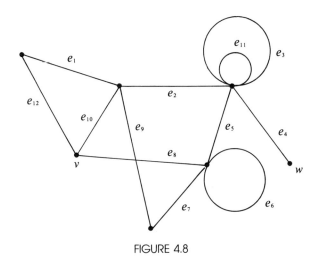

FIGURE 4.8

The **length** of a path is its number of edges. Thus, the four paths from v to w listed above have lengths 3, 3, 7, and 13, respectively. The **distance** between two vertices is the length of a shortest path between them. Thus, the distance between v and w is 3 and the distance from v to itself is zero.

A pseudograph is **connected** if each pair of distinct vertices can be joined by a path.

A path is **closed** if it begins and ends at the same vertex.

A **circuit** is a very special type of path that satisfies two conditions:

1. It begins and ends at the same vertex (so it's a closed path).

2. No edge is repeated.

Note that we did *not* require of a circuit that no vertex be repeated. If a circuit also satisfies this condition, it is said to be a **simple circuit**. For example, in Figure 4.8, $e_{12}, e_1, e_9, e_7, e_5, e_3, e_2, e_{10}$ is a circuit of length 8 at v; and e_{10}, e_2, e_5, e_8 is a simple circuit of length 4 at v.

A trivial sort of closed path begins at vertex v, travels to vertex w, and then returns to v by repeating the same edges in reverse order. It is useful to know that, apart from this trivial case, every closed path at v contains a simple circuit (which might, however, not go through v).

A **subpseudograph** H of a pseudograph G is a subset of vertices and edges of G such that (1) H is in itself a pseudograph, and (2) all the incidence relations in H are also incidence relations in G.

A subpseudograph of G can be thought of as being formed by erasing parts of G subject to the condition that if a vertex is erased, then each edge incident with that vertex must also be erased. Trivially, G and the empty graph are subpseudographs of any pseudograph G. Subgraphs of $K_{m,n}$ are called **bipartite** graphs. Finally, a **component** of a pseudograph is a "largest" connected subpseudograph in the sense that there are no paths between its vertices and other vertices of G not in the subpseudograph. Figure 4.9 illustrates the components of a particular pseudograph G.

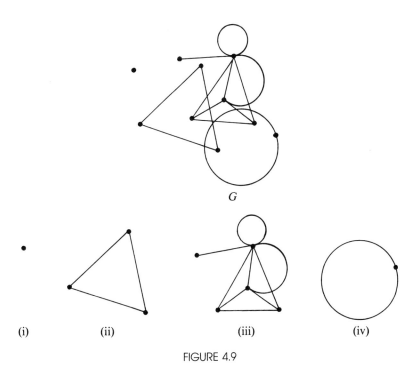

G

(i)   (ii)   (iii)   (iv)

FIGURE 4.9

Since the adjacency matrix of a graph is square, it can be raised to powers. Do these powers have any significance? Let's look at a simple example. The graph in Figure 4.10 has adjacency matrix

$$A = \begin{bmatrix} 0 & 1 & 0 & 1 \\ 1 & 0 & 1 & 1 \\ 0 & 1 & 0 & 1 \\ 1 & 1 & 1 & 0 \end{bmatrix}$$

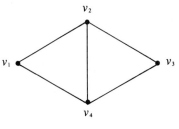

FIGURE 4.10

Then,
$$A^2 = \begin{bmatrix} 2 & 1 & 2 & 1 \\ 1 & 3 & 1 & 2 \\ 2 & 1 & 2 & 1 \\ 1 & 2 & 1 & 3 \end{bmatrix}$$

The (i, j)-entry in this matrix is the number of paths of length two from vertex v_i to vertex v_j. For example, the $(1, 3)$-entry is 2. We obtained 2 by adding the products $[(1, 2)\text{-entry} \times (2, 3)\text{-entry}] + [(1, 4)\text{-entry} \times (4, 3)\text{-entry}]$. The other products were zero. There is an edge from v_1 to v_2 and from v_2 to v_3. Together they make a path of length 2 from v_1 to v_3. There is an edge from v_1 to v_4 and from v_4 to v_3. Together they make a path of length 2 from v_1 to v_3. There are no other edges from v_1 to a vertex with an edge to v_3. In general, the (i, j)-entry in A^2 is obtained by combining edges from vertex v_i with edges to vertex v_j. Similarly, the (i, j)-entry in A^3 gives the number of paths of length 3 from vertex v_i to vertex v_j. Since

$$A^3 = \begin{bmatrix} 2 & 5 & 2 & 5 \\ 5 & 4 & 5 & 5 \\ 2 & 5 & 2 & 5 \\ 5 & 5 & 5 & 4 \end{bmatrix}$$

there are 4 paths of length 3 from v_4 to itself:

(i) v_4, v_1, v_2, v_4
(ii) v_4, v_2, v_3, v_4
(iii) v_4, v_3, v_2, v_4
(iv) v_4, v_2, v_1, v_4

In general, the (i, j)-entry of A^n is the number of paths of length n from v_i to v_j. In particular, (i, i)-entries on the diagonal are the number of closed paths of length n at v_i.

The **degree** of a vertex in a pseudograph is the number of edge-ends that hit it. Thus, a loop at a vertex is counted twice when calculating degree. For the purposes of calculating degree, each edge contributes two; thus, the sum of all the degrees of all the vertices is twice the number of edges; that is, an even number. It follows that there cannot be an odd number of vertices with odd degree.

For an amusing application of that last observation, consider the graph associated with a dinner party as follows. The vertices correspond to party guests, and we'll draw an edge between the vertices of guests who shake hands. Then the degree of a vertex corresponds to the number of handshakes by that guest. Our observation about degree translates into the fact that there is an even number of people who shake hands an odd number of times. (Note that zero is even, so perhaps no one shakes hands an odd number of times.)

In Figure 4.11 (which is a copy of Figure 4.3(a)) the degrees of the vertices are as follows:

vertex	degree
v_1	4
v_2	3
v_3	3
v_4	4
v_5	4

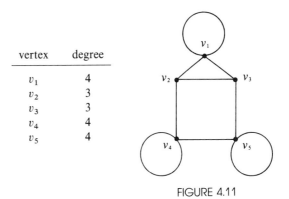

FIGURE 4.11

In some applications it is necessary to assign a direction to each edge of a pseudograph, obtaining a **directed pseudograph**. A directed edge from a vertex a to a vertex b is called an **arc** with **initial vertex** a and **terminal vertex** b. In drawing a directed pseudograph, an arc from a to b is $a \longrightarrow b$ and a loop from a to a is $a \bigcirc$. Note that $a \mathbin{\bigcirc} b$ is *not* a multiple connection, but $a \mathbin{\bigcirc} b$ *is* a multiple connection. A directed pseudograph with no loops or multiple connections is a directed graph, usually called a **digraph**.

In the adjacency matrix for a directed pseudograph, the entry at address (a, b) is the number of edges from a to b. The arcs in a path in a directed pseudograph must be traversed in their direction. Thus, if e_i and e_{i+1} are successive arcs in a path, then the terminal vertex of e_i must be the initial vertex of e_{i+1}. If A is the adjacency matrix of a directed pseudograph and n is a positive integer, then, just as with pseudographs, the (a, b)-entry of A^n is the number of paths of length n from a to b.

If S is a set and R is a binary relation on S, the **directed pseudograph of R** is defined as follows. The vertices are the elements of S; there is an arc from a to b if and only if $a \text{ R } b$.

EXAMPLE 4.2   If $S = \{2, 3, 4, 5, 6\}$ and R is the relation "is a divisor of," then the directed pseudograph of R is shown in Figure 4.12.

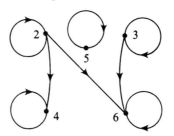

FIGURE 4.12

E X E R C I S E S

In Exercises 1–16 determine the incidence and adjacency matrices for the given pseudograph. Also, indicate the degree of each vertex.

1.

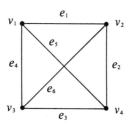

2.

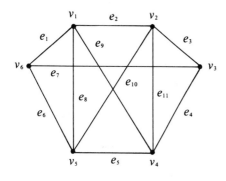

3.

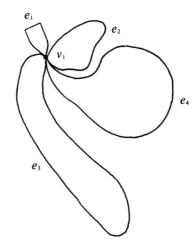

4.

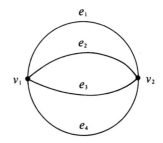

5.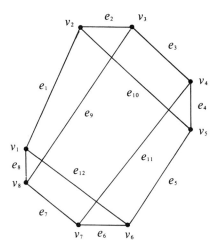

6.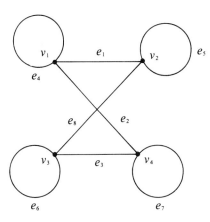

7.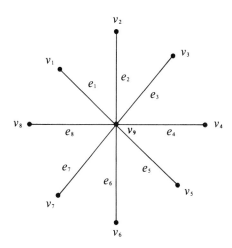

8.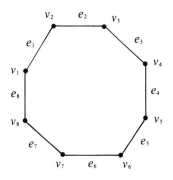

9. $\dot{v}_1 \quad \dot{v}_2 \quad \dot{v}_3 \quad \dot{v}_4 \quad \dot{v}_5$

10.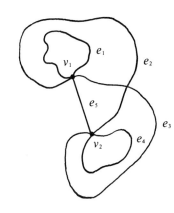

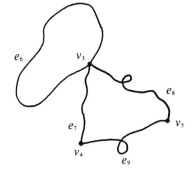

11. K_4

12. K_5

13. $K_{3,3}$

14. $K_{4,4}$

15. $K_{2,6}$

16. $K_{3,5}$

17. Describe the adjacency matrix for K_n.

18. What is the degree of each vertex in K_n? in $K_{n,n}$?

19. Draw pictures of K_3 and K_6.

20. Draw pictures of $K_{2,2}$ and $K_{5,5}$.

21. Draw a connected graph with four vertices, each of which has degree 5.

22. Draw a connected graph with five vertices, each of which has degree 4.

In Exercises 23–34 determine whether the given matrix is an adjacency matrix, incidence matrix, both, or neither. If the matrix is an adjacency matrix, draw a picture of the corresponding pseudograph. If the matrix is an incidence matrix, draw a picture of the corresponding pseudograph. For each pseudograph drawn, give the degree of each vertex.

23.
$$\begin{bmatrix} 1 & 0 & 0 \\ 0 & 1 & 0 \\ 0 & 0 & 1 \\ 1 & 0 & 0 \\ 0 & 0 & 1 \end{bmatrix}$$

24.
$$\begin{bmatrix} 1 & 0 & 1 \\ 1 & 1 & 0 \\ 0 & 1 & 1 \end{bmatrix}$$

25.
$$\begin{bmatrix} 0 & 0 & 0 & 0 \\ 0 & 0 & 0 & 0 \\ 0 & 0 & 0 & 0 \\ 0 & 0 & 0 & 0 \end{bmatrix}$$

26.
$$\begin{bmatrix} 1 & 1 & 1 & 1 & 1 \\ 1 & 1 & 1 & 1 & 1 \\ 1 & 1 & 1 & 1 & 1 \\ 1 & 1 & 1 & 1 & 1 \\ 1 & 1 & 1 & 1 & 1 \end{bmatrix}$$

27.
$$\begin{bmatrix} 1 & 1 & 0 & 0 & 0 & 0 \\ 1 & 0 & 1 & 0 & 0 & 0 \\ 0 & 1 & 0 & 1 & 0 & 0 \\ 0 & 0 & 1 & 0 & 0 & 0 \\ 0 & 0 & 0 & 0 & 1 & 1 \\ 0 & 0 & 0 & 0 & 1 & 1 \end{bmatrix}$$

28.
$$\begin{bmatrix} 0 & 0 & 1 & 0 & 0 \\ 0 & 1 & 0 & 1 & 0 \\ 1 & 0 & 0 & 0 & 1 \\ 0 & 1 & 0 & 1 & 0 \\ 0 & 0 & 1 & 0 & 1 \end{bmatrix}$$

29.
$$\begin{bmatrix} 1 & 0 & 1 & 0 & 0 & 0 & 0 \\ 0 & 1 & 1 & 0 & 0 & 0 & 1 \\ 0 & 0 & 0 & 1 & 1 & 0 & 1 \\ 0 & 0 & 0 & 1 & 0 & 1 & 0 \\ 0 & 0 & 0 & 0 & 1 & 1 & 1 \end{bmatrix}$$

30.
$$\begin{bmatrix} 1 & 1 & 1 \\ 1 & 1 & 1 \\ 1 & 1 & 1 \\ 1 & 1 & 1 \end{bmatrix}$$

31.
$$\begin{bmatrix} 0 & 1 & 0 & 0 & 0 & 0 \\ 1 & 0 & 1 & 0 & 0 & 0 \\ 0 & 1 & 0 & 1 & 0 & 0 \\ 0 & 0 & 1 & 0 & 1 & 0 \\ 0 & 0 & 0 & 1 & 0 & 1 \\ 0 & 0 & 0 & 0 & 1 & 0 \end{bmatrix}$$

32. I_n, the $n \times n$ **identity matrix**; that is, the $n \times n$ matrix with 1's on the main (upper left to lower right) diagonal and 0's everywhere else.

33. $[1 \quad 1 \quad 1 \quad 1 \quad 1]$

34. $\begin{bmatrix} 1 \\ 1 \\ 1 \\ 1 \\ 1 \end{bmatrix}$

35. List all simple circuits starting at v for the graph shown.

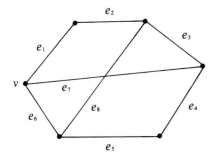

36. Explain how to calculate the degree of a vertex directly from the incidence matrix.

37. List all 3×3 matrices, all of whose entries are either 0's or 1's, that are both incidence and adjacency matrices.

38. How many 4×4 matrices have all entries either 0's or 1's? How many of these matrices are both incidence and adjacency matrices?

39. Prove that a graph with n vertices that has a vertex of degree $n - 1$ must be connected.

40. Prove that a connected graph is bipartite if and only if each circuit is of even length. (*Hint:* To prove that G is bipartite if all circuits are of even length, try a proof by contradiction. Let v be a vertex, V be

the set of all vertices an even distance from v, and W the set of all vertices an odd distance from v. Suppose two vertices u and w of V are adjacent. Connect them both to v to obtain a contradiction.)

In Exercises 41 and 42 use the adjacency matrix to determine the number of paths of length 3 from v_1 to v_3. List the paths.

41.

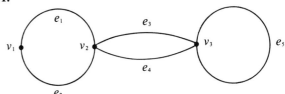

42.

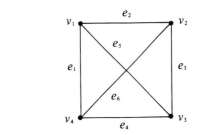

43. Find the total number of paths of length 4 in the digraph shown.

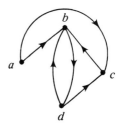

44. Find all paths of length 8 from a to b in the digraph of Exercise 43.

Trees and Searching

4.2

A **tree** is a connected graph with no simple circuits. Recall that a graph is connected if it is possible to travel between any two vertices along edges. A **simple circuit** is a circuit, each of whose vertices are incident with exactly two of its edges. In Figure 4.13 we have drawn all the trees with n vertices for $1 \leqslant n \leqslant 6$. Trees arise in many places, often rather unexpectedly. Among the applications of trees are storage and retrieval of data, coding of messages, estimation of errors in numerical calculations, sorting and merging, and analyzing complicated counting problems.

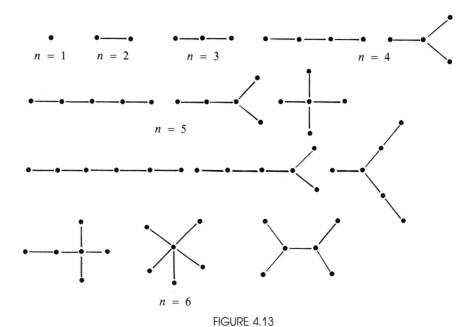

FIGURE 4.13

One nonexample is in order at this point. Your family tree, in which vertices correspond to your ancestors and edges represent the parent-child relationship, cannot be a tree as a graph, even though the part with which you are familiar probably is. It is easy to show this. You have 2 parents; 4 grandparents; 8 great-grandparents; and, in general, 2^n ancestors n generations back. If we allow about 30 years per generation and retreat 1800 years, your complete tree would have 2^{60} ancestors listed in generation 60. Now 2^{60} is about 1.15×10^{18}, while there are only about 7.9×10^{17} square inches of surface area on the earth, counting the oceans. If all your ancestors were different, they would have had no place to stand in A.D. 100. It follows that many of the branches in your tree return to common ancestors. That is, there are ancestors to which you are related by two (or more) different paths of descent. Connect two of these paths to obtain a closed path that contains a simple circuit in your family tree.

There are two important characterizations of trees. The following statements about a finite graph G are equivalent:

1. G is a tree.
2. Each two vertices of G are joined by one and only one **simple path**, that is, a path with no vertex repeated.
3. G is connected and the number of edges in G is one less than the number of vertices in G.

We establish this equivalence by proving a **circle of implications** as follows: $1 \Rightarrow 2$, $2 \Rightarrow 3$, $3 \Rightarrow 1$. From this it follows that each of 1, 2, 3 is equivalent to the other two.

$1 \Rightarrow 2$ Suppose G is connected. We will prove the contrapositive, which is logically equivalent to what we need: if G does *not* satisfy Condition 2, then G does *not* satisfy Condition 1. Suppose that G does not satisfy Condition 2. Then G must have two vertices u and v that are joined by two different simple paths P and Q. Since P and Q are different, there is a vertex w in P that is not in Q. Travel along P from w toward u until you reach the first vertex a that is in Q. (Perhaps a is u.) Travel along P from w toward v until you reach the first vertex b that is in Q. (Perhaps b is v.) Then a simple circuit of G is obtained by traveling from a to b along P and back to a along Q; so G does not satisfy Condition 1.

$2 \Rightarrow 3$ Suppose G satisfies Condition 2 and has n vertices. Then G is connected. We prove by induction on n that G has exactly $n - 1$ edges. First, if G has only 1 vertex v, then it cannot have an edge e since e and v constitute different (although fairly trivial) simple paths from v to v. It is also easy to check that the result is true for graphs with 2 or 3 vertices. Now suppose that any graph with n vertices and unique simple paths between each two vertices has $n - 1$ edges. Suppose G has $n + 1$ vertices with a unique simple path between each two. We must prove that G has exactly $n + 1 - 1 = n$ edges. Let P be a simple path in G of greatest possible length. Let v be the last vertex in P and let e be the edge of P incident with v. We claim that e is the only edge of G incident with v. Suppose a second edge f is incident with v. Let w be the other vertex on f. If w is in P, then f and that part of P joining w to v are each simple paths between v and w, contradicting the assumption about unique simple paths. If w is not in P, then P followed by f is a simple path longer than P, contradicting our choice of P. Thus, e is the only edge incident with v. Now remove v and e from G. The remaining graph has n vertices and a simple path between each two of them; so by our inductive assumption, it has $n - 1$ edges. Then G has $n - 1 + 1 = n$ edges.

$3 \Rightarrow 1$ This will be a proof by contradiction. Suppose G is connected, has n vertices and $n - 1$ edges, but is not a tree. Then G must contain a simple circuit. Remove any edge from this circuit, but not the vertices on that edge. The remaining graph is still connected, has n vertices, but has fewer than $n - 1$ edges. If this remaining graph still has a simple circuit, then repeat the edge-removal maneuver. Eventually you will reach a connected graph with n vertices, fewer than $n - 1$ edges, and *no* simple circuits. But such a graph is a tree; so, as we have proven, it has exactly $n - 1$ edges, not fewer than $n - 1$ edges. Thus, the original graph was a tree. This concludes the proof of the equivalence of Conditions 1, 2, and 3.

Rooted Trees

A **rooted tree** is a tree with one vertex labeled as the **root**. It is traditional to draw a rooted tree with its root either at the top or bottom and with all edges leading down or up as shown in Figure 4.14.

In a traditional rooted tree with root at the top, some common terminology seems natural. For example, we view the tree on the right in Figure 4.14 as a "genealogical tree." Then v_1 is the **parent** of v_5 and v_4. The vertices v_5 and v_4 are

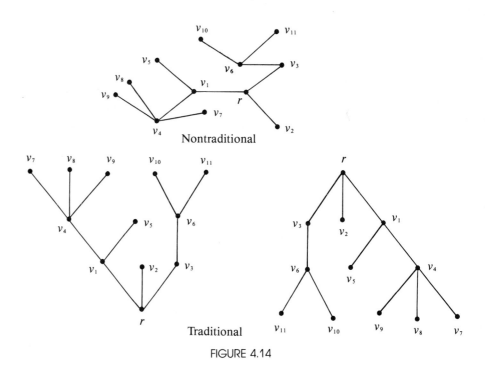

FIGURE 4.14

children. The vertex v_3 is an **ancestor** of vertices v_6, v_{11}, and v_{10}. These last three named vertices are *descendants* of v_3 and, of course, of r. The vertices v_2, v_5, v_{11}, v_{10}, v_9, v_8, and v_7 are often called **leaves**. This terminology makes more sense for the root-at-the-bottom representation on the left in Figure 4.14. In fact, the root-at-the-bottom representation is the origin of the term *tree*. In the root-at-the-top representation, leaves are sometimes called **terminal** vertices.

One other notion inspired by the tree on the left in Figure 4.14 will prove useful. The **height** of a vertex is the number of edges in the shortest path from it to the root. Thus, in Figure 4.14 the root r has height 0. The vertices v_1, v_2, and v_3 have height 1. Vertices v_4, v_5, and v_6 have height 2. Vertices v_7, v_8, v_9, v_{10}, and v_{11} have height 3.

A **binary** rooted tree is one in which each vertex has at most two children. One way to change the tree of Figure 4.14 into a binary tree is to remove vertices v_2 and v_8 and the edges on them.

Complicated Counts

Trees can be used to assist in complicated counts. In this application the tree is used to list all possible cases. For example, consider the following question: How many patterns of games are there for a best-four-out-of-seven series (such as the World Series)? Consider such a series between two teams called A and B. Let A denote the team that wins the first game. In Figure 4.15 we have drawn all possible cases where A means "A wins the game" and B means "B wins the game." The labels on the leaves also denote the team that wins the series. To list the outcomes in this fashion requires a rooted tree of height 6.

By counting A's and B's we can quickly determine that if A wins the first

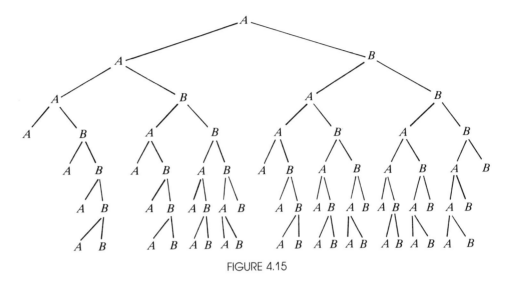

FIGURE 4.15

game, there are 20 ways for *A* to win the series and 15 ways for *B* to win. Of course, *B* might win the first game, in which case there will be 20 ways for *B* to win the series and 15 ways for *A* to win. There are 70 different patterns. The tree answers not only the given question but also questions such as: How many ways can the series last exactly five games? The answer: $14 \times 2 = 28$ ways. (Just count the leaves of height 4. Don't forget, Figure 4.15 shows only *half* of the complete series tree.)

Trees can even come in handy when there are too many branches to draw. Here they are used as an aid to thinking. For a very simple example, consider the problem of counting the number of length three permutations of the English alphabet. In Figure 4.16 we show part of a tree. In this case we have placed the

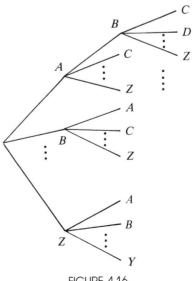

FIGURE 4.16

root to the left. We note that there are 26 vertices of height one. For each vertex of height one, there are 25 vertices of height two: total $= 26 \times 25 = 650$ vertices of height two. Finally, for each of these vertices of height two there are 24 vertices of height three: total $= 650 \times 24 = 15{,}600$ permutations.

Algebraic Expressions

The arithmetic operations $+$, $-$, $\cdot$, and $\div$ are binary operations. This means, for example, that we can add only two numbers at a time: "$a + b + c$" means either "$(a + b) + c$" or "$a + (b + c)$." The **Rules on the Order of Arithmetic Operations** eliminate the need for many parentheses. For instance, an expression such as

$$a + b \cdot c - (c \div d + e) + e \cdot f \cdot g$$

is to be interpreted as

$$\{[a + (b \cdot c)] - [(c \div d) + e]\} + [(e \cdot f) \cdot g]$$

Once all the parentheses have been inserted, such an algebraic combination can be represented by a binary tree. In Figure 4.17(a) we have drawn a detailed representation of the indicated algebraic expression. In Figure 4.17(b) is a simplified version of the same tree. In this representation the circled operations stand for the combination of the two branches coming up into that operation

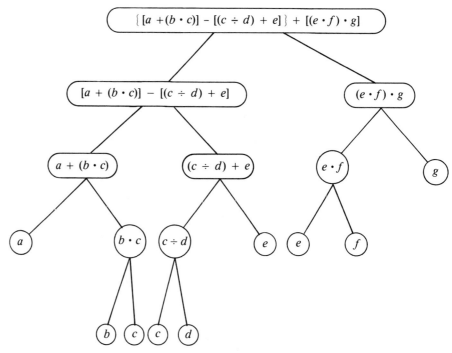

The binary tree for the expression $\{[a + (b \cdot c)] - [(c \div d) + e]\} + [(e \cdot f) \cdot g]$.

FIGURE 4.17(a)

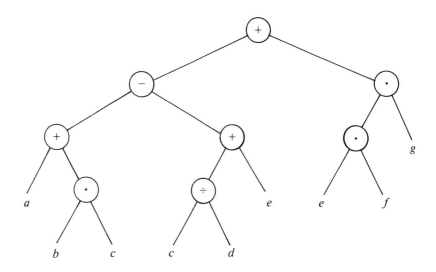

Simplified binary tree for the expression $\{[a + (b \cdot c)] - [(c \div d) + e]\} + [(e \cdot f) \cdot g]$.

FIGURE 4.17(b)

from below. You will note that one can easily recover the detailed tree at the top from the simplified one at the bottom. Trees such as the bottom one are called **process graphs** by W. Dorn and D. McCracken in their text *Numerical Methods with Fortran IV Case Studies* (Wiley, 1972). In Section 5.4 we shall use such process graphs to trace the accumulation of round-off errors through a sequence of machine-performed binary operations. It turns out that certain orders of performance generate smaller errors than others.

Huffman Codes

Rooted binary trees can be used to help efficiently code messages. A simple way to convert written text to a binary code is to assign a five-digit binary number to each letter. For example, A: 00001; B: 00010; ...; R: 10010; ...; Y: 11001; Z: 11010. If numbers and punctuation must also be encoded, then at least six digits will be needed. The observation underlying Huffman codes is simply that some letters occur more frequently than others. It might make sense to use a short code for A, E, or T, for example, saving the longer codes for X, J, and Q. We will first show how to derive a Huffman code from a tree. Next we will describe how to construct the best tree for a given text.

In Figure 4.18 we show a rooted binary tree with the edges labeled with 0's and 1's. We have labeled the leaves with the letters in a shortened alphabet: A, E, H, R, S, and T. We assign codes to the letters by stringing together the edge labels on the unique path from the root to the letter. Thus, E corresponds to 00; R to 01; A to 100; H to 101; S to 110; and T to 111. Note that the height of the leaf is the length of its code. To encode words, we simply place the codes for the letters next to each other *without spaces*. For example, the word *THE* is encoded

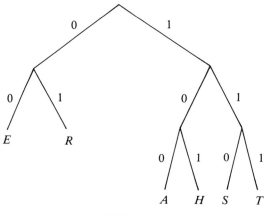

FIGURE 4.18

11110100. Now you ask, "That's fine, but how can I possibly decode a word without knowing where one letter code ends and the next begins?" The beauty of Huffman codes is that the tree makes decoding just as easy as encoding. To decode 11110100, start at the root and follow the "directions" until a leaf is reached. Thus, the first digit, 1, says "go on the right branch;" the next 1 says "take the right branch again;" the third 1 says "take the next right branch." We now arrive at T, the first letter. Return to the root and begin decoding the rest of the string, 10100. The first 1 says "take the right branch." From there the 0 tells us to move to the left; the third 1 tells us to go to the right. We have now arrived at H, the second letter. Again, we return to the root and begin again with the rest of the string: 00. The first 0 says "go left." The second 0 says "go left from there." We arrive at E, the third letter. Note that if we encode the six letters with ordinary binary digits: A: 001, E: 010, H: 011, R: 100, S: 101, T: 110, then THE requires nine characters instead of eight.

To determine the most efficient codes, we use a **weighted binary tree**. This is a rooted binary tree with weights (numbers) assigned to each leaf. Suppose T is a weighted binary tree with leaves $v_1, \ldots, v_n$ and respective weights $w_1, \ldots, w_n$. Then the **weight** of the tree T is defined to be the sum

$$h_1 w_1 + \cdots + h_n w_n$$

where h_i is the height of the leaf v_i. For example, in Figure 4.19 we have added weights to the leaves of the tree of Figure 4.18. The total weight of this tree is then

$$2 \times 3 + 2 \times 3 + 3 \times 2 + 3 \times 1 + 3 \times 2 + 3 \times 3 = 36$$

The original tree arose because we were trying to encode the silly message

THE REST ARE STARS

Note that the letters have frequency: A: 2; E: 3; H: 1; R: 3; S: 2; T: 3. We want short codes for the more frequent letters. If we construct a tree whose leaves have

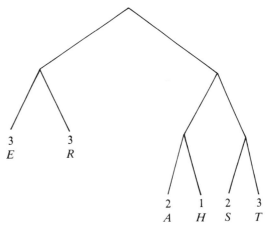

FIGURE 4.19

weights 2, 3, 1, 3, 2, and 3, we will want the heavier weights near the root. For example, the leaf with weight 3 should be close to the root since its corresponding letter, E, occurs frequently. To construct the appropriate tree for a given message:

1. Compute the frequency of each letter (or symbol).
2. Construct a minimal weight rooted binary tree whose leaves have the computed frequency as weights.

Thus, letters far from the root will have small weights and letters near the root will have large weights. That is, the less frequent letters will have the longer codes.
    Here is a recursive algorithm for Step 2. If you follow this algorithm for the weights 2, 3, 1, 3, 2, and 3, you will obtain the tree of Figure 4.18.

□ ALGORITHM 4.1   **To find a minimal weight rooted tree for the n weights $w_1, ..., w_n$.**

1. Assign the given weights $w_1, ..., w_n$ to n distinct points.
2. If there are not at least two vertices with assigned weights, go to Step 4.
3. a. Pick two vertices with the smallest remaining weights.
    b. Call the vertices v_1 and v_2 and their weights u_1 and u_2.
    c. Add a new vertex w and edges from w to v_1 and v_2.
    d. Erase the weights u_1 and u_2 and assign the weight $u_1 + u_2$ to w.
    e. Go to Step 2.
4. Call the last numbered vertex the root, erase its weight, and relabel the original n points with their original weights. STOP.   □

EXAMPLE 4.1   Construct a minimal weight binary tree for the weights 1, 3, 5, 6, 8, 9, 14.

SOLUTION   Each of the six trips through Step 3 is shown in Figure 4.20. In the last representation we have redrawn the tree so that the heights of the vertices are more readily apparent.

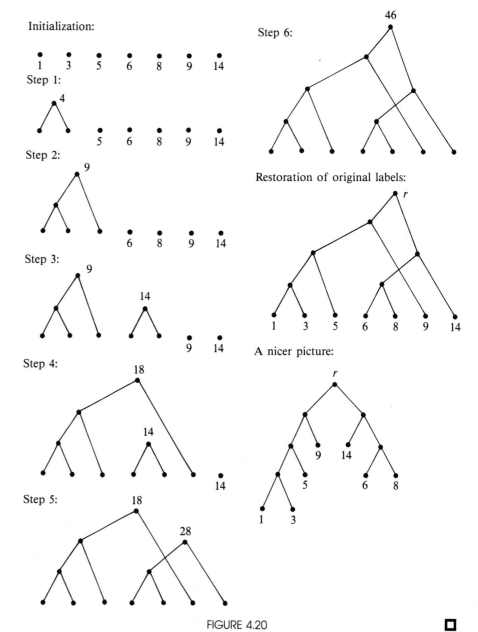

FIGURE 4.20

As a final and more realistic example we consider the problem of coding English.

EXAMPLE 4.2   Big Brother listens in on all communication lines. You want to send a Huffman-coded version of the novel *1984* to a friend. To save time, you are willing to forget punctuation and paragraphing; you won't distinguish capital or italic letters; and you will spell numbers as needed. Also, instead of coding a "word-space," you will simply leave a space between words. Develop the appropriate Huffman code.

SOLUTION   Presuming that the first three paragraphs are not unusual, we determine the relative frequency of each letter there and use the percentages to predict the relative frequency for the entire novel. Here is the result in terms of occurrences per 1000:

A: 79	*B*: 15	*C*: 28	*D*: 39	*E*: 111	*F*: 31
G: 23	*H*: 63	*I*: 73	*J*: 1	*K*: 7	*L*: 44
M: 23	*N*: 60	*O*: 76	*P*: 17	*Q*: 2	*R*: 59
S: 59	*T*: 97	*U*: 29	*V*: 12	*W*: 30	*X*: 0
Y: 19	*Z*: 3				

We next use the algorithm to construct the tree as shown in Figure 4.21 on the next page. Finally, we can read off the codes:

A: 1110	*B*: 101100	*C*: 00110	*D*: 10111
E: 010	*F*: 10011	*G*: 00100	*H*: 1010
I: 1100	*J*: 0010110001	*K*: 0010111	*L*: 11111
M: 111101	*N*: 1000	*O*: 1101	*P*: 101101
Q: 001011001	*R*: 0110	*S*: 0111	*T*: 000
U: 00111	*V*: 001010	*W*: 10010	*X*: 0010110000
Y: 111100	*Z*: 00101101		

Here is the first sentence of the novel *1984* in code:
1100000 1001011100111 1110 10110001101100001001010000
0011011011111110111 101111110111100 11001000
11101011010110110011111, 1110100010111 0001010010
0011011111101001100010111 0111 100100100110010
0111000011011000010111110010000010 0 000101011000110000010 0 101000

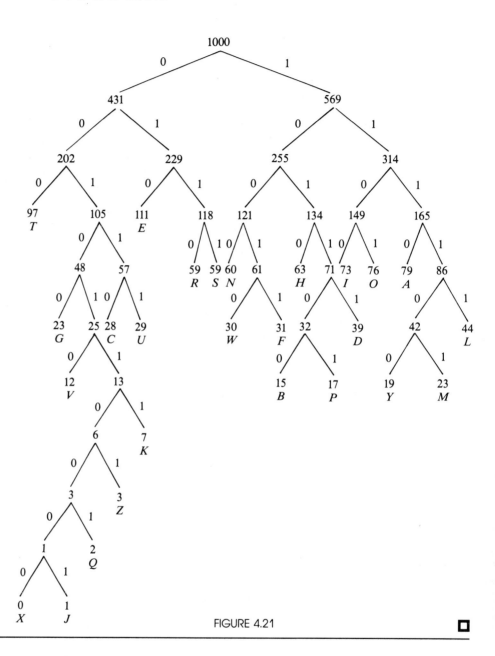

FIGURE 4.21

Searching   It is often useful to be able to list the vertices of a rooted tree in a systematic fashion. Such a list is usually called a **tree search** or **tree traversal**. We will describe five types of tree traversals:

1. Depth-first search
2. Breadth-first search

3. Pre-order traversal of a binary tree

4. In-order traversal of a binary tree

5. Post-order traversal of a binary tree.

All these searches presume that the tree is drawn with its root at the top.

Depth-First Search.   In Figure 4.22(a) we have numbered the vertices in the order they were obtained in a depth-first search. First, we went as far down the tree as we could, *keeping to the left**. We encountered vertices 1, 2, 3, and 4. Since vertex 4 is terminal, we then went back up to the first vertex where we could have made another choice: vertex 3. We took the next (and only) path to the right to vertices 5 and 6. Then we went back to vertex 5, down to vertex 7, and then back to vertex 5 and down to vertex 8. From vertex 8 we returned to vertex 2, the next vertex with unchosen edges. We went down to vertex 9 and then returned to the root to select the next path to the right. That got us to vertex 10. We returned again to the root and proceeded to visit the vertices on the right side of the tree in a similar fashion. When we actually write the result of a depth-first search, we list the vertices only the first time they are encountered. In Figure 4.22(a) our depth-first search yields

1, 2, 3, 4, 5, 6, 7, 8, 9, 10, 11, 12, 13, 14, 15, 16, 17, 18, 19, 20

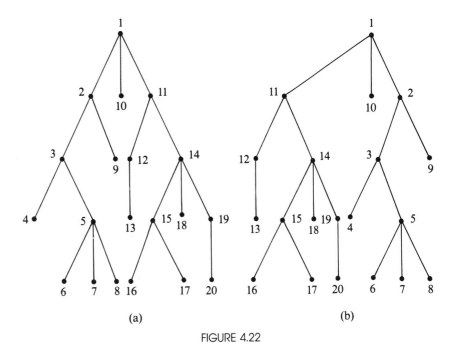

(a)   (b)

FIGURE 4.22

---

* Keeping to the left is just a convention, which serves to remove ambiguity.

Note that the order obtained depends not only on the tree but also very heavily on how it is drawn. For example, the tree in Figure 4.22(b) is exactly the same as the tree in (a). We have simply switched the branches from vertices 2 and 11. For this very same tree, a depth-first search yields

1, 11, 12, 13, 14, 15, 16, 17, 18, 19, 20, 10, 2, 3, 4, 5, 6, 7, 8, 9

Breadth-First Search.   A breadth-first search lists vertices in order of height. First is the root; then come vertices of height 1 in order *from left to right**; then all vertices of height 2; and so forth. In Figure 4.22(a):

Height 0: 1

Height 1: 2, 10, 11

Height 2: 3, 9, 12, 14

Height 3: 4, 5, 13, 15, 18, 19

Height 4: 6, 7, 8, 16, 17, 20

We thus obtain

1, 2, 10, 11, 3, 9, 12, 14, 4, 5, 13, 15, 18, 19, 6, 7, 8, 16, 17, 20

Just as with depth-first search, the way a tree is drawn is a major factor in the result. The result of a breadth-first search in Figure 4.22(b) is

1, 11, 10, 2, 12, 14, 3, 9, 13, 15, 18, 19, 4, 5, 16, 17, 20, 6, 7, 8

To compare the two methods of searching a tree, consider the simple maze in Figure 4.23. We have indicated decision points by L (turn left), R (turn right),

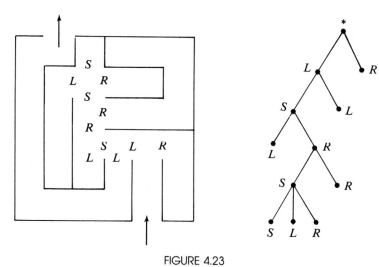

FIGURE 4.23

---

* Again, this is just a convention.

and S (go straight). To get through the maze, one makes two left turns and then completes the maze without having another decision. We have also drawn a decision tree for the particular labeling of the maze. A depth-first search pursues a path until it dead-ends. Then it backtracks to the most recent decision point and follows another path until it dead-ends. For our tree a depth-first search yields

$$*, L, S, L \text{ (dead-end)}; R, S, S \text{ (dead-end)}; L \text{ (dead-end)};$$
$$R \text{ (dead-end)}; R \text{ (dead-end)}; L \text{ (and we're out)}$$

In a breadth-first search we go to the first decision point and try each decision to see if we're done. If not, we try all paths that require two decisions, etc. For our tree a breadth-first search yields

$$*, L, R, S, L \text{ (and we're out)}$$

For that particular tree a breadth-first search is quicker. However, it is easy to redraw the tree (or the maze) to make a depth-first search the best.

Pre-Order Traversal of a Binary Tree.   It turns out that pre-order traversal of a binary tree is simply a depth-first search. However, we will present it recursively to relate it to in-order and post-order traversal. The mnemonic for pre-order traversal is

ROOT-LEFT-RIGHT

We illustrate the application of this rule on the binary tree in Figure 4.24. To apply any of these tree traversals, the child of each degree two vertex must be

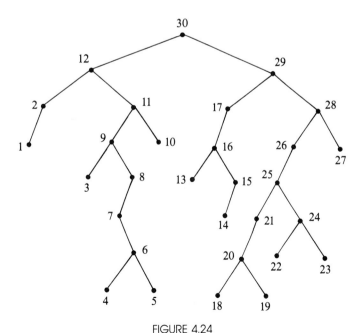

FIGURE 4.24

placed either to the left or right. Thus, in Figure 4.24 vertex 1 is a left vertex and vertex 10 is a right vertex. The ROOT-LEFT-RIGHT rule is applied recursively as follows. List the root. Then move left and regard the left vertex as the root of the tree below it. Apply the ROOT-LEFT-RIGHT rule to this smaller tree until all its terminal vertices are labeled. Return to the original root and move right. Regard this right vertex as the root of the tree below it. Apply the ROOT-LEFT-RIGHT rule to this tree until the terminal vertices are labeled. Here is the list that results from Figure 4.24.

30. We list the root.

12. We move left and are now applying the rule to the tree with root 12, which we just listed.

2. We move left and are now applying the rule to the tree with root 2, which we just listed.

1. We move left and list the new root 1. That finishes the left branch from vertex 12. We move right.

11. This is the new root.

9. We move left.

3. Left again.

8. Now right from vertex 9.

7.

6.

4.

5. That finishes the left side from vertex 11. We now pick up the right.

10. That finishes vertex 11. It also finishes vertex 12. We are back to the original root, 30, and are ready to go right.

29.

17.

16.

13.

15.

14. This finishes the left branch from vertex 29.

28.

26.

25.

21.

20.

18.

19.

24.

22.

23.

27.

You should check that this is a recursive way to carry out a depth-first search of the tree.

In-Order Traversal of a Binary Tree.   The mnemonic for in-order traversal is

LEFT-ROOT-RIGHT

In this case you do not list the root until you have applied the rule to the tree below the left vertex. Then list the root. Finally, we apply the rule to the tree below the right vertex. Here's what happens in Figure 4.24.

Don't list 30. Move left first.

Don't list 12 either. Move left first.

Don't list 2. Move left.

1. We list the left vertex.

2. We list the root. There is no right vertex.

12. We list the root. Now we move right.

Don't list 11 yet; move left first.

Don't list 9.

3.

9. Now move right from 9.

Don't list 8. Move left first.

7. There is no left vertex from 7, so we list it as the root and move right.

Don't list 6.

4. Left.

6. Root.

5. Right.

We have finished the left side from the root vertex 8, so we list it.

8.

11.

10.

30. Finally, we are back to the main root and ready to move right.

13.

16.

14.

15.

17.

29.

18.

20.

19.

21.

25.

22.

24.

23.

26.

28.

27.

Post-Order Traversal of a Binary Tree.   In this case the mnemonic is

LEFT-RIGHT-ROOT

The application is the same. You move immediately to the left vertex and start over. Once you reach a terminal vertex, you do the right side. Finally, you list the root. Figure 4.24 is labeled according to post-order traversal.

An interesting thing happens when binary tree traversal is applied to the process graphs for algebraic expressions. Pre-order traversal yields Polish notation. In-order traversal yields **infix notation**, which is the usual algebraic order, after parentheses are supplied. Post-order traversal yields reverse Polish notation. Here are the three traversals for Figure 4.17:

Pre-order traversal:

$$+ - + a \cdot bc + \div cde \cdot \cdot efg$$

In-order traversal:

$$a + b \cdot c - c \div d + e + e \cdot f \cdot g$$

This is the order in which the symbols are ordinarily written in algebra, but without parentheses.

Post-order traversal:

$$abc \cdot + cd \div e + - ef \cdot g \cdot +$$

This is the order in which you must enter the quantities and operation symbols to do the calculation on a calculator that uses reverse Polish notation. More precisely, you need to input this:

a, enter, b, enter, c, $\cdot$, $+$, c, enter, d, $\div$, e, $+$, $-$, e, enter, f, $\cdot$, g, $\cdot$, $+$

The "enter" key needs to be used four times to tell the calculator where one number ends and the next begins.

EXERCISES

1. Draw all 11 trees with seven vertices.
2. Draw all 23 trees with eight vertices.
3. *A* and *B* play at most six games. The first to win two games in a row wins the match. How many different patterns of wins and losses are there?
4. Draw a tree to represent all possible outcomes of a best-three-of-five series.
5. I have a bag containing four red and five blue balls. I remove them one at a time (without replacement) until I have removed three red ones. In how many ways can this be done?
6. Use an abbreviated tree to count the number of permutations of three letters in which no two vowels (*A, E, I, O, U*) are adjacent.

In Exercises 7–10 draw process graphs for the given algebraic expressions.

7. $(a + b) + (c + d)$ and $((a + b) + c) + d$
8. $(a \cdot b) + (c \cdot d)$ and $[a \cdot (b + c)] \cdot d$
9. $a \div b + c - d + e \cdot f$
10. $\{[(a + b) \div (c \cdot d)] - [e + f]\} \cdot g$

In Exercises 11 and 12 recover the algebraic expression from the given process graph.

11.

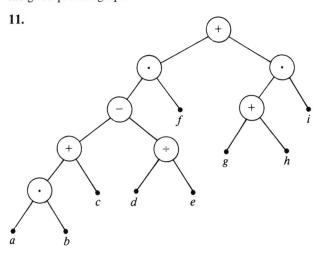

12.

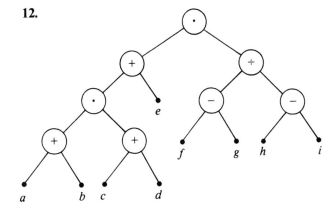

13. Decode the first sentence of *1984*. (See page 133.)
14. Encode the first phrase of the second sentence of *1984*: Winston Smith, his chin nuzzled into his breast in an effort to escape the vile wind

In Exercises 15 and 16 construct the minimal weighted binary tree for the given weights.

15. 1, 2, 2, 5, 6, 7, 8, 9
16. 1, 4, 6, 9, 10, 13, 21, 23

In Exercises 17 and 18 use letter frequency as weights to construct an appropriate Huffman code for the given words. Then use your code to encode the phrase.

17. We the people of the United States.
18. Fourscore and seven years ago our.

In Exercises 19–22 list the result of depth-first and breadth-first searches of the given tree.

19.

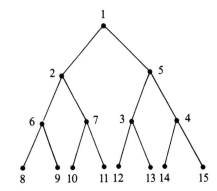

20.

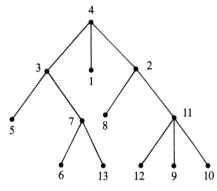

21.

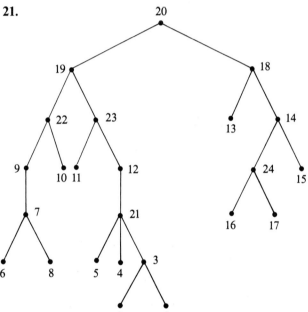

22.

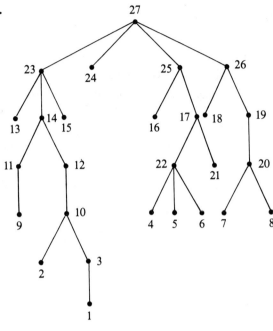

23. My house has five rooms, each one of which has two desks with three drawers each. There is a diamond ring in one of the desk drawers in my house. Describe a depth-first and a breadth-first search to find the ring.

24. I have drugged three captured spies with truth serum so that they will always tell the truth. Only a spy who was on the airbase could have the information I want. In fact, if the spy wasn't on the airbase, I will not ask that spy any more questions. Of those on the airbase, only someone who had been in the airplane could have the information. If they weren't in the airplane, for them to hear the next question would compromise our side. Finally, only a spy who had actually handled the bombsight could have the information I need. Describe a depth-first and a breadth-first search to find the spy with the information.

25. Describe a breadth-first search method to find a path between two given vertices u and v in a connected graph. Apply your procedure to the graph below Exercise 26 with

a. $u = v_1$, $v = v_7$.

b. $u = v_1$, $v = v_5$.

26. Describe a depth-first search method to find a path between two given vertices u and v in a connected graph. Apply your procedure to the graph below with

a. $u = v_1$, $v = v_8$.

b. $u = v_1$, $v = v_6$.

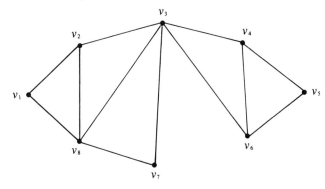

In Exercises 27–30 list the results of pre-order, in-order, and post-order traversals of the given binary tree.

27.

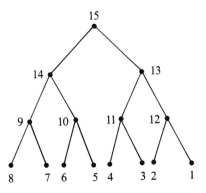

28.

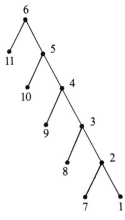

29.

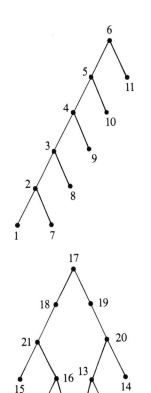

30.

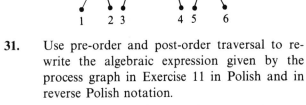

31. Use pre-order and post-order traversal to re-write the algebraic expression given by the process graph in Exercise 11 in Polish and in reverse Polish notation.

32. Use pre-order and post-order traversal to re-write the algebraic expression given by the process graph in Exercise 12 in Polish and in reverse Polish notation.

33. Use pre-order and post-order traversal to re-write the algebraic expression in Exercise 9 in Polish and in reverse Polish notation.

34. Use pre-order and post-order traversal to re-write the algebraic expression in Exercise 10 in Polish and in reverse Polish notation.

Eulerian Graphs and Hamiltonian Circuits

Leonhard Euler (pronounced "oiler"; 1707–1783) invented graph theory with the publication in 1736 of his paper *Solutio problematis ad geometriam situs pertinentis*. In this article he generalized and solved the famous Königsberg Bridge Problem. In 1736 Königsberg was a city in East Prussia, home of the 12-year-old fledgling philosopher Immanuel Kant. Now it is the city of Kaliningrad in the Russian Soviet Federated Socialist Republic of the U.S.S.R. It was located on the Pregel (now the Pregolya) River. Two islands were linked to each other and to both banks by footbridges as shown in Figure 4.25. The problem on

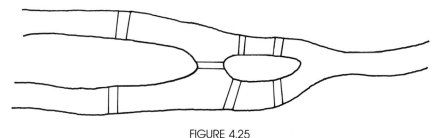

FIGURE 4.25

everyone's mind at the time was: "Is it possible to take a walk so that you cross each of the seven bridges exactly once and return to the same place you began?" If we represent the land areas by vertices and the bridges by edges, we obtain the pseudograph in Figure 4.26. The problem, restated for this pseudograph, now becomes: "Is it possible to find a circuit that includes each edge exactly once?"

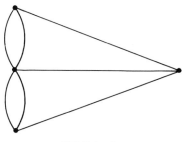

FIGURE 4.26

Pseudographs that contain a circuit that includes every edge exactly once are called **Eulerian**. An **Eulerian path** is a path that includes every edge exactly once. Such a path need not end where it begins. Euler discovered precisely which pseudographs are Eulerian.

Sir William Rowan Hamilton (1805–1865) was an Irish mathematician who made important contributions to algebra. In 1859 he invented and marketed a game called "Around the World" which amounted to finding a circuit that goes through each vertex of the graph in Figure 4.27 exactly once. (The actual game involved finding a circuit that went exactly once through each vertex of a regular **dodecahedron** (a solid with twelve pentagonal faces); but that

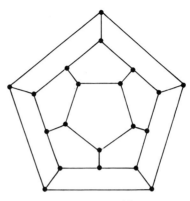

FIGURE 4.27

is equivalent to finding the same sort of circuit in the graph of Figure 4.27.) A **Hamiltonian pseudograph** is one that contains a circuit that visits each vertex exactly once. Of course, we also have the notion of a **Hamiltonian path**, which visits each vertex exactly once but does not necessarily begin and end at the same place. Unlike Euler, Hamilton did not find a characterization for the pseudographs that bear his name. This is no great disgrace, however, since to this day neither has anyone else.

In this section we discuss Eulerian and Hamiltonian pseudographs and present algorithms for finding Eulerian and Hamiltonian paths and circuits, provided they exist. We begin with a selection of applications illustrating each type of pseudograph.

EXAMPLE 4.2   There are many practical situations in which an Eulerian circuit is particularly useful. Consider a city street map to be a graph in which the edges are streets and the vertices are intersections. Then street cleaners, garbage men, letter carriers, milk deliverers, political canvassers, etc. benefit from knowledge of an Eulerian circuit since it enables them to go down each and every street exactly once. To make the situation more realistic for a person visiting homes, a pseudograph might be more appropriate. Let the vertices correspond to street corners and the edges to rows of houses on a block. Thus, any street with houses on both sides would be represented by two edges. (See Exercise 9.)   □

Since few city street patterns turn out to be Eulerian or contain Eulerian paths, a more general approach to the problem is needed. One method is to calculate the length of each edge and then find a minimal length route that traverses each edge at least once. We will discuss such minimization problems in the next section.

EXAMPLE 4.3   A similar situation is encountered by inspectors of networks of power lines, railways, telephone lines, etc., and even by museum visitors who are in a hurry to see all the exhibits. Here an Eulerian circuit is great, an Eulerian path is probably okay, but failing these, a minimal length circuit including each edge is needed.   ■

EXAMPLE 4.4   The classical example involving Hamiltonian circuits is the Traveling Salesman Problem. Recall that the **complete graph** on n vertices is the graph K_n, with an edge between each pair of its n vertices. Label the vertices $v_1, \ldots, v_n$; let e_{ij} denote the edge from v_i to v_j. Then the edges $e_{12}, e_{23}, \ldots, e_{n-2,n-1}, e_{n-1,n}, e_{n,1}$ form a Hamiltonian circuit. The Traveling Salesman Problem concerns the complete graph of n cities and interconnecting roadways (or airways). A salesman needs to visit each of n cities exactly once and return home. Naturally, he wants his Hamiltonian circuit to be as short as possible. Of course, it is reasonable to object that a complete graph is not the appropriate model. While it is certainly possible to travel between any two cities, the only (or only reasonable) route might incidentally go through another one of the cities on the itinerary. Thus, the edge from city v_i to city v_j might in reality be a road that goes through city v_k "unofficially." This situation is illustrated in Figure 4.28.

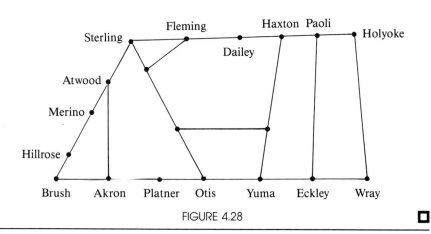

FIGURE 4.28   ■

If we view the roadmap itself as a pseudograph with cities as vertices and roads as edges, there is no guarantee that it has a Hamiltonian circuit. Thus, we also need an algorithm for finding Hamiltonian paths and circuits, when they exist.

We begin with Euler's Theorem of 1736 characterizing Eulerian pseudographs. It turns out to be quite simple.

□ THEOREM 4.1   **(Euler's Theorem)** A connected pseudograph G is Eulerian if and only if each vertex has even degree.

PROOF   Suppose the pseudograph is Eulerian. Let C denote an Eulerian circuit. Since no edge is repeated, whenever C goes into a vertex, it goes out on a *different* edge. Thus, the edges at each vertex occur in pairs; and so there must be an even number of edges at each vertex.

Now suppose that each vertex of G has even degree. Pick any vertex v of G. Form a path beginning at v. Since each vertex of G has even degree, each time a vertex is encountered it is possible to continue the path without backtracking; there is always an unused edge waiting. Of course, you might run into trouble if the vertex v has degree 2. In that case when you return to v, you will have no way out without repeating an edge. So continue the path begun at v; don't repeat any edges; and stop when you complete a circuit at v. (Since v is the only place you might get stuck, you will eventually return there.) Now if this process happens to use up all the edges of G, we have our Eulerian circuit. Otherwise, check all the edges in this circuit and call it C_0. The subgraph of unchecked edges and their vertices will probably not be connected. However, each vertex in the subgraph will have even degree since an even number of edges were checked at each vertex in the circuit C_0 (0 is also an even number). Start back around the circuit C_0. We will call the first vertex which is also a vertex of an unchecked edge, v_1. (If the degree of v is not 2, then v_1 will be v.) Starting at v_1, form a circuit of unchecked edges. We temporarily call this circuit C and check all its edges. The circuit C_1 is formed as follows. Go around C_0 to v_1; then go all the way around C; then finish C_0 back to v. If this circuit uses up all of G, we are done. Otherwise, consider the subgraph of unchecked edges and their vertices. Even if this subgraph is not connected, each vertex in it will still have even degree. Starting at v, travel around C_1 until you hit a vertex of an uncheckmarked edge. Call this vertex v_2. (Of course, v_2 might be v_1.) From v_2 form the circuit C of unchecked edges. Now add C to C_1 as before to form C_2. Check the edges of C_2 and keep going until you have used up all the edges of G.   □

The constructive nature of this proof is illustrated in Figure 4.29, where we have shown what might happen for a particular choice of v.

In view of this theorem the Königsberg Bridge Problem is easy. Since *no* vertex has even degree, the pseudograph fails to be Eulerian. In fact, according to the next theorem, it does not even contain an Eulerian path.

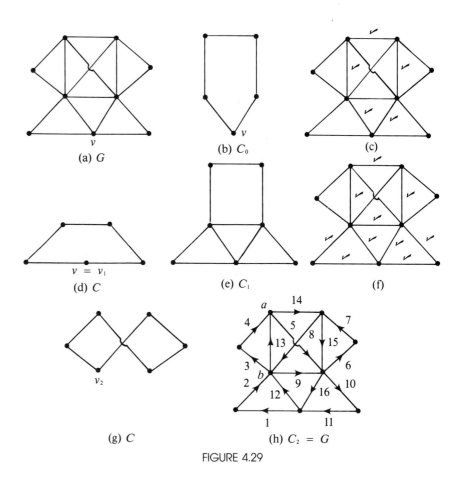

FIGURE 4.29

☐ THEOREM 4.2   A connected pseudograph G contains an Eulerian path P that is not a circuit if and only if it has exactly two vertices of odd degree.

PROOF   Suppose the pseudograph has an Eulerian path from v to w that is not a circuit. Then the argument in Euler's Theorem shows that each vertex except v and w has even degree. It is easy to see that v and w have odd degree since the first edge of P is out from v, and P does not end at v. Thus, if P ever returns to v, it also leaves again. Similarly for w. Conversely, suppose each vertex of G except v and w has even degree. Add a new edge e' from v to w to obtain the pseudograph G'. Then each vertex of G' has even degree, so by the previous theorem, G' has an Eulerian circuit C', which we may traverse beginning at w and going along e' to v. Now remove e' and traverse the rest of C' as before but beginning at v, to obtain an Eulerian path from v to w.   ☐

For example, if edge 13 in Figure 4.29(h) were missing, then an Eulerian path from a to b would be 14, 15, 16, 1, 2, 3, 4, 5, 6, 7, 8, 9, 10, 11, 12.

The problem of finding a minimal length closed path that includes each edge *at least* once will be discussed in the next section.

The situation for Hamiltonian circuits is not as satisfactory. No one has found an easy way to tell if a given pseudograph has a Hamiltonian circuit. Even if a pseudograph has a Hamiltonian circuit, no easy way of finding it is known. There are a few computer algorithms for checking a pseudograph for Hamiltonian circuits. Although none is famous for its efficiency, the one by Roberts and Flores (1966) is not too bad for pseudographs of reasonable size. As we will see in a moment, the Roberts and Flores Algorithm is really a depth-first search for Hamiltonian paths and circuits.

The Roberts and Flores Algorithm uses a table of neighboring vertices that is set up as follows:

1. Name the vertices of the pseudograph. (Do *not* use $v_1, v_2, \ldots, v_n$ as names.)

2. Write the names in a row.

3. Below each vertex name write in a column the names of each adjacent vertex.

Consider, for example, the graph in Figure 4.30. We have named the vertices a, b, c, d, e, f. In column a we write b and e. (It doesn't matter in which order.) The complete table is

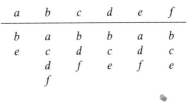

a	b	c	d	e	f
b	a	b	b	a	b
e	c	d	c	d	c
	d	f	e	f	e
	f				

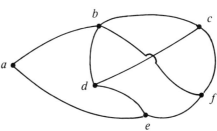

FIGURE 4.30

The algorithm begins labeling the vertices $v_1, v_2, \ldots$. At any step a **new vertex** is one that is not yet labeled. The word *first* means uppermost in the column.

PROGRAM 4.1   The Roberts and Flores Algorithm for finding Hamiltonian paths and circuits in a graph with n vertices.

1. Label a vertex v_1. Let v_1 be the first element of a list of the vertices in the path or circuit to be found

2. $i \leftarrow 1$

3. If the column of v_i has no new vertex go to 12

4. Label the first new vertex in the column of v_i, v_{i+1} and put it in the list
5. $i \leftarrow i + 1$
6. If $i \neq n$ go to 3
7. "$v_1, \ldots, v_n$ are the vertices of a Hamiltonian path."
8. If there is no edge from v_n to v_1 go to 12
9. "The path is a Hamiltonian circuit."
10. If you want to search for another Hamiltonian path or circuit go to 12
11. STOP
12. If $i \neq 1$ go to 14
13. "You have found all Hamiltonian circuits, if any, and all Hamiltonian paths, if any, that begin at v_1." STOP
14. $v \leftarrow v_i$
15. Delete v_i from the list
16. $i \leftarrow i - 1$
17. If there is no vertex in the column of v_i below v go to 12
18. Go to 4   ■

In running this algorithm for the graph shown above, we shall use a shorthand. For example, the step abc,3 means $v_1 = a$, $v_2 = b$, $v_3 = c$, $i = 3$; the step $abcde,f$,5 means $v_1 = a$, $v_2 = b$, $v_3 = c$, $v_4 = d$, $v_5 = e$, $v = f$, $i = 5$. Also, P means Hamiltonian path and C means Hamiltonian circuit. Note that in each step the value of i is simply the length of the path.

a,1	$abcd,e$,4	abc,f,3
ab,2	abc,d,3	ab,c,2
abc,3	$abcf$,4	abd,3
$abcd$,4	$abcfe$,5	$abdc$,4
$abcde$,5	$abcfed$,6 P	$abdcf$,5
$abcdef$,6 P	$abcfe,d$,5	$abdcfe$,6 C
$abcde,f$,5	$abcf,e$,4	

We *could* STOP here. If we want *all* paths and circuits, the steps would go on as follows:

$abdef,e$,5	$abfc$,4	abf,e,3
$abdc,f$,4	$abfcd$,5	ab,f,2
abd,c,3	$abfcde$,6 C	a,b,1
$abde$,4	$abfcd,e$,5	ae,2
$abdef$,5	$abfc,d$,4	aed,3
$abdefc$,6 P	abf,c,3	$aedb$,4
$abdef,c$,5	$abfe$,4	$aedbc$,5
$abde,f$,4	$abfed$,5	$aedbcf$,6 P
abd,e,3	$abfedc$,6 P	$aedbc,f$,5
ab,d,2	$abfed,c$,5	$aedb,c$,4
abf,3	$abfe,d$,4	$aedbf$,5 *(continued on next page)*

aedbfc,6 *P*	*aed,c*,3	*aefc*,4
aedbf,c,5	*ae,d*,2	*aefcb*,5
aedb,f,4	*aef*,3	*aefcbd*,6 *P*
aed,b,3	*aefb*,4	*aefcb,d*,5
aedc,4	*aefbc*,5	*aefc,b*,4
aedcb,5	*aefbcd*,6 *P*	*aefcd*,5
aedcbf,6 *P*	*aefbc,d*,5	*aefcdb*,6 *C*
aedcb,f,5	*aefb,c*,4	*aefcd,b*,5
aedc,b,4	*aefbd*,5	*aefc,d*,4
aedcf,5	*aefbdc*,6 *P*	*aef,c*,3
aedcfb,6 *C*	*aefbd,c*,5	*ae,f*,2
aedcf,b,5	*aefb,d*,4	*a,e*,1
aedc,f,4	*aef,b*,3	STOP

Thus, the graph of Figure 4.30 has precisely four Hamiltonian circuits and ten Hamiltonian paths that begin with *a* and are not circuits. There are other Hamiltonian paths that are not circuits, such as *eabfcd*. To find all such paths, we would have to run the algorithm for each possible choice of v_1. Of course, each such run would rediscover the four circuits. For example, the run with $v_1 = e$ would find *eabdcf*, which is the same as our first circuit *abdcfe*.

It is enlightening to recognize the Roberts and Flores Algorithm as a depth-first search of a particular tree associated with the graph. The tree for the graph in Figure 4.30 is shown in Figure 4.31. We have labeled the root *a*. Then we have

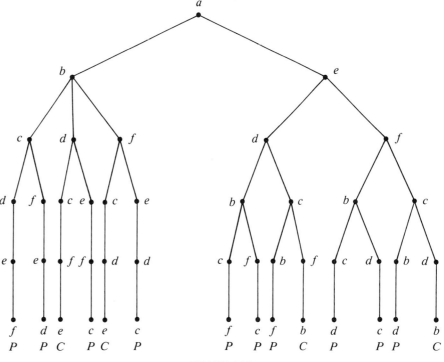

FIGURE 4.31

drawn edges from a to b and e since there are edges from a to b and e in the original graph. Now there are edges from b to a, c, d, and f in the original graph. Our tree also includes these edges, but does not repeat the edge to a. In general, we insert an edge in the tree if there is a corresponding edge in the graph, but we do not repeat any vertices along paths from the root. In fact, the tree includes all paths from a with no repeated vertices. These are precisely the candidates for Hamiltonian paths and circuits. In the case of Figure 4.31, each path of length 5 from the root corresponds to a Hamiltonian path. The path can be converted to a circuit if there is an edge from its terminal vertex to a. The Roberts and Flores Algorithm saves you the trouble of drawing the tree. The savings can be considerable if you need only one Hamiltonian circuit.

Gray Codes.   Gray codes are an interesting application of many of the previous topics in this text. First, they are a code, in the usual sense of the word. For any positive integer n, a Gray code associates a unique n-digit binary number from 0 to $2^n - 1$ to each integer from 0 to $2^n - 1$. Furthermore, this assignment has a special property. The Gray codes of consecutive integers must differ in precisely one place. We also consider 0 and $2^n - 1$ to be consecutive, as they would be in arithmetic modulo 2^n. We write the binary numbers from 0 to $2^n - 1$ with enough leading zeros to make them have n places as we did in Batcher's Sorting Method and in finding minimal disjunctive forms. In fact, we will represent binary numbers as ordered n-tuples of 0's and 1's. For example, we will write the number 0 0 1 1 0 1 as $(0, 0, 1, 1, 0, 1)$. This is so that we can view binary numbers geometrically in the following discussion. Here is an example for $n = 3$:

number	code
0	$(0, 0, 0)$
1	$(0, 0, 1)$
2	$(0, 1, 1)$
3	$(0, 1, 0)$
4	$(1, 1, 0)$
5	$(1, 1, 1)$
6	$(1, 0, 1)$
7	$(1, 0, 0)$

You should check that this is a Gray code. For example, the code for 4: $(1, 1, 0)$ and the code for 5: $(1, 1, 1)$ differ only in the third place.

Gray codes can be obtained recursively. Here are codes for $n = 1$ and $n = 2$:

$n = 1$:

number	code
0	0
1	1

$n = 2$:	number	code
	0	$(0, 0)$
	1	$(0, 1)$
	2	$(1, 1)$
	3	$(1, 0)$

Now to obtain a code for $n = 3$, put 0 as the first coordinate and these four codes as second and third coordinates. Then put 1 as the first coordinate and use these four codes as the second coordinates, but use them in order from bottom to top. That is,

$$(0, \text{code for } 0)$$
$$(0, \text{code for } 1)$$
$$(0, \text{code for } 2)$$
$$(0, \text{code for } 3)$$
$$(1, \text{code for } 3)$$
$$(1, \text{code for } 2)$$
$$(1, \text{code for } 1)$$
$$(1, \text{code for } 0)$$

In this way we obtain the code for $n = 3$ listed above. In general, if $c_0, \ldots, c_{2^n - 1}$ are codes for n, then

$$(0, c_0)$$
$$(0, c_1)$$
$$\vdots$$
$$(0, c_{2^n - 2})$$
$$(0, c_{2^n - 1})$$
$$(1, c_{2^n - 1})$$
$$(1, c_{2^n - 2})$$
$$\vdots$$
$$(1, c_1)$$
$$(1, c_0)$$

are codes for $n + 1$.

You may be wondering why Gray codes are in a section with Hamiltonian circuits. Well, they can also be regarded as Hamiltonian circuits for a particular graph. For n a positive integer, the **unit n-cube** is defined to be the graph with vertices the n-place binary numbers. Two numbers are adjacent if they differ in precisely one place. A Hamiltonian circuit through that graph is clearly a Gray code since adjacent vertices differ in exactly one place. Since we have a recursive way to obtain Gray codes, we know that there is a Hamiltonian circuit for each n. Why the graph is called the unit n-cube is illustrated in Figure 4.32. For $n = 3$, we can draw the graph in three-dimensional space so it looks like an ordinary cube. For this reason all the graphs are called cubes. In fact, a 2-cube is a square and a 4-cube is a four-dimensional object called a **hypercube** or **tesseract**. In the figure the lines from the inside cube to the outside cube are in the "fourth" direction.

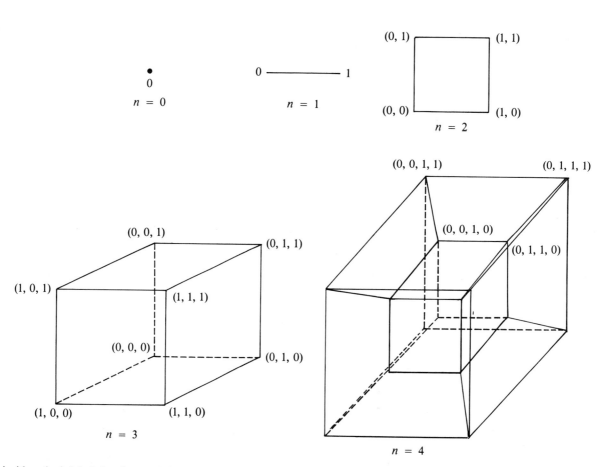

The inside cube is labeled as for $n = 3$, but with a 0 added as last coordinate. The outside cube is labeled as for $n = 3$ but with 1 as last coordinate.

FIGURE 4.32

E X E R C I S E S

In Exercises 1–8 determine which of the pseudographs have Eulerian paths or circuits. Construct an Eulerian path or circuit whenever it is possible to do so.

1.

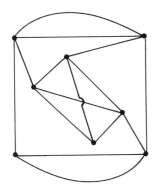

2.

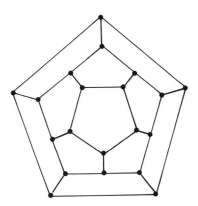

3.

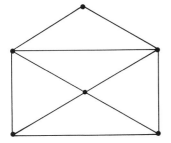

4.

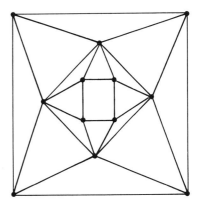

5.

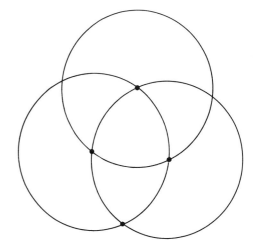

6.

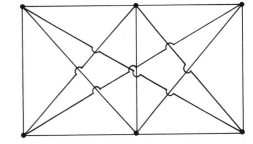

7. K_5

8. K_6

9. My neighborhood is a partially completed housing development with streets and houses as indicated on the following map. I am running for the office of

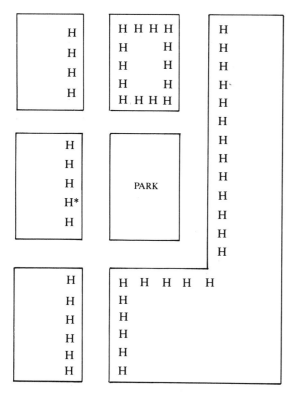

Development Philologist and would like to distribute my campaign literature as efficiently as possible. Find a route that takes me by each house exactly once. My house is marked with a *. Can my distribution route begin and end at my home?

10. *The World of Mathematics*, edited by James R. Newman, contains many very interesting articles

on mathematics. Among these is an excerpt from a treatment of the Königsberg Bridge Problem by Euler. In that article he also examines another (but fictitious) river with two islands and 15 bridges as shown. Analyze this map and determine if it is possible to traverse each bridge exactly once.

11. I am going on a trip to Connecticut, Massachusetts, New Hampshire, New Jersey, New York, Pennsylvania, and Vermont. I want to cross each boundary between pairs of these states exactly once. Which states are the only ones in which my trip can begin and end?

12. Convert the instructions in the proofs of Euler's Theorem and the theorem following it to a program to find an Eulerian circuit or path in a graph.

In Exercises 13–16 use the Roberts and Flores Algorithm to find a Hamiltonian circuit in the graph *as labeled*. Also, draw the tree associated to the graph.

13.

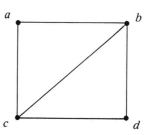

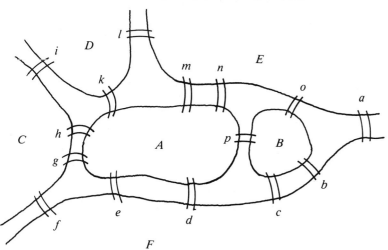

14.

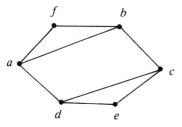

15.

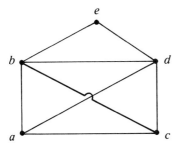

16.

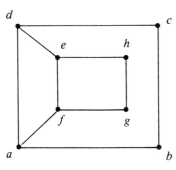

In Exercises 17 and 18 use the Roberts and Flores Algorithm
to show that no Hamiltonian circuit exists in the given graph.

17.

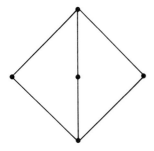

18.

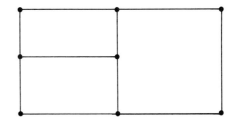

19. Find a Hamiltonian circuit in Hamilton's Around
the World game (Figure 4.27).

20. Use the Roberts and Flores Algorithm to find *all*
Hamiltonian circuits in the graph.

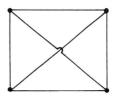

21. Use the Roberts and Flores Algorithm to find *all*
Gray codes for $n = 3$.

22. For the following Gray code:

number	code
(in binary)	$f\ g\ h$
0 0 0	0 0 0
0 0 1	1 0 0
0 1 0	1 0 1
0 1 1	0 0 1
1 0 0	0 1 1
1 0 1	1 1 1
1 1 0	1 1 0
1 1 1	0 1 0

design three switching circuits (one for f, one for g,
and one for h) that yield the three digits of the Gray
code.

4.4

Minimal Paths and Circuits

In this section we are concerned with connected pseudographs whose edges have been assigned numbers called weights. These weights might represent lengths, times, costs, etc. Road maps indicating mileages or traveling times are a natural example. We will present algorithms for two problems. The first is Dijkstra's Algorithm to find a minimal weight path between two given vertices in a connected pseudograph. The second is an algorithm presented by Christofides (in *Graph Theory: An Algorithmic Approach*, Academic Press, 1975, page 205). This algorithm locates a minimal weight circuit that traverses each edge of a connected pseudograph at least once. If we interpret the weight as length, then such a circuit would be of interest to a postman, street cleaner, inspector of power lines, etc. If the pseudograph has an Eulerian circuit, then that circuit, since it includes each edge only once, has minimal weight. Otherwise, a minimal weight circuit must include some edges more than once.

We begin with Dijkstra's Algorithm for finding a shortest path between a given pair of vertices in a pseudograph.

Figure 4.33 shows a graph in which each edge has been given a "weight."

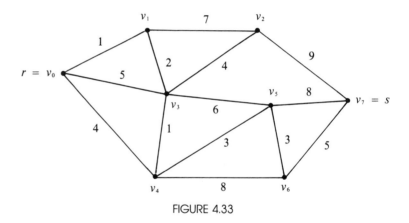

FIGURE 4.33

Note that the given weight has nothing to do with the geometric length of the line segment which represents the edge. Trial and error is not a very good method for finding minimal length paths, even for small graphs. For example, the shortest path through a graph might be obtained by choosing the longest edge available at each vertex reached. See Exercises 8 and 9.

Dijkstra's Algorithm requires some notation. First, $w(v_i, v_j)$ denotes the weight of the edge from vertex v_i to vertex v_j. If there is more than one edge, then $w(v_i, v_j)$ denotes the smallest weight of all such edges. The weights of the other edges are ignored as are edges that form loops at vertices. For example, in Figure 4.33, $w(v_3, v_5) = 6$, $w(v_5, v_7) = 8$, and $w(v_1, v_4)$ is not defined.

Second, we will use the notation $\min[a, b]$ to denote the smaller of the numbers a and b. The **infinity symbol**, ∞, is used to represent a very large number. How large is it? Well, it is always the larger of any pair of numbers.

□ ALGORITHM 4.2   **Dijkstra's Algorithm. Given a weighted pseudograph G and distinct vertices r and s in it, to find a path (or all paths) from r to s of minimal weight.**

0. For each two distinct adjacent vertices u, v of G, let $w(u, v)$ be the least weight of an edge joining u and v.
1. $L(r) \leftarrow 0$; for all vertices $u \neq r$, $L(u) \leftarrow \infty$.
2. Pick an uncircled vertex v with minimal $L(v)$. Circle v.
3. For each uncircled vertex u adjacent to v, $L(u) \leftarrow \min[L(u), L(v) + w(u, v)]$.
4. If s is uncircled, go to 2; otherwise, STOP.   □

To read all answers, construct a tree with root s at the top and a branch from v down to u if and only if $L(v) - w(u, v) = L(u)$. The answers are all paths in this tree from r to s. (Obviously, if only one answer is desired, only one path in the tree need be drawn.) If we replace Step 4 in the algorithm with

4. If there is an uncircled vertex, go to 2; if not, STOP.

then $L(u)$ gives the weight of a minimal weight path from r to u for every vertex u. This information will come in handy when we look for minimal weight circuits. It is not hard to see how Dijkstra's Algorithm works. It first finds a vertex "closest" to r. Then it looks for a closest vertex two edges away from r, etc. The closest vertices get circled along the way.

EXAMPLE 4.5   We will find a minimal weight path from r to s in the graph in Figure 4.33. Pick r. $L(r) \leftarrow 0$. Circle r.

$L(v_1) \leftarrow \min[\infty, 0 + 1] = 1$.
$L(v_3) \leftarrow \min[\infty, 0 + 5] = 5$.
$L(v_4) \leftarrow \min[\infty, 0 + 4] = 4$.
Circle v_1.
$L(v_2) \leftarrow \min[\infty, 1 + 7] = 8$.
$L(v_3) \leftarrow \min[5, 1 + 2] = 3$.
Circle v_3.
$L(v_2) \leftarrow \min[8, 3 + 4] = 7$.
$L(v_5) \leftarrow \min[\infty, 3 + 6] = 9$.
$L(v_4) \leftarrow \min[4, 3 + 1] = 4$.
Circle v_4.
$L(v_5) \leftarrow \min[9, 4 + 3] = 7$.
$L(v_6) \leftarrow \min[\infty, 4 + 8] = 12$.
Circle v_2. (v_5 could also be chosen.)

$L(s) \leftarrow \min[\infty, 7+9] = 16.$

Circle v_5.

$L(s) \leftarrow \min[16, 7+8] = 15.$

$L(v_6) \leftarrow \min[12, 7+3] = 10.$

Circle v_6.

$L(s) \leftarrow \min[15, 10+5] = 15.$

Circle s. STOP.

ANSWERS $rv_1v_3v_4v_5s$

rv_4v_5s

$rv_1v_3v_4v_5v_6s$

$rv_4v_5v_6s$

each of weight 15. Figure 4.34 shows the associated tree.

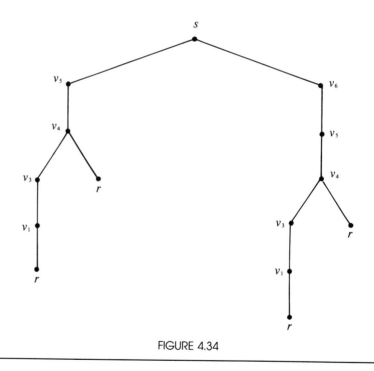

FIGURE 4.34

We now turn our attention to minimal weight circuits. Suppose we are given a connected pseudograph G whose edges have been assigned weights. If G contains an Eulerian circuit, then that circuit has minimal weight since it traverses each edge exactly once. If G does not contain an Eulerian circuit, then we must decide which edges to repeat.

First, recall that the only reason a pseudograph won't have an Eulerian circuit is because it has vertices of odd degree. Next, recall that there must be an even number of such vertices. It turns out that we must traverse certain paths between pairs of odd degree vertices more than once. Dijkstra's Algorithm helps to determine which paths we will repeat. The easiest way to indicate a repeated edge is to add another copy of it to the pseudograph. That is, we draw some edges more than once. The first time we go along an edge we will use one representation; the second time we will use the other. In the following algorithm we form a pseudograph G' by adding to G carefully selected second (or third, etc.) copies of edges that must be used more than once. Then G' will have an Eulerian circuit that represents the minimal weight circuit in G. That is, we will use Euler's Theorem (Section 4.3) to find an Eulerian circuit in G'. Each time we traverse an edge in G' that is not in G, we interpret it to mean that we are repeating the corresponding edge in G. Of course, the trick is to add the right edges. We want not only for G' to have an Eulerian circuit but also for its Eulerian circuit to represent a minimal weight circuit in G.

□ ALGORITHM 4.3

To find a minimal length circuit containing all edges of a weighted connected pseudograph.

1. If there are no vertices of odd degree, go to 7.

2. Let $u_1, \ldots, u_{2m}$ denote the vertices of odd degree.

3. Use Dijkstra's Algorithm to find the minimum distance and a minimum weight path from u_i to u_j for each pair of odd-degree vertices.

4. List the odd-degree vertices in pairs so that the total weight of all minimal weight paths between paired-off vertices is minimal. (What this means and how it is done are explained in detail below.)

5. Duplicate any edge of G that occurs in a minimal path between vertices in any pair in the pairing selected in Step 4. Call the new pseudograph so formed G'.

6. Find an Eulerian circuit for G'. This corresponds to a minimal weight circuit for G. Any edge not in G is simply traversed more than once. STOP.

7. The Eulerian circuit for G is the minimal weight circuit. STOP.   □

An explanation of how to accomplish Step 4 is in order. The approach that we will use is known as "brute force." Simply list all possible pairings. In Exercise 10 you will be asked to verify that there are $(2m - 1)(2m - 3) \cdot \cdots \cdot 3 \cdot 1$ of them. For each pairing list the total distance involved and then select a pairing for which the distance is minimal. There are more efficient algorithms for the "Minimal Pairing Problem." Unfortunately, a description of one would take us too far from our topic. On the other hand, small problems, such as those in the exercises, can be effectively handled by a consideration of all cases.

We illustrate the algorithm for the graph in Figure 4.35. Note that we have used letters for the vertices so as to reduce the number of numbers appearing on the graph.

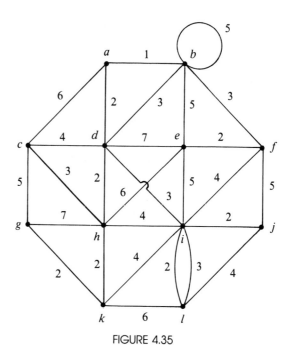

FIGURE 4.35

There are four vertices of odd degree: a, e, g, and j.

Dijkstra's Algorithm applied to the six pairs yields the following minimal weight paths:

$w(a, e) = 6$; path: $a - b - e$ (or $a - b - f - e$).
$w(a, g) = 8$; path: $a - d - h - k - g$.
$w(a, j) = 7$; path: $a - d - i - j$.
$w(e, g) = 10$; path: $e - h - k - g$.
$w(e, j) = 7$; path: $e - f - j$ (or $e - i - j$).
$w(g, j) = 8$; path: $g - k - i - j$.

There are three ways to split the four vertices a, e, g, and j into pairs, with weight sums as follows:

1. $w(a, e) + w(g, j) = 6 + 8 = 14$.
2. $w(a, g) + w(e, j) = 8 + 7 = 15$.
3. $w(a, j) + w(e, g) = 7 + 10 = 17$.

We choose the first pairing and add the corresponding paths ($a - b - e$ and $g - k - i - j$) to the graph G to obtain the graph G' as shown in Figure 4.36. The added edges are indicated by dotted lines. Note that each vertex of G' has even degree and so G' has an Eulerian circuit. Euler's Theorem (Section 4.3) will find many Eulerian circuits for the pseudograph G'. In the following one we have

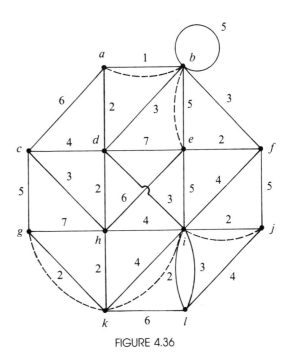

FIGURE 4.36

listed each edge by giving its endpoint vertices. We have also listed the weight of each edge. The symbol * indicates the second traversal of an edge.

ab	1		ef	2
bb	5		fi	4
bd	3		ij	2
dc	4		ji*	2
ch	3		il	3
hg	7		li	2
gk	2		id	3
ki	4		da	2
ik*	4		ab*	1
kh	2		bf	3
hi	4		fj	5
ie	5		jl	4
eh	6		lk	6
hd	2		kg*	2
de	7		gc	5
eb	5		ca	6
be*	5			

The total weight of this circuit is 121.

E X E R C I S E S

In Exercises 1–9 use Dijkstra's Algorithm to find the minimal
weight path from the vertex labeled *r* to the vertex labeled *s*.

1.

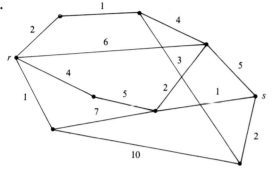

4.

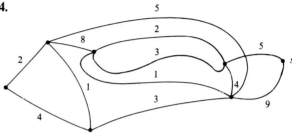

2.

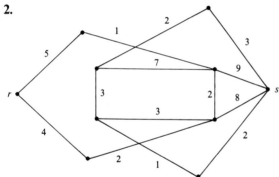

5.

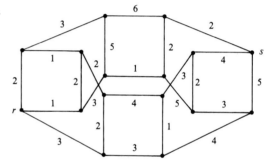

3.

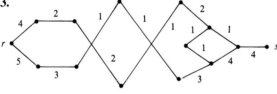

6.

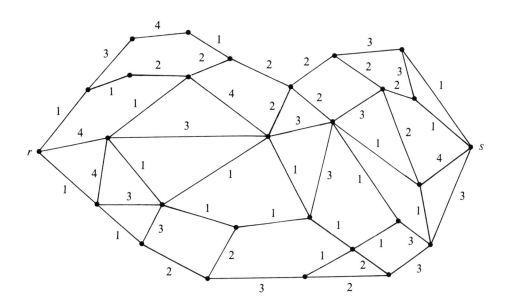

7.

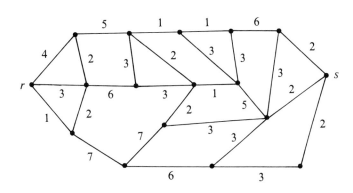

8.

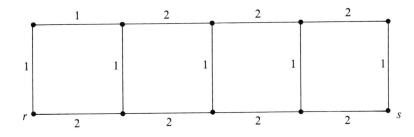

9.

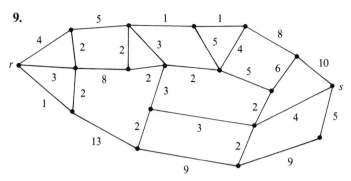

10. Show that there are $(2m-1)(2m-3) \cdot \cdots \cdot 3 \cdot 1$ pairings of $2m$ vertices.

In Exercises 11–14 find a minimal weight circuit that includes each edge at least once.

11.

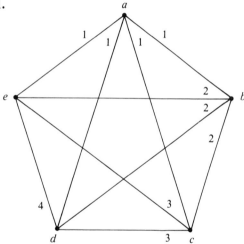

12.

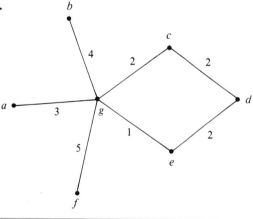

13.

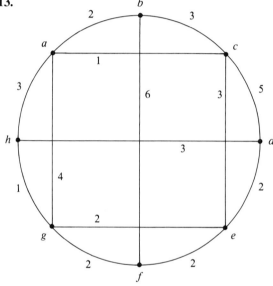

14.

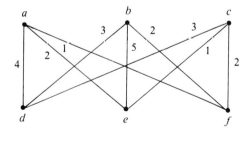

4.5

Spanning Trees

A **spanning tree** in a connected pseudograph G is a subgraph that is a tree that includes all the vertices of G. In Figure 4.37 we show a graph together with a spanning tree. In Figure 4.38 we list all the spanning trees of the graph G, given in the center.

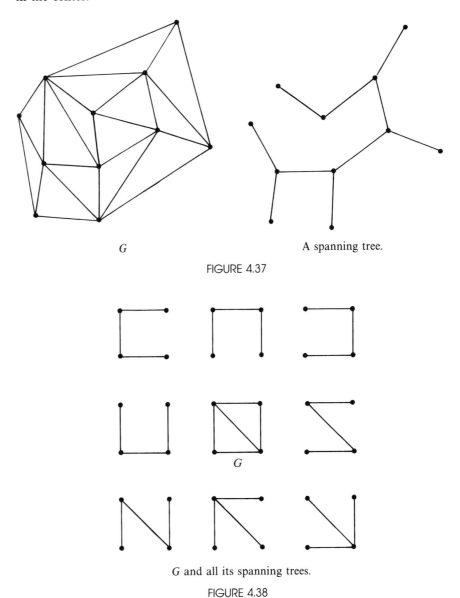

FIGURE 4.37

G and all its spanning trees.

FIGURE 4.38

Spanning trees are minimal sets of edges that reach all the vertices. For example, we have considered road maps to be pseudographs where the vertices are cities and the edges are roads connecting them. Then each spanning tree is a minimal road system, in the sense that if any edge is removed from the tree, there will be at least two cities that the road system no longer connects. In times of financial hardship it might be necessary to consider all such minimal road systems and then maintain only the least expensive one. If each road costs the same amount per mile to maintain, then we would be seeking a shortest spanning tree. In this section we present algorithms to solve the following three problems:

Problem I.   Find a spanning tree in a given connected pseudograph G.

Problem II.   Find a minimal weight spanning tree in a given connected pseudograph G whose edges have been assigned weights.

Problem III.   Determine the number of spanning trees in a connected graph.

We begin with a simple algorithm to determine whether or not a pseudograph contains a circuit. This program will be needed in two of the algorithms that follow. The program removes from G all edges and vertices that cannot be part of a circuit. There are two possible outcomes: either all of G is removed (so G has no circuit), or one or more circuits are discovered.

■ PROGRAM 4.2   **To determine if the pseudograph G contains a circuit.**

1. $G \leftarrow G$ with all vertices of degree zero deleted

2. If G has a vertex go to 4

3. "The pseudograph has no circuits." STOP

4. If G has a vertex of degree one go to 6

5. "The pseudograph has a circuit." STOP

6. $G \leftarrow G$ with all vertices of degree one and the edges incident with them deleted

7. Go to 1   ■

Here are two examples:

EXAMPLE 4.6 G:

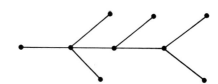

1. Remove vertices of degree zero:

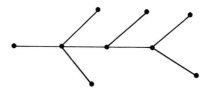

6. Remove vertices of degree one and the edges on them:

There are no vertices of degree zero.
6. Remove vertices of degree one and the edges on them:

•

1. Remove the vertex of degree zero:
$G = \emptyset$.
3. The graph has no circuits. STOP   □

EXAMPLE 4.7 G:

1. Remove vertices of degree zero:

6. Remove vertices of degree one and the edges on them:

There are no vertices of degree zero.
G has a vertex.
There are no vertices of degree one.
5. The graph has a circuit. STOP   □

Problem 1:
A Spanning Tree

It is quite easy to locate a spanning tree in a pseudograph G with n vertices and m edges. We use a fact about trees from Section 4.2: a tree with n vertices has $n-1$ edges. First, erase all the edges from G, leaving only the n vertices. Then redraw the edges of G one at a time, but omit those edges that would close a circuit. As soon as $n-1$ edges have been drawn, a spanning tree has been found. Here's a short program to do this.

■ PROGRAM 4.3

To find a spanning tree in a connected pseudograph with n vertices and edges e_1, ..., e_m, where $n > 1$.

1. Form an ordered list L. Initialize: $L \leftarrow \varnothing, j \leftarrow 0, i \leftarrow 1$
2. $j = n - 1$? If no go to 4
3. "L is the edge set of a spanning tree." STOP
4. $H \leftarrow$ the subgraph of G with edge set $L \cup \{e_i\}$
5. Does H have a circuit? (See Program 4.2.) If yes go to 7
6. $L \leftarrow L \cup \{e_i\}, j \leftarrow j + 1$
7. $i \leftarrow i + 1$
8. Go to 2

■

We illustrate Program 4.3 for the graph of Figure 4.39. Since the graph has 8 vertices, we set $n = 8$. In the program the index i tells which edge to try to include next. The index j keeps track of the number of edges included in the spanning tree L under construction.

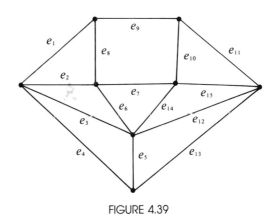

FIGURE 4.39

Step I. The program first includes edges e_1, e_2, e_3, e_4 in the spanning tree L (Figure 4.40). At this point $i = 5$ (e_5 is next) and $j = 4$ (there are 4 edges in L so far).

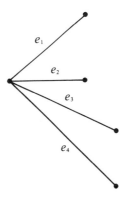

FIGURE 4.40

Step II.   We try to add edges e_5 and e_6, but discover they would introduce a circuit. Now $i = 7$ and $j = 4$.

Step III.   We add e_7. The edge e_8 would cause a circuit, but we can add edge e_9. The edge e_{10} makes a circuit, but we can add e_{11}. Now there are 7 edges in L. Since $7 = 8 - 1$, L is now a spanning tree (Figure 4.41).

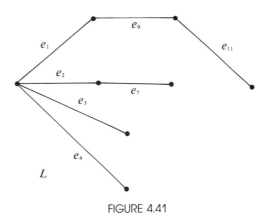

FIGURE 4.41

Problem 2:
A Minimal Weight
Spanning Tree

If the edges of a pseudograph G have been assigned weights, it is possible to ask for a spanning tree with minimal weight. For example, if the edges are labeled with lengths or costs, then we can seek a shortest or cheapest spanning tree. Kruskal's Algorithm solves this problem. The idea is fairly simple. First, erase all the edges of G, leaving only its n vertices. Then put the edges back one at a time in order of increasing weight, but omit any edge that would complete a circuit. Stop when $n - 1$ edges have been inserted.

ALGORITHM 4.4   **Kruskal's Algorithm to find a minimal weight spanning tree in a connected pseudograph G with n vertices and m edges.**

1. List and sort the edges of G according to weight. Label them $e_1, \ldots, e_m$, where the weight associated to e_i is less than or equal to the weight associated to e_{i+1} for $1 \leqslant i \leqslant m-1$. Call S the graph consisting of only the vertices of G.
2. $i \leftarrow 1$.
3. If the graph S has $n-1$ edges, go to 7.
4. If adding edge e_i to S would introduce a circuit, go to 6.
5. Add to S the edge e_i as it appears in G. Call this new graph S.
6. $i \leftarrow i+1$, go to 3.
7. "S is a minimal weight spanning tree." STOP.

EXAMPLE 4.8   Use Kruskal's Algorithm to find a minimal weight spanning tree for the graph of Figure 4.42.

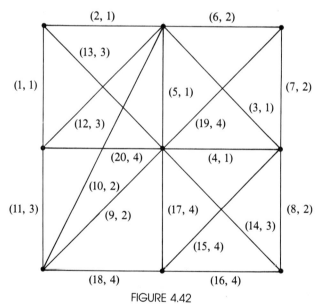

FIGURE 4.42

The edges have been labeled with ordered pairs (a, b), where a is the number of the edge and b is its weight. Note that we have already arranged for the weight of e_i to be less than or equal to the weight of e_{i+1} for $i = 1, \ldots, 19$. Let S be the graph with 9 vertices and no edges.

$i = 1$: $S = \{e_1\}$
$i = 2$: $S = \{e_1, e_2\}$
$i = 3$: $S = \{e_1, e_2, e_3\}$

$i = 4$: $S = \{e_1, e_2, e_3, e_4\}$

$i = 5$: Since e_3, e_4, e_5 form a circuit, we cannot add e_5 to S.

$i = 6$: $S = \{e_1, e_2, e_3, e_4, e_6\}$

$i = 7$: Since e_3, e_6, e_7 form a circuit, we cannot add e_7 to S.

$i = 8$: $S = \{e_1, e_2, e_3, e_4, e_6, e_8\}$

$i = 9$: $S = \{e_1, e_2, e_3, e_4, e_6, e_8, e_9\}$

$i = 10$: Since e_3, e_4, e_9, e_{10} form a circuit, we cannot add e_{10} to S.

$i = 11$: Since $e_1, e_2, e_3, e_4, e_9, e_{11}$ form a circuit, we cannot add e_{11} to S.

$i = 12$: Since e_1, e_2, e_{12} form a circuit, we cannot add e_{12} to S.

$i = 13$: Since e_2, e_3, e_4, e_{13} form a circuit, we cannot add e_{13} to S.

$i = 14$: Since e_4, e_8, e_{14} form a circuit, we cannot add e_{14} to S.

$i = 15$: $S = \{e_1, e_2, e_3, e_4, e_6, e_8, e_9, e_{15}\}$

Since S has eight elements, we stop. The result is shown in Figure 4.43. The total weight is 14.

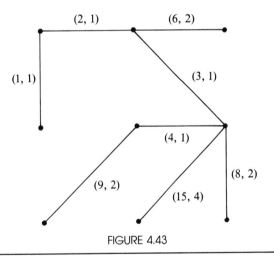

FIGURE 4.43   ◻

For another algorithmic solution to this problem (Prim's Algorithm) see the exercises.

Problem 3:
The Number of Spanning Trees in a Graph

For the remainder of this section we suppose that G *is a graph; that is, we assume that* G *has at most one edge between any pair of distinct vertices and no loops at any vertex.* We can determine the number of spanning trees of a graph by using a result reported by Kirchhoff in 1847. (G. B. Kirchhoff (1824–1887) may be familiar to you from **Kirchhoff's Laws** for electrical circuits.) For this purpose we need the notion of the **determinant** of a square matrix. (See Section 2.4, Exercises 20–34 for a different approach to determinants.) A square matrix is **upper**

triangular if all the entries below the main diagonal are zero. It is **lower triangular** if all the entries above the main diagonal are zero. The determinant of a square matrix A is denoted det A and is the real number determined by the following properties:

1. If A is a square matrix and A' is obtained from A by the row operation of adding a multiple of one row to another, then det $A =$ det A'.

2. If A is a square matrix and A' is obtained from A by switching two rows, then det $A = -$det A'.

3. If A is upper or lower triangular, then det A is the product of the elements on its main diagonal.

These three rules determine det A for any square matrix A since it is possible to use Properties (1) and (2) to reduce A to an upper or lower triangular matrix whose determinant is easily calculated by Property (3). Since by (1) and (2) the determinant of this upper or lower triangular matrix is either $\pm$det A, this process also computes the determinant of A. While these three properties are sufficient, the following two additional properties can make the calculations even easier.

4. If A is a square matrix and A' is obtained from A by adding a multiple of one column to another, then det $A =$ det A'.

5. If A is a square matrix and A' is obtained from A by switching two columns, then det $A = -$det A'.

6. If A is a square matrix and A' is obtained from A by multiplying a row or column of A by the number r, then det $A' = r$ det A.

EXAMPLE 4.9 Calculate the determinants of the following matrices.

a. $\begin{bmatrix} 1 & 2 & 1 & -1 \\ 2 & 3 & 1 & 4 \\ 1 & 2 & -1 & 3 \\ 0 & 1 & 2 & 4 \end{bmatrix}$

b. $\begin{bmatrix} a & b \\ c & d \end{bmatrix}$

c. $\begin{bmatrix} -1 & 2 & 4 \\ 2 & -3 & 1 \end{bmatrix}$

SOLUTION a.

$$\det\begin{bmatrix} 1 & 2 & 1 & -1 \\ 2 & 3 & 1 & 4 \\ 1 & 2 & -1 & 3 \\ 0 & 1 & 2 & 4 \end{bmatrix} = \det\begin{bmatrix} 1 & 2 & 1 & -1 \\ 0 & -1 & -1 & 6 \\ 0 & 0 & -2 & 4 \\ 0 & 1 & 2 & 4 \end{bmatrix}$$

$$= \det\begin{bmatrix} 1 & 2 & 1 & -1 \\ 0 & -1 & -1 & 6 \\ 0 & 0 & -2 & 4 \\ 0 & 0 & 1 & 10 \end{bmatrix}$$

$$= \det\begin{bmatrix} 1 & 2 & 1 & -1 \\ 0 & -1 & -1 & 6 \\ 0 & 0 & -2 & 4 \\ 0 & 0 & 0 & 12 \end{bmatrix}$$

$$= (1)(-1)(-2)(12) = 24$$

b. If $a \neq 0$, then

$$\det\begin{bmatrix} a & b \\ c & d \end{bmatrix} = \det\begin{bmatrix} a & b \\ 0 & (ad-bc)/a \end{bmatrix}$$
$$= a[(ad-bc)/a]$$
$$= ad - bc$$

If $a = 0$, then

$$\det\begin{bmatrix} a & b \\ c & d \end{bmatrix} = -\det\begin{bmatrix} c & d \\ 0 & b \end{bmatrix}$$
$$= -bc$$
$$= ad - bc \text{ (since } a = 0)$$

c. The matrix is not square so it has no determinant. ∎

We are now ready to calculate the number of spanning trees in a graph G.

□ THEOREM 4.3   Let G be a finite graph with vertices $v_1, \ldots, v_n$ and adjacency matrix $A = [a_{ij}]_{n \times n}$. Let $B = [b_{ij}]_{n \times n}$, where $b_{ij} = -a_{ij}$ for $i \neq j$ and $b_{ii} =$ degree of v_i. Let S be the $(n-1) \times (n-1)$ matrix obtained by erasing from B row 1 and column 1. Then the number of spanning trees of G is $\det S$. (If S' is B with row i and column j erased, then $\det S = (-1)^{i+j} \det S'$.)

EXAMPLE 4.10   Determine the number of spanning trees in the graph of Figure 4.44.

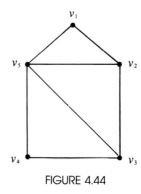

FIGURE 4.44

SOLUTION   The adjacency matrix for the graph as labeled is

$$A = \begin{bmatrix} 0 & 1 & 0 & 0 & 1 \\ 1 & 0 & 1 & 0 & 1 \\ 0 & 1 & 0 & 1 & 1 \\ 0 & 0 & 1 & 0 & 1 \\ 1 & 1 & 1 & 1 & 0 \end{bmatrix}$$

Then $-A$ is the matrix:

$$-A = \begin{bmatrix} 0 & -1 & 0 & 0 & -1 \\ -1 & 0 & -1 & 0 & -1 \\ 0 & -1 & 0 & -1 & -1 \\ 0 & 0 & -1 & 0 & -1 \\ -1 & -1 & -1 & -1 & 0 \end{bmatrix}$$

The degrees of the vertices are

vertex: v_1 v_2 v_3 v_4 v_5
degree: 2   3   3   2   4

We insert these as diagonal entries to obtain the matrix B:

$$B = \begin{bmatrix} 2 & -1 & 0 & 0 & -1 \\ -1 & 3 & -1 & 0 & -1 \\ 0 & -1 & 3 & -1 & -1 \\ 0 & 0 & -1 & 2 & -1 \\ -1 & -1 & -1 & -1 & 4 \end{bmatrix}$$

Note as a check that each row sums to zero. A quick check also reveals that if we delete the *last* row and *last* column, we will have an easier determinant to compute than if we delete the first row and column. Since these are the 5th row and column, we must multiply the determinant by $(-1)^{5+5} = 1$. The matrix S is

$$S = \begin{bmatrix} 2 & -1 & 0 & 0 \\ -1 & 3 & -1 & 0 \\ 0 & -1 & 3 & -1 \\ 0 & 0 & -1 & 2 \end{bmatrix}$$

Add $\frac{1}{2}$ row one to row 2:

$$\begin{bmatrix} 2 & -1 & 0 & 0 \\ 0 & \frac{5}{2} & -1 & 0 \\ 0 & -1 & 3 & -1 \\ 0 & 0 & -1 & 2 \end{bmatrix}$$

Add $\frac{2}{5}$ row 2 to row 3:

$$\begin{bmatrix} 2 & -1 & 0 & 0 \\ 0 & \frac{5}{2} & -1 & 0 \\ 0 & 0 & \frac{13}{5} & -1 \\ 0 & 0 & -1 & 2 \end{bmatrix}$$

Add $\frac{5}{13}$ row 3 to row 5:

$$\begin{bmatrix} 2 & -1 & 0 & 0 \\ 0 & \frac{5}{2} & -1 & 0 \\ 0 & 0 & \frac{13}{5} & -1 \\ 0 & 0 & 0 & \frac{21}{13} \end{bmatrix}$$

we can now multiply to find the determinant:

$$(2)(\tfrac{5}{2})(\tfrac{13}{5})(\tfrac{21}{13}) = 21$$

Thus, there are 21 spanning trees.   ∎

EXAMPLE 4.11   Determine the number of spanning trees in K_n.

SOLUTION   In K_n there is an edge between each pair of distinct vertices, and each vertex has degree $n-1$. Thus, the matrix S will be an $(n-1) \times (n-1)$ matrix consisting entirely of -1's except for the main diagonal, which will consist entirely of

$n - 1$'s. In this matrix

1. Subtract the first row from each of the other rows.
2. Add columns 2 through $n - 1$ to the first column.

The matrix that results is upper triangular with a main diagonal consisting of 1 followed by $n - 2$ entries that are all n. Thus, the determinant of this matrix is n^{n-2}. ■

This result was first discovered in 1874 by the English mathematician Arthur Cayley (1821–1895), who also invented matrices.

THEOREM 4.4   **(Cayley's Formula)** The number of spanning trees in the graph K_n is n^{n-2}.

E X E R C I S E S

1. Write each step of Program 4.2 for the following graph.

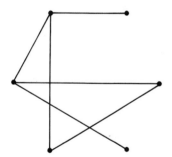

2. Write each step of Program 4.2 for the following graph.

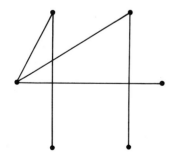

In Exercises 3–6 use Program 4.3 to find a spanning tree for the given graph *as labeled.*

3.

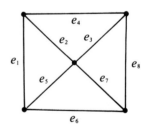

4.

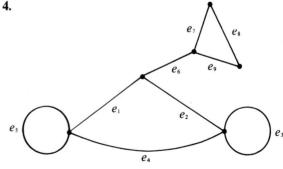

5.

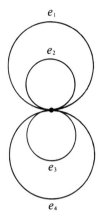

8.

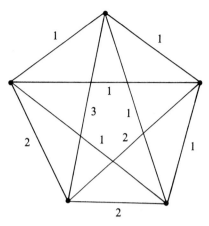

6.

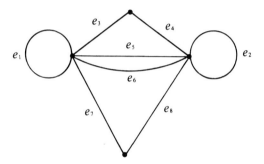

In Exercises 7–10 use Kruskal's Algorithm to find a minimal weight spanning tree for the given graph. The numbers indicate edge weight.

9.

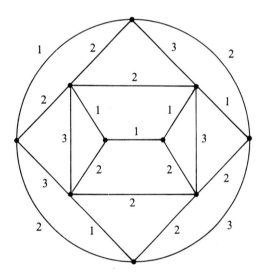

7.

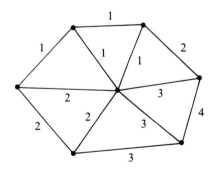

10.

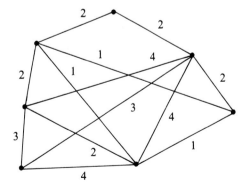

Another algorithm to find a spanning tree of minimum weight is **Prim's Algorithm**, which works as follows for a connected weighted graph with n vertices.

1. Let T be an edge of least weight.
2. Pick an edge of least weight that has exactly one vertex in T and add it to T. Call the resulting tree T and return to Step 2.
3. Stop when T has $n - 1$ edges.

11. Write an IMCOM program for Prim's Algorithm.

In Exercises 12–14 use Prim's Algorithm to find minimal spanning trees for the given graphs.

12. The graph of Exercise 8.

13. The graph of Exercise 9.

14. The graph of Exercise 10.

In Exercises 15–18 calculate the determinant of the given matrix.

15. $\begin{bmatrix} 1 & 2 & 1 \\ 2 & 1 & 2 \\ 3 & 2 & 1 \end{bmatrix}$

16. $\begin{bmatrix} 1 & 3 & 3 & 6 \\ 2 & 1 & 1 & 3 \\ 3 & 1 & 2 & 4 \\ 1 & -1 & 2 & 6 \end{bmatrix}$

17. $\begin{bmatrix} 0 & 4 & -1 & 0 \\ 0 & 3 & 2 & 1 \\ -1 & 2 & 1 & 4 \\ 1 & 3 & -1 & 3 \end{bmatrix}$

18. $\begin{bmatrix} a & b & c \\ d & e & f \\ g & h & i \end{bmatrix}$

In Exercises 19–22 determine the number of spanning trees for the given graph.

19.

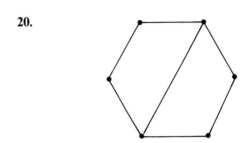

20.

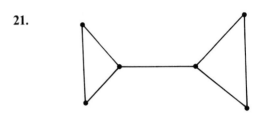

21.

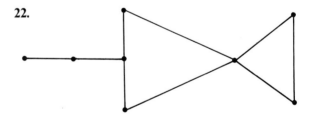

22.

23. Calculate the number of spanning trees for K_4. Evaluate the determinant by the two steps suggested in the text to verify Cayley's formula in this case.

24. Calculate the number of spanning trees for K_5. Evaluate the determinant by the two steps suggested in the text to verify Cayley's formula in this case.

25. Calculate the number of spanning trees in $K_{2,2}$. Draw them all.

26. Calculate the number of spanning trees in $K_{3,3}$.

27. Your instructor just assigned you the task of drawing all spanning trees in the complete graph on 10 points, K_{10}. Suppose you program your computer to generate all spanning trees and actually draw them with a plotter. Suppose it takes one second to generate and draw each spanning tree. Suppose 50 trees fit on one page and a stack of 500 pages of computer paper is one inch thick. How long will it take to generate the list? How tall will the complete list be?

C H A P T E R

F I V E

Graph Algorithms

5.1 Planarity

5.2 Graph Coloring

5.3 Networks

5.4 Error Propagation

OUR INTRODUCTION TO graph theory in Chapter Four has prepared us to move on to study some more complex problems. In this chapter we investigate four separate topics. First, we present an algorithm that tries to draw a graph in the plane so that its edges touch only at vertices. This algorithm fails precisely when the graph cannot be drawn in this way. Second, we consider graph coloring because its practical applications extend beyond merely coloring a graph. The idea is to assign "colors" (numbers or other attributes) to the vertices of a graph so that adjacent vertices have different colors. The goal is to accomplish this with as few different colors as possible. The third topic is an important one for business management. We present an algorithm to find the maximum amount of material that can be sent through a network, such as a system of railroads, phone lines, or pipelines. Finally, we will use graph theory to solve an important computer science problem, namely, how to arrange arithmetic calculations so as to minimize accumulated round-off errors.

Planarity

A pseudograph is said to be **planar** if it can be drawn in a two-dimensional plane in such a way that its edges intersect only at the vertices. We have been drawing pictures of pseudographs to aid in our study. However, any given pseudograph has several different possible representations by lines and dots. For example, in Figure 5.1 we have drawn three geometrical representations for the graph with the following adjacency matrix:

$$\begin{bmatrix} 0 & 1 & 1 & 1 & 1 \\ 1 & 0 & 1 & 0 & 0 \\ 1 & 1 & 0 & 1 & 1 \\ 1 & 0 & 1 & 0 & 1 \\ 1 & 0 & 1 & 1 & 0 \end{bmatrix}$$

The first representation is not a planar representation; the other two are. A question that immediately comes to mind is the following: "Given a pseudo-

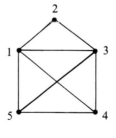
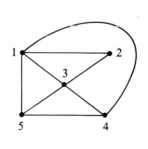
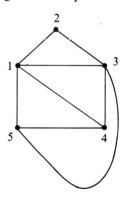

FIGURE 5.1

graph, how can we tell if it has a planar representation?" One obvious practical application is to the manufacture of printed circuits. Given a complicated electrical circuit diagram, is it possible to print it on one side of a circuit board so that wires (the edges) intersect only at electrical components (the vertices)? We will admit that this is not as practical as it may seem, since nowadays circuit boards are usually printed on *both* sides. Thus, the manufacturer really wants to know whether or not the circuit can be represented by two planar pseudographs connected at various vertices. (These connections are made through holes in the board.) Although this latter problem has also been solved, we shall restrict our attention to determining whether or not a given pseudograph is planar.

The most famous planar graph problem is familiar to children as the "gas, water, light problem." A very small town has three residents and three feuding utility companies. The feud has gone beyond reason to the point where none of the utilities will allow their lines to be crossed by those of the other companies. The problem is to connect each house to each utility in such a way that no pair of lines intersect. See Figure 5.2.

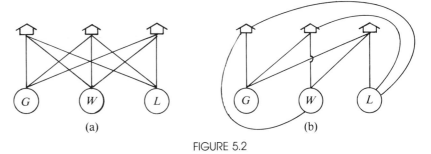

(a)   (b)

FIGURE 5.2

In (a) we have illustrated the arrangement before the feud. In (b) we have eliminated all but one crossing. Can you do any better? We hope that you recognize our problem as that of representing the bipartite graph $K_{3,3}$ as a planar graph.

Down the road is a town in the dense jungle where five couples live in isolated huts arranged roughly in a circle. Although each couple likes to visit each of the other couples, it is taboo in their primitive society for trails to cross. Thus, they each try to cut four trails through the dense underbrush with the hope that none of their four trails cross any other trail. See Figure 5.3. Can you help them out?

In this problem we are trying to find a planar representation for K_5, the complete graph on five vertices.

Although it is instructive to search for planar representations, merely failing to find one is no proof that one does not exist. Many people still try to solve the gas, water, light problem feeling that, if they tried only a bit harder, they would find the solution.

The first important result on planarity was named for Leonhard Euler, whom you will recall invented graph theory with his solution to the Königsberg Bridge Problem.

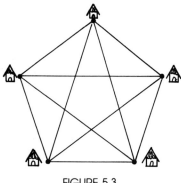

FIGURE 5.3

Euler's Formula uses the concept of **face** of a planar pseudograph. Every planar pseudograph divides the plane into regions called faces. These are the "smallest" areas bounded by circuits. If you were to draw a planar representation of the pseudograph on a piece of paper and then cut along each edge, each resulting puzzle piece of paper would correspond to a face. The traditional version of Euler's Formula requires that you interpret the region outside the pseudograph as an infinite face. In the scissors-and-paper description this is reasonable since the region outside the pseudograph is one of the resulting pieces. Figure 5.4 shows three examples to clarify the definition.

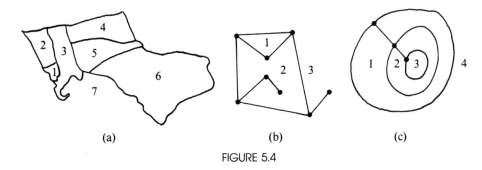

(a)   (b)   (c)

FIGURE 5.4

EULER'S FORMULA

In a connected planar pseudograph, let V denote the number of vertices, E the number of edges, and F the number of faces. Then

$$V - E + F = 2$$

In Figure 4(a): $V = 12$, $E = 17$, and $F = 7$. In Figure 4(b): $V = 8$, $E = 9$, and $F = 3$. In Figure 4(c): $V = 3$, $E = 5$, and $F = 4$.

The proof of Euler's Formula is most easily accomplished by induction on the number of faces. If the pseudograph has no circuits, it is a tree and so by the equivalences proved at the beginning of Section 4.2, it will have n vertices, $n-1$ edges, and 1 face. Then

$$n - (n-1) + 1 = 2 \checkmark$$

It is easy to check that if the pseudograph has only one circuit, then $V = E$. See Figure 5.5. Of course, in this case $F = 2$ and the formula is valid. Now suppose

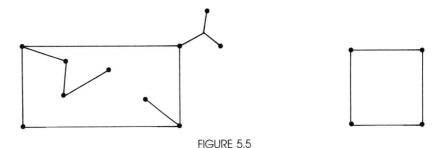

FIGURE 5.5

the formula is valid for a pseudograph with k faces and let G be a pseudograph with $k+1$ faces. Eliminate one face from G by erasing edges that are on the "outside" of the pseudograph. In Figure 5.6 we show three examples of what might happen. Dashed lines indicate the edges that might be erased.

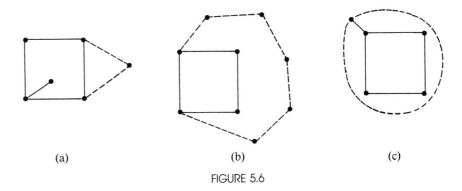

(a)   (b)   (c)

FIGURE 5.6

Since the new pseudograph G' has k faces, Euler's Formula holds for it. Let V', E', and F' denote the number of vertices, edges, and faces of this smaller pseudograph. Then

$$V' - E' + F' = 2$$

Suppose that we removed e edges from G to obtain G'. Then $E = E' + e$, $V = V' + e - 1$, and $F = F' + 1$. Thus,

$$\begin{aligned} V - E + F &= (V' + e - 1) - (E' + e) + (F' + 1) \\ &= V' - E' + F' = 2 \end{aligned}$$

and Euler's Formula is proved.

We can use Euler's Formula to prove that the graphs $K_{3,3}$ and K_5 encountered in the two preceding puzzles are not planar. For $K_{3,3}$ we count $V = 6$ and $E = 9$. If we could draw $K_{3,3}$ in the plane, then Euler's Formula would apply and $F = 5$. We will show that $V = 6$, $E = 9$, and $F = 5$ is impossible for $K_{3,3}$. First, we show that each face has at least four edges in its bounding circuit. Suppose some circuit had only three edges. Since each edge goes from a house to a utility, one vertex corresponds to a house and another to a utility. But then the third vertex must be a house since it is connected to a utility, but it *can't* be a house since it is connected to a house. Thus, each circuit has at least four edges. Thus, the planar representation must have at least $4F/2$ edges. (Since no vertex has degree 1, each edge bounds two faces. Therefore, $4F$ counts each edge twice. Of course, some faces might have more than four edges in a bounding circuit.) That is, $4F \leqslant 2E$. But $F = 5$ and $E = 9$. It follows that $K_{3,3}$ is not planar.

The reasoning is similar for K_5. From inspection we see that $V = 5$ and $E = 10$. Then by Euler's Formula, $F = 7$. Since each face has at least 3 edges in its bounding circuit and since each edge bounds two faces, we have $3F/2 \leqslant E$. But substituting for F and E yields $\frac{21}{2} \leqslant 10$, a contradiction. Thus, K_5 is not planar.

You may wonder why we are spending so much time investigating $K_{3,3}$ and K_5. The reason is the following surprising result published in 1930 by the Polish mathematician Kasimir Kuratowski (the "K" of $K_{m,n}$ and K_n). Kuratowski proved that every nonplanar graph contains a subgraph that is $K_{3,3}$ or K_5 or is obtained from one of these by the addition of one or more vertices of degree two. For example, the graphs in Figure 5.7 are not $K_{3,3}$ and K_5 because we have added a vertex v of degree two. However, it is obvious that as far as planarity is concerned, the graphs are equivalent to $K_{3,3}$ and K_5.

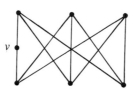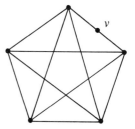

FIGURE 5.7

The proof of Kuratowski's Theorem is too hard for this text. We shall instead present an algorithm described in the text *Graph Theory with Applications*, by J. A. Bondy and U. S. R. Murty (American Elsevier Publishing Co., New York, 1976). The algorithm itself is by Demoucron, Malgrange, and Pertuiset (1964) and tells you how to draw any given graph in the plane—provided, of course, it is possible to do so. If the given graph cannot be drawn in the plane, the algorithm will tell you that.

Note that we said that the algorithm will tell you about *graphs*—not pseudographs. We shall take a moment to explain why knowing the answer for graphs is enough. Suppose G is a pseudograph. Form the graph G' by removing all loops at vertices and all but one edge in each multiple connection. Now use the algorithm described below to draw G' in the plane. If you can't, then since G' is a subgraph of G, you can't draw G in the plane either. On the other hand, suppose you can draw G' in the plane. Then you can also draw the edges you erased from G to form G'. It is easy to draw a loop at any vertex. And simply draw the other edges in each multiple connection right along side the corresponding edge of G' that is already drawn in the plane. For example, in Figure 5.8(a) we have a pseudograph that we wish to draw in the plane. Figure 5.8(b) shows the graph G' obtained from the pseudograph by removing the loops and all but one edge in each multiple connection. Figure 5.8(c) shows a planar representation of the graph of (b). We obtained this by inspection, but we could have used the algorithm. Figure 5.8(d) shows a planar representation for the original pseudograph.

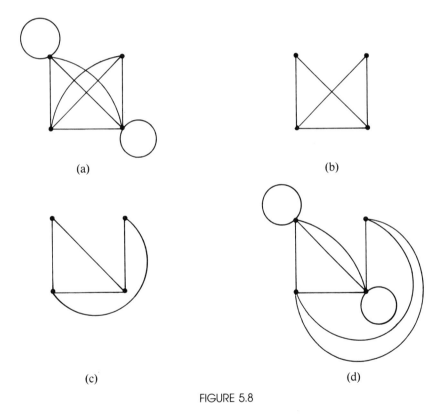

(a)

(b)

(c)

(d)

FIGURE 5.8

For the rest of our discussion, we will assume that we are trying to draw a graph in the plane.

To describe the algorithm, we need two new concepts. For a graph G and a subgraph S we define the **complement** of S, denoted S', to be the subgraph of G consisting of all the edges in G that are not in S, together with the vertices incident with these edges. Figure 5.9 shows two examples.

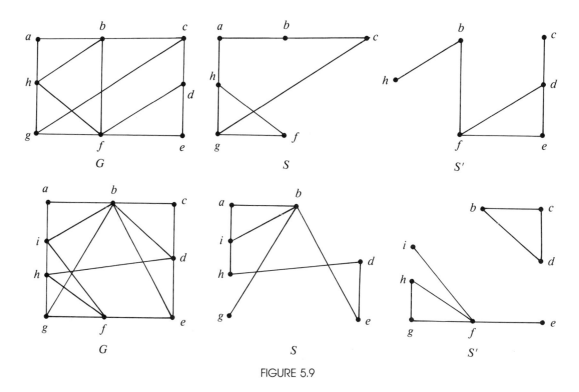

FIGURE 5.9

To define our next concept, it is useful to have the notion of initial and terminal vertex in a simple path. Recall from Section 4.1 that a path P of edges $e_1, e_2, \ldots, e_n$ is simple if it is a simple circuit or else has no repeated edges or vertices. The **initial vertex** of the path P is the vertex of e_1 *not* incident with e_2. The **terminal vertex** of the path P is the vertex of e_n *not* incident with e_{n-1}. In the case of a simple circuit, the initial and terminal vertices are the same vertex, which may be chosen to be any vertex in the circuit. Intuitively, the initial vertex is the vertex where the path starts, and the terminal vertex is the vertex where it ends.

The second concept we need is that of a **bridge** for a subgraph S of a graph G. Here is a set of properties such a bridge has:

1. A bridge for S in G is a connected subgraph of S' consisting of one or more edges.

2. Each edge in the complement S' is in precisely one bridge.

3. If an edge in the complement has both of its vertices in S, then that edge is a bridge all by itself.

4. Two edges are in the same bridge if they are in a simple path whose initial and terminal vertices are the only vertices in common with S.

It turns out that Property (4) is sufficient to define a bridge, but it is handy to know the other three properties as well. A depth-first search can be used to find bridges. In Figure 5.10 the square near the middle with darker edges is the subgraph S.

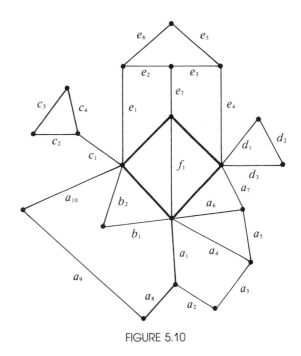

FIGURE 5.10

Let's find the bridges for the subgraph S of the entire graph shown. First, pick an edge not in S. For example, we decided to pick the edge labeled a_1. Continue following a path until you hit S or run out of unchosen edges. We followed the path a_1, a_2, a_3, a_4. Now we cannot choose either edges b_1 or a_6 since our path would have a vertex other than an initial or terminal vertex in common with S. So we backtrack to the first place we had another choice: a_5. Now we may select a_6. We backtrack again to pick up a_7. Again we hit S. We may not continue our current path. We backtrack all the way back to pick up a_8, a_9, and a_{10}. That's all for that bridge. Next we picked up the bridges $\{b_1, b_2\}$, $\{c_1, c_2, c_3, c_4\}$, and $\{d_1, d_2, d_3\}$. The bridge labeled with $e_1, ..., e_7$ was picked in the order listed. After we chose e_6, we backtracked because we had used all available edges, not because we hit S. The edge f_1 is a bridge all by itself since its two vertices are vertices of S.

As an exercise you should find the bridges of the two subgraphs in Figure 5.9. The first subgraph has three bridges: $\{bh\}$, $\{bf\}$, and $\{cd, df, de, fe\}$, where we have indicated an edge by its vertices. The second subgraph has four bridges: $\{hg\}$, $\{if, hf, gf, fe\}$, $\{bc, cd\}$, and $\{bd\}$. The **vertices of attachment** of a bridge are the vertices it has in common with S. Thus, in the top graph in Figure 5.9, $\{bh\}$ has vertices of attachment b and h, while $\{cd, df, de, fe\}$ has vertices of attachment c and f. In the bottom graph in Figure 5.9, the bridge $\{if, hf, gf, fe\}$ has vertices of attachment i, h, g, and e.

Each face of a planar graph has a bounding circuit. (The "outside" face is bounded by the "outside" edges.) We **list** a face by writing down the vertices of its bounding circuit. For example, in Figure 5.11 the faces are *abd, bcd, acdef, ghi*, and the "outside" face *abceghif*. For the following algorithm it does not matter in what order we list the vertices of a bridge or face. Finally, it is fairly obvious, but also follows at once from Kuratowski's Theorem, that if a graph does not contain a circuit, then it is planar.

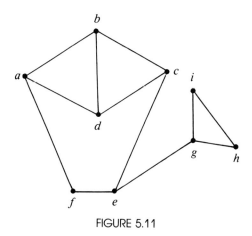

FIGURE 5.11

□ ALGORITHM 5.1   **Planarity algorithm to draw a graph *G* in the plane, if possible.**

1. If the graph *G* has no circuit, go to 8.

2. Draw any circuit of the graph in the plane. Call this circuit *S*.

3. If *S = G*, go to 9.

4. If there is a bridge *B* of *S* in *G* that contains only one vertex of *S*, attach a planar subgraph of *B* (perhaps only one edge) in one face of *S*. Call the resulting graph *S*. Go to 3.

5. For each bridge *B* for *S* in *G*, let *F(B)* denote the number of faces of *S* that contain *all* the vertices of attachment for *B*. If there is a bridge for which *F(B)* = 0, go to 7.

6. If there is a bridge for which *F(B)* = 1, choose such a bridge and call it *B*. Otherwise, call any bridge *B*. Let *F* be a face of *S* that contains all the vertices of attachment of *B*. Pick any two vertices of attachment of *B* and attach a path in *B* between them in *F*. Call the resulting subgraph *S*. Go to 3.

7. The graph is not planar. STOP.

8. Draw the graph in the plane.

9. The graph is drawn in the plane. STOP.   □

We provide two examples of this algorithm. One for the case of a planar graph and one to show that $K_{3,3}$ is not planar.

EXAMPLE 5.1   Draw a planar representation (if possible) of the graph with eight vertices shown in Figure 5.12.

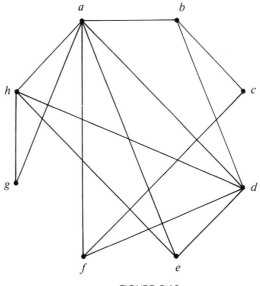

FIGURE 5.12

SOLUTION   To use the program efficiently, you should draw as much of the graph as possible at each step. Thus, when selecting the circuit, choose the longest one you can find. In our case such a circuit is *abcfdehg*. In fact, if you select this circuit, it is easy to see how to draw the rest of the graph in the plane without using the algorithm. To better illustrate the program, we will not take such a reasonable way out. We choose instead the circuit *aedf* illustrated simply in Figure 5.13.

FIGURE 5.13

In Figure 5.14 we have drawn the circuit as it appears in the original graph so we can better identify the bridges. There are three bridges: $\{a_1, a_2, a_3, a_4, a_5\}$, $\{b_1, b_2, b_3, b_4\}$, and $\{c_1\}$. The bridge labeled with *a*'s attaches to the circuit S at a, e, and d. The bridge labeled with *b*'s attaches at a, d, and f. The bridge c_1 attaches at a and d. Each bridge attaches in both faces of the circuit. We arbitrarily add the path a_4, a_2, a_3 to the inside face of S. The result is shown in Figure 5.15.

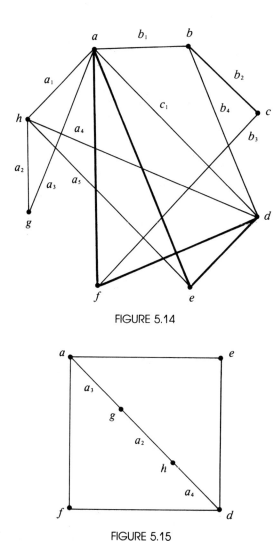

FIGURE 5.14

FIGURE 5.15

In Figure 5.16 we have drawn the current subgraph S as it appears in the original graph G and identified the bridges. There are now four bridges:

a_1 attaches in faces *aghde* and *afdhg*.

d_1 attaches in face *aedhg* only.

$b_1 b_2 b_3 b_4$ attaches in faces *afdgh* and *aefd*.

c_1 attaches in faces *aghde*, *aghdf*, and *aedf*.

The algorithm insists we next include the bridge d_1 since it attaches to only one face. Suppose we foolishly ignore that step and insert edge c_1 as shown in Figure 5.17. Now it is impossible to include d_1 in the plane since vertices e and h are

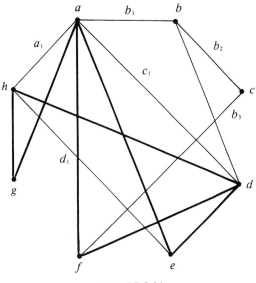

FIGURE 5.16

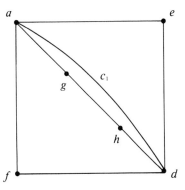

FIGURE 5.17

separated. Thus, we would get unnecessarily stuck. The algorithm is designed to guarantee that you will get stuck only when the graph is *not* planar. Instead we attach d_1 as shown in Figure 5.18. The bridges are the same as in Figure 5.16 (except, of course, d_1 is now part of S) and each attaches in two faces. We insert a_1 in the face *aghe*. The result is shown in Figure 5.19.

Finally, we are left with the "*b*" and "*c*" bridges of Figure 5.14. First, attach the path b_1, b_4, then attach the path b_2, b_3, and finally attach c_1. The graph is now drawn in the plane, Figure 5.20.

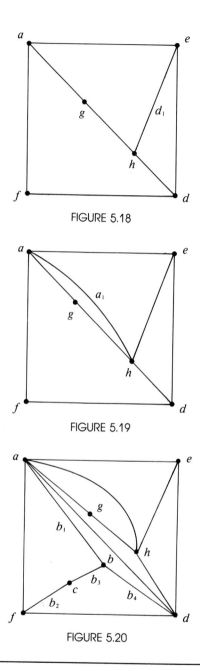

FIGURE 5.18

FIGURE 5.19

FIGURE 5.20

■

EXAMPLE 5.2   As a second example we will use the algorithm to attempt to draw $K_{3,3}$ in the plane. In Figure 5.21(a) we label the six vertices of $K_{3,3}$, and in Figure 5.21(b) we have drawn the longest circuit we could find in the graph.

In Figure 5.22(a) we have drawn the three bridges as they appear in the

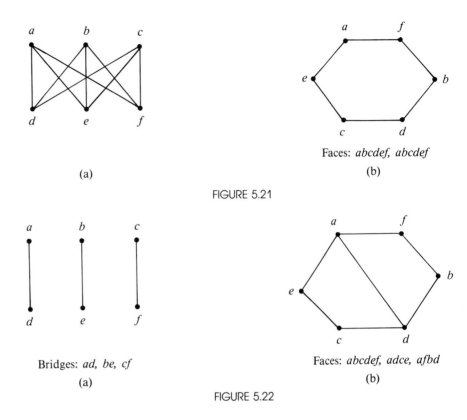

Faces: *abcdef, abcdef*

(a)   (b)

FIGURE 5.21

Bridges: *ad, be, cf*   Faces: *abcdef, adce, afbd*

(a)   (b)

FIGURE 5.22

original graph. Each bridge will fit in either face. We decide to include the bridge *ad* in Figure 5.22(b). In Figure 5.23(a) we have drawn the remaining two bridges. Each bridge fits only in the outside face. In Figure 5.23(b) we have included the bridge *be*. Now we have only the bridge *cf* left. Since it cannot be drawn in any of the four faces, we conclude that the graph is not planar.

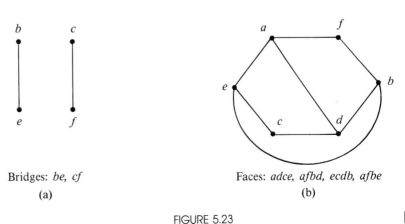

Bridges: *be, cf*   Faces: *adce, afbd, ecdb, afbe*

(a)   (b)

FIGURE 5.23   □

E X E R C I S E S

In Exercises 1–4 verify Euler's Formula for the given graph.

1.

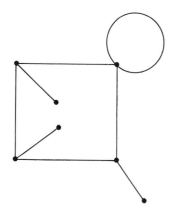

2.

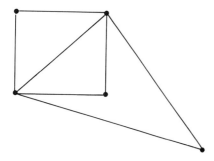

3.

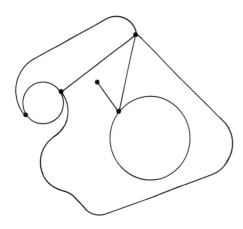

4.

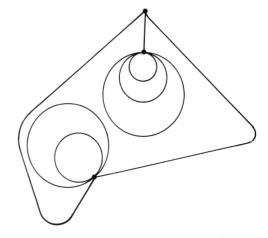

5. Write a program that in any graph *G* either finds a circuit or determines that none exists.

6. Use Algorithm 5.1 to show that K_5 is nonplanar.

7. Use Algorithm 5.1 to show that $K_{4,4}$ is nonplanar.

For the graphs in Exercises 8–11 either draw a planar representation or show that none exists.

8.

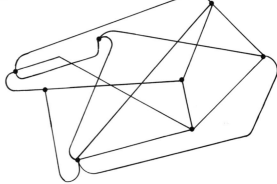

9.

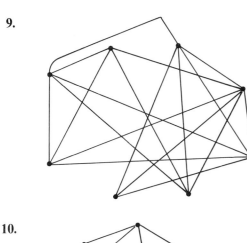

11.

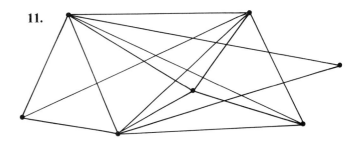

10.

5.2

Graph Coloring

Graph coloring is one of the most celebrated problems of mathematics.

"In 1852, a few months after he had completed his studies at University College London, Francis Guthrie wrote a letter to his brother Frederick, who was still at the college as a student of the mathematician Augustus De Morgan [of De Morgan's Laws]. Francis pointed out to Frederick that it seemed that every map drawn on a sheet of paper can be colored with only four colors in such a way that countries sharing a common border have different colors. He asked if there was any way to prove this mathematically. Frederick did not know, and he asked De Morgan, who did not know either. For the next 124 years Guthrie's four-color problem, the problem of proving that every map requires at most four colors or of drawing a map that requires five colors, intrigued professional mathematicians, amateur mathematicians, and high school students who felt that all unsolved problems remain so only because of the incompetence of the older generation.

"In 1976 we solved the four-color problem. Guthrie's conjecture was proven mathematically.*"

Some interpretation of the four-color-problem is necessary. First, by common border, one must mean an edge, not just a vertex. Thus, in a map of the United States, Arizona and Colorado can be given the same color. Second, a country must be in one piece. This rules out states like Kentucky, that consist of two separate pieces. (If you don't believe that Kentucky is in two pieces, check the southwest corner of that state on any good road map. By the way, the Mackinaw bridge makes one piece out of Michigan.)

It is easy to convert a map to a graph. Each country, state, or region corresponds to a vertex. Two vertices are joined by an edge if the countries have a common boundary. In Figure 5.24 we show the graph corresponding to the map of the Western (continental, contiguous) United States.

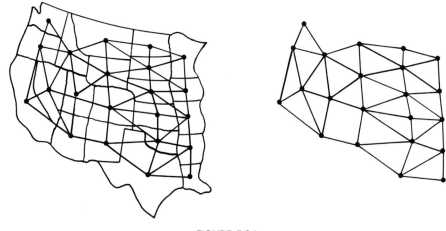

FIGURE 5.24

It is not hard to see that any map "drawn on a piece of paper" yields a planar graph. The problem then is, "Can the vertices of a planar graph be colored using four colors in such a way that adjacent vertices have different colors?" Appel and Haken proved that the answer is yes.

The *Scientific American* article referred to above is the best source for a description of the proof. During the 124 years between Guthrie's question and the final resolution, two processes were at work. First, mathematicians kept reducing the problem to the point that it could be settled by looking at cases. Second, computer scientists improved computers to the point that they were fast enough to consider the inordinate number of cases necessary. The final solution required 1200 hours of computer time.

---

* From: Kenneth Appel and Wolfgang Haken, "The Solution to the Four-Color-Map Problem," *Scientific American*, October 1977, page 108.

Although some might regard the four-color problem as an exercise in academic irrelevance, the problem of graph coloring in general has important applications. One of these is to scheduling problems. Since we mentioned academic irrelevance, let's suppose that you are in charge of scheduling final examinations at your college. There is a slight problem: the maintenance crews want to paint classrooms during exam week and so you are required to use as few exam times as possible. To find this minimum number, construct a graph as follows. Let the vertices correspond to sections of courses. Join two vertices with an edge if the two sections have one or more students in common. Now find the minimal number of colors necessary to color the vertices so that adjacent vertices have different colors. Then each color corresponds to an examination time.

One expects that the graph obtained for this scheduling problem is not planar. For such problems the four-color theorem is useless. What we need is a method to determine how to find and use the minimum number of colors needed to color the vertices of any graph. In 1972 J. Randall Brown published a graph-coloring algorithm designed to do just that. This algorithm was used to schedule final examinations at the Massachusetts Institute of Technology. (The answer was obtained in 0.4 second: 15 examination periods were needed.) The efficiency of the algorithm is understood only through statistical analysis of test cases. Other algorithms are available, but this is one of the easiest to describe.

First, note that we may restrict our attention to graphs instead of pseudographs. What matters in graph coloring is the adjacency of vertices. The number of edges connecting a pair of vertices is irrelevant. Only the fact that they are connected is important. Edges that form loops at a vertex do not make sense in the context of coloring since they make a vertex adjacent to itself and hence uncolorable. Second, we may as well assume that the graph is connected. Otherwise, we simply use the algorithm to color each component separately.

The algorithm is presented in two parts. Program 5.1 numbers the vertices and then Program 5.2 colors them. The way in which the vertices are labeled is important. Label any vertex v_1. Label as v_2 any vertex adjacent to v_1. Now, if possible, pick for v_3 any vertex adjacent to both v_1 and v_2. Failing that, pick v_3 adjacent to either v_1 or v_2. On to v_4. Pick any vertex adjacent to all three of v_1, v_2, and v_3 to be v_4. If there is no such vertex, pick any vertex adjacent to two of v_1, v_2, and v_3. Failing that, let v_4 be any vertex adjacent to v_1, v_2, or v_3. Continue in this way, picking vertices adjacent to as many labeled vertices as possible, until the entire graph is labeled. Here is a short program to do this.

PROGRAM 5.1   **Graph labeling, for a graph with n vertices.**

1. Label any vertex v_1

2. $i \leftarrow 2$

3. Label as v_i an unlabeled vertex adjacent to as many previously labeled vertices as possible

4. If $i = n$ STOP

5. $i \leftarrow i + 1$, go to 3   ■

Having labeled the vertices, we are now ready to color the graph. Program 5.2 begins by asking you to number the colors. The adjectives "highest" and "lowest" as applied to vertices and colors refer to the numbers which we have indicated by subscripts. The algorithm begins by finding some acceptable coloring assignments. Then backtracking is used to try to find improvements. Each time the last vertex, v_n, is recolored, the coloring assignment uses fewer colors. The algorithm stops when backtracking reaches the first vertex, v_1.

■ **PROGRAM 5.2**   **Graph Coloring**

1. Use Program 5.1 to label the vertices $v_1, \ldots, v_n$. Call the colors $c_1, \ldots, c_n$. $i \leftarrow 1$

2. Color v_i with the lowest color not used for adjacent vertices

3. If $i = n$ then go to 5

4. $i \leftarrow i + 1$. Go to 2

5. Let C denote the current vertex color assignment. $C_Q \leftarrow$ highest color used

6. $c_q \leftarrow$ highest color used
   $v_r \leftarrow$ highest vertex colored c_q
   $v_s \leftarrow$ highest vertex adjacent to v_r, $s < r$
   $c_t \leftarrow$ color of v_s

7. If $s \neq 1$ go to 9

8. "C is a color assignment using fewest colors." STOP

9. $j \leftarrow s$

10. $c_u \leftarrow$ lowest color with $u > t$ not assigned to any v_k, with $k < s$, adjacent to v_j

11. If $u < Q$ go to 13

12. Erase all colors for vertices v_k with $k > j$. Go to 6

13. Color v_s with c_u. $j \leftarrow s + 1$

14. $c_v \leftarrow$ lowest color not assigned to any vertex adjacent to v_j

15. If $v < Q$ go to 17

16. $j \leftarrow j - 1$. Go to 12

17. Recolor v_j with the lowest feasible color

18. If $j = n$ go to 5

19. $j \leftarrow j + 1$. Go to 14   ■

Let us illustrate this program for the map of Figure 5.25(a). First we convert the map to a graph as in Figure 5.25(b). Next use Program 5.1 to label the vertices of this graph. We arbitrarily choose vertex a to label as v_1. Now there are three vertices adjacent to v_1: b, c, and d. We arbitrarily let b be vertex v_2. Now vertices c,

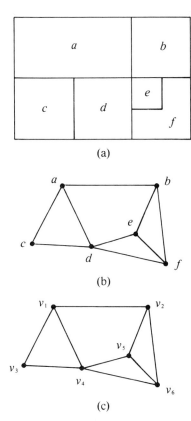

FIGURE 5.25

d, e, and f are each adjacent to exactly one of v_1 and v_2; we pick c to serve as v_3. There is no vertex adjacent to all three of v_1, v_2, and v_3. However, d is the only vertex adjacent to two of them. So we must pick d as v_4. Now e and f are each adjacent to two labeled vertices. We let e be v_5 and f be v_6. The graph is now labeled as in Figure 5.25(c) and we are ready to color.

We first find an assignment of colors so that adjacent vertices have different colors:

$$\begin{bmatrix} v_1 & v_2 & v_3 & v_4 & v_5 & v_6 \\ \hline c_1 & c_2 & c_2 & c_3 & c_1 & c_4 \end{bmatrix}$$

$$Q = 4; \ q = 4; \ r = 6; \ s = 5; \ t = 1$$

Since s is not 1, we continue. $j = s = 5$; $u = 4$; u is not less than Q. We erase the color on v_6 and go to step 6.

Now $q = 3$; $r = 4$; $s = 3$; $t = 2$. Since s is not 1, we let $j = s = 3$ and continue. $u = 3$. Now $u < Q = 4$ so we go to step 13 and recolor:

$$\begin{bmatrix} v_1 & v_2 & v_3 & v_4 & v_5 & v_6 \\ \hline c_1 & c_2 & c_3 & c_2 & c_1 & c_3 \end{bmatrix}$$

$$Q = 3; \ q = 3; \ r = 6; \ s = 5; \ t = 1$$

Since s is not 1, we set $j = s = 5$ and continue. $u = 3$; since $u = Q$, we erase all colors for $i > j = 5$. We are left with

$$\left[\begin{array}{ccccc} v_1 & v_2 & v_3 & v_4 & v_5 \\ \hline c_1 & c_2 & c_3 & c_2 & c_1 \end{array}\right.$$

$$q = 3; \ r = 3; \ s = 1; \ t = 1$$

Since $s = 1$, we stop. The last complete assignment of colors involves the fewest possible colors for this map and graph. We have indicated this coloring by shading the map in Figure 5.26. Of course, planar maps may require as many as four colors, while graphs in general may require even more than that.

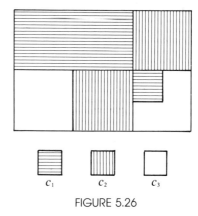

FIGURE 5.26

EXERCISES

In Exercises 1–6 color the given graph with as few colors as possible. In Exercises 5 and 6 use the given vertex labels.

1.

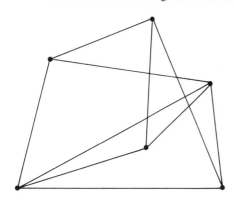

2.

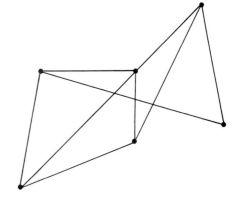

3.

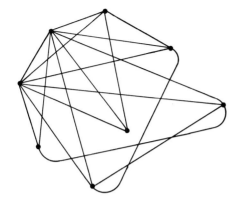

4.

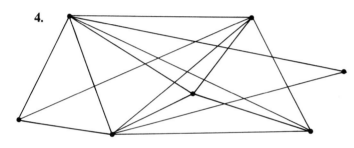

5.

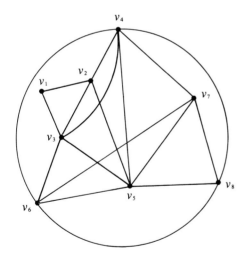

6.

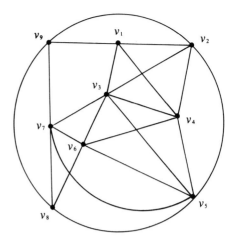

In Exercises 7–10 color the given maps with as few colors as possible.

7.

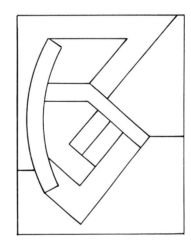

8.

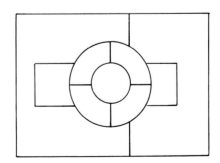

9.

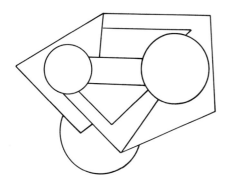

10.

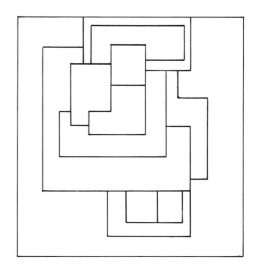

11. How many colors are necessary to color K_n?

12. How many colors are necessary to color $K_{m,n}$?

Networks

In 1955 T. E. Harris, in conjunction with General F. S. Ross (Ret.), asked how to determine how much could be shipped from one place to another in a complicated railroad network, where each segment of the network had restrictions on the amount that could be shipped. The result of this question was the book *Flows in Networks* by L. R. Ford and D. R. Fulkerson (Princeton University Press, 1962). The Ford-Fulkerson labeling method is the algorithm of this section. Two hundred years earlier in his *Dictionary of the English Language*, Samuel Johnson defined a **network** to be "anything reticulated or decussated at equal distance with interstices between the intersections." For our purposes we will need to modify his formulation. While "reticulated" (resembling a net; having lines crossing) and "interstices" (spaces) are pertinent to what we have in mind, "decussated" (shaped like an X) and "equal distance" are not. With all due respect to Dr. Johnson, when we say **network** we mean a graph or pseudograph in which the edges have been assigned numbers representing capacities. Here are two examples.

EXAMPLE 5.3   (Pipeweed shipment in The Shire) The governing council of The Shire has placed limits on the number of wagonloads of pipeweed that can travel per season on each of the paved connecting roads between the central towns. Leaf is produced in small quantities around many towns, but the most (and best) comes from around Longbottom. In this network, shown in Figure 5.27, the vertices are

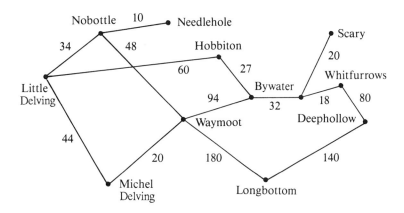

FIGURE 5.27

the towns, the edges are paved roads, and the numbers on the edges give the restrictions. □

EXAMPLE 5.4 (The Telephone Company) When Gulliver returned to England after his voyage to Laputa, he complained that communication between the places he had visited was extremely difficult. Ye Olde Englishe Belle immediately sent representatives to acquire property rights, and soon microwave towers dotted all horizons. The result was the telephone network shown in Figure 5.28. A line (or edge) between

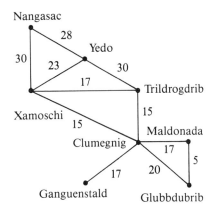

FIGURE 5.28

two cities (the vertices) indicates that there is a direct telephone connection between them. The numbers on the edges indicate the number of calls that can be carried simultaneously between connected cities.   ◻

While there are many questions one can ask, we will limit ourselves to just one: Given two vertices in a network, what is the largest amount of material that can be sent between them at one time without exceeding any of the edge restrictions? For example, in The Shire the residents of Nobottle want as much Longbottom leaf as possible. The direct route can handle some 48 wagonloads, but by routing through Bywater they can get an additional 27 wagonloads. They want to know if this is the best they can do. Again, all telephone calls from Nangasac to Glubbdubdrib must be routed through other towns. The phone company needs to know how many calls can be transmitted simultaneously because they want to expand their system if it is not large enough to meet average peak demand.

Let us call a particular movement of material through a network a **flow**. We are looking for a maximal (largest) flow. Other applications should come to mind. What is the maximal flow through a network of railways, a system of oil pipelines, a network of power plants? It is even possible to interpret the assignment of persons to jobs as a network flow problem. A network must satisfy the following three conditions before the algorithm can be applied. However, all three restrictions are met in real-life problems.

1. Each edge in the network must have a carrying capacity. In real-life situations these capacities might be fractional, although by changing units (that is, multiplying by a least common denominator), it would be possible to avoid fractions altogether. For example, if three edges in a gold supply network have capacities $\frac{5}{12}$, $\frac{1}{3}$, and $\frac{3}{4}$ in troy pounds, then in troy ounces their capacities are 5, 4, and 9, respectively. It is also possible to apply the labeling method if some edges have infinite capacity. *All edges of all networks in this text will have finite positive integer capacities.*

2. Each edge must be directed; that is, each edge must have an arrow indicating the direction of flow. No flow can go against the arrow. Although this may seem to be an unreasonable assumption in some problems, it is actually not restrictive at all. For example, if an undirected edge with capacity 5 appears in your network:

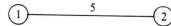

simply replace it with two directed edges, each with capacity 5:

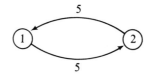

This does introduce more edges, but it really does not change the problem. It is essential that all edges be directed in order to apply the Ford-Fulkerson algorithm.

3. All material that flows through the network must originate at one single vertex, called the **source**, and end at one single vertex, called the **sink**. It turns out that this is not really a restriction either. Later in this section we will show how to turn a network with many sources and sinks into one with one source and one sink in such a way that the answer will not be changed. We will always call the source (s) and the sink (t) (for "terminal").

Figure 5.29 is an example of a directed capacitated network with a single source and a single sink. Our aim is to move as many items from (s) to (t) as

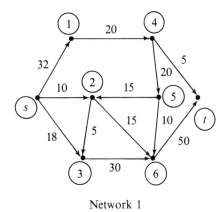

Network 1

FIGURE 5.29

possible without exceeding any edge capacities and without moving against any arrows. For small networks it is often possible to locate a maximal flow by trial and error. However, for large networks a systematic approach adaptable to computers is needed. Beyond that, even if you do find a flow you think is maximal, how can you be *certain* it is maximal? The Ford-Fulkerson labeling algorithm addresses both these needs.

The following program outlines the Ford-Fulkerson algorithm for finding a maximal flow in a directed network. The method is easy to apply but difficult to illustrate in a book. Following the outline we will carefully describe each step and then apply it to the network shown in Figure 5.29.

□ ALGORITHM 5.2   **(Outline) To find a maximal flow.**

1. Label the edges with a possible flow.

2. Use the edge labels to determine a labeling of vertices. Begin by labeling the source.

3. If the sink is labeled, go to 5.

4. "The listed flow is maximal." STOP.

5. Use the vertex labels to determine a relabeling of edges. After thus increasing the flow, erase the vertex labels. Go to 2.   □

Step I.   We indicate a possible flow by writing a number next to the capacity number on the edges.

Step II.   We begin by labeling the source. Proceeding from there, we label vertices adjacent to labeled vertices according to the rules set out below. The aim is to label the sink. However, if the flow is maximal, the labeling rules will tell us to stop before this happens.

Step III.   If the sink has been labeled, its label will indicate an amount by which the flow can be increased. The labels on the other vertices indicate how to alter the flow so it will be increased by that amount. We increase the flow, erase all vertex labels, and return to Step II. If this step has to be performed many times by hand, a lot of erasing or recopying will be required. For this purpose a chalkboard may be handy.

We now give a detailed explanation of each of these steps, illustrating the entire procedure with Network 1 as we go along.

Step I.   When indicating a possible flow, you must follow two rules:

(i)   Do not exceed the capacity of any edge.

(ii)   Except for the source and sink, there must be exactly as many items entering a vertex as leaving it.

It can be shown that if all the edge capacities are given by integers, then fractions will not appear in the answer or in the solution. So it is never necessary to use fractions in any flows. Also, if you follow the two rules given above, there will be exactly the same number of items leaving the source as entering the sink. This is guaranteed by Rule (ii): everything shipped out gets through. No items are left hanging around a vertex.

The simplest initial flow for any computer, including IMCOM, is a flow of 0 on each edge. However, if you are working a problem by hand, it will generally take a long time for the algorithm to turn a flow of zero into a maximal flow. The best idea when working by hand is to try to determine a maximal flow immediately by inspecting the network. If you are lucky and actually do stumble onto a maximal flow right off, Steps II and III will verify this for you rather quickly. However, in your eagerness to obtain a maximal flow do not forget the two rules given above.

We will use ordered pairs to label the edges. The first entry will be the edge capacity; the second entry will denote the current flow. Since the edge capacities are part of the information describing the network, the first entries will not change as we proceed through the solution.

There are many ways to do Step 1. Figure 5.30 shows our initial flow.

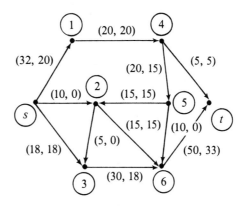

FIGURE 5.30

You may be able to see better ways to begin, but do check that we have satisfied Rules (i) and (ii). For example, at vertex ④:

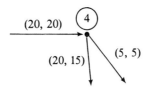

we have 20 coming in and $15 + 5 = 20$ going out.

Step II.   We now use the edge labels to label the vertices with ordered pairs. The following program outlines the procedure. This program will help you understand the main idea. However, it does not explain how to label the vertices. We will take care of that aspect soon.

□ ALGORITHM 5.3   **Vertex Labeling (Step 2 of Algorithm 5.2 in Outline).**

1. Label the source $(-, \infty)$.
2. If there is a vertex with a label but no ✓, go to 4.
3. "The labeling is complete." STOP.
4. If ⓣ has been labeled, go to 3.
5. Choose a labeled vertex that has no ✓. Call it v.
6. Attempt to label each unlabeled vertex adjacent to v. This attempt may fail as explained below.
7. Put a ✓ by v. Go to 2.   □

Before we describe how to label a given vertex, there are two matters that deserve clarification:

1. In Step 1 we used the infinity symbol, ∞, in the label for the source. The symbol ∞ stands for a number that is bigger than any edge capacity in the problem.

2. In Step 6 we say "attempt to label" since the following rules may not allow you to label a vertex. In fact, as the flow increases, the number of vertices that can be labeled decreases.

We now describe the specifics of the labeling process. There are two cases.

Case I.   The edge is directed *out from* the labeled vertex.

or

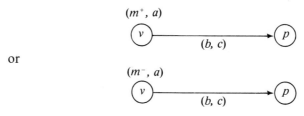

If $b = c$, do not label vertex $\widehat{p}$.
If $b > c$, label vertex $\widehat{p}$

$$(v^+, d)$$

where d is the smaller of the numbers $b - c$ and a.

PROBLEM 5.1   (This has nothing to do with Network 1.) Label vertex $\widehat{9}$ in each of the following cases:

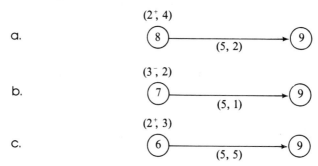

SOLUTION   (a) According to the label on the edge, it has capacity 5, of which 2 are being used. The second entry in the vertex label means that 4 items can be brought to vertex $\widehat{8}$. However, we can ship only $3 = 5 - 2$ more of them on to vertex $\widehat{9}$. To indicate the fact that they came from vertex $\widehat{8}$, we label vertex $\widehat{9}$:

$$(8^+, 3)$$

The label means "we can bring 3 *more* from vertex ⑧ to vertex ⑨."

(b) There is room for $4 = 5 - 1$ more on the edge from ⑦ to ⑨, but the label on vertex ⑦ tells us we have only 2 available for shipment. In this case vertex ⑨ is labeled

$$(7^+, 2)$$

(c) The label on the edge from ⑥ to ⑨ indicates that this edge is completely filled. We cannot ship any more from ⑥ to ⑨ than are already being shipped. Therefore, we do not label vertex ⑨.   ∎

Case II.   The edge is directed *in toward* the labeled vertex.

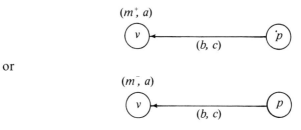

or

If $c = 0$, do not label vertex ⑨.
If $c > 0$, label vertex ⑨

$$(v^-, d)$$

where d is the smaller of the numbers c and a.

PROBLEM 5.2   (This has nothing to do with Network 1.) Label vertex ⑨ in each of the following cases:

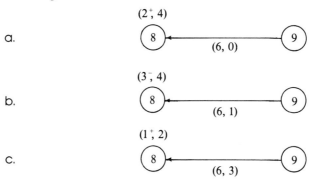

SOLUTION   The labeling process begins at the source. We began at the source and labeled vertices until we got out to vertex ⑧. Now we want to label vertex ⑨. The arrow indicates that it is impossible to use this edge to ship anything directly from vertex ⑧ to vertex ⑨. The edge is "backwards." The best we can do is to ship fewer items from ⑨ to ⑧.

(a) In this case we are not shipping anything along this edge. We certainly do not want to change that. Vertex ⑨ remains unlabeled.

(b) In this case 1 unit is "going backwards." We want to subtract and reroute it. We label vertex ⑨ $(8^-, 1)$. This label means

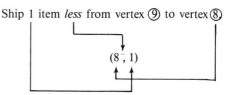

(c) In this case we would like to reroute all 3 items on the edge. However, the second entry of the label at vertex ⑧ indicates that there are only 2 items there. Thus, we can reschedule 2 of the 3 items. Vertex ⑨ is labeled

$$(8^-, 2) \qquad \blacksquare\square$$

We will rarely consider pseudograph networks with more than one edge between any two vertices. Of course, whenever the algorithm is applied to an undirected graph, it is first turned into a pseudograph by replacing each edge with a pair of edges. For that reason we present the following extreme example to help you understand what to do if you need to label a vertex and there are several edges between it and an adjacent labeled vertex.

PROBLEM 5.3   Label vertex ⑨ in Figure 5.31.

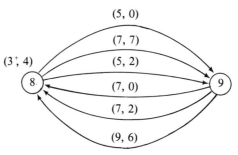

FIGURE 5.31

SOLUTION   We can label vertex ⑨ in many ways. Four of the six edges could be used. Numbering from the top, the labels are given by

Edge	Label for ⑨
1	$(8^+, 4)$
3	$(8^+, 3)$
5	$(8^-, 2)$
6	$(8^-, 4)$

Mathematically, it does not matter which label we use. Practically, we should use either $(8^+, 4)$ or $(8^-, 4)$ if we want to have fewer steps in the solution of the problem.   ■

If it is possible to label a vertex, you must do so. Do not simply look at the second edge in Problem 5.3 and say that ⑨ cannot be labeled. Once a vertex is labeled, this label remains until all the labels are erased after the flow is increased.

We illustrate Algorithm 5.3 for Network 1. In general, there will be many different choices for unchecked vertices, and so there will be many different ways to implement this algorithm. One is shown in Figure 5.32.

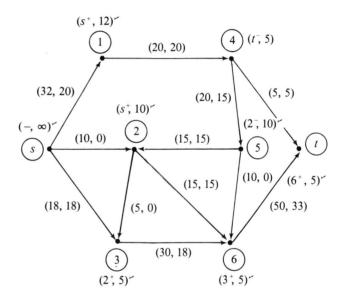

FIGURE 5.32

The full sequence of steps used in obtaining this labeling is as follows:

1. Label ⓢ $(-, \infty)$.
2. Label ① $(s^+, 12)$.
3. Label ② $(s^+, 10)$.
4. ③ cannot (yet) be labeled.
5. Check off ⓢ.
6. Choose ①. (② could have been chosen instead.)
7. ④ cannot be labeled.
8. Check off ①.
9. Choose ②. (There is no other choice at this point.)

10. Label ③ $(2^+, 5)$.
11. Label ⑤ $(2^-, 10)$.
12. Check off ②.
13. Choose ③.
14. Label ⑥ $(3^+, 5)$.
15. Check off ③.
16. Choose ⑥.
17. ⑤ is labeled.
18. Label t $(6^+, 5)$.
19. Check off ⑥.
20. Choose t.
21. Label ④ $(t^-, 5)$.
22. Check off t.
23. Choose ④.
24. ⑤ is labeled.
25. Check off ④.
26. Choose ⑤.
27. Check off ⑤.
28. The labeling is complete.

Step III.   If the sink has not been labeled by Algorithm 5.3, the flow is a maximal one. Since there may be other ways to ship the same maximal amount through, we say *a* maximal flow instead of *the* maximal flow. This algorithm does not find all maximal flows. If the sink has been labeled, it is possible to increase the flow by the amount indicated by the second coordinate of the sink label. In fact, once the sink is labeled, there is no reason to continue labeling vertices. Thus, in labeling Network 1, we would stop at Step 18 when the sink was labeled $(6^+, 5)$. That 5 in the second coordinate indicates that we can increase the flow by 5. We now ignore the second coordinates of all the vertex labels. *We begin by examining the sink label and proceed systematically back to the source, following the directions given by the first coordinates of the vertex labels.* There are two cases.

Case I.   A vertex is labeled

$$ⓐ(b^+, c) ✓$$

Increase the flow along the edge between ⓑ and ⓐ by the amount indicated in the *sink label*. If there is more than one edge, apply this increase to the flow on the one used in obtaining the label on vertex ⓐ. Now examine vertex ⓑ.

Case II.   A vertex is labeled

$$\text{(a)}(b^-, c) \checkmark$$

Now decrease the flow along the edge between b and a (used to obtain the label) by the amount indicated in the *sink label*. Now examine vertex b.

In both cases the number c is ignored.
Here are the steps involved in our particular example.

1. The sink is labeled $(6^+, 5)$. The flow can be increased by 5. In particular, we increase the flow from 6 to t from 33 to 38. Now examine vertex 6.
2. At vertex 6 the label $(3^+, 5)$ tells us to increase the flow from vertex 3 to vertex 6 by 5. We increase the flow from 18 to 23 and go to vertex 3.
3. At vertex 3 we find a label with a 2^+ as first coordinate. We increase the flow from 2 to 3 by 5 and go to vertex 2.
4. At vertex 2 we find the label $(s^+, 10)$. We increase the flow from s to 2 by 5 (*not* by 10). Since we have reached the source, we erase all vertex labels and return to Algorithm 5.3.

Note that we used only the labels on vertices in a path from s to t. Thus, when applying the algorithm by hand, try to label a path to the sink as quickly as possible. If we make all these changes, we obtain the new edge labeling shown in Figure 5.33. For clarity, the changes are underlined; usually they are not.

It is easy to see that if you alter the flow according to the rules in Step 5 of Algorithm 5.2, it will still satisfy the conditions in Step 1. We now label again, only this time we will label just a path to the sink (and vertex 1, which turned out to be a blind alley). See Figure 5.34.

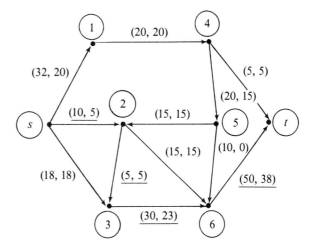

FIGURE 5.33

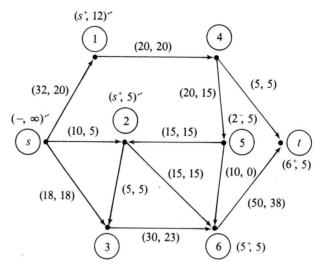

FIGURE 5.34

We are now ready for Step 5 of Algorithm 5.2 again.

1. Increase the flow from ⑥ to ⓣ by 5.
2. Increase the flow from ⑤ to ⑥ by 5.
3. Decrease the flow from ② to ⑤ by 5.
4. Increase the flow from ⓢ to ② by 5.

In the network of Figure 5.35 we not only indicate the new flow but we also give the new labels.

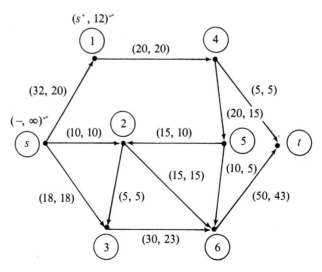

FIGURE 5.35

Since the rules in Step 2 will not allow us to label any vertices except (s) and (1), the flow of 48 units is maximal.

You should now go back to our original labeling and note that if we had labeled vertex (6) with $(2^-, 10)$ instead of $(3^+, 5)$, we would have found the maximal flow with one labeling. You should watch for such shortcuts.

The Minimal Cut   A **cut** in a network is any edge blockade that completely cuts off the flow from (s) to (t). The **cut capacity** is the total capacity of all edges involved in the cut. Here are three examples with our network.

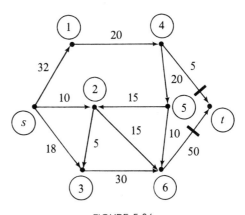

FIGURE 5.36

This cut has capacity $50 + 5 = 55$.

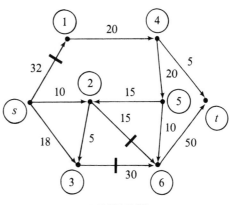

FIGURE 5.37

In this case we are blocking $32 + 15 + 30 = 77$ units.

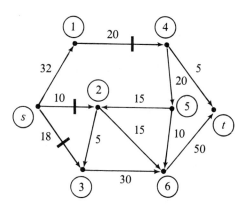

FIGURE 5.38

Now we have completely stopped the flow by blocking $20 + 10 + 18 = 48$ units. In all these examples note that the cut capacity is obtained from the edge capacities, not from any flow. In fact, we have not even indicated a flow in our illustrations of cuts.

There is a rather close relationship between cuts and flows. In the first place, a cut completely blocks the flow. It follows that each item in the flow must pass some cut barricade. Thus, no flow can exceed any cut capacity. In our case, since we have found a cut with capacity 48, we know that it is impossible to ship more than 48 through the network. Similarly, since we have found a flow of 48, we know that it is impossible to find a smaller cut. Thus, a flow of 48 is maximal and a cut of 48 is minimal.

In general, in any network, if you can find a flow and a cut with the same capacity, then the flow is maximal and the cut is minimal. It is easy to use the Ford-Fulkerson algorithm to find a minimal cut:

1. Use Step 2 to label as many vertices as possible.
2. Form two sets: $L =$ the set of labeled vertices; $U =$ the set of unlabeled vertices.
3. The minimal cut consists of a blockade at each edge in the network that goes *from* a vertex in L *to* a vertex in U.

Note that we must not block edges from vertices in U to vertices in L.

In our case

$$L = \{ \text{\textcircled{s}}, \text{\textcircled{1}} \}$$
$$U = \{ \text{\textcircled{2}}, \text{\textcircled{3}}, \text{\textcircled{4}}, \text{\textcircled{5}}, \text{\textcircled{6}}, \text{\textcircled{t}} \}$$

and a minimal cut consists of the edges from \textcircled{s} to \textcircled{2}, \textcircled{s} to \textcircled{3}, and \textcircled{1} to \textcircled{4} as indicated in the third example above.

Multiple Sources and Sinks It is easy to handle a network with more than one source or sink. Suppose we are given a network that begins and ends as follows.

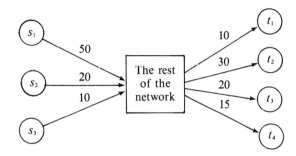

Simply enlarge the network.

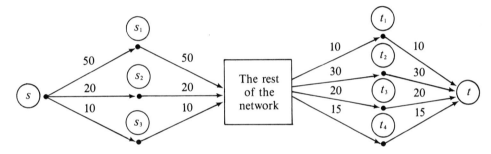

This converts the original network into a network with exactly one source and one sink. We solve the problem exactly as before and then erase ⓢ, ⓣ, and the edges we added.

E X E R C I S E S

1. What is the maximal number of wagonloads of pipeweed that can be legally transported from Longbottom to Nobottle in one season?

2. What is the maximal number of calls that can be made from Nangasac to Glubbdubdrib simultaneously?

In Exercises 3–16 find the maximal flow and minimal cut for the given network.

3.

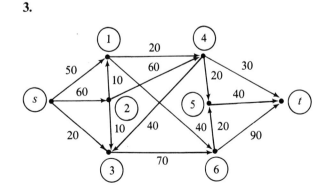

4.

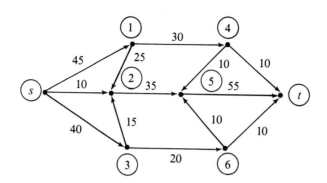

5.

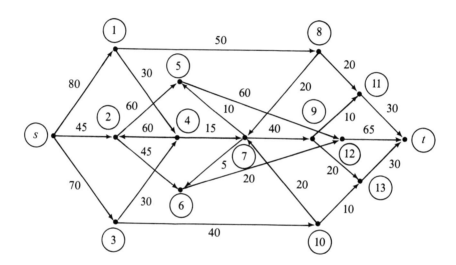

6.

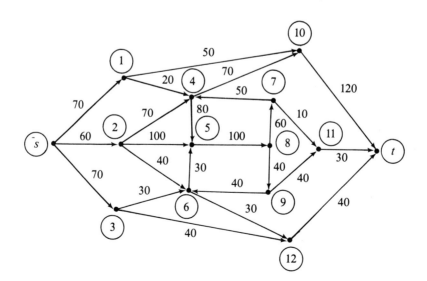

7.

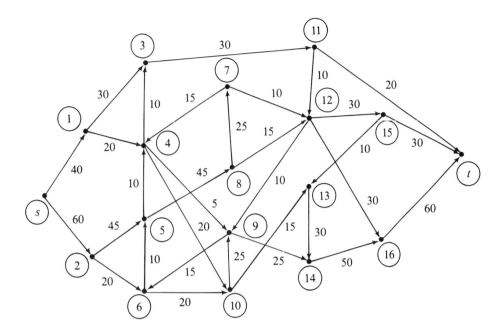

8.

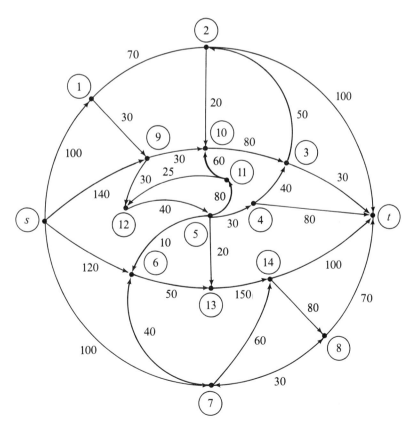

9.

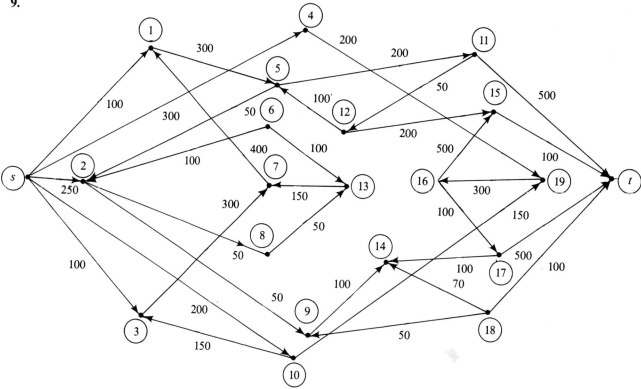

10.

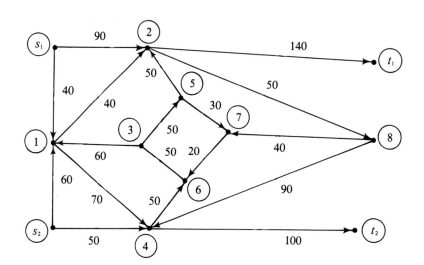

11.

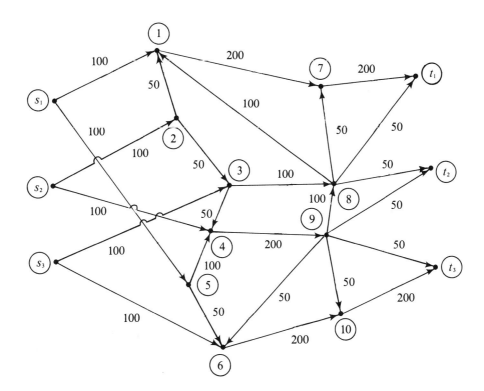

12.

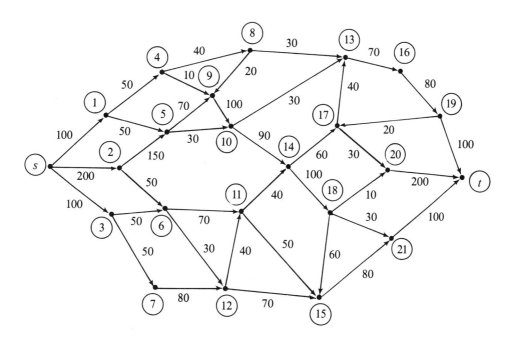

13.

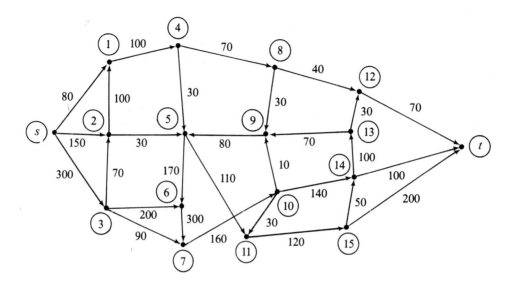

14.

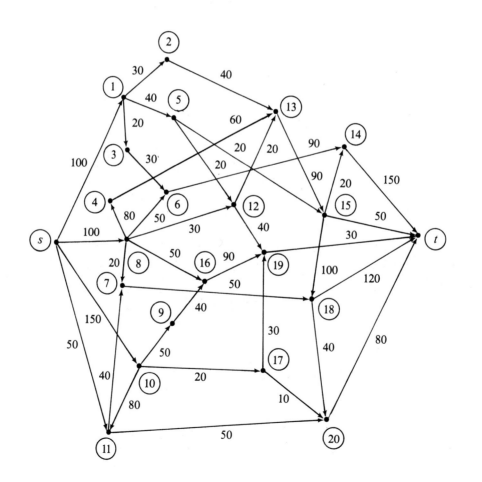

15.

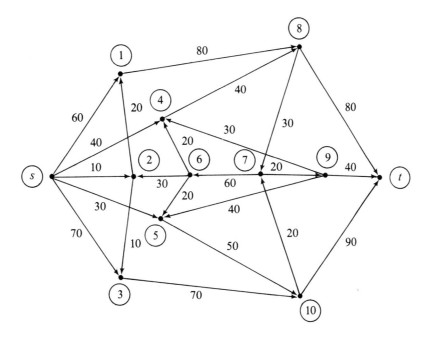

16.

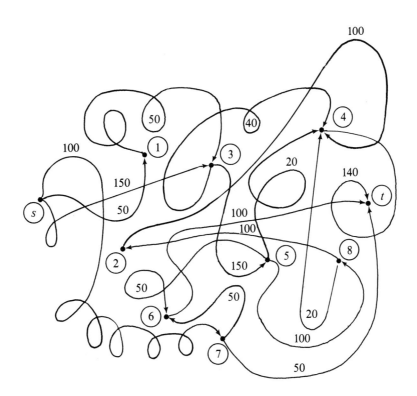

17. a. The following network represents an oil pipeline system. What is the maximal flow for the network?

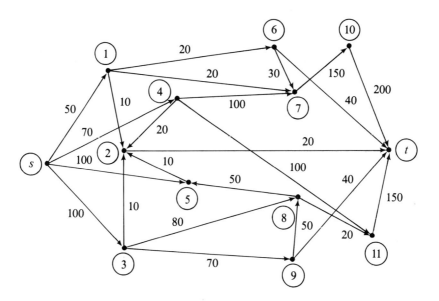

b. The owners of the pipeline system intend to build a pipeline between vertices ④ and ⑤. Which direction should it go and what should be its capacity?

Error Propagation

In Section 4.2 **process graphs** were introduced to represent algebraic expressions. For example, to analyze the general quadratic $ax^2 + bx + c$, first insert parentheses and then draw a tree diagram, such as one of those shown in Figure 5.39. For another example, consider the sum of four numbers, $a + b + c + d$. There are several ways in which parentheses can be inserted to obtain this sum. Figure 5.40 illustrates two of them.

The presentation in this section is modeled on the excellent treatment of William S. Dorn and Daniel D. McCracken, who in *Numerical Methods with Fortran IV Case Studies* (John Wiley & Sons, Inc., 1972) use such trees to understand how errors accumulate in a sequence of arithmetic calculations.

In real-world problems most data consist of approximations. Nearly all measurements of physical quantities are necessarily approximate, no matter how accurate. It is therefore important to have information regarding the ways in which errors are increased or decreased by each calculation in a long sequence of arithmetic operations. Nevertheless, our concern is not with approximations,

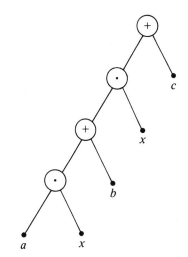

The process graph for $(ax + b)x + c = ax^2 + bx + c.$

FIGURE 5.39(a)

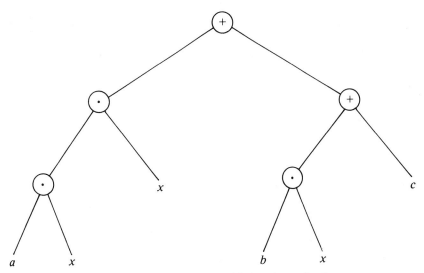

The process graph for $((ax)x) + ((bx) + c) = ax^2 + bx + c.$

FIGURE 5.39(b)

estimates, or "outright blunders" in the input data. Let us accept the fact that most input data are bound to contain errors, and study how these errors are affected by the errors introduced by our computer. Here we might hope to have some control. First, let's see why computers, unless doing simple, small-integer arithmetic, almost always introduce errors into each calculation. The real culprit is the unfortunate fact that machines can use only a few digits of any number's decimal, binary, or hexadecimal representation. Few numbers have a short,

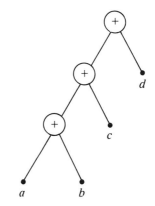

The process graph for $((a + b) + c) + d$.

FIGURE 5.40(a)

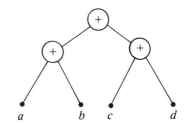

The process graph for $(a + b) + (c + d)$.

FIGURE 5.40(b)

terminating, decimal expression. The ugly consequence is the creation of errors with each calculation. There is really no way to avoid these errors. One must be content with merely keeping them within known bounds.

When I ask my home computer, "What is $\sqrt{2}$?" It responds with $\sqrt{2}$ = 1.414213562. This happens to be correct as far as it goes. To get more digits, I have it calculate

$$10^n\sqrt{2} - \lfloor 10^n\sqrt{2} \rfloor$$

for various values of n. To my surprise, I discover that my machine seems to be confused about the next digits. For $n = 1$, it says 4 is the next digit. (The next digits are actually 373, so this is correct if we round off.) For $n = 2$, it says 61 are the next digits. For $n = 3$, it gives 965. It is clear that it doesn't really know what comes next. When I ask for $\sqrt{3}$, it gives 1.73205081. Since the correct answer to twelve places is 1.732050807568, I guess that my computer has, in general, seven correct digits, but rounds to obtain the eighth. This is a fairly common procedure for small computers and pocket calculators. In "extended precision," larger computers might be programmed to deal with 15 digits. However, it takes longer to do calculations in extended precision, so it is used only in special circumstances.

IMCOM is a very smart computer, but it keeps only four significant figures. Thus, if a user inputs the numbers

$$17384$$
$$389{,}965$$
$$3.7126$$
$$.0013624$$
$$\tfrac{2}{3}$$
$$\sqrt{2}$$

IMCOM immediately rounds and stores these:

$$17380$$
$$390000$$
$$3.713$$
$$.001362$$
$$.6667$$
$$1.414$$

In actual practice it stores four digits and then uses another digit to keep track of the location of the decimal point. That is, it uses **scientific notation**, so that 390,000 is really stored as 3.900×10^5, and .001362 is stored as 1.362×10^{-3}. When called upon to do a numerical calculation, IMCOM uses four significant figures, does *exact* arithmetic with all of them, and then rounds to four significant digits before proceeding to the next calculation. By rounding we mean: leave the fourth digit alone if the fifth digit is less than five; otherwise, add one to the fourth digit. To save time, some machines "chop" (or truncate); that is, they ignore all digits beyond a certain point. We will soon discover that the error caused by rounding never exceeds the error caused by chopping; thus, many machines are programmed to round.

Machine errors are due to rounding. These rounding errors make machine arithmetic very different from exact arithmetic. For example, in theory, addition and multiplication of numbers are **associative**. That is, for any numbers a, b, and c,

$$a + (b + c) = (a + b) + c$$

$$a(bc) = (ab)c$$

In the world of a real computer, these rules do not always hold. To illustrate this point, here are four arithmetic problems for IMCOM.

PROBLEM 5.4   Add: $32{,}130 + (2312 + 24)$.

SOLUTION
$$32{,}130 + (2312 + 24) = 32{,}130 + 2336$$
$$= 34{,}466$$

Since this answer has five digits, IMCOM rounds and responds:

$$32{,}130 + (2312 + 24) = 34{,}470 \qquad \blacksquare$$

PROBLEM 5.5   Add: $(32{,}130 + 2312) + 24$.

SOLUTION
$$(32{,}130 + 2312) + 24 = 34{,}442 + 24$$

Since IMCOM must round after each calculation, this result is changed to $34{,}440 + 24 = 34{,}464$, which is rounded to yield the response:

$$(32{,}130 + 2312) + 24 = 34{,}460 \qquad \blacksquare$$

Problems 1 and 2 can be somewhat unsettling since they show that *addition is not associative in a computer.*

PROBLEM 5.6   Multiply: $(2.31 \times 2.64) \times 3$.

SOLUTION
$$(2.31 \times 2.64) \times 3 = 6.0984 \times 3$$

IMCOM rounds before proceeding:

$$= 6.098 \times 3$$
$$= 18.294$$

The answer: 18.29. $\qquad \blacksquare$

PROBLEM 5.7   Multiply: $2.31 \times (2.64 \times 3)$.

SOLUTION
$$2.31 \times (2.64 \times 3) = 2.31 \times 7.92$$
$$= 18.2952$$

The answer: 18.30. $\qquad \blacksquare$

The errors in Problems 5.6 and 5.7 are small. However, if we were to do several thousand calculations, even relatively small errors could begin to contribute to a significant part of the answer. Some arithmetic operations, such as division, tend to magnify errors. For example, let's divide 1673 by the "answers" to our previous multiplication:

$$1673/18.29 \doteq 91.47$$

$$1673/18.2952 \doteq 91.45$$

$$1673/18.30 \doteq 91.42$$

Here we have a possible error of as much as .03.

Having briefly investigated the origins of errors, we are now ready to begin a detailed analysis. The **error** is usually defined as the true value minus the approximation. Given a number x, we let $a(x)$ denote the **approximation** and

$e(x)$ denote the **error**. Then

$$e(x) = x - a(x)$$

or
$$x = a(x) + e(x)$$

For example, in the answer to Problem 5.4 we have a true value, $x = 34{,}466$; an approximation, $a(x) = 34{,}470$; and an error, $e(x) = -6$:

$$34{,}464 = 34{,}470 + (-6)$$

Note that errors may be positive, negative, or zero.

A more useful concept is that of **relative error**, $r(x)$, which is defined as the ratio of the error to the approximation:

$$r(x) = e(x)/a(x)$$

A more natural definition of relative error is $e(x)/x$, the ratio of the error to the true value. However, as Dorn and McCracken point out, one does not generally know the true value. We will usually know $a(x)$ and have bounds on the size of $e(x)$. Thus, defining $r(x) = e(x)/a(x)$ is more useful and gives a result nearly equal to the more natural quotient.

For Problem 5.4 we have

$$r(x) = -6/34{,}470 \doteq -.0001741$$

or about $-.01741\%$.

Of course, we rarely know $e(x)$ or $r(x)$ exactly. If we did, we could adjust our approximation and present the correct answer. However, we can obtain bounds for these errors and thus have information regarding the accuracy of our approximations. In particular, we can determine how many decimal places of an answer are certain to be correct.

Let's first investigate **symmetric rounding**. To simplify our presentation we will restrict our attention to positive numbers. The sign of a number can be handled separately. We shall see that the size of the round-off error depends upon the number of significant digits kept by the computer. Let t denote this number. For IMCOM, $t = 4$; for many home computers, $t = 8$. Next, given a nonzero number x, we write

$$x = a \times 10^e + b \times 10^{e-t}$$

where a has exactly t digits, $1 \leqslant a < 10$, and $0 \leqslant b < 10$. A few examples will make this clear. Here are three nonzero numbers:

$$x = 37.826140917$$

$$y = 174286.320031$$

$$z = .031430207812$$

If $t = 4$, we can write

$$x = 37.826140917$$
$$= 3.782 \times 10^1 + 6.140917 \times 10^{1-4}$$
$$= 3.782 \times 10^1 + 6.140917 \times 10^{-3}$$

In this case $a = 3.782$, $e = 1$, $b = 6.140917$, and $e - t = 1 - 4 = -3$.

$$y = 174286.320031$$
$$= 1.742 \times 10^5 + 8.6320031 \times 10^{5-4}$$
$$= 1.742 \times 10^5 + 8.6320031 \times 10^1$$

Here we have $a = 1.742$, $e = 5$, $b = 8.6320031$, and $e - t = 5 - 4 = 1$.

$$z = .031430207812$$
$$= 3.143 \times 10^{-2} + .207812 \times 10^{-2-4}$$
$$= 3.143 \times 10^{-2} + .207812 \times 10^{-6}$$

Here $a = 3.143$, $e = -2$, $b = .207812$, and $e - t = -2 - 4 = -6$.

If $t = 8$, we can write

$$x = 37.82614097$$
$$= 3.7826140 \times 10^1 + 9.7 \times 10^{1-8}$$
$$= 3.7826140 \times 10^1 + 9.7 \times 10^{-7}$$

In this case $a = 3.7826140$, $e = 1$, $b = 9.7$, and $e - t = 1 - 8 = -7$.

$$y = 174286.320031$$
$$= 1.7428632 \times 10^5 + .031 \times 10^{5-8}$$
$$= 1.7428632 \times 10^5 + .031 \times 10^{-3}$$

Here we have $a = 1.7428632$, $e = 5$, $b = .031$, and $e - t = 5 - 8 = -3$.

$$z = .031430207812$$
$$= 3.1430207 \times 10^{-2} + 8.12 \times 10^{-2-8}$$
$$= 3.1430207 \times 10^{-2} + 8.12 \times 10^{-10}$$

Here $a = 3.1430207$, $e = -2$, $b = 8.12$, and $e - t = -2 - 8 = -10$. Note that the exponent, e, is the same for any number of significant digits.

The decision on rounding is determined by the size of b. If $b < 5$, we ignore it and use the approximation

$$a(x) = a \times 10^e$$

If $b \geqslant 5$, we add one to the last digit of a. Adding 1 to this last digit is equivalent to adding 10^{-t+1} to a. Thus, we use the approximation

$$a(x) = (a + 10^{-t+1}) \times 10^e = a \times 10^e + 10^{e-t+1}$$

The actual errors in each case are easy to determine:

Case I. $b < 5$:

$$e(x) = a \times 10^e + b \times 10^{e-t} - a \times 10^e$$
$$= b \times 10^{e-t}$$

Case II. $b \geqslant 5$:

$$e(x) = a \times 10^e + b \times 10^{e-t} - (a \times 10^e + 10^{e-t+1})$$
$$= b \times 10^{e-t} - 10^{e-t+1}$$
$$= (b - 10) \times 10^{e-t}$$

We can now determine and bound the relative round-off errors, $r(x)$ in each case.

Case I. $b < 5$:

$$|r(x)| = (b \times 10^{e-t})/(a \times 10^e) = b/a \times 10^{-t}$$

Now how large can this relative error be? The fraction b/a takes on its largest value when b is as large as possible and a is as small as possible; that is, when $b = 5$ and $a = 1$. We obtain the result:

$$|r(x)| \leqslant 5 \times 10^{-t}$$

Case II. $b \geqslant 5$:

$$\begin{aligned} |r(x)| &= |((b - 10) \times 10^{e-t})/((a + 10^{-t+1}) \times 10^e)| \\ &= |(b - 10)/(a + 10^{-t+1})| \times 10^{-t} \end{aligned}$$

Now $|a + 10^{-t+1}|$ can be very slightly less than 1 (if a is near -1) and $|b - 10| \leqslant 5$. Thus, in this case as well,

$$|r(x)| \leqslant 5 \times 10^{-t}$$

If we decide not to round, but *chop* instead, we take $a \times 10^e$ as our approximation in every case. Thus, the **relative chopping error**, $c(x)$, is computed as in Case 1:

$$|c(x)| = |(b \times 10^{e-t})/a \times 10^e| = b/a \times 10^{-t}$$

But now all we know is that $1 \leqslant a$ and $b < 10$. We thus obtain $|c(x)| < 10 \times 10^{-t}$. It follows that rounding is generally more accurate, and therefore probably worthwhile if you can spare the machine time to do it.

To analyze errors, we need one fact from algebra, namely, the **triangle inequality**. This says that if $x_1, \ldots, x_n$ are numbers, then

$$|x_1 + \cdots + x_n| \leqslant |x_1| + \cdots + |x_n|$$

For an outline of the proof see Exercises 29 and 30.

Now we are ready to use process graphs to determine the effect of arithmetic on absolute and relative errors.

Addition.   Suppose we add two numbers:

$$x = a(x) + e(x)$$

and $$y = a(y) + e(y)$$

If, for the moment, we ignore the round-off error introduced by the addition, we can determine the error that results if we approximate the sum by adding the approximations of x and y:

$$x + y = a(x) + a(y) + e(x) + e(y)$$

Thus, $e(x + y) = e(x) + e(y)$. We will also need the relative error:

$$r(x + y) = \frac{e(x) + e(y)}{a(x) + a(y)}$$

$$= \frac{e(x)}{a(x) + a(y)} + \frac{e(y)}{a(x) + a(y)}$$

$$= \frac{a(x)}{a(x) + a(y)}\left(\frac{e(x)}{a(x)}\right) + \frac{a(y)}{a(x) + a(y)}\left(\frac{e(x)}{a(y)}\right)$$

$$= \frac{a(x)}{a(x) + a(y)}r(x) + \frac{a(y)}{a(x) + a(y)}r(y)$$

Subtraction.　Now suppose we wish to subtract two numbers:

$$x = a(x) + e(x)$$

and

$$y = a(y) + e(y)$$

Then

$$x - y = a(x) - a(y) + e(x) - e(y)$$

Thus, $e(x - y) = e(x) - e(y)$. We will also need the relative error:

$$r(x - y) = \frac{e(x) - e(y)}{a(x) - a(y)}$$

$$= \frac{e(x)}{a(x) - a(y)} - \frac{e(y)}{a(x) - a(y)}$$

$$= \frac{a(x)}{a(x) - a(y)}\left(\frac{e(x)}{a(x)}\right) - \frac{a(y)}{a(x) + a(y)}\left(\frac{e(x)}{a(y)}\right)$$

$$= \frac{a(x)}{a(x) - a(y)}r(x) - \frac{a(y)}{a(x) - a(y)}r(y)$$

Multiplication.　We next consider multiplication. Again we take

$$x = a(x) + e(x)$$

$$y = a(y) + e(y)$$

$$xy = (a(x) + e(x))(a(y) + e(y))$$
$$= a(x)a(y) + e(x)a(y) + a(x)e(y) + e(x)e(y)$$

Thus, the error in using the product of the approximations to approximate the product is

$$e(xy) = e(x)a(y) + a(x)e(y) + e(x)e(y)$$

To obtain a nice formula for the relative error, we must approximate. If we are being reasonable, our errors will be fairly small. Thus, $e(x)$ and $e(y)$ will be small numbers. Then their product, $e(x)e(y)$ will be extraordinarily small. In fact, it will be so small it will be insignificant in comparison to $e(x)$ or $e(y)$. For example, if $e(x) = e(y) = .0001$, an error of one digit in the fourth decimal place, then $e(x)e(y) = .00000001$, an error of one digit in the eighth decimal place. This place is irrelevant if our errors are affecting the fourth decimal place. The point is, we are going to ignore the products of errors. Thus, the error in using the product of the approximations to approximate the product is approximately

$$e(xy) \approx e(x)a(y) + a(x)e(y)$$

We compute the relative error:

$$r(xy) = \frac{e(x)a(y) + a(x)e(y)}{a(x)a(y)}$$

$$= \frac{e(x)}{a(x)} + \frac{e(y)}{a(y)}$$

$$= r(x) + r(y)$$

Division. Finally, we turn to division. Again we take

$$x = a(x) + e(x)$$

$$y = a(y) + e(y)$$

Then

$$\frac{x}{y} = \frac{a(x) + e(x)}{a(y) + e(y)}$$

$$= \frac{a(x) + e(x)}{a(y)} \left[\frac{1}{1 + e(y)/a(y)} \right]$$

We now use polynomial long division to divide the term in square brackets:

$$\frac{x}{y} = \frac{a(x) + e(x)}{a(y)} [1 - e(y)/a(y) + (e(y)/a(y))^2 - \cdots]$$

Again we ignore all terms involving products of errors or, in this case, powers of errors.

$$\frac{x}{y} \approx \frac{a(x) + e(x)}{a(y)} [1 - e(y)/a(y)]$$

$$\approx a(x)/a(y) + e(x)/a(y) - [a(x)e(y)]/(a(y))^2$$

Once again we have ignored a product of errors, namely, $[e(x)e(y)]/(a(y))^2$. It follows that the error caused by approximating a quotient by the quotient of the approximations is

$$e(x/y) \approx e(x)/a(y) - [a(x)e(y)]/(a(y))^2$$

To obtain the relative error, we divide this error by $a(x)/a(y)$; that is, we multiply it by $a(y)/a(x)$. The result is

$$r(x/y) \approx e(x)/a(x) - e(y)/a(y)$$

$$= r(x) - r(y)$$

SUMMARY

Suppose $a(x)$ and $a(y)$ are approximations of x and y containing relative errors of $r(x)$ and $r(y)$. Then, ignoring the relative round-off errors in the arithmetic operation, the relative errors in the sum, difference, product, and quotient are

ADDITION:

$$r(x + y) = \frac{a(x)}{a(x) + a(y)}r(x) + \frac{a(y)}{a(x) + a(y)}r(y)$$

SUBTRACTION:

$$r(x - y) = \frac{a(x)}{a(x) - a(y)}r(x) - \frac{a(y)}{a(x) - a(y)}r(y)$$

MULTIPLICATION: $r(xy) \approx r(x) + r(y)$

DIVISION: $r(x/y) \approx r(x) - r(y)$

The Triangle Inequality: If $x_1, \ldots, x_n$ are numbers, then

$$|x_1 + \cdots + x_n| \leqslant |x_1| + \cdots + |x_n|$$

To make use of process graphs in the analysis of errors, we must first decorate the tree. Each edge leading up to a multiplication symbol is labeled with a 1. The left edge leading up to a division symbol is labeled 1, the right edge, -1. See Figure 5.41.

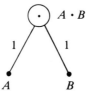 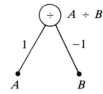

FIGURE 5.41

For edges up to addition and subtraction vertices, the labels depend upon the quantities at the lower end of the edges. In our representation a circled arithmetic operation actually stands for a quantity. We describe two examples. In Section 4.2, where we first introduced process graphs, we agreed to write

          as

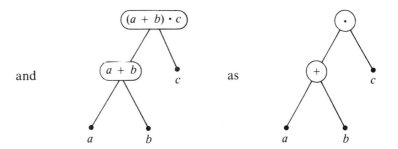

and   as

Thus, the quantity represented by a circled operation may be complicated. If we let A and B represent the quantities at the ends of edges leading into an addition or subtraction vertex, then the edges are labeled as shown in Figure 5.42.

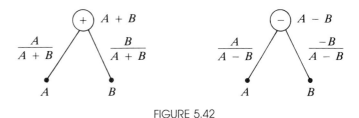

FIGURE 5.42

Note that for each arithmetic operation the edge labels are the factors multiplying the relative errors in the boxed summary above. Here is an example of the labeling process. In Figure 5.43(a) we have drawn a process graph for $[((a + b) \cdot c) + (d \div e)] - f$. In Figure 5.43(b) we have labeled the operation vertices with the quantities present. Finally, Figure 5.43(c) shows the edge labels.

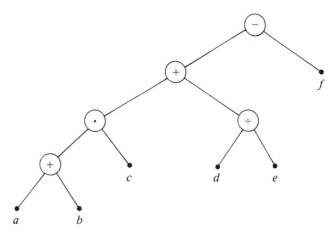

FIGURE 5.43(a)

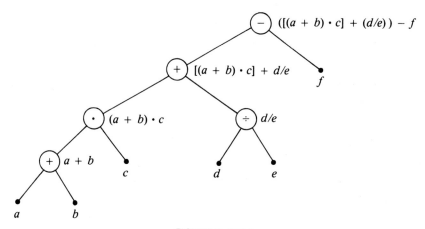

FIGURE 5.43(b)

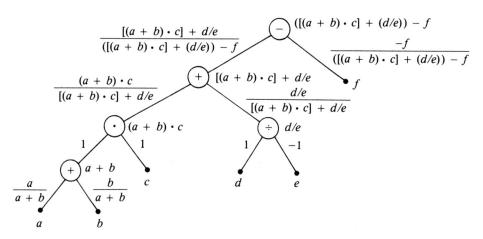

FIGURE 5.43(c)

Now suppose we wish to compute the relative error at a vertex v as shown in Figure 5.44. We have called the edge labels F_1 and F_2 since, without specifying the operation at v, we can't tell which of the four sets of labels described above are appropriate. According to our boxed summary of relative

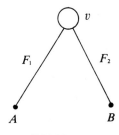

FIGURE 5.44

errors, the relative error at v is

$$F_1 r(A) + F_2 r(B)$$

This takes into account only the relative errors in A and B. It ignores the relative round-off error in the operation at v. Call this relative round-off error r. We can now take the round-off error into account and obtain the total relative error at the vertex v:

$$r(v) = F_1 r(A) + F_2 r(B) + r$$

If our process graph continued above v, this is the relative error we would use in our next calculation. It would take the place of $r(A)$ or $r(B)$ as we move up to the next vertex.

Let's now compare the relative round-off errors in the sums

$$((a + b) + c) + d \quad \text{and} \quad (a + b) + (c + d)$$

assuming the input numbers are exactly correct. Figure 5.45 shows Figure 5.40(a) with the appropriate edge labels. We have also numbered and labeled the

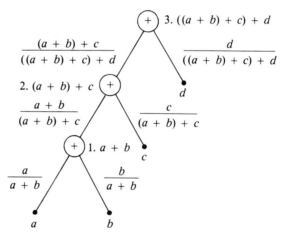

FIGURE 5.45

vertices to make the edge labels less mysterious. Let r_1, r_2, r_3 denote the relative round-off errors in the additions at vertices 1, 2, and 3, respectively. We assume that the input data is exactly correct, so

$$r(a) = r(b) = r(c) = r(d) = 0$$

The relative error at vertex 1 is

$$(a/(a + b))r(a) + (b/(a + b))r(b) + r_1$$

Since $r(a) = r(b) = 0$, this relative error is *all* round-off error:

$$r(v_1) = r_1$$

We now move on to compute the relative error at vertex 2:

$$r(v_2) = [(a+b)/(a+b+c)]r(v_1) + [c/(a+b+c)]r(c) + r_2$$

Then, since $r(c) = 0$, and $r(v_1) = r_1$, we obtain

$$r(v_2) = [(a+b)/(a+b+c)]r_1 + r_2$$

Finally, we move to vertex 3 to compute the relative error in our answer. Let $S = a + b + c + d$. Then

$$r(v_3) = [(a+b+c)/S]r(v_2) + (d/S)r(d) + r_3$$

Since $r(d) = 0$, we have

$$r(v_3) = \{[(a+b)/(a+b+c)]r_1 + r_2\}[(a+b+c)/S] + r_3$$

If we multiply both sides of this equation by S and simplify, we obtain the error in the sum as

$$e(S) = r_1(a+b) + r_2(a+b+c) + r_3 S$$

Thus,

$$
\begin{aligned}
|e(S)| &= |r_1(a+b) + r_2(a+b+c) + r_3(a+b+c+d)| \\
&= |a(r_1 + r_2 + r_3) + b(r_1 + r_2 + r_3) + c(r_2 + r_3) + dr_3| \\
&\leqslant |a(r_1 + r_2 + r_3)| + |b(r_1 + r_2 + r_3)| + |c(r_1 + r_2)| + |dr_3|
\end{aligned}
$$

When we studied symmetric rounding earlier in this section, we found that each round-off error is bounded by 5×10^{-t}, where t is the number of significant figures kept by the computer. It follows that

$$|e(S)| \leqslant |(3a + 3b + 2c + d)| \times 5 \times 10^{-t}$$

A surprising fact emerges. It is better to add the smallest numbers first since the first numbers added contribute most to this error bound.

Before moving on to the process graph for $(a+b)+(c+d)$, we investigate the case in which a, b, c, and d are nearly equal. That is, we assume that

$$b = a + e_1$$

$$c = a + e_2$$

$$d = a + e_3$$

where e_1, e_2, and e_3 are all very small. Then

$$3a + 3b + 2c + d = 3a + 3a + 3e_1 + 2a + 2e_2 + a + e_3$$
$$\approx 9a$$

and the error in the sum is

$$|e[((a+b)+c)+d)]| \leqslant 9|a| \times 5 \times 10^{-t}$$

In Figure 5.46 we have labeled the process graph for $(a+b)+(c+d)$. Again we assume that there is no error in the input numbers. Then the only errors at the first two pluses are the relative round-off errors, r_1 and r_2. The

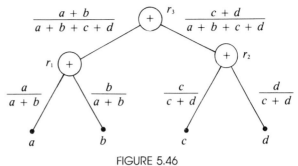

FIGURE 5.46

relative error at v_3 is

$$r(v_3) = r_1[(a+b)/S] + r_2[(a+b)/S] + r_3$$

Here again, $S = a + b + c + d$. Then the actual error is obtained by multiplying the relative error by S:

$$e(S) = r_1(a+b) + r_2(c+d) + r_3 S$$

Finally,

$$|e(S)| \leqslant |2a + 2b + 2c + 2d| \times 5 \times 10^{-t}$$

Note that in the case of nearly equal numbers we have

$$|e(S)| \leqslant 8|a| \times 5 \times 10^{-t}$$

Again we encounter an unexpected result. When adding four nearly equal numbers, it is better to add them as $(a+b)+(c+d)$ than $((a+b)+c)+d)$.

As a final example we turn to the process graph of Figure 5.39(a): $y = (ax+b)x + c$. In Figure 5.47 we have shown the graph with edge labels. For this

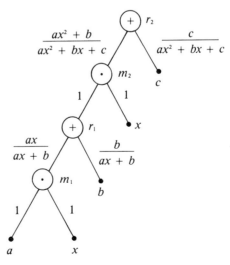

FIGURE 5.47

example we let $r(a)$, $r(b)$, $r(c)$, and $r(x)$ be the relative errors in a, b, c, and x, respectively. We will assume that these relative errors are all round-off errors so that each is less than or equal to 5×10^{-t}. We let m_1 and m_2 denote the relative round-off errors in the multiplications; we let r_1 and r_2 denote the relative round-off errors in the additions. Finally, for this example we will assume that $|x| \leqslant 1$.

We ascend the tree. At the first vertex we have a relative error of

$$r(v_1) = r(a) + r(x) + m_1$$

At the next vertex we have

$$r(v_2) = [r(a) + r(x) + m_1](ax/(ax + b)) + (b/(ax + b))r(b) + r_1$$

At the third vertex we have

$$r(v_3) = [r(a) + r(x) + m_1](ax/(ax + b)) + (b/(ax + b))r(b) + r_1 + r(x) + m_2$$

To save space, we let $y = ax^2 + bx + c$. Then finally, at the last vertex we have

$$r(y) = \{[r(a) + r(x) + m_1](ax/(ax + b)) + (b/(ax + b))r(b) \\ + r_1 + r(x) + m_2\}(ax^2 + bx)/y + [c/y]r(c) + r_2$$

If we multiply both sides by y, we obtain the absolute error in y:

$$e(y) = \{[r(a) + r(x) + m_1](ax/(ax + b)) + (b/(ax + b))r(b) \\ + r_1 + r(x) + m_2\}(ax^2 + bx) + cr(c) + r_2 y$$

$$e(y) = \{[r(a) + r(x) + m_1]ax + br(b) \\ + (r_1 + r(x) + m_2)(ax + b)\}x + cr(c) + r_2 y$$

Or, rearranging:

$$e(y) = ax^2[r(a) + 2r(x) + m_1 + r_2 + r_1 + m_2] \\ + bx[r(b) + r_1 + r(x) + m_2 + r_2] + c(r(c) + r_2)$$

Our assumptions on all the relative errors and on the size of x allow us to simplify this to obtain

$$|e(y)| \leqslant (7|a| + 5|b| + 2|c|) \times 5 \times 10^{-t}$$

EXERCISES

1. Write an expression that equals the nth digit to the right of the decimal point of a given number x.

2. Show that $\lfloor x + 0.5 \rfloor$ rounds x to the nearest unit.

3. Write an expression that rounds x to the nearest .001.

4. Write an expression that chops x at the third digit to the right of the decimal point.

5. Write $.2 = \frac{1}{5}$ in binary by using long division to divide 1 by 101_2.

6. Write $.6 = \frac{3}{5}$ in hexadecimal by dividing 3 by 5 in base 16.

7. Work the following problems as IMCOM would and compare your answers.

   a. $(3.7184 + .0002) + .0003$

   b. $3.7184 + (.0002 + .0003)$

8. Work the following problems as IMCOM would and compare your answers.

   a. $(2.31 \times 2.46) \times 3.2$

   b. $2.31 \times (2.46 \times 3.2)$

In Exercises 9–18 given two of x, $a(x)$, $e(x)$, and $r(x)$, find the other two.

9. $x = 37.246$, $a(x) = 37.25$.

10. $x = .0012478$, $a(x) = .001248$.

11. $a(x) = 1.327$, $e(x) = .0003$.

12. $a(x) = 276.5$, $e(x) = -.0002$.

13. $x = 7.1284$, $e(x) = .0004$.

14. $x = 384,729$, $e(x) = -29$.

15. $r(x) = .02$, $a(x) = 3.1$.

16. $r(x) = .0013$, $a(x) = -76.4$.

17. $r(x) = .012$, $e(x) = -.0012$.

18. $r(x) = .0045$, $e(x) = .036$.

In Exercises 19–22 write each given number x in the form $a \times 10^e + b \times 10^{e-t}$, where a has exactly t digits, $1 \leqslant |a| < 10$, and $0 \leqslant |b| < 10$, for the given number t.

19. $x = 378.26170917$, $t = 6$

20. $x = 174986.320031$, $t = 3$

21. $x = .031402007812$, $t = 6$

22. $x = 3.141592653589793238$, $t = 15$

23. Verify that in Exercise 19, rounding x to t digits is equivalent to adding 10^{-t+1} to a.

24. Verify that in Exercise 20, rounding x to t digits is equivalent to adding 10^{-t+1} to a.

25. Calculate $r(x)$ directly for rounding x in Exercise 19 at the sixth significant digit.

26. Calculate $r(x)$ directly for rounding x in Exercise 20 at the third significant digit.

In Exercises 27 and 28 let $x = 2.1$, $a(x) = 2$, $y = 6.03$, $a(y) = 6$.

27. a. Verify the first result in the boxed summary on page 238.

   b. Calculate the error in using the approximation in the third result in the boxed summary.

28. a. Verify the second result in the boxed summary on page 238.

b. Calculate the error in using the approximation in the fourth result in the boxed summary.

In Exercises 29 and 30 we will verify the triangle inequality.

29. If $x_1 \geqslant 0$, then $-|x_1| \leqslant 0 \leqslant x_1 = |x_1|$. If $x_1 \leqslant 0$, then $-|x_1| = x_1 \leqslant 0 \leqslant |x_1|$. Thus, in either case,

$$-|x_1| \leqslant x_1 \leqslant |x_1|$$

Similarly for x_2. Recall that $|x| \leqslant a$ is equivalent to $-a \leqslant x \leqslant a$, provided that $a \geqslant 0$. Use these facts to verify that

$$|x_1 + x_2| \leqslant |x_1| + |x_2|$$

30. Use induction and Exercise 29 to prove that the triangle inequality is valid for any finite number of numbers $x_1, \ldots, x_n$.

31. Pretend you are IMCOM and consider the following numbers:

$$
\begin{array}{l}
.0000063 \\
.000021 \\
.00054 \\
.0043 \\
.012 \\
.94 \\
3.8 \\
12.0
\end{array}
$$

Add them in the order given and then in the reverse order and compare the results.

32. Add as if you were IMCOM:

   a. $(6.123 + 6.124) + (6.125 + 6.127)$

   b. $((6.123 + 6.124) + 6.125) + 6.127$

and compare the results.

In Exercises 33–38 draw a process graph for the given algebraic expression and label the edges appropriately.

33. $(((a + b) + c) + d) + e$

34. $((ab)c)d$

35. $(ab)(cd)$

36. $a + (b - (c + d))$

37. $a \cdot ((b - c) + d)$

38. $(a - b) - (c - d)$

Let m_1, m_2, m_3 denote the relative round-off errors in the multiplications, and $r(a)$, $r(b)$, $r(c)$, and $r(d)$ denote the relative errors in the input numbers. In Exercises 39 and 40 use a process graph to determine the relative error in the given expression.

39. $((ab)c)d$

40. $(ab)(cd)$
What can you conclude?

41. Label the edges of the process graph in Figure 5.39(b). With the same assumptions on the quantities

as made in the example on page 244, calculate the absolute error in the quadratic $((ax)x + bx) + c$. Compare this method of evaluation to the one given by Figure 5.39(a).

42. (From Dorn and McCracken) Assume that the numbers a, b, and x are positive and exactly correct. Use process graphs to show that the error bounds for $ax + b(x^2)$ and $x(a + bx)$ are the same. Use $a = 0.7625$, $b = 0.6947$, and $x = 0.4302$ (with four-place arithmetic a la IMCOM) to show that the errors themselves might not be equal.

CHAPTER
SIX

Relations, Algebraic Systems, and Machines

6.1 Relational Closures and Equivalence Relations

6.2 Posets, Lattices, and Boolean Algebras

6.3 Monoids and Groups

6.4 Symmetries, Permutations, Rings, and Fields

6.5 Machines

RELATIONS WERE INTRODUCED in Section 1.3. If A and B are sets, a **binary relation** from A to B is a subset R of the cartesian product $A \times B$. The statement $(a, b) \in$ R is written a R b. Three types of relations are of great importance in computer science and mathematics: equivalence relations, partial orders, and functions. Equivalence relations and partial orders are the subjects of the first two sections of this chapter. Functions were defined in Section 1.3 and have already been studied in several parts of this book. A special type of function called a binary operation will be defined and used in several sections of this chapter, as will an important way of combining functions, called composition. Finally, ideas of functions, arrays, and directed pseudographs will be combined to create fundamental mathematical models of computers, known as machines.

6.1
Relational Closures and Equivalence Relations

Let R be a relation from a set A to a set B. Suppose A and B are finite but not empty; say $A = \{a_1, ..., a_m\}$ and $B = \{b_1, ..., b_n\}$. Then R may be conveniently represented by its **characteristic matrix**, which is the $m \times n$ matrix $[r_{ij}]$, where r_{ij} is 1 if a_i R b_j and 0 otherwise.

EXAMPLE 6.1   The characteristic matrix of the relation "less than" from $\{1, 2, 4\}$ to $\{1, 2, 3, 5\}$ is

$$\begin{bmatrix} 0 & 1 & 1 & 1 \\ 0 & 0 & 1 & ① \\ 0 & 0 & 0 & 1 \end{bmatrix}$$

The circled entry, r_{24}, is 1, because $a_2 = 2$ is less than $b_4 = 5$.   ■

EXAMPLE 6.2   An integer a **divides** an integer b if there is an integer c such that $b = ac$. In that case we write $a|b$. For example, $3|6$, $5|20$, but 4 does not divide 18. The characteristic matrix of the relation "divides" from $\{1, 2, 3\}$ to $\{1, 2, 4, 6\}$ is

$$\begin{bmatrix} 1 & 1 & 1 & 1 \\ 0 & 1 & 1 & 1 \\ 0 & 0 & 0 & 1 \end{bmatrix}$$

■

By a **relation on** a set A we mean a relation from A to A.

A relation R on A is **reflexive** if

$$x \text{ R } x, \text{ for all } x \text{ in } A \tag{1}$$

EXAMPLE 6.3   On any set the relation "equals" is reflexive. On any set of integers the relation "divides" is also reflexive. On any nonempty set the relation "does not equal" is not reflexive.   ■

Any relation R on a nonempty set of n elements has an $n \times n$ *square* characteristic matrix $[r_{ij}]$. Such a relation is reflexive if and only if each entry on the **main diagonal**—$r_{11}, r_{22}, \ldots, r_{nn}$—is 1. If R is not reflexive, we may **extend** it to a reflexive relation by adjoining more ordered pairs. If a pair (a_i, a_i) is not in R, then it must be adjoined. Once all such pairs are adjoined, the extended relation will be reflexive, and no more pairs need be adjoined. This extended relation is called the **reflexive closure** of R and is denoted $\bar{R}^r$. For example, the reflexive closure of the relation "less than" on the integers is "less than or equal."

To summarize: $\bar{R}^r$ is an extension of R (that is, $R \subset \bar{R}^r$) and is reflexive. Moreover, if Q is any reflexive extension of R, then $\bar{R}^r \subset Q$. In other words, the reflexive closure of a relation is its minimal reflexive extension. The reflexive closure of a relation on a finite set is easily found from its characteristic matrix, as shown in Program 6.1. In this algorithm c counts the number of entry changes from 0 to 1.

PROGRAM 6.1   **To check whether or not a relation R on a finite nonempty n-element set is reflexive, and if it is not, to find $\bar{R}^r$.**

1. $i \leftarrow 1; c \leftarrow 0$
2. If $r_{ii} = 0$ go to 6
3. $i \leftarrow i + 1$
4. If $i = n + 1$ go to 7
5. Go to 2
6. $r_{ii} \leftarrow 1; c \leftarrow c + 1$, go to 3
7. If $c = 0$ go to 9
8. "R is not reflexive. The characteristic matrix of $\bar{R}^r$ is $[r_{ij}]$." STOP
9. "R is reflexive." STOP   ■

A relation R on a set A is **symmetric** if

$$x \, R \, y \text{ implies } y \, R \, x, \text{ for all } x \text{ and } y \text{ in } A \qquad (2)$$

EXAMPLE 6.4   On any set the relations "equals" and "does not equal" are symmetric. On any set of numbers that contains more than one number the relation "less than" is not symmetric. On any set of positive integers with more than one number the relation "divides" is not symmetric either.   ■

If A is nonempty and finite, then R is symmetric if and only if its characteristic matrix $[r_{ij}]$ is symmetric, in the sense that, for all i and j, $r_{ij} = r_{ji}$. The **symmetric closure** $\bar{R}^s$ of R is the symmetric extension of R that is contained in every symmetric extension of R. This closure is easily obtained from any relation R on $A = \{a_1, \ldots, a_n\}$ as follows. For each i, j with $1 \leqslant i < j \leqslant n$, if $a_i \, R \, a_j$, then adjoin (a_j, a_i), if it is not already in R. In terms of $[r_{ij}]$ we have Program 6.2.

■ PROGRAM 6.2   **To check whether or not a relation R on a finite n-element set is symmetric and, if it is not, to find $\bar{R}^s$.**

1. $i \leftarrow 1; c \leftarrow 0$
2. $j \leftarrow i + 1$
3. If $j = n + 1$ go to 7
4. If $r_{ij} = r_{ji}$ go to 6
5. $r_{ij} \leftarrow 1; r_{ji} \leftarrow 1; c \leftarrow c + 1$
6. $j \leftarrow j + 1$, go to 3
7. $i \leftarrow i + 1$
8. If $i = n$ go to 10
9. Go to 2
10. If $c \neq 0$ go to 12
11. "R is symmetric." STOP
12. "R is not symmetric. The characteristic matrix of $\bar{R}^s$ is $[r_{ij}]$." STOP   ■

EXAMPLE 6.5   A **proper divisor** of an integer $n \neq 0$ is a divisor other than $-n, -1, 1,$ or n. For instance, the proper divisors of 6 are $-3, -2, 2, 3$; the integer 7 has no proper divisors. Let R be the relation "is a proper divisor of" on the set $\{2, 3, 4, 6\}$. The characteristic matrix of R is

$$\begin{bmatrix} 0 & 0 & 1 & 1 \\ 0 & 0 & 0 & 1 \\ 0 & 0 & 0 & 0 \\ 0 & 0 & 0 & 0 \end{bmatrix}$$

The characteristic matrix of $\bar{R}^r$ is

$$\begin{bmatrix} 1 & 0 & 1 & 1 \\ 0 & 1 & 0 & 1 \\ 0 & 0 & 1 & 0 \\ 0 & 0 & 0 & 1 \end{bmatrix}$$

This is the relation |, "divides."

The matrix of $\bar{R}^s$ is

$$\begin{bmatrix} 0 & 0 & 1 & 1 \\ 0 & 0 & 0 & 1 \\ 1 & 0 & 0 & 0 \\ 1 & 1 & 0 & 0 \end{bmatrix}$$

This is the relation "is a proper divisor or a proper multiple of."

The matrices of $\bar{R}^{rs}$ and $\bar{R}^{sr}$ are the same (Exercise 25):

$$\begin{bmatrix} 1 & 0 & 1 & 1 \\ 0 & 1 & 0 & 1 \\ 1 & 0 & 1 & 0 \\ 1 & 1 & 0 & 1 \end{bmatrix}$$

This is the relation "is a divisor or a multiple of." □

A relation R on a set A is **transitive** if

$$x \, R \, y \text{ and } y \, R \, z \text{ implies } x \, R \, z, \text{ for all } x, y, \text{ and } z \text{ in } A \qquad (3)$$

EXAMPLE 6.6   On any set the relation "is equal to" is transitive. On any set with more than one element "is not equal to" is not transitive: although Implication (3) will hold for some choices of x, y, z, it will not hold for *all*. On any set of integers the relation "divides" is transitive, as you should verify algebraically. □

If A is nonempty and finite, then R is transitive if and only if, for all i, j, k,

$$r_{ik} = 1 \text{ and } r_{kj} = 1 \text{ implies } r_{ij} = 1 \qquad (4)$$

If for some i, j, k, Implication (4) does not hold, then it must be that $r_{ik} = 1$, $r_{kj} = 1$, and $r_{ij} = 0$. Then extend the relation R by replacing r_{ij} by 1. If the extended relation is still not transitive, then there will be some i, j, k for which (4) fails; then extend again. Eventually you will reach the **transitive closure** $\bar{R}^t$ of R: the transitive extension of R that is contained in every transitive extension of R. (It is not obvious from this argument that every relation on an infinite set has a transitive closure. This is, however, true.)

It is harder to devise a reasonably efficient algorithm for transitive closure than it was for reflexive and symmetric closures. One such algorithm, due to S. Warshall in 1962, is Program 6.3. The idea is to first find each case of

Implication (4) with $k = 1$ that does not hold, and replace r_{ij} by 1 whenever required; then do the same with $k = 2$, and so on through $k = n$.

■ PROGRAM 6.3   **Warshall's Algorithm for transitive closure.**

    1. $k \leftarrow 1, c \leftarrow 0$

    2. $i \leftarrow 1$

    3. $j \leftarrow 1$

    4. If $r_{ij} = 1$ go to 8

    5. If $r_{kj} = 0$ go to 8

    6. If $r_{ik} = 0$ go to 8

    7. $r_{ij} \leftarrow 1, c \leftarrow c + 1$

    8. If $j = n$ go to 10

    9. $j \leftarrow j + 1$, go to 4

    10. If $i = n$ go to 12

    11. $i \leftarrow i + 1$, go to 3

    12. If $k = n$ go to 14

    13. $k \leftarrow k + 1$, go to 2

    14. If $c = 0$ go to 16

    15. "R is not transitive. The characteristic matrix of $\bar{R}^t$ is $[r_{ij}]$." STOP

    16. "R is transitive." STOP   ■

EXAMPLE 6.7   Let $A = \{a_1, a_2, a_3, a_4\}$ and $R = \{(a_1, a_2), (a_2, a_3), (a_3, a_4)\}$. Then, for instance, Implication (4) fails for $i = 1, j = 3, k = 2$. Program 6.3 adjoins pairs to R in the following order:

$$k = 1: \text{none}$$

$$k = 2: (a_1, a_3)$$

$$k = 3: (a_1, a_4), (a_2, a_4)$$

$$k = 4: \text{none}$$

Thus,

$$\bar{R}^t = \{(a_1, a_2), (a_1, a_3), (a_1, a_4), (a_2, a_3), (a_2, a_4), (a_3, a_4)\}$$

The reader should write the characteristic matrix of R, follow its modifications to STOP, and check that $\bar{R}^t$ is transitive.   ▢

It is not obvious that $\bar{R}^t$ as constructed by Warshall's Algorithm really is the transitive closure of R. We present a proof that it is. First, since the algorithm begins with the characteristic matrix of R and never replaces a 1 by a 0, $\bar{R}^t$ is an extension of R. Next, to show that $\bar{R}^t$ is transitive, suppose that $a_i\,\bar{R}^t\,a_m$ and $a_m\,\bar{R}^t\,a_j$. Let p be the smallest integer such that $a_i\,\bar{R}^t\,a_p$ and $a_p\,\bar{R}^t\,a_j$. It might be that r_{ij} is already 1 before k reaches p. If not, then while $k = p$, r_{ij} will be replaced by 1. Hence, $a_i\,\bar{R}^t\,a_j$, and so $\bar{R}^t$ is transitive. Finally, suppose T is a transitive extension of R and $a_i\,\bar{R}^t\,a_j$. For $1 \leqslant m \leqslant n$, let R_m be R together with all ordered pairs added by the algorithm for $1 \leqslant k \leqslant m$. Then $\bar{R}^t$ is R_n. If $a_i\,R_1\,a_j$, then either $a_i\,R\,a_j$, in which case $a_i\,T\,a_j$, or $a_i\,R\,a_1$ and $a_1\,R\,a_j$, in which case $a_i\,T\,a_1$ and $a_1\,T\,a_j$, which implies $a_i\,T\,a_j$. Thus, $R_1 \subset T$. If $a_i\,R_2\,a_j$, then either $a_i\,R_1\,a_j$, in which case $a_i\,T\,a_j$, or $a_i\,R_1\,a_2$ and $a_2\,R_1\,a_j$, in which case $a_i\,T\,a_2$ and $a_2\,T\,a_j$, which implies $a_i\,T\,a_j$. Thus, $R_2 \subset T$. Continuing like this, we eventually have $R_n \subset T$; that is, T is an extension of $\bar{R}^t$.

An **equivalence relation** on a set A is a relation on A that is reflexive, symmetric, and transitive.

EXAMPLE 6.8   On any set "is equal to" is an equivalence relation. On any set of propositions "is equivalent to" is an equivalence relation.   ◻

Another example of an equivalence relation is congruence on the set **Z** of integers. Let n be a positive integer. Two integers a and b are **congruent modulo n** if their difference is an integer multiple of n. For example, 12 is congruent to 77 modulo 5, since $12 - 77 = -65 = 5(-13)$. The statement "a is congruent to b modulo n" is written

$$a \equiv b(\bmod\ n)$$

Thus, $12 \equiv 77(\bmod\ 5)$, $8 \equiv 120(\bmod\ 14)$, and $79 \equiv 13(\bmod\ 2)$. Two integers are congruent modulo 2 if and only if they are either both odd or both even.

EXAMPLE 6.9   Congruence modulo n is an equivalence relation on **Z**.

(i) Reflexive: If $x \in \mathbf{Z}$, then $x - x = n \cdot 0$, so

$$x \equiv x(\bmod\ n)$$

(ii) Symmetric: Suppose $x \equiv y(\bmod\ n)$; say $x - y = nq$. Then $y - x = n(-q)$, so

$$y \equiv x(\bmod\ n)$$

(iii) Transitive: Suppose $x \equiv y(\bmod\ n)$ and $y \equiv z(\bmod\ n)$; say $x - y = nq_1$ and $y - z = nq_2$. Then $x - z = (x - y) + (y - z) = n(q_1 + q_2)$, so

$$x \equiv z(\bmod\ n)$$ ◻

If an integer x is divided by a positive integer n, there will be a quotient q and a nonnegative remainder r less than n. That is, $x = nq + r$, $0 \leqslant r \leqslant n - 1$. Then $x - r = nq$, so $x \equiv r(\bmod\ n)$. Thus, every integer is congruent modulo n to one of the integers $0, 1, \ldots, n - 1$. For instance, 79 divided by 8 gives a quotient of 9 and a remainder of 7: $79 = 8 \cdot 9 + 7$; so $79 \equiv 7(\bmod\ 8)$. Similarly, every integer is congruent modulo 8 to one of 0, 1, 2, 3, 4, 5, 6, 7.

Suppose that an integer x is congruent modulo n to r_1 and to r_2, where $0 \leqslant r_1 \leqslant n - 1$ and $0 \leqslant r_2 \leqslant n - 1$. Then $r_1 \equiv r_2(\bmod\ n)$, so $r_1 - r_2$ is an integer multiple of n. Now $r_1 - r_2$ is between $-(n - 1)$ and $(n - 1)$, and the integer multiples of n are $0, n, -n, 2n, -2n, \ldots$. Hence, $r_1 - r_2$ must be 0, so $r_1 = r_2$. We have shown that every integer is congruent modulo n to one and only one integer in the set

$$\mathbf{Z}_n = \{0, 1, \ldots, n - 1\}$$

This set is called the **integers modulo n**.

Congruence modulo n **preserves** addition and multiplication in the following sense. For all x, x_1, y, y_1 in $\mathbf{Z}$, if

$$x \equiv x_1(\bmod\ n) \text{ and } y \equiv y_1(\bmod\ n)$$

then $\qquad\qquad x + y \equiv x_1 + y_1(\bmod\ n) \text{ and } xy \equiv x_1 y_1(\bmod\ n) \qquad$ **(5)**

We prove this directly. Suppose $x - x_1 = nq_1$ and $y - y_1 = nq_2$ for some q_1, q_2 in $\mathbf{Z}$. Then $x + y - (x_1 + y_1) = x - x_1 + y - y_1 = nq_1 + nq_2 = n(q_1 + q_2)$. Then since $q_1 + q_2$ is an integer, $x + x_1 \equiv y + y_1(\bmod\ n)$. Also, $xy - x_1 y_1 = xy - (x - nq_1)(y - nq_2) = xy - (xy - xnq_2 - nq_1 y + nq_1 nq_2) = xy - xy + xnq_2 + nq_1 y - nq_1 nq_2 = n(xq_2 + q_1 y - q_1 nq_2)$. Then since $xq_2 + q_1 y - q_1 nq_2$ is an integer, $xy \equiv x_1 y_1(\bmod\ n)$.

Since every integer is congruent modulo n to one and only one element of $\mathbf{Z}_n$, we may, in view of Result (5), restrict the operations $+$ and $\times$ to $\mathbf{Z}_n$ without losing any information modulo n. These restrictions are called **addition modulo n** and **multiplication modulo n** and are denoted $+_n$ and $\times_n$. (The subscript n is omitted when n has been specified elsewhere, and $a \times_n b$ is then written simply ab.) Consider, for example, $n = 5$. $\mathbf{Z}_5 = \{0, 1, 2, 3, 4\}$. Now $3 + 4 = 7$ and $7 \equiv 2(\bmod\ 5)$. Thus, if $x \equiv 3(\bmod\ 5)$ and $y \equiv 4(\bmod\ 5)$, then $x + y \equiv 2(\bmod\ 5)$. We may express this by simply writing $3 +_5 4 = 2$. Similarly, $2 \times 4 = 8 \equiv 3(\bmod\ 5)$; so $2 \times_5 4 = 3$. The complete addition and multiplication tables for $\mathbf{Z}_5$ and $\mathbf{Z}_6$ are as follows:

$+_5$	0	1	2	3	4
0	0	1	2	3	4
1	1	2	3	4	0
2	2	3	4	0	1
3	3	4	0	1	2
4	4	0	1	2	3

$\times_5$	0	1	2	3	4
0	0	0	0	0	0
1	0	1	2	3	4
2	0	2	4	1	3
3	0	3	1	4	2
4	0	4	3	2	1

$+_6$	0	1	2	3	4	5
0	0	1	2	3	4	5
1	1	2	3	4	5	0
2	2	3	4	5	0	1
3	3	4	5	0	1	2
4	4	5	0	1	2	3
5	5	0	1	2	3	4

$\times_6$	0	1	2	3	4	5
0	0	0	0	0	0	0
1	0	1	2	3	4	5
2	0	2	4	0	2	4
3	0	3	0	3	0	3
4	0	4	2	0	4	2
5	0	5	4	3	2	1

We shall have more to say about modular arithmetic in Sections 6.3 and 6.4.

A **partition** of a nonempty set A is a family of nonempty subsets of A such that each element of A is in one and only one member of the family.

EXAMPLE 6.10   Let $A = \{1, 2, 3, 4, 5\}$. Then $\{\{1, 2\}, \{3\}, \{4, 5\}\}$, $\{\{1\}, \{2\}, \{3\}, \{4\}, \{5\}\}$, and $\{\{1, 2, 3, 4, 5\}\}$ are three different partitions of A. The family $\{\{1, 2, 4\}, \{5\}\}$ is not a partition of A, because 3 is in no member. The family $\{\{1, 2, 3\}, \{3, 4, 5\}\}$ is not a partition of A because 3 is in two members. The family $\{\{1, 2, 3\}, \{4, 5, 6\}\}$ is not a partition of A, because $\{4, 5, 6\}$ is not a subset of A. □

There is a close connection between partitions of A and equivalence relations on A, which is established with the following notation. If R is an equivalence relation on A and $a \in A$, the **equivalence class** of a under R is

$$[a] = \{x \in A : x \mathrel{R} a\} \tag{6}$$

EXAMPLE 6.11   Let $A = \{1, 2, 3, 4, 5\}$ and R be congruence modulo 3. Then

$$[1] = \{1, 4\}, \; [2] = \{2, 5\}, \; [3] = \{3\}, \; [4] = [1], \text{ and } [5] = [2] \qquad □$$

THEOREM 6.1   Let A be a nonempty set. If R is an equivalence relation on A, then the family of all equivalence classes of elements of A under R is a partition of A. If P is a partition of A, then there is one and only one equivalence relation on A, the family of whose equivalence classes is P.

PROOF   Let R be an equivalence relation on A and let P be the family of all equivalence classes of elements of A:

$$P = \{[a] : a \in A\}$$

By Definition (6) each member of P is a subset of A. If $a \in A$, then $a \in [a]$, since $a \mathrel{R} a$; so each member of P is nonempty, and each element of A is in at least one member of P. Suppose that c is in two elements, $[a]$ and $[b]$ of P. We show that $[a] = [b]$. If $x \in [a]$, then $x \mathrel{R} a$. Since $c \in [a]$, $c \mathrel{R} a$. Then by symmetry, $a \mathrel{R} c$.

Then by transitivity, $x\,\mathsf{R}\,a$ and $a\,\mathsf{R}\,c \Rightarrow x\,\mathsf{R}\,c$. Since $c \in [b]$, $c\,\mathsf{R}\,b$. Then by transitivity, $x\,\mathsf{R}\,c$ and $c\,\mathsf{R}\,b \Rightarrow x\,\mathsf{R}\,b$; so $x \in [b]$. Similarly, if $x \in [b]$, then $x \in [a]$. Hence, $[a] = [b]$. We have shown that each element of A is in one and only one member of P. Thus, P is a partition of A.

Now suppose that P is a partition of A. Define a relation R on A as follows: $x\,\mathsf{R}\,y$ if and only if x and y are in the same member of P. We will show that R is an equivalence relation on A. Obviously, R is reflexive and symmetric. Suppose $x\,\mathsf{R}\,y$ and $y\,\mathsf{R}\,z$. Then x and y are in the same member, say B, of P; and y and z are in the same member, say C, of P. Then y is in B and C; so, since P is a partition, $B = C$. Then x and z are in the same member of P; that is, $x\,\mathsf{R}\,z$. Thus, R is transitive and hence is an equivalence relation on A.

We must now show that the family of all equivalence classes of the relation R is P. Suppose $a \in A$. Say a is in the member B of P. Then

$$[a] = \{x \in A : x \text{ and } a \text{ are in the same member of } P\}$$
$$= \{x \in A : x \in B\} = B$$

Thus, each equivalence class is a member of P. Conversely, if B is a member of P and $a \in B$, then as we have just shown, $B = [a]$. Thus, each member of P is an equivalence class.

We have shown that the family of all equivalence classes of R is P. Finally, suppose R' is an equivalence relation on A, the family of whose equivalence classes is P. We must show that $\mathsf{R}' = \mathsf{R}$. Suppose $a\,\mathsf{R}'\,b$. The equivalence class of a under R' is a member B of P, which contains a and b. Since a and b are in the same member of P, $a\,\mathsf{R}\,b$. Conversely, suppose $a\,\mathsf{R}\,b$, say a and b are in the same member B of P. Since $a \in B$, the equivalence class of a under R' is B. Then since $b \in B$, we have $b\,\mathsf{R}'\,a$ and hence $a\,\mathsf{R}'\,b$. We have shown that, for all a and b in A, $a\,\mathsf{R}'\,b$ if and only if $a\,\mathsf{R}\,b$. Thus, $\mathsf{R}' = \mathsf{R}$.

This concludes the proof.   □

We see from this theorem that the connection between partitions and equivalence relations is indeed close: they are, in fact, two versions of the same idea.

EXERCISES

In Exercises 1–4 write the characteristic matrix of the given relation.

1. "precedes in alphabetical order," from {a, c, d, e} to {b, c, d, g}.

2. "precedes in alphabetical order," from {every, good, girl} to {studies, computer, science}.

3. "is not equal to," from {2, 4, 6, 8} to itself.

4. "is less than or equal to," from {2, 4, 6, 8} to itself.

In Exercises 5–12 find a relation on the set of all integers that has the stated properties.

5. not reflexive, not symmetric, not transitive.

6. not reflexive, not symmetric, transitive.

7. not reflexive, symmetric, not transitive.

8. reflexive, not symmetric, not transitive.

9. not reflexive, symmetric, transitive.

10. reflexive, not symmetric, transitive.

11. reflexive, symmetric, not transitive.

12. reflexive, symmetric, transitive.

Let R_1 and R_2 be relations on $\{a_1, a_2, a_3, a_4\}$ with respective characteristic matrices

$$\begin{bmatrix} 1 & 0 & 1 & 0 \\ 0 & 0 & 1 & 1 \\ 1 & 0 & 0 & 0 \\ 1 & 1 & 0 & 1 \end{bmatrix} \text{ and } \begin{bmatrix} 0 & 0 & 0 & 1 \\ 1 & 0 & 0 & 0 \\ 0 & 1 & 0 & 1 \\ 1 & 0 & 1 & 0 \end{bmatrix}$$

In Exercises 13–18 find the characteristic matrix of the given relation.

13. $\bar{R}_1^r$ **14.** $\bar{R}_2^r$

15. $\bar{R}_1^s$ **16.** $\bar{R}_2^s$

17. $\bar{R}_1^t$ **18.** $\bar{R}_2^t$

Let $A = \{1, 2, 3, 4, 5\}$. In Exercises 19–22 use Warshall's Algorithm to find the transitive closures of the given relation on A.

19. $R = \{(1, 1), (1, 2), (1, 3), (2, 3), (2, 4), (3, 2), (4, 1), (4, 3)\}$.

20. $R = \{(1, 2), (1, 4), (1, 5), (2, 1), (2, 3), (4, 1), (4, 2), (4, 5)\}$.

21. $R = $ "does not equal."

22. $R = $ "is exactly two less than or exactly one more than."

The reflexive closure of the symmetric closure of a relation R on a set is denoted $\bar{R}^{rs}$, with similar notations for other multiple closures. In Exercises 23–26 use Exercises 13–18 to find the characteristic matrix of the given relations.

23. $\bar{R}_1^{rr}$ and $\bar{R}_1^{rrr}$

24. $\bar{R}_2^{ss}$ and $\bar{R}_2^{sss}$

25. $\bar{R}_1^{rs}$ and $\bar{R}_1^{sr}$

26. $\bar{R}_2^{st}$ and $\bar{R}_2^{tr}$

27. Show that for any relation R on a set A, $\bar{R}^{rs} = \bar{R}^{sr}$.

28. (*Hard*) Show that for any relation R on a set A, $\bar{R}^{rt} = \bar{R}^{tr}$.

29. Find a relation R on $\{1, 2\}$ such that $\bar{R}^{st} \neq \bar{R}^{ts}$.

30. For any relation R on a set A, for $i = r$, s, or t, and for n a positive integer, let $\bar{R}^{ni}$ be $\bar{R}^{ii\cdots i}$, with n i's. Show that $\bar{R}^{ni} = \bar{R}^i$.

In Exercises 31 and 32 perform the indicated modular operations.

31. $4 + 5(\text{mod } 6)$; $3 \cdot 4(\text{mod } 8)$; $3 + 4(\text{mod } 9)$

32. $12 \cdot 12(\text{mod } 15)$; $6 + 9(\text{mod } 15)$; $3 \cdot (5 + 7)(\text{mod } 9)$

You can define modular division in the same way ordinary division is defined. Thus, we say $a \div b(\text{mod } n)$ is the number which, when multiplied (mod n) by b, yields a. Sometimes there is no such number, in which case we say the division cannot be done. In Exercise 33 perform the modular divisions or else show that they cannot be done.

33. $2 \div 3(\text{mod } 5)$, $4 \div 3(\text{mod } 7)$, $3 \div 4(\text{mod } 12)$, $1 \div 4(\text{mod } 11)$

34. Write modular addition tables for $n = 4$, 7, and 8.

35. Write modular multiplication tables for $n = 4$, 7, and 8.

36. Show that if $a \equiv b(\text{mod } n)$ and c is any integer, then $a + c \equiv b + c$ and $ac \equiv bc(\text{mod } n)$.

37. Show that if $a \equiv b(\text{mod } n)$, then $a^2 \equiv b^2$, $a^3 \equiv b^3$, $a^k \equiv b^k(\text{mod } n)$, $k = 1, 2, \ldots$.

38. Show that $a \equiv b(\text{mod } 1)$ for all a and b.

39. a. For which integers m does $0 | m$?

  b. Show that $a \equiv b(\text{mod } 0)$ if and only if $a = b$.

40. Let A be the set of integers from 0 to 9 inclusive. For each prime number p in A, list the equivalence classes under congruence modulo p.

41. Consider the following partition of the set A of Exercise 40: $\{\{0, 4, 5, 9\}, \{1, 2, 6\}, \{3, 7, 8\}\}$. Find a word description of the equivalence relation obtained. (*Hint:* Consider the names of the digits.)

In Exercises 42–44 find the worst-case efficiency of the given algorithm by counting the number of queries made about an entry of the characteristic matrix. (See Section 2.4.)

42. Program 6.1

43. Program 6.2

44. Program 6.3 (Just find the order in terms of big oh.)

6.2

Posets, Lattices, and Boolean Algebras

A **poset** (short for *partially ordered set*) is a set A together with a relation R on A, called a **partial order**, such that, for all x, y, and z in A:

(i) $x \, \mathsf{R} \, x$ (**reflexive law**)

(ii) if $x \, \mathsf{R} \, y$ and $y \, \mathsf{R} \, x$, then $x = y$ (**antisymmetry law**)

(iii) if $x \, \mathsf{R} \, y$ and $y \, \mathsf{R} \, z$, then $x \, \mathsf{R} \, z$ (**transitive law**)

As the following illustrations demonstrate, the variety of posets is enormous.

ILLUSTRATIONS

1. A: any set of numbers; R: $\leqslant$ (is less than or equal to).

2. A: any set of positive integers; R: $|$ (divides).
   The restriction to positive integers is made to ensure that the antisymmetry law holds. Otherwise, we might have, say, $3|-3$ and $-3|3$.

3. A: any set of sets; R: $\subset$ (contained in).

4. (See Section 3.3.) A: any set of statements; R: $\Rightarrow$ (implies).
   Here, to ensure that the antisymmetry law holds, we define two statements to be equal if they are equivalent; that is, $a = b$ means $a \equiv b$.

5. A: any set of words; R: **lexicographic order**, that is, alphabetical order as used in dictionaries. Thus, a R an, an R an, and R any, any R cab.   ■

In discussing an arbitrary poset A, the order relation is customarily denoted by $\leqslant$ and the poset by $(A, \leqslant)$. In this section the symbol $\leqslant$ is not necessarily the relation "is less than or equal to." There is no one commonly accepted way to read the statement $a \leqslant b$; a reasonable reading is "a part of b."

Two elements x, y of a poset $(A, \leqslant)$ are said to be **comparable** if $x \leqslant y$ or $y \leqslant x$, and **noncomparable** if they are not comparable. The poset $(A, \leqslant)$ is **linear** (also called linearly or totally ordered) if

(iv) each two elements of A are comparable   (**comparability law**)

The posets of Illustrations 1 and 5 are linear; those of the other three illustrations may or may not be linear, depending upon the set A. Thus, in Illustration 2, if $A = \{1, 2, 4, 8\}$, the relation is linear, but if $A = \{1, 2, 3, 4\}$, it is not; and in Illustration 3, if $A = \{\varnothing, \{1\}, \{1, 2\}, \{1, 2, 3\}\}$, the relation is linear, but if $A = \{\varnothing, \{1\}, \{1, 2\}, \{2, 3\}\}$, it is not.

For the poset $(A, \leqslant)$ we define $x \geqslant y$ to mean $y \leqslant x$; $x < y$ to mean $x \leqslant y$ and $x \neq y$; and $x > y$ to mean $y < x$. It is almost obvious that every linear poset $(A, \leqslant)$ satisfies the following statement:

(v) for all x and y in A exactly one of the statements
   $x < y$, $x = y$, $x > y$ is true   (**trichotomy law**)

Let B be a subset of a poset $(A, \leqslant)$. An element u of A is an **upper bound** of B if

$$\text{for all } b \text{ in } B, \, b \leqslant u \tag{1}$$

An element l of A is a **lower bound** of B if

$$\text{for all } b \text{ in } B, l \leqslant b \tag{2}$$

In Illustration 2 suppose A is the set of all positive integers. If $B = \{6, 8\}$, then 24, 48, and 96 are among the upper bounds of B, while 1 and 2 are the only lower bounds of B. Again in Illustration 2, if we let P be the set of all prime integers, then P has no upper bound and only 1 as a lower bound.

Suppose that in the poset $(A, \leqslant)$ the set A itself has an upper bound u. If v is also an upper bound of A, then $u \leqslant v$ since $u \in A$ and v is an upper bound; and $v \leqslant u$ since $v \in A$ and u is an upper bound; hence, $v = u$. Thus, the upper bound of A itself is unique, if it exists. Similarly, the lower bound for A is unique, if it exists. The lower and upper bounds of A, when they exist, are called the **least** and **greatest** elements of A. Often the least element of A is denoted by 0 and the greatest element is denoted by 1. In Section 3.3 we denoted a contradiction by 0 and a tautology by 1. This agrees with the present notation when applied to the posets of Illustration 4: If A contains a contradiction 0, then 0 is the least element of A; and if A contains a tautology 1, then 1 is the greatest element of A.

Let B be a subset of a poset $(A, \leqslant)$. An element u of A is a **least upper bound** of B if (1) u is an upper bound of B, and (2) for all upper bounds v of B, $u \leqslant v$. If w is also a least upper bound of B, then $u \leqslant w$ since w is an upper bound and u is a least upper bound; and $w \leqslant u$ since u is an upper bound and w is a least upper bound; hence, $u = w$. Therefore, the least upper bound of B is unique, if it exists at all.

An element l of B is a **greatest lower bound** of B if (1) l is a lower bound of B, and (2) for all lower bounds x of B, $l \geqslant x$. As with least upper bounds, the greatest lower bound of B is unique, if it exists at all. The least upper and greatest lower bounds of B, if they exist, are denoted lub B and glb B, respectively. (Some authors write sup A [supremum A] for lub A and inf A [infimum A] for glb A.)

EXAMPLE 6.12   In the set A of all real numbers with order relation $\leqslant$ (is less than or equal to), let $B = (x : x^2 < 3\}$. If $x \geqslant 2$, then $x^2 \geqslant 4$, so if $x^2 < 3$, we must have $x < 2$. Thus, $x < 2$ for all x in B; that is, 2 is an upper bound of B. Now it can similarly be shown that for all x in B, $x < 1.8$; so 2 is not the *least* upper bound of B. On the other hand, 1.71 is not an upper bound of B since $(1.72)^2 = 2.9584 < 3$. In fact, of course, lub $B = \sqrt{3}$. Also, glb $B = -\sqrt{3}$.   ◻

EXAMPLE 6.13   In the poset of Illustration 2, the set E of all even numbers has no upper bounds, and hence no least upper bound. But glb $E = 2$.   ◻

Let x and y be elements of a poset $(A, \leqslant)$. The subset $\{x, y\}$ of A has two elements if $x \neq y$ and only one element if $x = y$. The least upper bound and greatest lower bound of such a set, when they exist, have special notations. We write

$$\text{lub } \{x, y\} = x \vee y, \quad \text{glb } \{x, y\} = x \wedge y \tag{3}$$

and read "x cup y" and "x cap y," respectively. The symbols $\vee$ and $\wedge$ have, of course, been used before to denote "and" and "or." We will now show that Notation (3) includes this previous use as a special case. Let A be a set of statements with the order relation ($\leqslant$) of implication ($\Rightarrow$), where, as in Illustration 4, equivalent statements are considered to be equal. Suppose A contains the four statements $a, b, (a$ and $b), (a$ or $b)$. Since $a \Rightarrow a$ or b, and $b \Rightarrow a$ or b, we see that $a \leqslant a$ or b and $b \leqslant a$ or b; that is, a or b is an upper bound of $\{a, b\}$. Suppose c is also an upper bound of $\{a, b\}$. Then $a \Rightarrow c$ and $b \Rightarrow c$. But then a or $b \Rightarrow c$; that is, a or $b \leqslant c$. Hence, a or b is the *least* upper bound of $\{a, b\}$; that is, $a \vee b = a$ or b. Similarly, $a \wedge b = a$ and b.

EXAMPLE 6.14   Let S be a set. Let A be the poset of all subsets of S with order relation $\subset$ (Illustration 3). If $B \in A$ and $C \in A$ (that is, $B \subset S$ and $C \subset S$), then $B \vee C = B \cup C$ and $B \wedge C = B \cap C$.   ◻

EXAMPLE 6.15   Let A be the set of all positive integers with order relation | (Illustration 2). If $m \in A$ and $n \in A$, then $m \wedge n = \gcd(m, n)$ and $m \vee n = \text{lcm}(m, n)$. Here gcd denotes "greatest common divisor" and lcm denotes "least common multiple."   ◻

Let a and b be elements of a poset $(A, \leqslant)$. If $a \leqslant b$, then $a \leqslant b$ and $b \leqslant b$; so $a \vee b \leqslant b$. But $b \leqslant a \vee b$; so $a \vee b = b$. Conversely, if $a \vee b = b$, then $a \leqslant a \vee b = b$; so $a \leqslant b$. Thus, $a \leqslant b$ if and only if $a \vee b = b$. Similarly, $a \leqslant b$ if and only if $a \wedge b = a$. To summarize:

In any poset the following statements are equivalent:

$$a \leqslant b, \ a \vee b = b, \ a \wedge b = a \tag{4}$$

A **lattice** is a poset in which each set of two elements $\{a, b\}$ has a least upper bound $a \vee b$ and a greatest lower bound $a \wedge b$. We have already seen several examples of lattices. Let a and b be elements of a poset $(A, \leqslant)$. We say that a **is covered by** b (or b **covers** a), written $a \lhd b$ (or $b \rhd a$) if $a < b$ and there is *no* element c of A such that $a < c < b$ (that is, $a < c$ and $c < b$).

EXAMPLE 6.16   In the lattice of all subsets of $\{a, b, c\}$ ordered by $\subset$, $\{a\}$ is covered by $\{a, b\}$.   ◻

EXAMPLE 6.17   In the lattice $\{2, 4, 8, 16\}$, ordered by |, 2 is *not* covered by 8, since $2|4$ and $4|8$; but 4 is covered by 8.   ◻

Any finite poset $(A, \leqslant)$ may be depicted in a **Hasse diagram** (pronounce the name "HASS uh"). Each element is shown by a dot ·, and if $a \lhd b$, an upward-slanting or vertical line segment is drawn from a to b.

PROBLEM 6.1 Draw a Hasse diagram of the poset $(A, \leqslant)$, where $A = \{a, b, c, d\}$ and $a < c < d$, $b < c$.

SOLUTION See Figure 6.1.

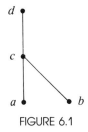

FIGURE 6.1

Note that $(A, \leqslant)$ is not a lattice, because $a \wedge b$ does not exist.   ◻

PROBLEM 6.2 Diagram the lattice of all subsets of $S = \{1, 2, 3\}$ under $\subset$.

SOLUTION See Figure 6.2. Note that this lattice has a least element 0, namely $\varnothing$, and a greatest element 1, namely S.

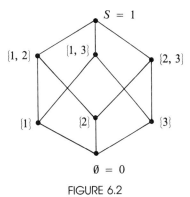

FIGURE 6.2   ◻

A lattice $(L, \leqslant)$ is **distributive** if, for all a, b, c in L,

$$a \wedge (b \vee c) = (a \wedge b) \vee (a \wedge c) \text{ and } a \vee (b \wedge c) = (a \vee b) \wedge (a \vee c) \qquad \textbf{(5)}$$

In Figure 6.3 we see the diagram of a lattice that is *not* distributive: we have $a \wedge (b \vee c) = a \wedge 1 = a$, but $(a \wedge b) \vee (a \wedge c) = 0 \vee 0 = 0$. On the other hand, the

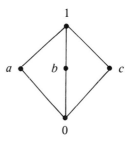

FIGURE 6.3

lattice of all positive integers, ordered by |, is distributive. For example, $6 \wedge (8 \vee 15) = 6 \wedge 120 = 6$ and $(6 \wedge 8) \vee (6 \wedge 15) = 2 \vee 3 = 6$. (Of course, this example doesn't prove that the distributive laws hold for *all a, b, c* in this lattice; but they do.)

Take another look at the laws of Boolean algebra (pages 91–92). The distributive law does not hold in all lattices, as we have seen. But some of the other laws do always hold. It's easy to see that the idempotent, commutative, associative, and absorption laws hold in all lattices. The other laws certainly don't always hold, since not all lattices have a greatest element 1 or a least element 0. If a lattice does have a 0 or 1, then the bound laws will obviously hold. Let's investigate the laws involving negation.

In a lattice $(L, \leqslant)$ with 0 and 1, we define a **complement** of an element *a* to be any *x* such that

$$a \vee x = 1 \text{ and } a \wedge x = 0 \tag{6}$$

In switching circuits, each element *a* has a unique complement *a′*. This is not necessarily true in lattices with 0 and 1. In Figure 6.4 *a* has no complement, and in Figure 6.5 *a* has two complements, *b* and *c*.

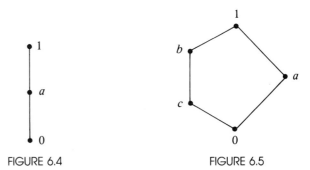

FIGURE 6.4　　　　　　　　FIGURE 6.5

A lattice is said to be **complemented** if it has 0 and 1 and if each element has at least one complement. A **Boolean algebra** is a distributive complemented lattice. In a Boolean algebra $(B, \leqslant)$ *all* the laws of Boolean algebra hold. We first show that each element *a* of *B* has a unique complement. Suppose *a* has complements x and y. Then

$$
\begin{aligned}
x &= x \wedge 1 \\
&= x \wedge (a \vee y) \\
&= (x \wedge a) \vee (x \wedge y) \\
&= 0 \vee (x \wedge y) \\
&= (y \wedge a) \vee (x \wedge y) \\
&= y \wedge (a \vee x) \\
&= y \wedge 1 \\
&= y
\end{aligned}
$$

that is, $x = y$. We may then denote *the* complement of a by a'. The involution and De Morgan's laws are now easy to prove.

EXAMPLE 6.18   The set of all subsets of $S = \{1, 2, 3\}$, diagramed in Figure 6.2, is a Boolean algebra. Indeed, the set of all subsets of *any* set, ordered by set inclusion, is a Boolean algebra.   ∎

Boole's original work, *The Laws of Thought*, contains, essentially, the observation that any set of statements that contains a contradiction, a tautology, the negations of each of its statements, and the conjunction and disjunction of each two of its statements is a Boolean algebra under implication.

By means of Result (4) it is possible to define a Boolean algebra solely in terms of the unary operation ' and the binary operations $\vee$ and $\wedge$. This approach is explored in the exercises.

EXERCISES

In Exercises 1–6 determine which of the pairs $(A, \leqslant)$ are posets. For those that are not posets, state which laws are violated.

1. A: any set of numbers; $\leqslant$: $\geqslant$.

2. A: any set of numbers; $\leqslant$: $<$.

3. A: any set of sets; $\leqslant$: $\supset$.

4. A: any set; $\leqslant$: $=$.

5. $A = \{1, 2, 3\}$; $\leqslant \, = \{(1, 1), (2, 2), (3, 3), (1, 2), (1, 3)\}$.

6. $A = \{1, 2, 3\}$; $\leqslant \, = \{(1, 1), (1, 2), (2, 2), (2, 3), (3, 3)\}$.

7. Show that every linear poset is a lattice.

8. Show that the set of all finite sets of integers, ordered by $\subset$, is a lattice.

9. Exhibit a nonempty subset of the lattice of Exercise 8 that does not have an upper bound.

10. Exhibit a nonempty *linear* subset of the lattice of Exercise 8 that does not have an upper bound.

11. Prove that the greatest lower bound of a subset B of a poset $(A, \leqslant)$ is unique, if it exists at all.

12. Suppose a set of statements, ordered by $\Rightarrow$, contains a, b, (a and b). Prove that $a \wedge b = (a$ and $b)$.

13. Let a and b be elements in the lattice $(L, \leqslant)$. Prove that $a \leqslant b$ if and only if $a \wedge b = a$.

14. In the lattice of all subsets of $\{1, 2, 3, 4\}$, ordered by $\subset$, let $a = \{2, 3, 4\}$ and $b = \{3\}$. Find all c such that $b \lhd c \lhd a$.

In Exercises 15–18 draw Hasse diagrams of the posets.

15. $A = \{2, 3, 4, 5, 6\}$; $\leqslant$: |.

16. $A = \{3, 6, 9, 12\}$; $\leqslant$: |.

17. A = the set of all subsets of $\{a, b, c\}$; $\leqslant$: ⊂.

18. A = the set of all subsets of $\{a, b, c\}$; $\leqslant$: ⊃.

19. Prove that the idempotent and commutative laws hold in every lattice.

20. Prove that the associative laws hold in every lattice.

21. Prove that the absorption laws hold in every lattice.

22. Prove that the involution law holds in every Boolean algebra.

23. Prove that De Morgan's laws hold in every Boolean algebra.

24. Prove that for any elements a, b in any Boolean algebra, the following statements are equivalent: $a \leqslant b$, $a' \vee b = 1$, $a \wedge b' = 0$.

One operational approach to Boolean algebra runs as follows. Let B be a set together with a unary operation $*$, two binary operations $+$ and $\cdot$ (omitted in writing), and two distinct elements 0 and 1 such that, for all elements a, b, c of B:

a. $a + b = b + a$ and $ab = ba$.

b. $a + (bc) = (a + b)(a + c)$ and $a(b + c) = (ab) + (ac)$.

c. $a + 0 = a$ and $a \cdot 1 = a$.

d. $a + a^* = 1$ and $aa^* = 0$.

Define a relation $\leqslant$ on B as follows: $a \leqslant b$ means $ab = a$. We wish to prove that $(B, \leqslant)$ is a Boolean algebra with least element 0, greatest element 1, and for all a, b: $a' = a^*$, $a \vee b = a + b$, and $a \wedge b = ab$. To do this, solve the following exercises.

25. Show that $a + a = a$ and $aa = a$.

26. Show that $a + 1 = 1$ and $a \cdot 0 = 0$.

27. Show that $a + (ab) = a$ and $a(a + b) = a$.

28. (*Hard*) Show that $(a + b) + c = a + (b + c)$ and $(ab)c = a(bc)$.

29. Show that if $a + x = 1$ and $ax = 0$, then $x = a^*$.

30. Show that $(a^*)^* = a$.

31. Show that $(a + b)^* = a^*b^*$ and $(ab)^* = a^* + b^*$.

32. Show that $(B, \leqslant)$ is a poset.

33. Show that $(B, \leqslant)$ is a lattice and $a \vee b = a + b$ and $a \wedge b = ab$.

34. Show that the least element of $(B, \leqslant)$ is 0 and the greatest element of $(B, \leqslant)$ is 1.

35. Show that $a' = a^*$.

Monoids and Groups

A **binary operation** on a set S is a function from the cartesian product $S \times S$ to S. If $f: S \times S \to S$ is a binary operation and $(x, y) \in S \times S$, we have introduced three notations for $f((x, y))$: prefix notation (also called Polish notation),

$$f((x, y)) = fxy$$

postfix notation (reverse Polish),

$$f((x, y)) = xyf$$

infix notation,

$$f((x, y)) = xfy$$

In this section we shall use mainly infix notation. We have already met many binary operations. Here are twenty-three examples from this text.

EXAMPLE 6.19

1. $+$ on the set of numbers.

2. $-$ on the set of numbers.

3. $\times$ on the set of numbers.

4. $\div$ on the set of nonzero numbers.

5. ∧ on the set of positive integers. (See Exercises 23 and 24 in Section 1.1.)

6. ∨ on the set of positive integers. (See Exercises 23 and 24 in Section 1.1.)

7. min on the set of numbers. (min (a, b) = the smaller of a and b.)

8. max on the set of numbers. (max (a, b) = the larger of a and b.)

9. ∩ on the set of all subsets of a given set.

10. ∪ on the set of all subsets of a given set.

11. ∼ on the set of all subsets of a given set.

12. × on the set of finite sets.

13. addition on the set of $n \times m$ matrices.

14. subtraction on the set of $n \times m$ matrices.

15. multiplication on the set of $n \times n$ matrices.

16. $\binom{n}{j}$ on the set of nonnegative integers, where $\binom{0}{0}$ is defined to be 1 and

$\binom{n}{j}$ is defined to be 0 if $n < j$.

17. ∧ on the set of propositions.

18. ∨ on the set of propositions.

19. approximate $+, -, \times, \div$ as defined in Section 5.4.

20. $+_n$ (modular addition) on the set Z_n.

21. $\times_n$ (modular multiplication) on the set Z_n.

22. ∧ in a lattice.

23. ∨ in a lattice. □

Mathematicians in the nineteenth century discovered that binary operations were a central theme in nearly all branches of their work. Different results in different areas turned out to be surprisingly similar when expressed in terms of binary operations. Furthermore, the language of binary operations provided a convenient framework for expressing many mathematical ideas. The study of binary operations for their own sake became what is now called algebra. In these next two sections we describe several of the most important mathematical systems in terms of their binary operations.

You may recall from algebra an important binary operation that has yet to be introduced in this text: function composition. Suppose f and g are functions from a set A to itself. The **composition** of f and g is denoted $f \circ g$ and is the function defined at an element x of A as follows:

$$f \circ g(x) = f(g(x))$$

Since $f \circ g$ is also a function from A to A, we see that composition, $\circ$, is a binary operation on the set of all functions from A to A. Here's an algebraic example of composition to make you feel more at home before we look at an example that is important to us.

EXAMPLE 6.20   Suppose f and g are functions defined by the following formulas:

$$f(x) = 5x + 1$$

$$g(x) = x^2 + 3x + 1$$

Then the compositions are these functions:

$$
\begin{aligned}
f \circ g(x) &= f(g(x)) \\
&= f(x^2 + 3x + 1) \\
&= 5(x^2 + 3x + 1) + 1 \\
&= 5x^2 + 15x + 6 \\
g \circ f(x) &= g(f(x)) \\
&= g(5x + 1) \\
&= (5x + 1)^2 + 3(5x + 1) + 1 \\
&= 25x^2 + 10x + 1 + 15x + 3 + 1 \\
&= 25x^2 + 25x + 5
\end{aligned}
$$

Note that $f \circ g(0) = 6$ and $g \circ f(0) = 5$. Thus, $f \circ g$ and $g \circ f$ are different functions.
■

EXAMPLE 6.21   Suppose f and g are functions from the set $A = \{1, 2, 3\}$ to itself defined as follows:

$$f(1) = 2, f(2) = 3, f(3) = 1$$

$$g(1) = 3, g(2) = 2, g(3) = 1$$

Then

$$
\begin{array}{ll}
f \circ g(1) = f(g(1)) = f(3) = 1 & g \circ f(1) = g(f(1)) = g(2) = 2 \\
f \circ g(2) = f(g(2)) = f(2) = 3 & g \circ f(2) = g(f(2)) = g(3) = 1 \\
f \circ g(3) = f(g(3)) = f(1) = 2 & g \circ f(3) = g(f(3)) = g(1) = 3 \\
f \circ f(1) = f(f(1)) = f(2) = 3 & g \circ g(1) = g(g(1)) = g(3) = 1 \\
f \circ f(2) = f(f(2)) = f(3) = 1 & g \circ g(2) = g(g(2)) = g(2) = 2 \\
f \circ f(3) = f(f(3)) = f(1) = 2 & g \circ g(3) = g(g(3)) = g(1) = 3
\end{array}
$$
■

Suppose A is a set and $*$ is a binary operation on A. Then $*$ is **associative** if, for each triple of elements a, b, c in A,

$$a * (b * c) = (a * b) * c \tag{1}$$

Many binary operations with which you are familiar are associative. But most binary operations are not associative. However, most binary operations studied in mathematics are associative, partly because associative operations tend to arise naturally and partly because it is easier to deal with associative operations. For example, in elementary school you learned that addition and multiplication are associative. Thus, apparently ambiguous expressions such as

$$23 + 56 + 87 \text{ or } 4 \times 6 \times 18$$

do not require parentheses since the answer is the same no matter which pair of numbers is combined first. Subtraction and division are nonassociative, however. For example,

$$12 - (6 - 3) = 9 \neq 3 = (12 - 6) - 3$$

$$16 \div (8 \div 2) = 4 \neq 1 = (16 \div 8) \div 2$$

An expression such as

$$12 - 6 - 3$$

makes sense only because there is a rule that says: "unless parentheses indicate otherwise, do the subtractions in order from left to right." Thus, $12 - 6 - 3$ means $(12 - 6) - 3$.

EXAMPLE 6.22 Is the operation $*$ defined on $A = \{a, b\}$ by $a*a = b$, $a*b = a$, $b*a = b$, $b*b = b$ associative?

ANSWER No. For example, $(a*a)*a = b*a = b$; but $a*(a*a) = a*b = a$. Thus,

$$(a*a)*a \neq a*(a*a) \qquad \blacksquare$$

A **semigroup** is a set with an associative binary operation. Apart from the set of numbers with $+$ or $\times$, examples of semigroups are the set of propositions with $\wedge$ or $\vee$; the set of finite sets with $\cup$ or $\cap$; and any lattice or Boolean algebra with $\wedge$ or $\vee$.

EXAMPLE 6.23 Suppose f, g, and h are functions from a set S to itself. Then for each element x in S,

$$
\begin{aligned}
[f \circ (g \circ h)](x) &= f([g \circ h](x)) \\
&= f(g(h(x))) \\
&= [f \circ g](h(x)) \\
&= [(f \circ g) \circ h](x)
\end{aligned}
$$

It follows that $f \circ (g \circ h)$ and $(f \circ g) \circ h$ define the same function; that is, $f \circ (g \circ h) = (f \circ g) \circ h$. Thus, *function composition is associative*; so the set of functions from S to S forms a semigroup. $\qquad \blacksquare$

Suppose x_1, x_2, x_3, x_4 are elements of a semigroup $(S, *)$. There are five ways to insert parentheses in the expression $x_1 * x_2 * x_3 * x_4$:

$$x_1 * (x_2 * (x_3 * x_4))$$

$$x_1 * ((x_2 * x_3) * x_4)$$

$$(x_1 * x_2) * (x_3 * x_4)$$

$$(x_1 * (x_2 * x_3)) * x_4$$

$$((x_1 * x_2) * x_3) * x_4$$

We claim that all five ways yield the same element of S. For instance, the first element equals the second by equation (1) with $a = x_2$, $b = x_3$, $c = x_4$. The first element equals the third by equation (1) with $a = x_1$, $b = x_2$, $c = x_3 * x_4$. The general result for inserting parentheses is called the **general associative law**.

THEOREM 6.2   Let $x_1, x_2, \ldots, x_n$ be elements of a semigroup $(S, *)$. Then every way of inserting parentheses in $x_1 * x_2 * \cdots * x_n$ gives the same element of S.

PROOF   We use strong induction on n (see Section 2.2). For $n = 3$, the result is simply the associative law. Suppose that $n > 3$ and that the result is true for $x_1 * x_2 * \cdots * x_k$ for all $k < n$. Consider an insertion of parentheses in $x_1 * x_2 * \cdots * x_n$. Say the last operation is the kth $*$ from the left. (For instance, in

$$[x_1 * ((x_2 * x_3) * x_4)] \overset{\downarrow}{*} (x_5 * x_6)$$ the last operation, marked $\downarrow$, is the 4th from

the left.) Then the result of this insertion of parentheses equals $[x_1 * \cdots * x_k] * [x_{k+1} * \cdots * x_n]$, and by assumption it doesn't matter how we insert parentheses in $x_1 * \cdots * x_k$ and in $x_{k+1} * \cdots * x_n$. If $k > 1$, insert parentheses like this:

$$[x_1 * (x_2 * \cdots * x_k)] * [x_{k+1} * \cdots * x_n]$$

By (1) this equals $x_1 * [(x_2 * \cdots * x_k) * (x_{k+1} * \cdots * x_n)]$, and this equals $x_1 * (x_2 * \cdots * x_n)$, where by assumption it doesn't matter how parentheses are inserted in $x_2 * \cdots * x_n$. Thus, every way of inserting parentheses in $x_1 * \cdots * x_n$ is equal to $x_1 * (x_2 * \cdots * x_n)$, so that the result is true for n. This completes the proof.   □

Suppose A is a set with a binary operation $*$. An **identity** for $*$ is an element e in A such that

$$e * a = a = a * e \text{ for all } a \text{ in } A$$

EXAMPLE 6.24   a. The identity for $+$ on the set of numbers is 0, since $0 + a = a = a + 0$ for any number a.

b. The identity for $\times$ on the set of numbers is 1, since $1 \times a = a = a \times 1$ for any number a.

c. The identity for $\cup$ on the set of finite sets is $\varnothing$, since $\varnothing \cup A = A = A \cup \varnothing$ for any set A.

d. The identity for $\cap$ on the set of subsets of a universal set $\mathcal{U}$ is $\mathcal{U}$, since $\mathcal{U} \cap A = A = A \cap \mathcal{U}$ for any set A.

e. The identity for $\wedge$ on the set of propositions is 1, the tautology, since $1 \wedge p \equiv p \equiv p \wedge 1$ for any proposition p.

f. The identity for $\vee$ on the set of propositions is 0, the contradiction, since $0 \vee p \equiv p \equiv p \vee 0$ for any proposition p. ■

A **monoid** is a semigroup with identity. That is, a monoid is a set with an associative binary operation with an identity. The six examples listed in Example 6.24 are all monoids.

□ THEOREM 6.3   A monoid M has exactly one identity element.

PROOF   Let e be the identity element of M guaranteed by the definition and let $*$ be the binary operation on M. Suppose e' is another "identity element," that is, suppose e' has the property

$$e' * a = a = a * e' \text{ for all } a \text{ in } M$$

Then $e' = e * e' = e$. Thus, e is the only identity element. □

EXAMPLE 6.25   Let S be a set and let e be the function from S to S defined by $e(x) = x$ for all elements x in S. Then

$$e \circ f(x) = e(f(x)) = f(x) = f(e(x)) = f \circ e(x)$$

It follows that e is the identity function and the set of functions from S to S forms a monoid. ■

Not all semigroups are monoids. For example, the set of finite sets with the operation $\cap$ has no identity. To see this, suppose some finite set E were the identity. Then necessarily $E \cap A = A = A \cap E$ for all finite sets A. Since E is finite, there is something, say x, not in E. Let $A = E \cup \{x\}$. Then $E \cap A = E \neq A$, so E must not be the identity after all.

EXAMPLE 6.26   A Boolean algebra is a monoid in two ways. It is a monoid with $\vee$ as the operation and 0 as the identity. It is also a monoid with $\wedge$ as the operation and 1 as the identity. ■

Suppose M is a monoid with the binary operation $*$ and identity e. If a is an element of M, then an **inverse** for a is an element b such that

$$a*b = e = b*a$$

In any monoid the identity e is always its own inverse since $e*e = e$. It can happen that e is the only element with an inverse. For example, in the monoid of positive integers with multiplication, only the identity 1 has an inverse, since if $n > 1$, then the only possible solution to $nx = 1$ is $x = 1/n$, which is not an integer. It is easy to show that if an element in a monoid has an inverse, it has only one.

☐ THEOREM 6.4   Suppose M is a monoid with binary operation $*$ and identity element e. Then if the element a in M has an inverse, it has only one inverse.

PROOF   Suppose b and c are inverses for a. Then

$$\begin{aligned}
b &= b*e \text{ (since } e \text{ is the identity)} \\
&= b*(a*c) \text{ (since } c \text{ is an inverse for } a) \\
&= (b*a)*c \text{ (since } * \text{ is associative)} \\
&= e*c \text{ (since } b \text{ is an inverse of } a) \\
&= c \text{ (since } e \text{ is the identity)}
\end{aligned}$$

☐

The inverse of an element a of a monoid, if it exists, is usually denoted a^{-1}, read "a inverse."

EXAMPLE 6.27   In Example 6.21 the function g is its own inverse since $g \circ g$ is the function e discussed in Example 6.25. It is not hard to find the inverse of f. Call the inverse h. Then $h \circ f = e$, so

$$h(f(1)) = 1, \; h(f(2)) = 2, \; h(f(3)) = 3$$

That is,

$$h(2) = 1, \; h(3) = 2, \; h(1) = 3$$

Note that $f \circ h$ is also e:

$$f(h(1)) = f(3) = 1$$
$$f(h(2)) = f(1) = 2$$
$$f(h(3)) = f(2) = 3$$

■

A **group** is a monoid in which each element has an inverse. Specifically, a group G is a set with a binary operation $*$ and identity e such that

a. $*$ is associative.

b. for each element g in G there is an element h such that $g*h = e = h*g$.

☐ THEOREM 6.5   Suppose S is a monoid with identity e such that for each element a there is an element b with $a*b = e$. Then S is a group.

PROOF   We must show that each element of S has a "two-sided" inverse. Let a be an element of S. Let b be an element such that $a*b = e$. Let c be an element such that $b*c = e$. Then

$$(b*a)*b = b*(a*b) = b*e = b$$

So $$[(b*a)*b]*c = b*c = e$$

Thus, $$e = [(b*a)*b]*c$$
$$= (b*a)*(b*c)$$
$$= (b*a)*e$$
$$= b*a$$

It follows that b is the inverse for a. Since a was an arbitrary element of S, we have shown that S is a group.   ☐

Theorem 6.5 can save a lot of trouble. For example, if you wish to check that a given square matrix A is the inverse of a square matrix B, it is enough to check that AB is the identity matrix, since then by Theorem 6.5 BA will also be the identity. In Example 6.27 we did not need to check that $f \circ h = e$ once we had determined that $h \circ g = e$.

EXAMPLE 6.28   a. One of the most familiar groups is the group Z of integers with the operation $+$. Addition is associative; 0 is the identity; and the inverse of an integer a is its negative, $-a$.

b. Other familiar examples of groups are the set of positive rational numbers or the set of positive real numbers with the binary operation $\times$. Multiplication is associative; the identity element is 1; and the inverse of a number a is its reciprocal, $1/a$.

c. In fact, the set of nonzero rationals and the set of nonzero reals also form groups under the operation $\times$.

d. The set $Z_n = \{0, 1, 2, \ldots, n-1\}$ forms a group under the operation $+_n$, addition modulo n. Thus, we see that for each positive integer n, there is at least one group with n elements. For some n the set $\{1, 2, \ldots, n-1\}$ forms a group under modular multiplication, $\times_n$. It is *not* a group for $n = 4$ since 2 has no inverse. (To see this, try every possibility: $1 \times_4 2 = 2$, $2 \times_4 2 = 0$, $2 \times_4 3 = 2$. Thus, no product with 2 is the identity.)   ◼

The collection of facts and theorems about groups forms a branch of mathematics called **group theory**. In mathematics the word "theory" means a "concise systematic view of a subject," not a body of opinion. Group theory is one of the richest areas in mathematics in terms of number of theorems, range of applications, and importance. Even the history of group theory is a rapidly growing area in itself. One major project of group theorists is to produce a list of all the different possible groups with a finite number of elements. This undertaking is described in Daniel Gorenstein's *Scientific American* article, "The Enormous Theorem" (December 1985, pp. 104–115). We will have to settle for a listing of all groups with 1, 2, 3, or 4 elements. Even this apparently simple task requires the following theorem on cancellation.

THEOREM 6.6   Suppose G is a group with binary operation $*$. Then

$$a*b = a*c \text{ implies } b = c$$

and $$b*a = c*a \text{ implies } b = c$$

That is, the element a may be canceled from both sides of an equation.

PROOF   Let e denote the identity in G and, following multiplicative notation, let a^{-1} denote the inverse of a. Then

$$a*b = a*c \text{ implies}$$

$$a^{-1}*(a*b) = a^{-1}*(a*c) \text{ implies}$$

$$(a^{-1}*a)*b = (a^{-1}*a)*c \text{ implies}$$

$$e*b = e*c \text{ implies}$$

$$b = c$$

The other result follows in the same way by multiplying on the right by a^{-1}.
□

This theorem implies an important fact about the multiplication table for a group. Below is the multiplication table for a group with eight elements e, r, s, t, h, v, d, and f. In the next section we will explain this strange choice of letters and show that the table really does define a group. It is difficult to see directly from the definition that this is a group, since verification of associativity requires 2048 multiplications. However, the first row and column announce loudly that e is the identity. It is also easy to find inverses by looking for identities in the table. For example, to find the inverse of t, we look for an e in its row and find one under r. Thus, $t*r = e$, and, since it really is a group, $r*t = e$ as well. Now look again at the table. Note that all eight elements appear exactly once in each row and in each column. (Ignore the row and column headings.) This always happens.

$*$	e	r	s	t	h	v	d	f
e	e	r	s	t	h	v	d	f
r	r	s	t	e	d	f	v	h
s	s	t	e	r	v	h	f	d
t	t	e	r	s	f	d	h	v
h	h	f	v	d	e	s	t	r
v	v	d	h	f	s	e	r	t
d	d	h	f	v	r	t	e	s
f	f	v	d	h	t	r	s	e

| THEOREM 6.7 | There is no repetition in any row or any column of the multiplication table for a group. Thus, each element appears exactly once in each row and in each column. |

PROOF   Suppose the row opposite an element w has the same element x in two columns: under y and under z. Then by the definition of the table,

$$w * y = x = w * z$$

But then by the cancellation theorem, $y = z$. So the two columns really are the same and the element x appears in only one column. The argument for columns is identical except that it uses the second cancellation property.   □

Armed with this theorem, we can find all groups with 1, 2, 3, or 4 elements. There is only one possible binary operation on a single element set $\{e\}$, namely, $e * e = e$. This operation defines a group, called the **trivial group**. Given a two-element set, we pick one element as the identity and label it e. The set is then $\{e, a\}$. Since e is the identity, we need only calculate $a * a$ to complete a multiplication table. We use Theorem 6.4. If $a * a = a = e * a$, then $a = e$ and the group has only one element. Thus, $a * a = e$. This multiplication defines a group, which really amounts to $\mathbf{Z}_2$ with $+_2$, where we have labeled 0 as e and 1 as a.

At this point we had better consider the question of what it means for two groups to be the same. Naturally, we require that two identical finite groups have the same number of elements. Here are two tables for two three-element groups. The first you should recognize as $\mathbf{Z}_3$ with $+_3$.

$+_3$	0	1	2		$*$	e	a	b
0	0	1	2		e	e	a	b
1	1	2	0		a	a	b	e
2	2	0	1		b	b	e	a

Can you see that the second table is really the same as the first? We have simply changed all the 0's to e's, all the 1's to a's, and all the 2's to b's. The way in which the elements are multiplied is the same.

Suppose A and B are finite sets with the same number of elements. Then the function F from A to B is a **relabeling** if each element in B has only one element in A corresponding to it. In our example the function F from $\{0, 1, 2\}$ to $\{e, a, b\}$ defined by

$$F(0) = e \qquad F(1) = a \qquad F(2) = b$$

is a relabeling. The function G defined by

$$G(0) = e \qquad G(1) = a \qquad G(2) = a$$

is not a relabeling since we have used a to relabel two different elements. A relabeling is also called a **one-to-one function**.

It is not enough to simply relabel. We must also be sure the multiplication is really the same. The notion of group isomorphism is designed to capture this idea. Suppose $(G_1, *_1)$ is a group with binary operation $*_1$ and $(G_2, *_2)$ is a group with binary operation $*_2$. An **isomorphism** F from G_1 to G_2 is a bijection from G_1 to G_2 that respects the binary operations. That is, for each pair of elements a and b of G_1,

$$F(a *_1 b) = F(a) *_2 F(b)$$

The word *isomorphism* is from Greek words meaning "equal form." Two groups are isomorphic if one is obtained from the other by simply renaming elements. Two groups are said to be **isomorphic** if there is an isomorphism between them. We will need only two properties of isomorphisms.

☐ THEOREM 6.8   Let F be an isomorphism from the group $(G_1, *_1)$ to the group $(G_2, *_2)$; let e_1 be the identity of G_1 and e_2 be the identity of G_2. Then $F(e_1) = e_2$ and, for all a in G_1, $F(a^{-1}) = [F(a)]^{-1}$.

PROOF $F(e_1) = F(e_1 *_1 e_1) = F(e_1) *_2 F(e_1)$, so by the cancellation law $F(e_1) = e_2$. Then $e_2 = F(e_1) = F(a *_1 a^{-1}) = F(a) *_2 F(a^{-1})$, so $F(a^{-1}) = [F(a)]^{-1}$.   ☐

It is not hard to write the multiplication table for the three-element group. The cancellation theorem leaves no choices in the construction of the table, so there is only one three-element group. Since $\mathbf{Z}_3$ is a three-element group under $+_3$, the group constructed must either be $\mathbf{Z}_3$ or be isomorphic to $\mathbf{Z}_3$.

The situation for a four-element set is much more interesting. Of course, $\mathbf{Z}_4$ is a four-element group under $+_4$. But there is another four-element group that is not isomorphic to $\mathbf{Z}_4$. It is called **Klein's 4-group** or simply the **four-group**. We will describe this group while we show that it is the only other four-element group. Let G be a four-element group with identity e. Let $a \neq e$ be another element of G. Now $a * a$ might be e, or it might be some other element of G. First, suppose $a * a = b \neq e$. Then the table for G looks like this:

*	e	a	b	c
e	e	a	b	c
a	a	b		
b	b			
c	c			

Now to complete the row opposite a, we cannot put c under c. Since c and e must appear in that row, they must appear in that order. Similarly for the column under a:

*	e	a	b	c
e	e	a	b	c
a	a	b	c	e
b	b	c		
c	c	e		

Now e and a must appear in the row opposite b, but e cannot appear twice in the last column. Similarly for the column under b. Finally, $c*c = b$, since b must appear in the last row and column. Here is the complete table:

*	e	a	b	c
e	e	a	b	c
a	a	b	c	e
b	b	c	e	a
c	c	e	a	b

The above table is really addition modulo 4 where we have relabeled: $e = F(0)$; $a = F(1)$; $b = F(2)$; $c = F(3)$. (You should check that F is an isomorphism.) Now suppose our four-element group has $a*a = e$. If we proceed as before, we find there is a choice at once. Either $b*b = e$ or $b*b = a$. The latter choice leads again to I_4, this time with the relabeling: $e = G(0)$; $a = G(2)$; $b = G(3)$; $c = G(1)$. If we let $b*b = e$, the rest of the table is determined and is as follows:

*	e	a	b	c
e	e	a	b	c
a	a	e	c	b
b	b	c	e	a
c	c	b	a	e

This table does *not* define Z_4.

How can we be sure about that? The key lies in the fact that each element in this group squares to the identity: $e = e*e = a*a = b*b = c*c$. Suppose F is an isomorphism from this group to $\mathbf{Z}_4$. We know by Theorem 6.8 that $F(e) = 0$. Now let x be the element in $\{e, a, b, c\}$ such that $F(x) = 3$. Then

$$0 = F(e) = F(x*x) = F(x) + F(x) = 3 + 3 = 2$$

It follows that there really are two different four-element groups.

Thus far all our groups have satisfied an additional axiom:

c. for each pair of elements a, b in G, $a*b = b*a$.

A group that satisfies this condition is called **commutative** or **abelian***. You have already seen one example of a **nonabelian** group, namely, the set of all invertible $n \times n$ matrices under matrix multiplication. In the next section we will discuss two additional examples, including the eight-element group whose table is listed on page 272. For now we simply note that it is not commutative since, for example, $h*r = f \neq d = r*h$.

---

* Niels H. Abel (1802–1829; note the age) was an important early contributor to modern algebra.

EXERCISES

In Exercises 1–10 either prove that the given binary operation is associative or else find a particular triple of elements that shows that it is not associative.

1. $\circ$ on the set of all rational numbers except 1, where $a \circ b = a + b - ab$.

2. $*$ on the set of integers, where $n * j = \binom{n}{j}$ as defined in Example 6.19 part 16.

3. $\square$ on the set of nonnegative integers, where $a \square b = \min(a, b)$.

4. $*$ on the set of nonnegative integers, where $a * b = \max(a, b)$.

5. $*$ on the set $\{1, 2, 4, 8, 12, 24\}$, where $a * b =$ the greatest common divisor of a and b.

6. $*$ on the set $\{1, 2, 4, 8, 12, 24\}$, where $a * b =$ the least common multiple of a and b.

7. $\sim$ on the set of subsets of a given nonempty set X.

8. $\triangle$ on the set of subsets of a set X, where $A \triangle B = (A \sim B) \cup (B \sim A)$. The binary operation $\triangle$ is called the **symmetric difference** of the two sets.

9. $-$ on the set of propositions, where $p - q = p \wedge q'$.

10. $\triangle$ on the set of propositions, where $p \triangle q = (p - q) \vee (q - p)$.

In Exercises 11–20 find an identity for the given binary operation or show that it has none.

11. The operation $\circ$ of Exercise 1.

12. The operation $*$ of Exercise 2.

13. The operation $\square$ of Exercise 3.

14. The operation $*$ of Exercise 4.

15. The operation $*$ of Exercise 5.

16. The operation $*$ of Exercise 6.

17. The operation $\sim$ of Exercise 7.

18. The operation $\triangle$ of Exercise 8.

19. The operation $-$ of Exercise 9.

20. The operation $\triangle$ of Exercise 10.

In Exercises 21–30 find the inverse of an arbitrary element or else find an element with no inverse.

21. The operation $\circ$ of Exercise 1.

22. The operation $*$ of Exercise 2.

23. The operation $\square$ of Exercise 3.

24. The operation $*$ of Exercise 5.

25. The operation $*$ of Exercise 6.

26. The operation $\sim$ of Exercise 7.

27. The operation $\triangle$ of Exercise 8.

28. The operation $\triangle$ of Exercise 10.

29. The operation $\cup$ on the set of all subsets of a universal set $\mathscr{U}$.

30. The operation $\cap$ on the set of all subsets of a universal set $\mathscr{U}$.

31. Write all tables for a binary operation on a two-element set $\{a, b\}$.

32. Show that if the binary operation $\circ$ on the set $\{a, b\}$ has an identity, then it is associative.

33. How many binary operations can be defined on a set with n elements?

34. How many binary operations with identity can be defined on a set with n elements?

35. Show that the operation $\circ$ of Exercise 1 makes the set of all rational numbers except 1 into an abelian group.

36. Show that the symmetric difference operation $\triangle$ of Exercise 8 makes the set of all subsets of a given universal set $\mathscr{U}$ into an abelian group.

37. Show that if $a_1, a_2, \ldots, a_n$ are elements of a group, then

$$\left(\prod_{i=1}^{n} a_i \right)^{-1} = \prod_{i=1}^{n} a_{n+1-i}^{-1}$$

38. Let a, b be elements of a group. Show that $(ab)^{-1} = a^{-1}b^{-1}$ if and only if $ab = ba$.

39. Use the group described by the table on page 272 to give an example of the *falsity* of the formula

$$\left(\prod_{i=1}^{n} a_i \right)^{-1} = \prod_{i=1}^{n} a_i^{-1}$$

6.4

Symmetries, Permutations, Rings, and Fields

Here is a square with its corners labeled 1, 2, 3, 4:

Suppose I pick the square up. Here is where it was:

How many different ways can I replace the square exactly where it was? I can rotate it through 90 degrees clockwise and replace it:

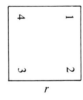

To make the numbers easier to read, let's agree to write them right side up even though they will really end up turned or flipped along with the square. Thus, the result of the motion called *r* (for "rotate") will be shown as

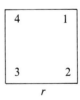

I can also rotate the square 180 degrees or 270 degrees clockwise:

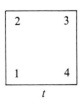

I can turn it over in four different ways along vertical, horizontal, or two diagonal lines:

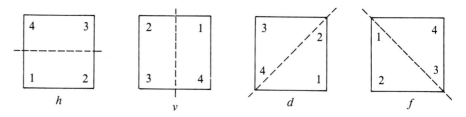

Note that these motions will actually make the corner labels disappear. They are shown moved back around to the front. Of course, I can also just set it back the way it was:

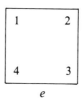

These eight motions are called the **symmetries** of a square and are the only ways to return it to its original location. The use of the word *symmetry* makes sense for the four flips around the lines *h*, *v*, *d*, and *f*, since the square is actually symmetric about each of those four lines.

We name the eight motions:

e: replace the square exactly as it was.

r: rotate through 90 degrees clockwise.

s: rotate through 180 degrees clockwise.

t: rotate through 270 degrees clockwise.

h: flip around a horizontal line.

v: flip around a vertical line.

d: flip around the top right to lower left diagonal.

f: flip around the other diagonal.

We can turn the set of eight motions into a group by defining composition as doing one motion after the other. Thus, *h∗r* means flip across a horizontal

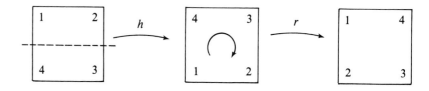

line then rotate 90 degrees clockwise. Note that this motion is the same as f. To see that the set of motions forms a group under composition, we note first that the composition of any two motions on our list is a motion on our list, since our list of motions is complete. We check associativity: if we do three motions one after the other, we can think of this action as doing the first two motions and then the third, or as doing the first motion and then the last two. Clearly, the identity is the "do-nothing" motion. As for inverses, no matter how you move the square, I can move it back the way it was.

The multiplication table for this eight-element group was written out in Section 6.3 (page 272), where we noted that it is nonabelian (i.e., not commutative).

The group of symmetries of the square is not the smallest nonabelian group. The smallest nonabelian group is a member of a whole family of groups we are about to describe. Further study of the groups in this family is an important piece of mathematics and computer science, but it cannot be undertaken in this text.

A preliminary idea is needed. Let A be a set. A **permutation** of A is a bijection from A to A. (The reader may wish to review the discussion of bijections in Section 1.3.) If f and g are permutations of A, then the composition $f \circ g$ is a function from A to A. We claim that $f \circ g$ is, in fact, a permutation of A:

$f \circ g$ is *injective*. Suppose $f \circ g(x_1) = f \circ g(x_2)$. Then $f(g(x_1)) = f(g(x_2))$, $g(x_1) = g(x_2)$ (since f is injective), and $x_1 = x_2$ (since g is injective).

$f \circ g$ is *surjective*. Suppose $y \in A$. There exists $z \in A$ such that $y = f(z)$ (since f is surjective). There exists $x \in A$ such that $z = g(x)$ (since g is surjective). Then $f \circ g(x) = f(g(x)) = f(z) = y$

Let $S(A)$ be the set of all permutations of A. We have just shown that function composition $\circ$ is a binary operation on $S(A)$. Since $\circ$ is always associative, $(S(A), \circ)$ is a semigroup. Let $e = i_A$, the identity function on A. Then e is a permutation; that is, $e \in S(A)$, and for all $f \in S(A)$, $e \circ f = f \circ e = f$. Thus, $(S(A), \circ)$ is a monoid. Finally, if $f \in S(A)$, then since f is a bijection, there is an inverse function f^{-1}. The function f^{-1} is also a bijection; so $f^{-1} \in S(A)$. From Section 1.3 we know that $f(f^{-1}(y)) = y$ for all y in A and $f^{-1}(f(x)) = x$ for all x in A; hence, $f \circ f^{-1} = f^{-1} \circ f = e$. Thus, $(S(A), \circ)$ is a group. To summarize:

> The set $S(A)$ of all permutations of a set A, with the operation $\circ$ of composition, is a group. This group is called the **symmetric group** on A.

It does not matter for the study of $S(A)$ what the elements of A are. If A is a finite set with n elements, we shall use $A = \{1, 2, 3, \dots, n\}$. The symmetric group $S(\{1, 2, 3, \dots, n\})$ is denoted S_n and is called the symmetric group of **degree** n. How many permutations f of $\{1, 2, 3, \dots, n\}$ are there? We have n choices for $f(1)$, $n - 1$ choices for $f(2)$, $\dots$, and finally one choice for $f(n)$; so there are $n(n - 1) \cdots 1 = n!$ permutations. Thus, S_n is a group with $n!$ elements.

The symmetric group S_3 has $3! = 6$ elements. The six permutations of $\{1, 2, 3\}$ may be denoted $f_0, f_1, \ldots, f_5$ and described by the following table:

	f_0	f_1	f_2	f_3	f_4	f_5
1	1	1	3	2	2	3
2	2	3	2	1	3	1
3	3	2	1	3	1	2

For instance, $f_4(1) = 2$, $f_4(2) = 3$, $f_4(3) = 1$. Let us calculate $f_1 \circ f_4$ and $f_4 \circ f_1$. We have $f_1 \circ f_4(1) = f_1(2) = 3$; $f_1 \circ f_4(2) = f_1(3) = 2$; and therefore $f_1 \circ f_4(3) = 1$. Checking the table, we see that $f_1 \circ f_4 = f_2$. Now $f_4 \circ f_1(1) = f_4(1) = 2$; $f_4 \circ f_1(2) = f_4(3) = 1$; and so $f_4 \circ f_1(3) = 3$. Then $f_4 \circ f_1 = f_3$. Thus, $f_1 \circ f_4 \neq f_4 \circ f_1$; so S_3 is a nonabelian group with six elements. The reader should calculate the entire multiplication table for S_3. It can be shown that S_3 is the only nonabelian group with six elements and that every group with fewer than six elements is abelian.

We turn now to a brief description of two other important algebraic structures. A **ring** is a set R together with two binary operations usually denoted $+$ and $\cdot$ (with the $\cdot$ usually omitted in writing) such that

1. $(R, +)$ forms a commutative group.
2. $\cdot$ is associative.
3. $a(b + c) = (ab) + (ac)$.
4. $(b + c)a = (ba) + (ca)$ for all a, b, and c in R.

Property (3) is the **distributive law**. The distributive law relates the addition and multiplication in the ring. Note that in a ring $+$ is always commutative. There is always a zero element 0 such that $a + 0 = a$ for all a in R.

ILLUSTRATIONS
1. $(\mathbf{Z}, +, \cdot)$, the ring of integers with ordinary addition and multiplication.
2. For n a positive integer, $(\mathbf{Z}_n, +_n, \times_n)$, the ring of integers modulo n, with addition modulo n and multiplication modulo n.
3. For n a positive integer, $R =$ the set of all $n \times n$ matrices with integer entries, with matrix addition and matrix multiplication.   ◻

An **identity** in a ring is an element denoted 1 such that $1 \neq 0$ and $1a = a = a1$ for all a in R. (Here 1 is merely a symbol, not necessarily the integer 1.) If R contains such an element, R is said to be a **ring with identity**. Thus, a ring with identity is a monoid under its multiplication operation. If R is a ring with identity, then the **inverse** of the element a is defined in the usual way as an element a^{-1} such that $a^{-1}a = 1 = aa^{-1}$. Theorem 6.4 shows that inverses are unique when they exist. A **unit** in a ring with identity is an element with an inverse.

□ THEOREM 6.9	Let R be a ring with identity and let U be the set of units in R. Then $(U, \cdot)$ is a group.
PROOF	First, 1 is a unit since it is its own inverse. Thus, U has an identity. Next, suppose a and b are units. Then so is ab since

$$(b^{-1}a^{-1})(ab) = b^{-1}a^{-1}ab$$
$$= b^{-1}1b$$
$$= b^{-1}b$$
$$= 1$$

Thus, ab has an inverse, namely $b^{-1}a^{-1}$. It follows that $\cdot$ is a binary operation on U. The operation $\cdot$ is given to be associative. It follows that $(U, \cdot)$ is a group. □

The next theorem shows that 0 is never a unit in a ring.

□ THEOREM 6.10	In any ring R, $0a = 0 = a0$ for any element a.
PROOF	$a0 = a(0 + 0) = a0 + a0$ (distributive law)

Now $a0$ has an inverse in the additive group $(R, +)$. If we add this inverse to both sides, the result follows. That $0a = 0$ follows from the other distributive law in exactly the same way. □

The units in the ring $\mathbf{Z}$ are just 1 and -1. It can be shown that the units in the ring of $n \times n$ integer matrices are precisely those matrices with determinant 1 or -1. The units in the ring $\mathbf{Z}_n$ depend on n. In $\mathbf{Z}_3$ every nonzero element is a unit:

$$1 \times_3 1 = 1$$
$$2 \times_3 2 = 1$$

Thus, each element is its own inverse. In $\mathbf{Z}_4$, 1 and 3 are their own inverses, but 2 has no inverse, as we noted in Example 6.28. You should check that in $\mathbf{Z}_5$

$$1^{-1} = 1$$
$$2^{-1} = 3$$
$$3^{-1} = 2$$
$$4^{-1} = 4$$

so that each nonzero element has an inverse. In $\mathbf{Z}_6$ only 1 and 5 have inverses.

Rings in which every nonzero element has an inverse are important. A **field** is a ring with identity $(F, +, \cdot)$ such that

1. $ab = ba$ for all a and b in F.

2. each nonzero element of F has an inverse.

Thus, $\mathbf{Z}_3$ and $\mathbf{Z}_5$ are fields, but $\mathbf{Z}_4$ and $\mathbf{Z}_6$ are not. We conclude with a theorem that tells precisely when $\mathbf{Z}_n$ is a field.

☐ THEOREM 6.11 $\mathbf{Z}_n$ is a field if and only if n is a prime number.

PROOF   First, suppose n is not prime. Then $n = ab$, where $1 < a < n$ and $1 < b < n$. Then $a \not\equiv 0 \pmod{n}$, $b \not\equiv 0 \pmod{n}$ and $ab \equiv 0 \pmod{n}$; so in $\mathbf{Z}_n$, $a \neq 0$, $b \neq 0$, and $a \times_n b = 0$. If $\mathbf{Z}_n$ were a field, then a would have an inverse a^{-1}. But then

$$\begin{aligned} b &= 1 \times_n b \\ &= (a^{-1} \times_n a) \times_n b \\ &= a^{-1} \times_n (a \times_n b) \\ &= a^{-1} \times_n 0 \\ &= 0 \end{aligned}$$

so $b = 0$, which is a contradiction. Thus, if n is not a prime number, then $\mathbf{Z}_n$ is not a field.

Now suppose n is a prime number p, $a \in \mathbf{Z}_p$ and $a \neq 0$. To show that $\mathbf{Z}_p$ is a field, we must show that a has an inverse in $\mathbf{Z}_p$. Let S be the set of all positive integers of the form $ax + py$, where x and y are integers. Note that $a = a \cdot 1 + p \cdot 0 \in S$. Let d be the smallest element of S; say $d = ab + pc$. Then $1 \leqslant d \leqslant a < p$. Divide p by d to get a quotient q and remainder r: $p = dq + r$, where $0 \leqslant r < d$. Then $r = p - dq = p - (ab + pc)q = a(-bq) + p(1 - cq)$, which is of the form $ax + py$; so either r is in S or $r = 0$. But d is the smallest element of S and $r < d$; hence, $r = 0$. Then $p = dq$, so d is a divisor of p. But p is prime and $1 \leqslant d < p$, so $d = 1$. Thus, $1 = ab + pc$. Now divide b by p to get a quotient s and a remainder a': $b = ps + a'$, where $0 \leqslant a' < p$. Then $a' \in \mathbf{Z}_p$. Now $1 = a(ps + a') + pc$, $aa' - 1 = p(-as - c)$; so $aa' \equiv 1 \pmod{p}$. Thus, in $\mathbf{Z}_p$, $a \times_p a' = 1$, and a' is the inverse of a. Hence, $\mathbf{Z}_p$ is a field.

EXERCISES

In Exercises 1–4 cut out a square, label its corners, and physically verify the given equation.

1. $r * h = d$.

2. $t * h = f$.

3. $d * t = v$.

4. $t * d = h$.

5. Each symmetry of a square can be viewed as a permutation. For example, h:

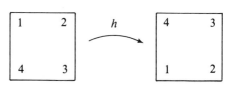

changes 1 to 4, 2 to 3, 3 to 2, and 4 to 1. That is, $h(1) = 4$, $h(2) = 3$, $h(3) = 2$, and $h(4) = 1$. Write r, s, and t as permutations.

6. (See Exercise 5.) Write v, d, and f as permutations.

7. (See Exercise 5.) Find a permutation of $\{1, 2, 3, 4\}$ that is not a symmetry of the square and thus show that the group of symmetries of the square is not S_4.

8. Find all symmetries of an equilateral triangle and show that the group of symmetries of an equilateral triangle is S_3.

9. Write the multiplication table for S_3.

10. Write the multiplication tables for S_2 and S_1.

11. Show that S_n is not commutative for $n > 2$.

Suppose H is a subset of a group G. Then H is a **subgroup** of G if H satisfies all the group axioms with the same binary operation as G.

12. Find a commutative subgroup (other than $\{e\}$) of S_3.

13. Find a commutative subgroup (other than $\{e\}$) of the group of symmetries of the square.

14. Find a commutative subgroup (other than $\{e\}$) of S_4.

It turns out that $\mathbf{Z}_5$ is the only group with 5 elements and $\mathbf{Z}_7$ is the only group with 7 elements. However, $\mathbf{Z}_8$ and the group of symmetries of the square are not the only groups with 8 elements. There are two other commutative groups with 8 elements. (There is also another noncommutative group with 8 elements, which we shall not describe.) Suppose $(G, *)$ and $(H, \circ)$ are groups. Define the **product group** to be the group of all ordered pairs of elements from G and H (that is, $G \times H$) with this product:

$$(g_1, h_1) \otimes (g_2, h_2) = (g_1 * g_2, h_1 \circ h_2)$$

In Exercises 15–18 you are asked to use this construction to describe the two other commutative groups with 8 elements.

15. Prove that $G \times H$ as described above is a group.

16. Show that $\mathbf{Z}_4 \times \mathbf{Z}_2$ is an eight-element group.

17. Let F denote the four-group. Show that $F \times \mathbf{Z}_2$ is an eight-element group.

18. Show that the groups constructed in Exercises 16 and 17 are different. Do this by showing that in the group of Exercise 17 each element is its own inverse, whereas there is an element in the group of Exercise 16 that is not its own inverse.

19. Recall that the symmetric difference of two sets A and B is $A \triangle B = (A \sim B) \cup (B \sim A)$. Show that the set of all subsets of a given set $\mathcal{U}$ forms a commutative ring with identity under the operations $\triangle$ (for $+$) and $\cap$ (for $\cdot$).

20. Find the units and their inverses in $\mathbf{Z}_7$ and $\mathbf{Z}_9$.

21. Find the units and their inverses in $\mathbf{Z}_8$ and $\mathbf{Z}_{11}$.

Let B be a Boolean algebra with $+$ and $\cdot$ as defined for Exercises 25–35 in Section 6.2. It is possible to turn B into a ring by defining

$$x \oplus y = (xy^*) + (x^*y)$$
$$x \otimes y = xy$$

In Exercises 22–27 you will verify that these definitions do indeed turn B into a ring.

22. Show that $\oplus$ and $\otimes$ are commutative.

23. Verify that $\oplus$ and $\otimes$ are associative.

24. Show that $\otimes$ distributes over $\oplus$.

25. Show that 0 is the identity for $\oplus$ and 1 is the identity for $\otimes$.

26. Show that $x \oplus x = 0$ for all x. That is, show that under $\oplus$ each element has an additive inverse, namely, itself.

Machines

Our previous work with switching circuits represents a simple mathematical model of the inner workings of a computer. In this section we take a more abstract approach, considering several mathematical models of computers in which no attention is paid to internal construction. This approach is an attempt to answer questions such as the following. Just what does it mean to "compute" a number or to "accept" a word? Are there precisely stated problems that can never be solved?

The models in this section are called **machines**. Machines read from, and some of them write on, a **tape** consisting of **frames** (Figure 6.6). The frames do

FIGURE 6.6

not have addresses. A frame may be blank or it may contain precisely one symbol chosen from a finite nonempty set A of symbols called an **alphabet**. The elements of A are called **letters**, although they may be different from the letters of the English alphabet. It is sometimes convenient to report that a frame is blank by placing the symbol $\#$ in it. Thus, $\#$ must not be a letter.

A **string** is a finite sequence of letters, written consecutively without punctuation. For instance, if $A = \{a, b, c\}$, then abc, $caaba$, and b are strings. The **length** of a string is the number of letters in it, counting repetitions. The **empty string** $\#$, consisting of no letters, has length zero. (Other commonly used symbols for the empty string are the Greek letters epsilon, ε, and lambda, λ, Λ.) A nonempty string is **stored** on a tape by placing its letters in order in consecutive frames. The empty string $\#$ may be stored in a blank frame. If X is a string and n is a positive integer, then X^n denotes the string $XX \cdots X$, with n X's. For instance, $(bca)^3 = bcabcabca$. Also, X^0 is defined to be $\#$.

EXAMPLE 6.29   If $A = \{a, b\}$, the strings of length at most 2 are $\#, a, b, a^2, ab, ba,$ and b^2. The set of all strings with letters in alphabetical order is $\{a^m b^n : m, n = 0, 1, 2, \ldots\}$.

The set of all strings that begin with b and end with a is $\{ba\} \cup \{bXa : X$ is a nonempty string$\}$. The set of all strings consisting of the string aba repeated at least once is $\{(aba)^n : n = 2, 3, \ldots\} = \{a(ba^2)^n ba, \ n = 1, 2, \ldots\}$. Note that aba is not such a string, because aba is *not* repeated.   ■

A frame is read by a machine's **sensor** (Figure 6.7). In some machines, the sensor can also erase a letter from a frame or write a letter on a frame. If such a

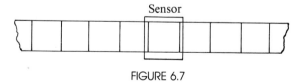

Sensor

FIGURE 6.7

machine is told to write a letter on a frame that already contains a letter, it automatically erases the old letter before it writes the new one. A machine can also move the tape through the sensor, one frame at a time. Some machines can move the tape only to the left; others can move it left or right. (Equivalently, you could think of the machine moving along a fixed tape. But be careful: moving the tape left is equivalent to moving the machine right, and vice versa.)

To **load** a sequence of strings $X_1, X_2, \ldots$ onto a previously blank tape, store the strings with one blank frame between consecutive strings. Obviously, loading the empty sequence of strings or loading any sequence in which each string is empty will simply leave the tape blank. To **place** a *nonblank* loaded tape into the sensor, insert the leftmost nonblank frame into the sensor. To place a *blank* tape, insert any frame.

A machine may be in any one of a finite nonzero number of **states**. The set S of all possible states of a machine is thus finite and nonempty. (This fact is emphasized by some authors, who call a machine a **finite state machine**.) The current state of a machine appears in a window below the sensor (Figure 6.8).

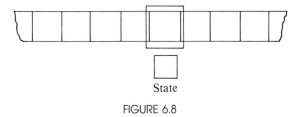

State

FIGURE 6.8

One or more states are designated **initial states**. To **run** a loaded tape, place the tape into a machine and set the machine to an initial state. We shall assume that, while it is running, the machine always takes at least one action per minute. (You may, of course, substitute any time unit you wish for our minute.) If the machine has taken no action for one minute, then it has **halted**. There could be situations in which a machine never halts.

The simplest kind of machine is called a **deterministic automaton**. (We'll explain these terms in a moment.) A deterministic automaton has exactly one initial state. The machine proceeds as follows:

1. Read the frame. If it is blank, do nothing; otherwise, proceed.

2. Move the tape one frame to the left.

3. Change to another state (which may be the same as the present state), and go to 1.

This machine is called an *automaton* because it cannot alter the tape by erasing or writing and it always moves the tape the same direction. If a blank tape is placed, the automaton will halt at once. If a tape loaded with a sequence of strings is placed, the automaton will halt after reading the first string. The machine is *deterministic* because it always begins in the same state (the unique initial state), and for each state s_i and letter x, the next state is uniquely determined. In other words, there is a **next-state function** $f: S \times A \to S$, where $f(s_i, x) =$ the next state, given the present state s_i and letter x in the sensor. The next-state function may be conveniently described by a table:

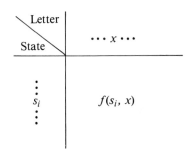

EXAMPLE 6.30 Consider the deterministic automaton with alphabet $A = \{a, b, c\}$, set of states $\{s_0, s_1, s_2, s_3\}$, initial state s_0, and the following next-state table:

	a	b	c
s_0	s_0	s_1	s_2
s_1	s_3	s_1	s_2
s_2	s_3	s_3	s_2
s_3	s_3	s_3	s_3

Here is how the machine runs for the string *abcb*:

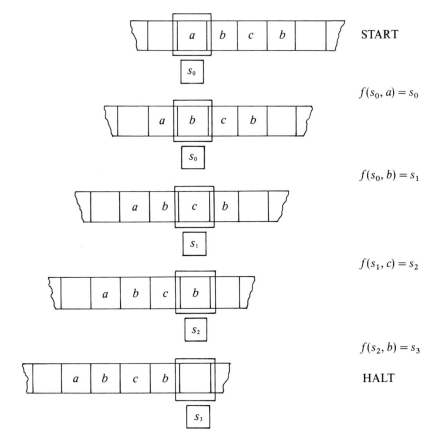

Here is the run for the string *abbc*.

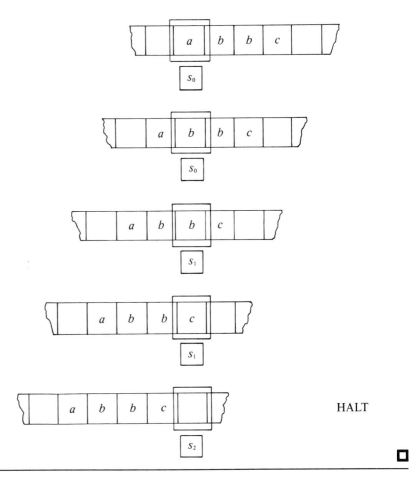

HALT

The **final state** of a machine for a given sequence of strings is the state it is in if it halts when that sequence is run. An automaton always halts. If some sequence of strings causes some machine to run forever, then that machine has no final state for that sequence. For the machine above, the final state for *abcb* is s_3 and the final state for *abbc* is s_2. The reader should run this machine for enough strings (Exercises 1–10, for example) to see that the final state of a string is s_3 if and only if the letters of the string are not in alphabetical order. More completely:

The final state is	for all strings of the form
s_0	a^n, $n = 0, 1, \ldots$
s_1	$a^m b^n$; $m = 0, 1, \ldots$; $n = 1, 2, \ldots$
s_2	$a^k b^m c^n$; $k, m = 0, 1, \ldots$; $n = 1, 2, \ldots$
s_3	none of the above

This machine can be used to accept precisely those strings that are in alphabetical order, by designating states s_0, s_1, and s_2 as **accepting** states. A machine **accepts** a string if its final state is an accepting state. A string that is accepted by a machine M is called a **word** of M. The set of all words of M is called the **language** of M and denoted $L(M)$. An accepting state will be indicated in the next-state table by an asterisk * before its row. An initial state will be indicated by a ∘ before its row. Then the full description of the deterministic automaton of Example 6.30 is given by the following table:

	a	b	c
∘*s_0	s_0	s_1	s_2
*s_1	s_3	s_1	s_2
*s_2	s_3	s_3	s_2
s_3	s_3	s_3	s_3

Two problems are immediately suggested:

I. Given a machine, describe its language.

II. Given a set of strings, describe a machine that has that set as its language.

It is often helpful for each of these problems to use the following representation of a machine as a directed graph†. Each state s_i, with the ∘ or * label if needed, is a vertex (s_i) If the machine is in state s_i, reads letter x, and can change to state j, draw $(s_i) \xrightarrow{x} (s_j)$, if $i \neq j$, and draw $(s_i) \circlearrowright x$ if $i = j$. (For deterministic machines, replace "can" in the previous sentence by "must.") For simplicity we may write $(s_i) \underset{y}{\overset{x}{\rightrightarrows}} (s_j)$ as $(s_i) \xrightarrow{x, y} (s_j)$ and $\underset{y}{\overset{x}{\circlearrowright}} (s_i)$ as $(s_i) \circlearrowright x, y$. The resulting representation is called the **digraph** of the machine. The digraph of the machine described above is shown in Figure 6.9. To run a string through the digraph, start at an initial vertex and follow the arrows in the order of the letters in the string. Thus, for the digraph above, the string ab^2cba starts at s_0 and runs to s_0, s_1, s_1, s_2, s_3, s_3, with final (nonaccepting) state s_3.

A state that a machine cannot leave once it enters is called a **trap**. For the machine above, s_3 is a trap. It is easy to recognize a trap from the next-state table (how?) or the digraph (how?). Traps have two uses: (1) as a nonaccepting state to dump partly read strings that will definitely not be accepted, and (2) as an accepting state for partly read strings that will definitely be accepted.

---

† Actually, it is a directed pseudograph, but we'll allow this abuse of language.

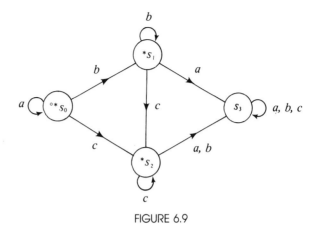

FIGURE 6.9

EXAMPLE 6.31   The deterministic automaton M shown in Figure 6.10 accepts only the string abc. Thus, $L(M) = \{abc\}$.

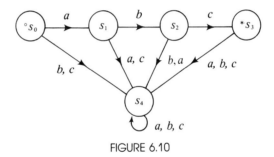

FIGURE 6.10   ☐

EXAMPLE 6.32   The deterministic automaton M shown in Figure 6.11 has $L(M) = \{cX: X$ is a string in $\{a, b, c\}\}$.

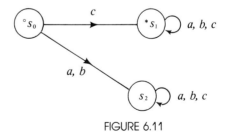

FIGURE 6.11   ☐

An optimization problem stemming from the problems above is this: given a machine M, find a machine M' with the smallest possible number of states such that $L(M) = L(M')$. For deterministic automata we shall present, without proof, an algorithm to do this. The algorithm requires two operations on machines: **reversing** and **determinizing**.

To **reverse** a deterministic automaton: (1) make the initial state an accepting state, (2) make each accepting state an initial state, and (3) reverse the direction of each arrow in the digraph representation. The resulting machine may be nondeterministic for any of several reasons: it may have several initial states; for some state–letter pairs, it may have no next state; and for some other state–letter pairs, it may have more than one next state. In practice it is easier to work with next-state tables than digraphs.

EXAMPLE 6.33   The deterministic automaton M, presented in next-state table form as well as digraph form (Figure 6.12), accepts all strings $(ab)^n$, $n = 1, 2, \ldots$.

M	a	b
$\circ s_0$	s_1	s_4
s_1	s_4	s_2
$*s_2$	s_3	s_4
s_3	s_4	s_2
s_4	s_4	s_4

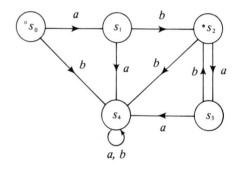

FIGURE 6.12

Its reverse, denoted RM, is also presented in both forms (Figure 6.13):

RM	a	b
$*s_0$	—	—
s_1	s_0	—
$\circ s_2$	—	$s_1 s_3$
s_3	s_2	—
s_4	$s_1 s_3 s_4$	$s_0 s_2 s_4$

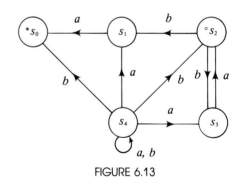

FIGURE 6.13

To get the entry in the RM table at address (s_4, a), run down column a of the M table and write all row addresses with entry s_4: since s_4 occurs in column a at rows s_1, s_3, and s_4, the entry is $s_1 s_3 s_4$, which is short for "any one of s_1 or s_3 or s_4." A search of column b of M reveals no s_3, so the entry in RM at address (s_3, b) is nothing, symbolized by —.   ◻

A nondeterministic automaton operates just as a deterministic one, except that for some state–letter pairs it may do nothing, and for some pairs it may change to any one of several states. Consider RM of Example 6.33. The machine must begin in s_2. If it reads a, then it does nothing. If it reads b, it changes to s_1 or s_3, moves the tape one frame left, and reads the next frame. The string ba could send the machine from s_2 to s_3 to s_2 or from s_2 to s_1 to s_0. A nondeterministic automaton accepts a string if for *some* run (perhaps not every run) of the string it halts in an accepting state. Thus, RM above accepts ba. (What else does it accept? See Exercise 19.)

The **determinization** of a nondeterministic automaton M, denoted DM, is a deterministic automaton that accepts precisely the same words as M does. The states of DM are subsets of the set S of all states of M—usually not *all* subsets of S, just some subsets. The states of DM are constructed recursively as follows. (1) The initial state of DM is the set of all initial states of M. (2) If A is a state of DM and x is a letter, then the next state of DM is the set of all next states to which M can change, given x, from any state in A. Finally, the accepting states of DM are each of its states that contain at least one accepting state of M. In the construction of DM we denote a set of states $\{s_i, s_j, ...\}$ simply as $s_i s_j \cdots$; the empty set, if needed (it usually is), is denoted $\varnothing$.

EXAMPLE 6.34 Let M be

M	a	b
○∗s_0	$s_1 s_2$	—
s_1	—	s_0
○s_2	s_3	$s_0 s_1$
∗s_3	—	—

The initial state of DM is $s_0 s_2$. For a, s_0 can change to s_1 or s_2, and s_2 can change to s_3. Then $s_1 s_2 s_3$ is a state of DM, which we list below the initial state of DM:

DM	a	b
○$s_0 s_2$	$s_1 s_2 s_3$	
$s_1 s_2 s_3$		

For b, s_0 can go to nothing, and s_2 can go to s_0 or s_1. Then:

DM	a	b
○$s_0 s_2$	$s_1 s_2 s_3$	$s_0 s_1$
$s_1 s_2 s_3$		
$s_0 s_1$		

For a, $s_1 s_2 s_3$ changes to s_3, because s_1 and s_3 can do nothing and s_2 can change only to s_3. Since s_3 can change to no state in M, it changes to $\varnothing$ (given either a

or b) in DM. Continuing, we finally reach this:

DM	a	b
t_0	$\circ *s_0 s_2$	$s_1 s_2 s_3$	$s_0 s_1$
t_1	$*s_1 s_2 s_3$	s_3	$s_0 s_1$
t_2	$*s_0 s_1$	$s_1 s_2$	s_0
t_3	$*s_3$	$\varnothing$	$\varnothing$
t_4	$s_1 s_2$	s_3	$s_0 s_1$
t_5	$*s_0$	$s_1 s_2$	$\varnothing$
t_6	$\varnothing$	$\varnothing$	$\varnothing$

Thus, DM has seven states. (The set S of all states of M has sixteen subsets; DM uses seven of them.) Those states of DM that contain s_0 or s_3 are accepting states of DM. To simplify notation, we rename the states of DM as $t_0, \ldots, t_6$ as shown above to obtain the following table:

DM	a	b
$*t_0$	t_1	t_2
$*t_1$	t_3	t_2
$*t_2$	t_4	t_5
$*t_3$	t_6	t_6
t_4	t_3	t_2
$*t_5$	t_4	t_6
t_6	t_6	t_6

■

A solution of the problem posed just after Example 6.32 is provided by the following result, for which we give no justification.

If M is a deterministic automaton, then a deterministic automaton M' with the smallest possible number of states such that $L(M') = L(M)$ is

$$M' = DRDRM$$

EXAMPLE 6.35   In Example 6.33 we considered an automaton M with 5 states and $L(M) = \{(ab)^n: n = 1, 2, \ldots\}$, and we constructed RM. Then:

DRM	a	b
t_0	$\circ s_2$	$\varnothing$	$s_1 s_3$
t_1	$\varnothing$	$\varnothing$	$\varnothing$
t_2	$s_1 s_3$	$s_0 s_2$	$\varnothing$
t_3	$*s_0 s_2$	$\varnothing$	$s_1 s_3$

that is:

DRM	a	b
$\circ t_0$	t_1	t_2
t_1	t_1	t_1
t_2	t_3	t_1
$*t_3$	t_1	t_2

Then:

RDRM	a	b
$*t_0$	—	—
t_1	$t_0 t_1 t_3$	$t_1 t_2$
t_2	—	$t_0 t_3$
$\circ t_3$	t_2	—

Then:

DRDRM	a	b
u_0	$\circ t_3$	t_2	$\varnothing$
u_1	t_2	$\varnothing$	$t_0 t_3$
u_2	$\varnothing$	$\varnothing$	$\varnothing$
u_3	$*t_0 t_3$	t_2	$\varnothing$

that is:

M′	a	b
$\circ u_0$	u_1	u_2
u_1	u_2	u_3
u_2	u_2	u_2
$*u_3$	u_1	u_2

which has the digraph shown in Figure 6.14. Note that $L(M') = L(M) = \{(ab)^n: n = 1, 2, \ldots\}$, but M' has only 4 states.

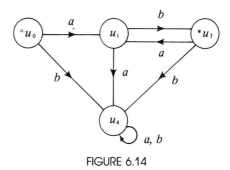

FIGURE 6.14

For the construction of algebraic processing programs, it would be useful to have an automaton that checks if parentheses are correctly placed. Such an automaton would, for instance, reject the expression $(a + b) + c)(d + (e - f)$, even though it has three left and three right parentheses. Let us suppress the variables and operation symbols in this expression to obtain $())(($. The machine would reject this expression because, in scanning it from left to right, there is a point at which more ")" have been read than "(." It may come as a surprise that *there is no automaton that can check parentheses.* We prove this assertion by contradiction. Suppose there is such an automaton. Then determinizing it, if necessary, there is a deterministic automaton M that accepts all correct parentheses expressions and does not accept any incorrect ones. Say M has n states. Consider the obviously correct expression $(^{n+1})^{n+1}$; that is,

$$\overbrace{((\ \ldots \ ((}^{n+1}\overbrace{)) \ \ldots \ ))}^{n+1}.$$

In scanning $(^{n+1}$, M starts in the initial state and changes to a next state n times. Then since M has only n states, it must be in the same state at two different points. Say M is in state s after reading $(^{i}$ and is again in state s after reading $(^{j}$, where $1 \leqslant i < j \leqslant n + 1$. Then whenever M is in state s and still has $(^{n+1-i})^{n+1}$ left to read, it will eventually halt in an accepting state. (That's the trouble with automatons: they don't "remember" how they got to a state.) Now feed M the expression $(^{n+1-i+j})^{n+1}$. This expression is obviously incorrect because it has $j - i$ more "(" than ")." M reads the first $(^{j}$ and finds itself in state s with $(^{n+1-i})^{n+1}$ still to read; so it goes on to accept this incorrect expression! Thus, there is no such automaton.

To get a parentheses checker, we must increase the abilities of our machines, allowing them to write and erase on the tape and to move the tape left or right. Such a machine is called a **Turing machine**, after Alan Turing (1912–1954), one of the founders of computer science. (Turing, a British mathematician, was instrumental in deciphering messages prepared by German "enigma" code machines during World War II. The book, *Alan Turing: the Enigma*, by Andrew Hodges (New York: Simon and Schuster, 1983) is recommended.) For a Turing machine the next-state table is expanded to a **next-action** table that includes the next state, what to write on the frame just read (or to erase the frame by "writing" $\#$ on it, or to do nothing), and which way to move the tape (L, R, or don't move). For example, the entries

	$\#$	a	b
s_0	$s_1 aR$	$s_2 L$	—

mean: if in state s_0 and the frame is blank, then go to state s_1, write a, and move tape right; if in s_0 and frame contains a, then go to state s_2, don't write or erase, and move tape left; if in s_0 and frame contains b, then do nothing (after one minute we would then realize that the machine has halted).

EXAMPLE 6.36   The following Turing machine is a parentheses checker. The alphabet is $\{(,), \dagger, \dagger\}$. The states are

s_0: searching for)

s_1: searching back for (to match a $\dagger$

s_2: searching back for an extra (

s_3: incorrect expression

s_4: correct expression

The next-action table is

	(	)	#	⊢	⊣
°s_0	$s_0 L$	$s_1 ⊣ R$	$s_2 R$	$s_0 L$	$s_0 L$
s_1	$s_0 ⊢ L$	$s_1 R$	s_3	$s_1 R$	$s_1 R$
s_2	s_3	$s_2 R$	s_4	$s_2 R$	$s_2 R$
s_3	—	—	—	—	—
*s_4	—	—	—	—	—

For the incorrect expression $(())) ($, the final position is

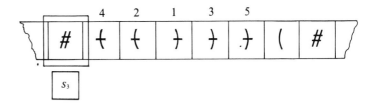

where we have indicated the order in which the machine wrote. For the correct expression $(()()(()))$, the final position is

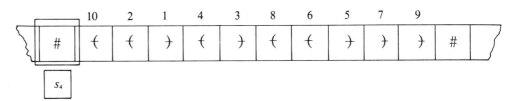

(The student should draw each step, as was done in Example 6.30.) It is easy to modify the machine to "skip over" other symbols such as $+$ or b and to "clean up" the final tape. In the following next-action table, x stands for all letters except (,), ⊢, and ⊣.

	(	)	#	⊢	⊣	x
°s_0	$s_0 L$	$s_1 ⊣ R$	$s_2 R$	$s_0 L$	$s_0 L$	$s_0 L$
s_1	$s_0 ⊢ L$	$s_1 R$	$s_3 L$	$s_1 R$	$s_1 R$	$s_1 R$
s_2	$s_3 R$	$s_2 R$	$s_4 L$	$s_2 R$	$s_2 R$	$s_2 R$
s_3	$s_3 R$	$s_3 R$	$s_5 L$	$s_3 R$	$s_3 R$	$s_3 R$
*s_4	$s_4 L$	$s_4 L$	—	$s_4 (L$	$s_4)L$	$s_4 L$
s_5	$s_5 L$	$s_5 L$	—	$s_5 (L$	$s_5)L$	$s_5 L$

Turing machines can do many things besides checking parentheses.

EXAMPLE 6.37   The following machine adds any two positive integers m and n, where a positive integer k is loaded as k consecutive 1's, and where two positive integers are separated by one blank frame.

	1	#
$\circ s_0$	$s_0 L$	$s_1 1 L$
s_1	$s_1 L$	$s_2 R$
s_2	$s_3 \#$	—
s_3	—	—

There is no accepting state.   ■

Turing machines are tremendously powerful. In fact, it is reasonable to define a computer science problem to be **solvable** if and only if it can be solved by a Turing machine. The student would do well to pursue further the study of mathematical machines, and the closely related topic of mathematical languages, perhaps in subsequent courses.

EXERCISES

In Exercises 1–10, run the machine of Example 6.30 for the given strings.

1. a^3 **6.** $a^2 c^2$

2. $a^2 b$ **7.** cab

3. ac^2 **8.** ba^2

4. $b^2 c$ **9.** $abc^2 b$

5. bc^3 **10.** $b^2 c^2 a$

In Exercises 11–20 describe the language of the automata.

11.

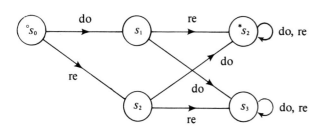

12.

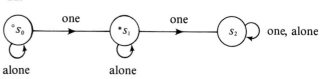

13.

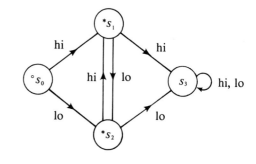

14.

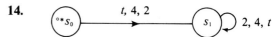

15.

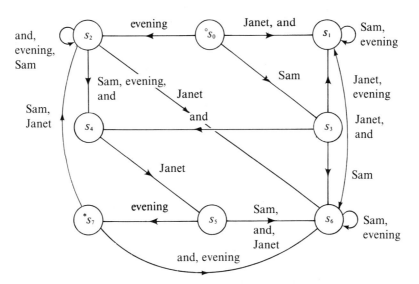

(Perhaps your parents or grandparents can explain this joke, if you tell them it was sung in *South Pacific* by Ezio Pinza.)

16.

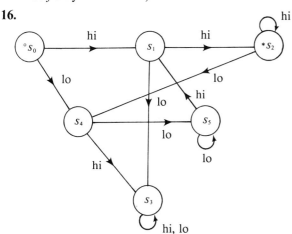

17.

	p	q	r
$\circ s_0$	s_1	s_3	s_2
$*s_1$	s_2	s_1	s_1
s_2	s_2	s_2	s_2
$*s_3$	s_3	s_2	s_3
s_4	s_2	s_2	s_3

18.

	t	u	v
$\circ s_0$	s_1	s_1	s_3
s_1	s_4	s_1	s_4
$*s_2$	s_3	s_3	s_2
$*s_3$	s_3	s_2	s_3
s_4	s_4	s_1	s_1

19. The automaton *RM* of Example 6.33.

20. The automaton *RDRM* of Example 6.35.

21. Design an **even parity checker**, that is, a deterministic automaton with alphabet $\{0, 1\}$ that accepts a string if and only if it contains an even number of 1's.

22. Define and then design an odd parity checker.

23. Define and then design a "divisible by 3" checker.

24. Define and then design a "congruent to 1 modulo 4" checker.

25. A string Y is **strongly contained** in a string X (also expressed: Y is a **substring** of X) if the letters of Y, in the order in which they appear in Y, including repetitions, appear as *consecutive* letters, in the same order, in X. For example, *bac* is strongly contained in each of *cbacb*, *bacb*, *abac*, and *bac*. Design a deterministic automaton with alphabet $\{a, b, c\}$ that accepts precisely those strings that strongly contain *baac*.

26. Repeat Exercise 25 with "strongly" replaced by "weakly" and "consecutive" deleted.

In Exercises 27 and 28 you are asked to prove the statements made in the text about the determinization *DM* of an automaton *M*.

27. Explain why every string accepted by *M* is accepted by *DM*.

28. Explain why every string accepted by *DM* is accepted by *M*.

In Exercises 29–34 find a deterministic automaton M' with the smallest possible number of states such that $L(M') = L(M)$.

29.

M	a	b
$\circ s_0$	s_3	s_2
$*s_1$	s_1	s_3
s_2	s_2	s_4
$*s_3$	s_1	s_3
s_4	s_2	s_2

30.

M	0	1
$\circ*s_0$	s_2	s_0
s_1	s_0	s_2
s_2	s_0	s_1

31.

M	0	1
$\circ s_0$	s_2	s_1
$*s_1$	s_4	s_1
s_2	s_4	s_3
$*s_3$	s_0	s_1
s_4	s_2	s_3
$*s_5$	s_4	s_5

32.

M	a	b
$\circ s_0$	s_2	s_1
$*s_1$	s_6	s_1
s_2	s_4	s_3
$*s_3$	s_2	s_5
s_4	s_5	s_4
s_5	s_5	s_4
s_6	s_6	s_1

33.

M	u	v	w
$\circ s_0$	s_4	s_5	s_1
s_1	s_4	s_5	s_2
$*s_2$	s_3	s_2	s_2
$*s_3$	s_3	s_3	s_3
s_4	s_7	s_7	s_9
s_5	s_6	s_5	s_5
s_6	s_6	s_6	s_6
s_7	s_7	s_8	s_7
$*s_8$	s_9	s_8	s_9
s_9	s_9	s_8	s_9

34.

M	0	1
$\circ s_0$	s_0	s_1
$*s_1$	s_2	s_3
$*s_2$	s_2	s_1
$*s_3$	s_0	s_3

For the following two exercises let M_1 be a deterministic automaton with alphabet $A_1 = \{a_{11}, a_{12}, ...\}$ and set state $S_1 = \{\circ s_{10}, s_{11}, ...\}$, and M_2 be a deterministic automaton with alphabet $A_2 = \{a_{21}, a_{22}, ...\}$ and set state $S_2 = \{\circ s_{20}, s_{21}, ...\}$.

35. Describe how to construct a deterministic automaton $M_1 \wedge M_2$ such that $L(M_1 \wedge M_2) = L(M_1) \cap L(M_2)$.

36. Describe how to construct a deterministic automaton $M_1 \vee M_2$ such that $L(M_1 \vee M_2) = L(M_1) \cup L(M_2)$.

37. Give an example of a string for which the Turing machine of Example 6.36 does not halt at the left end of the string.

38. What can be said about all examples that solve Exercise 37?

In Exercises 39–42 describe what the Turing machines do.

39.

	a	b
$\circ s_0$	$s_0 bL$	$s_0 aL$

40.

	a	b	c
$\circ s_0$	$s_0 aL$	$s_0 bL$	$s_0 \#L$

41.

	a	b	$\#$
$\circ s_0$	$s_1 R$	$s_1 R$	$s_1 a$
s_1	$s_1 L$	$s_1 L$	$s_2 b$
s_2	$s_2 R$	$s_2 R$	—

42.

	a	b	$\#$
$\circ s_0$	$s_1 L$	$s_2 L$	s_3
s_1	$s_1 L$	$s_1 L$	$s_3 a$
s_2	$s_2 L$	$s_2 L$	$s_3 b$
s_3	$s_3 R$	$s_3 R$	—

43. Design a Turing machine that will **concatenate** two nonempty strings from the alphabet $\{p, q\}$. Thus, given the strings pqp and pq, stored as usual, the machine will halt with $pqppq$.

44. Design a Turing machine to add two nonnegative integers, where a nonnegative integer n is represented by a $11\cdots1$, with $n+1$ ones.

45. Design a Turing machine that "tries" to write ha on every frame of a (possibly loaded, possibly blank) tape. Why do we say "tries"? Be careful, there may be some previous ha's on the tape.

Answers to Odd-Numbered Exercises

CHAPTER ONE

Section 1.1, page 6

1. Note that $x = -b/a$ unless $a = 0$.
   If $a \neq 0$, then the answer is $-b/a$.
   If $a = 0$ and $b \neq 0$, then there is no answer.
   If $a = 0$ and $b = 0$, then every number is an answer.

3. Note that $x = c/ab$, unless $ab = 0$.
   If $ab \neq 0$, then the answer is c/ab.
   If $ab = 0$ and $c \neq 0$, then there is no answer.
   If $ab = 0$ and $c = 0$, then every number is an answer.

5. Solve $ax + b = 0$.
   1. If $a = 0$, then go to 3
   2. "The answer is $-b/a$." STOP
   3. If $b = 0$, then go to 5
   4. "There is no answer." STOP
   5. "Every number is an answer." STOP

7. Solve $abx = c$.
   1. If $ab = 0$, then go to 3
   2. "The answer is c/ab." STOP
   3. If $c = 0$, then go to 5
   4. "There is no answer." STOP
   5. "Every number is an answer." STOP

9. b^2 **11.** ba **13.** 10

15. The program will not terminate. Therefore there will be an arbitrarily large, that is, "infinite" number of steps.

17. 16   **19.** 13, 11, 74

21.
$p = 5$	$p = 1$
"1"	$n = 2$
$n = 6$	"1"
"0"	$p = 0$
"0"	"0"
$p = 2$	
"1"	100110

23. 1100, 101111

25. Write n in ternary notation.
   1. $p \leftarrow 0$
   2. If $3^{p+1} > n$, go to 5
   3. $p \leftarrow p + 1$, go to 2
   4. If $3^p > n$, go to 12
   5. If $n - 3^p \geqslant 3^p$, go to 9
   6. "1"
   7. If $p = 0$, STOP
   8. $n \leftarrow n - 3^p$, $p \leftarrow p - 1$, go to 4
   9. "2"
   10. If $p = 0$, STOP
   11. $n \leftarrow n - 2 \cdot 3^p$, $p \leftarrow p - 1$, go to 4
   12. "0"
   13. If $p = 0$, then STOP
   14. $p \leftarrow p - 1$, go to 4

27. Group the binary digits by threes from the right. Replace each group of three digits with its octal equivalent.

$$101011110 \rightarrow 101\ 011\ 110$$
$$\rightarrow\ 5\quad 3\quad 6$$
$$\rightarrow\ 536$$

$$110000001101 \rightarrow 110\ 000\ 001\ 101$$
$$\rightarrow\ 6\quad 0\quad 1\quad 5$$
$$\rightarrow\ 6015$$

29. 2589; 718; 2989

31. Replace each digit with its four-place binary equivalent.

$$A1D \rightarrow 1010\ 0001\ 1101 \rightarrow 101000011101$$
$$2CE \rightarrow 0010\ 1100\ 1110 \rightarrow\ 1011001110$$
$$BAD \rightarrow 1011\ 1010\ 1101 \rightarrow 101110101101$$

Section 1.2, page 16

1. $(7, 4, 0, 3, 3)$

3. $a_5 = 3, a_2 = 1, a_9$ is not defined.

5. max $= 2$; min $= -3$

7. $i \leftarrow 1$
$m \leftarrow 2$
$i \leftarrow 2$
$m \leftarrow 1$
$i \leftarrow 3, 4, 5, 6, 7, 8$

The minimum is 1.

9. $i \leftarrow 1, j \leftarrow 1$
$m \leftarrow 2$
$i \leftarrow 2, j \leftarrow 2$
$m \leftarrow 1$
$i \leftarrow 3, 4, 5, 6, 7, 8$

The minimum is 1, which occurs at address(es) 2.

11. Selection sort requires 6 comparisons and no switches. Bubblesort requires 3 comparisons and no switches.

13. $k = 5$.
$i = 1, j = 1$.
$(3, 4, 4, 2, 1)$. $\{a_1 \leftrightarrow a_2\}$
$j = 1$.
$i = 2$.
$i = 3$.
$(3, 4, 2, 4, 1)$. $\{a_3 \leftrightarrow a_4\}$
$j = 3$.
$i = 4$.
$(3, 4, 2, 1, 4)$. $\{a_4 \leftrightarrow a_5\}$
$j = 4$.
$i = 5$.
$k = 4$.
$i = 1, j = 1$.
$i = 2$.
$(3, 2, 4, 1, 4)$. $\{a_2 \leftrightarrow a_3\}$
$j = 2$.
$i = 3$.
$(3, 2, 1, 4, 4)$. $\{a_3 \leftrightarrow a_4\}$

$j = 3$.
$i = 4$.
$k = 3$.
$i = 1, j = 1$.
$(2, 3, 1, 4, 4)$. $\{a_1 \leftrightarrow a_2\}$
$j = 1$.
$i = 2$.
$(2, 1, 3, 4, 4)$. $\{a_2 \leftrightarrow a_3\}$
$j = 2$.
$i = 3$.
$k = 2$.
$i = 1, j = 1$.
$(1, 2, 3, 4, 4)$. $\{a_1 \leftrightarrow a_2\}$
$j = 1$.
$i = 2$.
$k = 1$.
$i = k$.
$k = 1$.
$(1, 2, 3, 4, 4)$

15. a. A sequence in strictly decreasing order.
  b. A sequence already in increasing order.

17. $i \leftarrow 1, 2, 3, 4$
  b belongs in cell 5.

19. LINKED

21. 5, 7, 4, 6, 2, LAST, 3

23. 3, 5, 6, 7, 4, 2, LAST

25. *Program.* To find $\min(a_1, a_2, \ldots, a_n)$ and every address at which it occurs
  1. $i \leftarrow 1$
  2. $m \leftarrow a_i, j \leftarrow i$
  3. If $i = n$, then go to 6
  4. $i \leftarrow i + 1$
  5. If $a_i < m$, then go to 2; otherwise, go to 3
  6. $k \leftarrow j; h \leftarrow 1$
  {Now k is the first address of the minimum; h counts the number of occurrences of the minimum.}
  7. $j \leftarrow j + 1$
  8. If $j = n + 1$, then go to 11
  9. If $a_j \neq m$, then go to 7
  10. $h \leftarrow h + 1$, then go to 7
  11. If $h = 1$, then go to 14
  12. If $h = 2$, then go to 15
  13. Go to 18
  14. "The minimum is m, which occurs at address k." STOP
  15. $j \leftarrow j' + 1$
  16. If $a_j \neq m$, then go to 15
  17. "The minimum is m, which occurs at addresses k and j." STOP
  18. "The minimum is m, which occurs at addresses k,"
  19. $j \leftarrow k; g \leftarrow 1$
  20. $j \leftarrow j + 1$
  21. If $a_j \neq m$, then go to 20
  22. If $g = h$, then go to 25
  23. $g \leftarrow g + 1$
  24. "j,", then go to 20
  25. "and j." STOP

27. Here is a simple-minded program.
  Program. To determine whether two or more elements in a sequence $(a_1, \ldots, a_n)$ are equal.
  1. $i \leftarrow 1$
  2. $j \leftarrow i + 1$
  3. If $a_i = a_j$, go to 8
  4. If $j = n$ go to 6
  5. $j \leftarrow j + 1$, go to 3
  6. If $i = n - 1$ go to 9
  7. $i \leftarrow i + 1$, go to 2
  8. "The entries at addresses i and j are equal." STOP
  9. "No two entries are equal." STOP

29. A_5, A_2, A_4, A_1, A_3

31. Here is a modification of Program 1.7.
  Program. To put a sequence of sequences $(A_1, \ldots, A_n)$ where $A_i = (a_{i1}, \ldots, a_{in_i})$ in lexicographic order.
  1. $k \leftarrow n$
  2. $i \leftarrow 1, j \leftarrow 1$

3. If $i = k$ then go to 10
4. $m \leftarrow 1$
5. If $a_{im} > a_{i+1,m}$ go to 8
6. If $m = \min\{n_i, n_{i+1}\}$ then go to 9
7. $m \leftarrow m + 1$
8. $A_i \leftrightarrow A_{i+1}, j \leftarrow 1$
9. $i \leftarrow i + 1$, go to 3
10. If $k = 1$ then go to 12
11. $k \leftarrow j$, go to 2
12. "$(A_1, \ldots, A_n)$" STOP

33. The sequence is $(4, 1, 1, 5, 4)$. $n = 5$
$t = 0, 1, 2, 3$
$p = 4 = 100_2$
$q = 4; r = 0; d = 4; n - d = 1$
$i = 0$
$i \wedge p = 0 = r$
Compare a_1 with a_5. Don't switch.
$i = 1 = n - d$
$q = p$
$p \neq 1$
$p = 2 = 10_2$
$q = 4; r = 0; d = 2; n - d = 3$
$i = 0$
$i \wedge p = 0 = r$
Compare a_1 with a_3. Switch: $(1, 1, 4, 5, 4)$.
$i = 1$
$i \wedge p = 0 = r$
Compare a_2 with a_4. Don't switch.
$i = 2$
$i \wedge p = 2 \neq r$
$i = 3 = n - d$
$q \neq p$
$d = 2; q = 2; r = 2 = 10_2; n - d = 3$
$i = 0, 1, 2 = 10_2$
$i \wedge p = 10_2 = r$
Compare a_3 with a_5. Don't switch.
$i = 3 = n - d$
$q = p$
$p \neq 1$
$p = 1$
$q = 4; r = 0; d = 1; n - d = 4$
$i = 0$
$i \wedge p = 0 = r$
Compare a_1 with a_2. Don't switch.
$i = 1 \neq n - d$
$i \wedge p = 1 \neq r$
$i = 2 \neq n - d$
$i \wedge p = 0 = r$
Compare a_3 with a_4. Don't switch.
$i = 3 \neq n - d$
$i \wedge p = 1 \neq r$
$i = 4 = n - d$
$q \neq p$
$d = 3; q = 2; r = 1; n - d = 2$
$i = 0, 1$
$i \wedge p = 1 = r$
Compare a_2 with a_5. Don't switch.
$i = 2 = n - d$
$q \neq p$
$d = 1; q = 1; r = 1; n - d = 4$
$i = 0, 1$
$i \wedge p = 1 = r$
Compare a_2 with a_3. Don't switch.
$i = 2 \neq n - d$
$i \wedge p = 0 \neq r$
$i = 3 \neq n - d$
$i \wedge p = 1 = r$
Compare a_4 with a_5. Switch: $(1, 1, 4, 4, 5)$.
$i = 4 = n - d$
$q = p$
$p = 1$
STOP

$(1, 1, 4, 4, 5)$

Section 1.3, page 27

1. 4, 6, 8, 10   **3.** 23, 29

5. Washington, Adams

7. The set is empty.

9. $\{x: x$ is an even positive integer less than $10\}$, for example

11. $\{x: x$ was president of the United States in 1963 or 1972$\}$, for example

13. $\{x: x$ is a real number whose square is $-1\}$, for example

15. False. b is an element of A, but b is not either of the two elements in B.

17. True. a is the only element in common to A and B.

19. False. c is not an element of A and it is not either of the two elements of B.

21. 1   **23.** 2   **25.** By Venn diagrams:

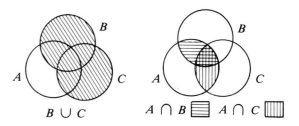

$B \cup C$ $A \cap B$▤ $A \cap C$▥

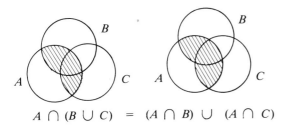

$$A \cap (B \cup C) = (A \cap B) \cup (A \cap C)$$

27. By Venn diagrams:

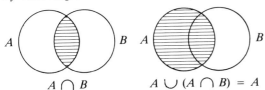

$$A \cap B \qquad A \cup (A \cap B) = A$$

29. *Program.* To find $A \cap B$ for finite sets $A = \{a_1, \ldots, a_m\}$ and $B = \{b_1, \ldots, b_n\}$.
  1. $C \leftarrow \emptyset$
  2. $i \leftarrow 1$
  3. If $i = m + 1$ go to 7
  4. If $a_i \in B$ go to 6
  5. $i \leftarrow i + 1$, go to 3
  6. $C \leftarrow C \cup \{a_i\}$, go to 5
  7. "$A \cap B = C$." STOP

31. If $x = u$ and $y = v$, then $\{x\} = \{u\}$, and $\{x, y\} = \{u, v\}$, so $(x, y) = \{\{x\}, \{x, y\}\} = \{\{u\}, \{u, v\}\} = (u, v)$. Now suppose $\{\{x\}, \{x, y\}\} = \{\{u\}, \{u, v\}\}$. Then $\{u\} \in \{\{x\}, \{x, y\}\}$. If $\{u\} = \{x\}$, then $u = x$. If $\{u\} = \{x, y\}$, then $u = x$ and $u = y$. In any case $u = x$. Also, $\{u, v\} \in \{\{x\}, \{x, y\}\}$. If $\{u, v\} = \{x\}$, then $u = v = x$. In that case $\{x, y\} = \{u\}$, so $x = y = u$. So $v = y$. If $\{u, v\} = \{x, y\}$, since $u = x$, $v = y$. In any case $v = y$.

33. $\{(a, a), (a, b), (b, a), (b, b), (c, a), (c, b)\}$

35. $\{(3, 3)\}$ **37.** $\{(3, 3)\}$ **39.** Only equals

41. $f = \{(1, 1), (2, 4), (3, 9), (4, 16)\}$

43. $f = \{(1, 3), (2, 3), (3, 5), (4, 4)\}$

45. Injection but not surjection

47. Surjection but not injection

49. Bijection; $f^{-1}(y) = 3 - y$

51. Neither surjection nor injection

53. Bijection; $f^{-1} = \emptyset$

Section 1.4, page 41

1. $-1, -10, 1$ **3.** $(1, 3), (2, 2), (2, 1)$

5. $x = -1, y = -5, z = 5, w = -10, u = 11$

7. There is no solution; the given matrix is the wrong size.

9. $\begin{bmatrix} 24 & -4 & -20 \\ -28 & 4 & 20 \\ -40 & 8 & 44 \end{bmatrix}$

11. For example, $k = 1/24$ and $C = \begin{bmatrix} 12 & -16 \\ -18 & 15 \end{bmatrix}$.

13. $\begin{bmatrix} 8 & -3 & -2 \\ -4 & 2 & 9 \\ -3 & -1 & 21 \end{bmatrix}$ **15.** $\begin{bmatrix} 4 & 1 & -8 \\ -10 & 0 & 1 \\ -17 & 5 & 1 \end{bmatrix}$

17. *Program.* Given k and $C = [c_{ij}]_{m \times n}$ to find kC.
  1. $i \leftarrow 1$
  2. $j \leftarrow 1$
  3. $a_{ij} \leftarrow k c_{ij}$
  4. If $j \neq n$, $j \leftarrow j + 1$ and go to 3
  5. If $i \neq m$, $i \leftarrow i + 1$ and go to 2
  6. "$[a_{ij}]$" STOP

19. $[6 \quad -1 \quad -5], [-7 \quad 1 \quad 5], [-10 \quad 2 \quad 11]$

21. $[-12]$ or -12

23. $\begin{bmatrix} -26 & 2 & -36 \\ 24 & 0 & 33 \\ 63 & -11 & 88 \end{bmatrix}$

25.   1. $3 = 3$
  2. $i = 1$
  3. $j = 1$
  4. $k = 1, c_{11} = 0$
  5. $c_{11} = c_{11} + 6 \cdot 2 = 0 + 12 = 12$
  6. $k = 2$
  7. $c_{11} = c_{11} + (-1)(3) = 12 - 3 = 9$
  8. $k = 3$
  9. $c_{11} = c_{11} + (-5)(7) = 9 - 35 = -26$
  10. $k = 3 = n$
  11. Store -26 at address $(1, 1)$
  12. $j = 2$
  13. $k = 1, c_{12} = 0$
  14. $c_{12} = c_{12} + (6)(-2) = 0 - 12 = -12$
  15. $k = 2$
  16. $c_{12} = c_{12} + (-1)(1) = -12 - 1 = -13$
  17. $k = 3$
  18. $c_{12} = c_{12} + (-5)(-3) = -13 + 15 = 2$
  19. $k = 3 = n$
  20. Store 2 at address $(1, 2)$

27. $m \times n$

29. $\begin{bmatrix} 4 & 5 & 6 & 5 & 4 \\ 7 & 8 & 9 & 8 & 7 \end{bmatrix} \begin{bmatrix} 1 & 0 \\ 0 & 1 \end{bmatrix} = \begin{bmatrix} 4 & 5 & 6 & 5 & 4 \\ 7 & 8 & 9 & 8 & 7 \end{bmatrix}$

31. $\begin{bmatrix} 6 & -1 & -5 \\ -21 & 3 & 15 \\ -10 & 2 & 11 \end{bmatrix}$ **33.** $\begin{bmatrix} 6 & -1 & -5 \\ -7 & 1 & 5 \\ -22 & 4 & 21 \end{bmatrix}$

35. $\begin{bmatrix} -10 & 2 & 11 \\ -7 & 1 & 5 \\ 6 & -1 & 5 \end{bmatrix}$

37. *Program.* To do $R_i \leftarrow kR_i$ on a matrix $A = [a_{jl}]_{m \times n}$.
1. $j \leftarrow 1$
2. $l \leftarrow 1$
3. If $j = i$, go to 5
4. $c_{jl} \leftarrow a_{jl}$, go to 6
5. $c_{jl} \leftarrow la_{jl}$
6. If $l \neq n$, $l \leftarrow l + 1$, go to 3
7. If $j \neq m$, $j \leftarrow j + 1$, go to 2
8. "$[c_{jl}]$" STOP

39. *Program.* To do $R_i \leftrightarrow R_j$ on a matrix $A = [a_{rs}]_{m \times n}$, where $i \neq j$.
1. $r \leftarrow 1$
2. $s \leftarrow 1$
3. If $r = i$ go to 6
4. If $r = j$ go to 7
5. $c_{rs} \leftarrow a_{rs}$, go to 8
6. $c_{rs} \leftarrow a_{js}$, go to 8
7. $c_{js} \leftarrow a_{is}$
8. If $s \neq n$, $s \leftarrow s + 1$, go to 3
9. If $r \neq m$, $r \leftarrow r + 1$, go to 2
10. "$[c_{rs}]$" STOP.

41. $\begin{matrix} R_1 + R_2 \\ \\ R_3 - 2R_2 \end{matrix} \begin{bmatrix} -1 & 0 & 0 \\ -7 & 1 & 5 \\ 4 & 0 & 1 \end{bmatrix}$

43. *Program.* To use R_i to clear C_j in a matrix $M = [m_{rs}]_{m \times n}$.
1. If $m_{ij} = 0$, "Cannot be done." STOP
2. $r \leftarrow 1$
3. $s \leftarrow 1$
4. If $r = i$, go to 6
5. $c_{rs} \leftarrow m_{rs} - m_{is}(m_{rj}/m_{ij})$, go to 7
6. $c_{rs} \leftarrow m_{rs}/m_{ij}$
7. If $s \neq n$, $s \leftarrow s + 1$, go to 4
8. If $r \neq m$, $r \leftarrow r + 1$, go to 3
9. "$[c_{ij}]$" STOP

45. $x = 1$, $y = 0$, $z = 1$

47. $x = \frac{1}{2} - (\frac{11}{8})z$, $y = \frac{3}{2} + (\frac{1}{8})z$, z is free.

49. $A^{-1} = \begin{bmatrix} -1 & -1 & 0 \\ -27 & -16 & -5 \\ 4 & 2 & 1 \end{bmatrix}$

51. Only 1×1 row matrices, since only they are square.

53.
$\left. \begin{matrix} 6x_1 - x_2 - 5x_3 = 1 \\ -7x_1 + x_2 - 5x_3 = 0 \\ -10x_1 + 2x_2 + 11x_3 = 0 \end{matrix} \right\}$

$\left. \begin{matrix} 6x_1 - x_2 - 5x_3 = 0 \\ -7x_1 + x_2 - 5x_3 = 1 \\ -10x_1 + 2x_2 + 11x_3 = 0 \end{matrix} \right\}$

$\left. \begin{matrix} 6x_1 - x_2 - 5x_3 = 0 \\ -7x_1 - x_2 - 5x_3 = 0 \\ -10x_1 + 2x_2 + 11x_3 = 1 \end{matrix} \right\}$

Algorithm 1.5 solves each of these systems simultaneously. The answer for each column of the inverse can be read all at once and put together on the right when the identity matrix appears on the left.

CHAPTER TWO

Section 2.1, page 54

1. 20   **3.** 1   **5.** 5   **7.** 7   **9.** $2^8 = 256$

11. a. $26^5 = 11,881,376$
    b. $26 \cdot 25 \cdot 24 \cdot 23 \cdot 22 = 7,893,600$

13. $\binom{5}{2} \cdot 5 \cdot 4 \cdot 21 \cdot 20 \cdot 19 = 1,596,000$

14. For each choice of five letters, there is exactly one way to alphabetize them. Thus, the answer is $\binom{26}{5} 1 = 65,780$.

15. Arrange the count by the number of repeated letters. No letters repeated: pick five, alphabetize.

(example: ACFGL) $\binom{26}{5} = 65,780$

One letter repeated: pick four, pick one to repeat, alphabetize.

(example: ADDRS) $4\binom{26}{4} = 59,800$

One letter three times: pick three, pick one to repeat.

(example: ADHHH) $3\binom{26}{3} = 7,800$

One letter three times, one twice: pick two, pick one for twice.

(example: SSYYY) $2\binom{26}{2} = 650$

Two letters twice: pick three, pick one not to repeat.

(example: PPXZZ) $3\binom{26}{3} = 7,800$

One letter four times: pick two, pick one to repeat.

(example: WXXXX) $2\binom{26}{2} = 650$

One letter five times: pick one letter to repeat.

(example: OOOOO) $\binom{26}{1} = \underline{26}$

Answer: 142,506

17. $x^k y^{n-k}$ **19.** $\binom{n}{k}x^k y^{n-k}$ **21.** 2^n

23. $2^n = (1+1)^n = \sum_{k=0}^{n} \binom{n}{k} 1^k 1^{n-k} = \sum_{k=0}^{n} \binom{n}{k}$

25. $D_5 = 44$

Section 2.2, page 61

1. $n=1$: $\sum_{k=1}^{1} 1^3 = 1(1+1)^2/4.$ ✓

Suppose $\sum_{k=1}^{n} k^3 = n^2(n+1)^2/4.$ Then

$$\sum_{k=1}^{n+1} k^3 = \sum_{k=1}^{n} k^3 + (n+1)^3$$
$$= n^2(n+1)^2/4 + (n+1)^3$$
$$= (n+1)^2[n^2/4 + n + 1]$$
$$= (n+1)^2[n^2 + 4n + 4]/4$$
$$= (n+1)^2(n+2)^2/4 \checkmark$$

3. The inductive step fails for $n=2$.

5. $\sum_{k=1}^{n} 2k = 2 \sum_{k=1}^{n} k = 2[n(n+1)/2] = n^2 + n$

7. First, $8! = 40,320$ while $4^8 = 65,536$. So the formula fails at $n = 8$. Next, $9! = 362,880 > 264,144$ so the formula works for $n = 9$. Answer: $n \geqslant 9$.

Proof. It works for $n = 9$. Suppose $n! > 4^n$. Then

$$(n+1)! = (n+1)n!$$
$$> (n+1)4^n$$
$$> 4 \cdot 4^n$$
$$= 4^{n+1}, \checkmark$$

provided $n + 1 > 4$, which we certainly have.

9. $1^2 = (2-1)^2 = 2(2^2-1)/6$ ✓

Suppose $1^2 + \cdots + (n-1)^2 = n(n^2-1)/6.$ Then

$$1^2 + 3^2 + \cdots + (n-1)^2 + (n+1)^2$$
$$= n(n^2-1)/6 + (n+1)^2$$
$$= (n+1)[n(n-1) + 6(n+1)]/6$$
$$= (n+1)(n^2 + 5n + 6)/6$$
$$= (n+1)(n+2)(n+3)/6$$
$$= (n+2)((n+2)^2 - 1)/6 \checkmark$$

11.

13.

15. Suppose $x = n + f$, where n is an integer and $0 < f < 1$. Then $\lfloor x \rfloor = n$ and $\lceil x \rceil = n + 1$. Thus, $f = 0$, and the only solutions are integers.

17. Let $y = \lg x$. Then by definition, $2^y = x$. So $\log 2^y = \log x$ or (by properties of log) $y \log 2 = \log x$. Thus, $y = \dfrac{\log x}{\log 2}$.

19. Result 2.1(7) is true for $n = 2$, since in that case it *is* Result 2.1(6). Now suppose that Result 2.1(7) holds for $i = n$. Suppose we are given $n + 1$ actions $1, 2, \ldots, n, n + 1$. The number of elements resulting from the first n actions is, by the inductive assumption, $N_1 \cdots N_n$. The number of elements from the $(n + 1)$st action is N_{n+1}. Thus, by Result 2.1(6), the total number of elements from the $n + 1$ actions is

$$(N_1 \cdots N_n)N_{n+1} = N_1 \cdots N_n N_{n+1}$$

and the result is proved.

21. Certainly, $f(1) = [f(1)]^1$. Now suppose $f(n) = [f(1)]^n$. Then $f(n + 1) = f(n)f(1) = [f(1)]^n f(1) = [f(1)]^{n+1}$.

Section 2.3, page 67

1. Approximately 10,812,763,900,000,000,000   **3.** 5

5. Characteristic equation: $x^2 - 5x + 6 = (x - 2)(x - 3)$
Roots: $r_1 = 2, r_2 = 3$
$g_n = 3^n p_1 + 2^n p_2$
$\left. \begin{array}{l} g_0 = p_1 + p_2 = -1 \\ g_1 = 3p_1 + 2p_2 = 0 \end{array} \right\}$
$p_1 = 2, p_2 = -3$
Answer: $a_n = 2 \cdot 3^n - 3 \cdot 2^n$

7. $a_n = 5^n(1 - n)$ **9.** $a_n = (\frac{1}{4})^{n-1} + 4^{n-1}$

11. Characteristic equation: $x^3 - 9x^2 + 26x - 24 = (x - 2)(x - 3)(x - 4)$
$a_n = p_1 2^n + p_2 3^n + p_3 4^n$
$\left. \begin{array}{l} p_1 + p_2 + p_3 = a_0 = \\ 2p_1 + 3p_2 + 4p_3 = a_1 = \\ 4p_1 + 9p_2 + 16p_3 = a_2 = \end{array} \right\} \begin{cases} 1 \\ 3 \\ 11 \end{cases}$
$p_1 = 1, p_2 = -1, p_3 = 1$
Answer: $a_n = 2^n - 3^n + 4^n$

13. $a_n = \frac{4}{3} + (\frac{1}{3})(-1)^n + (\frac{7}{6})2^n + (\frac{13}{6})(-2)^n$ **15.** $a_n = n!$

17.

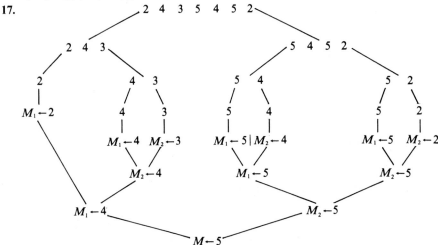

19. $i = 1.$
$j = 4.$
$k = 1.$
$a_1 \leqslant a_4$? No.
$b_1 = 2.$
$j = 5.$
$a_1 \leqslant a_5$? Yes.
$b_2 = 4.$
$i = 2.$
$a_2 \leqslant a_5$? No.
$b_3 = 4.$
$j = 6.$

$a_2 \leqslant a_6$? Yes.
$b_4 = 5.$
$i = 3.$
$a_3 \leqslant a_6$? No.
$b_5 = 6.$
$j = 7.$
$a_3 \leqslant a_7$? Yes.
$b_6 = 8.$
$i = 4.$
$b_7 = 9.$

$(2, 4, 4, 5, 6, 8, 9)$

21.

7 6 5 4 3 2 1
7 6 5   4 3 2 1
7   6 5   4 3   2 1
7   6   5   4   3 2   1
7   5 6   3 4   1 2
5 6 7   1 2 3 4
1 2 3 4 5 6 7

23. For a sequence (a_k) of length 1, LOCATE is:
1. If $b = a_k$, go to 3
2. $L = 0$; "b not yet found." STOP
3. "$b = a_k$." STOP

Suppose LOCATE is described for sequences of length i for $1 \leqslant i \leqslant n-1$, $n \geqslant 2$. Then LOCATE for $(a_1, \ldots, a_n)$ is:
1. LOCATE b in $(a_1, \ldots, a_{\lfloor n/2 \rfloor})$.
2. If $L = 0$, go to 4
3. "$b = a_L$." STOP
4. LOCATE b in $(a_{\lfloor n/2 \rfloor + 1}, \ldots, a_n)$
5. If $L = 0$, go to 7
6. "$b = a_L$." STOP
7. "b not yet found." STOP

25. It is greater than or equal to the entries before it and less than or equal to the entries after it.

Section 2.4, page 74

1. a. 5 **b.** 15 **c.** 15 **d.** 12 **e.** 14

3. $(n-1)n/2$

5. a. 3 **b.** 3 **c.** 5 **d.** 5

7. $\min(m, n)$

9. a. 7 **b.** 9 **c.** 11 **d.** 10 **e.** 8

11. $n2^{n-1}$ **13.** $m(2n-1)p$

15. $A(B+C)$: $np + m(2n-1)p$, $AB + AC$: $2m(2n-1)p + np$, which is larger by $m(2n-1)p$.

17. a. $\begin{bmatrix} 1 & 3 \\ 2 & 4 \end{bmatrix}$ **b.** $\begin{bmatrix} 1 \\ 2 \\ 3 \\ 4 \end{bmatrix}$ **c.** $\begin{bmatrix} 1 & 4 \\ 2 & 5 \\ 3 & 6 \end{bmatrix}$ **d.** unchanged

19. $n(n-1)/2$

21. a. $(x_1 - x_2)(x_1 - x_3)(x_2 - x_3)$ **b.** $n(n-1)/2$

23. $|A_1| = 1$. For $n \geqslant 2$, $|A_n| = n!/2$.

25. $\det[a_{ij}]_{1 \times 1} = a_{11}$,
$\det[a_{ij}]_{3 \times 3} = a_{11}a_{22}a_{33} - a_{11}a_{23}a_{32} + a_{12}a_{23}a_{31}$
$\qquad - a_{12}a_{21}a_{33} + a_{13}a_{21}a_{32} - a_{13}a_{22}a_{31}$

27. $a_{11}\begin{vmatrix} a_{22} & a_{23} \\ a_{32} & a_{33} \end{vmatrix} - a_{12}\begin{vmatrix} a_{21} & a_{23} \\ a_{31} & a_{33} \end{vmatrix} - a_{13}\begin{vmatrix} a_{21} & a_{22} \\ a_{31} & a_{32} \end{vmatrix} = $ result of Exercise 25. Similarly for $i = 2$.

29. $a_{11}a_{22} \cdots a_{nn}$

31. a. $\begin{vmatrix} a_{21} & a_{22} \\ a_{11} & a_{12} \end{vmatrix} = a_{21}a_{12} - a_{22}a_{11} = -(a_{11}a_{22} - a_{12}a_{21})$
b. Similar.

33. $\frac{2}{3}n^3 - \frac{1}{2}n^2 + \frac{5}{6}n$. This expression is 75 when $n = 5$.

CHAPTER THREE

Section 3.1, page 82

1.

3.

5.

7.

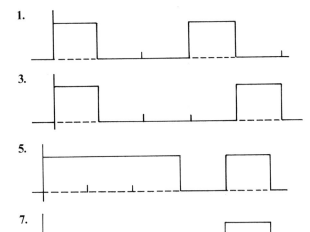

9. a_1 a_2 u_3 a_4

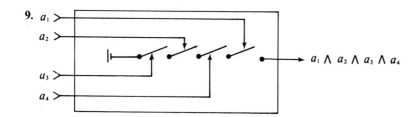

$a_1 \wedge a_2 \wedge a_3 \wedge a_4$

11.

a_1	a_2	a_3	a_4	$a_1 \wedge a_2 \wedge a_3 \wedge a_4$
0	0	0	0	0
0	0	0	1	0
0	0	1	0	0
0	0	1	1	0
0	1	0	0	0
0	1	0	1	0
0	1	1	0	0
0	1	1	1	0
1	0	0	0	0
1	0	0	1	0
1	0	1	0	0
1	0	1	1	0
1	1	0	0	0
1	1	0	1	0
1	1	1	0	0
1	1	1	1	1

17.

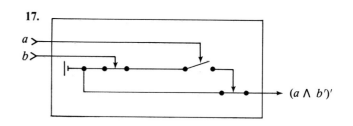

$(a \wedge b')'$

13.

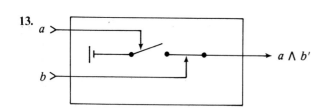

$a \wedge b'$

19.

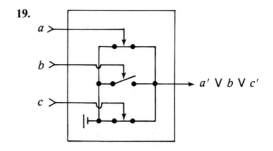

$a' \vee b \vee c'$

15.

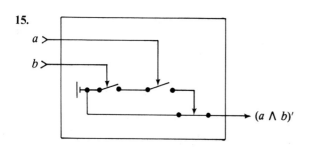

$(a \wedge b)'$

21.

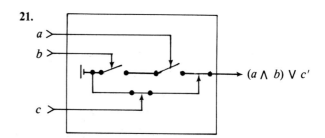

$(a \wedge b) \vee c'$

23.

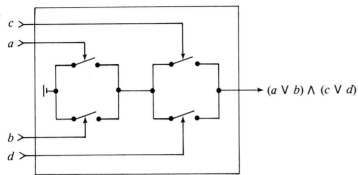

$(a \vee b) \wedge (c \vee d)$

25.

a	b	$a \wedge b'$
0	0	0
0	1	0
1	0	1
1	1	0

27.

a	b	c	$a' \vee b \vee c'$
0	0	0	1
0	0	1	1
0	1	0	1
0	1	1	1
1	0	0	1
1	0	1	0
1	1	0	1
1	1	1	1

29.

a	b	c	d	$(a \vee b) \wedge (c \vee d)$
0	0	0	0	0
0	0	0	1	0
0	0	1	0	0
0	0	1	1	0
0	1	0	0	0
0	1	0	1	1
0	1	1	0	1
0	1	1	1	1
1	0	0	0	0
1	0	0	1	1
1	0	1	0	1
1	0	1	1	1
1	1	0	0	0
1	1	0	1	1
1	1	1	0	1
1	1	1	1	1

Section 3.2, page 88

1.

a_1	a_2	f
0	1	$a_1' \wedge a_2$
1	0	$a_1 \wedge a_2'$

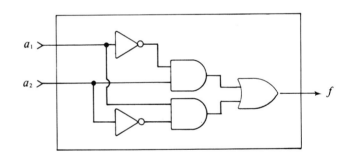

f

3.

a_1	a_2	f
0	0	$a_1' \wedge a_2'$

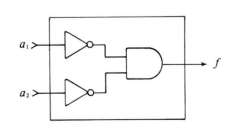

f

5.

a_1	a_2	a_3	f
0	0	1	$a_1' \wedge a_2' \wedge a_3$
0	1	0	$a_1' \wedge a_2 \wedge a_3'$
1	0	0	$a_1 \wedge a_2' \wedge a_3'$

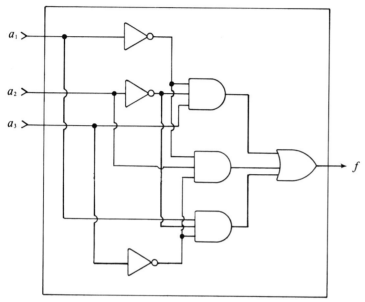

7.

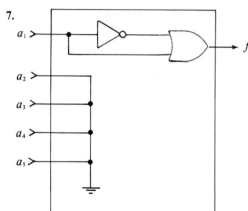

9.

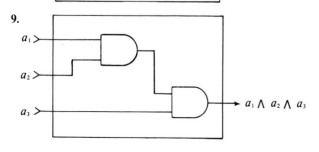

11.

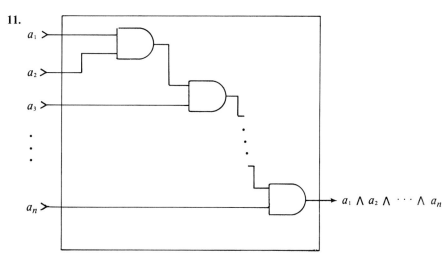

$n-1$ 2-input gates are needed no matter how the circuit is built. (More than $n-1$ could be *used*, but only $n-1$ are *needed*.)

13.

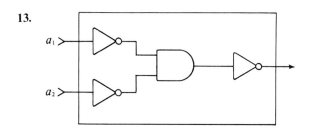

15. Make circuit. Replace each n-input AND gate, where $n > 2$, by $n-1$ 2-input AND gates. Replace each n-input OR gate, where $n > 2$, by $n-1$ 2-input OR gates. Finally, replace each 2-input OR gate by the circuit of Exercise 13.

17.

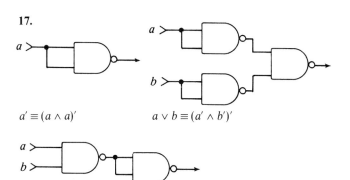

$a' \equiv (a \wedge a)'$

$a \vee b \equiv (a' \wedge b')'$

$a \wedge b \equiv ((a \wedge b)')$

19.

a_1	a_2	f	
0	0	0	
0	1	0	
1	0	0	
1	1	1	$a_1 \wedge a_2$

21.

a_1	a_2	a_3	f
1	1	1	1
otherwise			0

23. $\wedge \vee abc$ **25.** $\wedge \sim a \sim b$ **27.** $\sim \vee \sim a \sim b$

29. $(a \vee b) \wedge c$ **31.** $a' \wedge b'$ **33.** $(a' \vee b')'$

Section 3.3, page 98

1.

x	$x \wedge x$	$x \vee x$	$(x')'$
0	0	0	0
1	1	1	1

same

3.

x	y	$x \wedge y$	$y \wedge x$	$x \vee y$	$y \vee x$	$x \wedge (x \vee y)$	$x \vee (x \wedge y)$
0	0	0	0	0	0	0	0
0	1	0	0	1	1	0	0
1	0	0	0	1	1	1	1
1	1	1	1	1	1	1	1

5. $(x \vee z) \wedge (x \vee w) \wedge (y \vee z) \wedge (y \vee w)$
$\equiv [x \vee (z \wedge w)] \wedge [y \vee (z \wedge w)]$
$\equiv (x \wedge y) \vee (z \wedge w)$

7. $x \Rightarrow y \equiv x' \vee y \equiv y \vee x' \equiv (y')' \vee x' \equiv y' \Rightarrow x'$

9. $\equiv [(a_1 \vee a_2') \wedge a_3'] \vee [a_2 \vee (a_3 \vee a_1')']$
$\equiv [(a_1 \vee a_2') \wedge a_3'] \vee [a_2 \vee (a_3' \wedge a_1)]$
$\equiv (a_1 \wedge a_3') \vee (a_2' \wedge a_3') \vee a_2 \vee (a_3' \wedge a_1)$
$\equiv (a_1 \wedge a_3') \vee (a_2' \wedge a_3') \vee a_2$

11. $\equiv [a_1 \vee (a_2 \wedge a_3) \vee (a_2 \wedge a_1')] \wedge [a_1 \vee a_2' \vee a_3']$
$\equiv [a_1 \wedge (a_1 \vee a_2' \vee a_3')] \vee [(a_2 \wedge a_3) \wedge (a_1 \vee a_2' \vee a_3')]$
$\qquad \vee [(a_2 \wedge a_1') \wedge (a_1 \vee a_2' \vee a_3')]$
$\equiv a_1 \vee (a_2 \wedge a_3 \wedge a_1) \vee 0 \vee 0 \vee 0 \vee (a_2 \wedge a_1' \wedge a_3')$
$\equiv a_1 \vee (a_1' \wedge a_2 \wedge a_3)$

13. (9) $[(0 \vee 0') \wedge 1'] \vee [0' \wedge (1 \vee 0')]'$
$= [(0 \vee 1) \wedge 0] \vee [1 \wedge (1 \vee 1)]'$
$= (1 \wedge 0) \vee (1 \wedge 1)'$
$= 0 \vee 1'$
$= 0 \vee 0$
$= 0$
(11) The truth value is 0.

15. $\equiv (a_1' \wedge a_2 \wedge a_3 \wedge a_4')' \wedge (a_1' \wedge a_2 \wedge a_3' \wedge a_4)'$
$\qquad \wedge (a_1' \wedge a_2 \wedge a_3 \wedge a_4')' \wedge (a_1 \wedge a_2 \wedge a_3' \wedge a_4')'$
$\qquad \wedge (a_1 \wedge a_2' \wedge a_3 \wedge a_4')'$
$\equiv (a_1 \vee a_2' \vee a_3 \vee a_4) \wedge (a_1 \vee a_2 \vee a_3 \vee a_4')$
$\qquad \wedge (a_1 \vee a_2 \vee a_3' \vee a_4) \wedge (a_1 \vee a_2' \vee a_3 \vee a_4)$
$\qquad \wedge (a_1' \vee a_2 \vee a_3 \vee a_4)$

17. $s = 0; c = 0. \; s \Rightarrow c. \; 0 \Rightarrow 0 = 1.$ True.

19. $(s \vee c') \wedge (t' \wedge r)'.$
$(0 \vee 0') \wedge (1' \wedge 0)' = (0 \vee 1) \wedge (0 \wedge 0)' = 1 \wedge 0'$
$\qquad\qquad\qquad\qquad\qquad = 1 \wedge 1 = 1.$ True.

21.

a	b	$a \Rightarrow b$	$a \Rightarrow (a \Rightarrow b)$	
0	0	1	1	
0	1	1	1	
1	0	0	0	neither

23.

a	b	$a \Rightarrow b$	$b \Rightarrow a$	$(a \Rightarrow b) \vee (b \Rightarrow a)$	
0	0	1	1	1	
0	1	1	0	1	
1	0	0	1	1	
1	1	1	1	1	tautology

25.

a	b	$a \Rightarrow b$	$\sim a \Rightarrow \sim b$	$(a \Rightarrow b) \wedge (\sim a \Rightarrow \sim b)$	
0	0	1	1	1	
0	1	1	0	0	neither

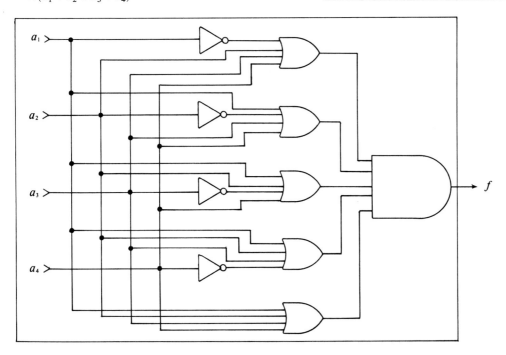

27.

a	b	c	$a \Rightarrow b$	$b \Rightarrow c$	$\wedge$	$a \Rightarrow c$	$\Rightarrow$
0	0	0	1	1	1	1	1
0	0	1	1	1	1	1	1
0	1	0	1	0	0	1	1
0	1	1	1	1	1	1	1
1	0	0	0	1	0	0	1
1	0	1	0	1	0	1	1
1	1	0	1	0	0	0	1
1	1	1	1	1	1	1	1

tautology

Section 3.4, page 108

1. No consensus.   **3.** $a \wedge b' \wedge e \wedge f$

5. $a \vee (b' \wedge c)$

7. $(b \wedge c \wedge d) \vee (a' \wedge b' \wedge d) \vee (a' \wedge b' \wedge c') \vee (a' \wedge c \wedge d)$

9. $(a' \wedge b \wedge c' \wedge d') \vee (a' \wedge b \wedge c \wedge d')$;
$(a' \wedge b' \wedge c' \wedge d) \vee (a' \wedge b \wedge c' \wedge d) \vee (a \wedge b' \wedge c' \wedge d)$
$\vee (a \wedge b \wedge c' \wedge d)$

11. $10101_2 = 21_{10}$; $01010_2 = 10_{10}$

13. $14_{10} = 1110_2 = a \wedge b \wedge c \wedge d'$;
$6_{10} = 0110_2 = a' \wedge b \wedge c \wedge d'$;
$2_{10} = 0010_2 = a' \wedge b' \wedge c \wedge d'$

15. $a \vee (b' \wedge c)$

17. $(b \wedge c \wedge d) \vee (a' \wedge b' \wedge d) \vee (a' \wedge b' \wedge c')$;
$(b \wedge c \wedge d) \vee (a' \wedge b' \wedge c') \vee (a' \wedge c \wedge d)$

19. $A: a \wedge c'$; $B: a \wedge b \wedge d'$; $C: a' \wedge c$; $D: a \wedge b \wedge e$;
$E: b' \wedge c' \wedge d' \wedge e'$; $F: b \wedge c \wedge d'$; $G: b \wedge c \wedge e$;
$H: a' \wedge b' \wedge d' \wedge e$
$A \vee C \vee E \vee B \vee G$; $A \vee C \vee E \vee B \vee D$;
$A \vee C \vee E \vee F \vee G$; $A \vee C \vee E \vee F \vee D$;
$A \vee C \vee H \vee F \vee G$; $A \vee C \vee H \vee F \vee D$;
$A \vee C \vee H \vee B \vee G$; $A \vee C \vee H \vee B \vee D$

21. $\equiv 1$; so minimal forms are $a \vee a'$, $b \vee b'$, $c \vee c'$, $d \vee d'$.

23. $(a' \wedge c) \vee (b \wedge c) \vee d' \vee (a \wedge b' \wedge c')$

CHAPTER FOUR

Section 4.1, page 120

1. The incidence matrix:

$$\begin{array}{c} \\ v_1 \\ v_2 \\ v_3 \\ v_4 \end{array} \begin{array}{cccccc} e_1 & e_2 & e_3 & e_4 & e_5 & e_6 \\ \begin{bmatrix} 1 & 0 & 0 & 1 & 1 & 0 \\ 1 & 1 & 0 & 0 & 0 & 1 \\ 0 & 0 & 1 & 1 & 0 & 1 \\ 0 & 1 & 1 & 0 & 1 & 0 \end{bmatrix} \end{array}$$

The adjacency matrix:

$$\begin{array}{c} \\ v_1 \\ v_2 \\ v_3 \\ v_4 \end{array} \begin{array}{cccc} v_1 & v_2 & v_3 & v_4 \\ \begin{bmatrix} 0 & 1 & 1 & 1 \\ 1 & 0 & 1 & 1 \\ 1 & 1 & 0 & 1 \\ 1 & 1 & 1 & 0 \end{bmatrix} \end{array}$$

All vertices have degree 3.

3. The incidence matrix:

$$\begin{array}{c} \\ v_1 \end{array} \begin{array}{cccc} e_1 & e_2 & e_3 & e_4 \\ \begin{bmatrix} 1 & 1 & 1 & 1 \end{bmatrix} \end{array}$$

The adjacency matrix:

$$\begin{array}{c} \\ v_1 \end{array} \begin{array}{c} v_1 \\ \begin{bmatrix} 4 \end{bmatrix} \end{array}$$

The degree of v_1 is 8.

5. The incidence matrix:

	e_1	e_2	e_3	e_4	e_5	e_6	e_7	e_8	e_9	e_{10}	e_{11}	e_{12}
v_1	1	0	0	0	0	0	0	1	0	0	0	1
v_2	1	1	0	0	0	0	0	0	0	1	0	0
v_3	0	1	1	0	0	0	0	0	1	0	0	0
v_4	0	0	1	1	0	0	0	0	0	0	1	0
v_5	0	0	0	1	1	0	0	0	0	1	0	0
v_6	0	0	0	0	1	1	0	0	0	0	0	1
v_7	0	0	0	0	0	1	1	0	0	0	1	0
v_8	0	0	0	0	0	0	1	1	1	0	0	0

The adjacency matrix:

	v_1	v_2	v_3	v_4	v_5	$v_6,$	v_7	v_8
v_1	0	1	0	0	0	1	0	1
v_2	1	0	1	0	1	0	0	0
v_3	0	1	0	1	0	0	0	1
v_4	0	0	1	0	1	0	1	0
v_5	0	1	0	1	0	1	0	0
v_6	1	0	0	0	1	0	1	0
v_7	0	0	0	1	0	1	0	1
v_8	1	0	1	0	0	0	1	0

All vertices have degree 3.

7. The incidence matrix:

	e_1	e_2	e_3	e_4	e_5	e_6	e_7	e_8
v_1	1	0	0	0	0	0	0	0
v_2	0	1	0	0	0	0	0	0
v_3	0	0	1	0	0	0	0	0
v_4	0	0	0	1	0	0	0	0
v_5	0	0	0	0	1	0	0	0
v_6	0	0	0	0	0	1	0	0
v_7	0	0	0	0	0	0	1	0
v_8	0	0	0	0	0	0	0	1
v_9	1	1	1	1	1	1	1	1

7. *(continued)*   The adjacency matrix:

	v_1	v_2	v_3	v_4	v_5	v_6	v_7	v_8	v_9
v_1	0	0	0	0	0	0	0	0	1
v_2	0	0	0	0	0	0	0	0	1
v_3	0	0	0	0	0	0	0	0	1
v_4	0	0	0	0	0	0	0	0	1
v_5	0	0	0	0	0	0	0	0	1
v_6	0	0	0	0	0	0	0	0	1
v_7	0	0	0	0	0	0	0	0	1
v_8	0	0	0	0	0	0	0	0	1
v_9	1	1	1	1	1	1	1	1	0

All vertices, except v_9, have degree 1; the degree of v_9 is 8.

9. The incidence matrix: there is none. The adjacency matrix: a 5×5 matrix of zeros. All vertices have degree zero.

11. Same as Exercise 1.

13. Label the graph as follows:

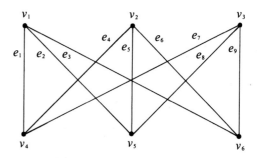

The incidence matrix:

	e_1	e_2	e_3	e_4	e_5	e_6	e_7	e_8	e_9
v_1	1	1	1	0	0	0	0	0	0
v_2	0	0	0	1	1	1	0	0	0
v_3	0	0	0	0	0	0	1	1	1
v_4	1	0	0	1	0	0	1	0	0
v_5	0	1	0	0	1	0	0	1	0
v_6	0	0	1	0	0	1	0	0	1

13. (*continued*) The adjacency matrix:

	v_1	v_2	v_3	v_4	v_5	v_6
v_1	0	0	0	1	1	1
v_2	0	0	0	1	1	1
v_3	0	0	0	1	1	1
v_4	1	1	1	0	0	0
v_5	1	1	1	0	0	0
v_6	1	1	1	0	0	0

All vertices have degree 3.

15. Label the graph as shown below.
The incidence matrix:

	e_1	e_2	e_3	e_4	e_5	e_6	e_7	e_8	e_9	e_{10}	e_{11}	e_{12}
v_1	1	1	1	1	1	1	0	0	0	0	0	0
v_2	0	0	0	0	0	0	1	1	1	1	1	1
v_3	1	0	0	0	0	0	1	0	0	0	0	0
v_4	0	1	0	0	0	0	0	1	0	0	0	0
v_5	0	0	1	0	0	0	0	0	1	0	0	0
v_6	0	0	0	1	0	0	0	0	0	1	0	0
v_7	0	0	0	0	1	0	0	0	0	0	1	0
v_8	0	0	0	0	0	1	0	0	0	0	0	1

15. (*continued*) The adjacency matrix:

	v_1	v_2	v_3	v_4	v_5	v_6	v_7	v_8
v_1	0	0	1	1	1	1	1	1
v_2	0	0	1	1	1	1	1	1
v_3	1	1	0	0	0	0	0	0
v_4	1	1	0	0	0	0	0	0
v_5	1	1	0	0	0	0	0	0
v_6	1	1	0	0	0	0	0	0
v_7	1	1	0	0	0	0	0	0
v_8	1	1	0	0	0	0	0	0

Degrees:
$v_1 : 6;\ v_2 : 6;\ v_3 : 2;\ v_4 : 2;\ v_5 : 2;\ v_6 : 2;\ v_7 : 2;\ v_8 : 2$

17. It is an $n \times n$ matrix with each entry off the main diagonal equal to 1 and each entry on the main diagonal equal to 0.

19. K_3: K_6:

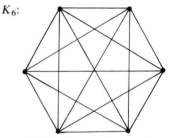

21. It is impossible to draw a *graph* with the stated properties, but here is a pseudograph that meets all the other conditions:

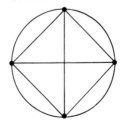

$K_{2,6}$:

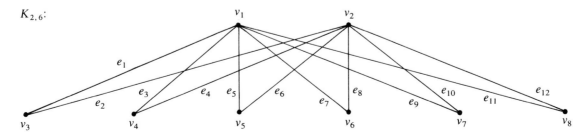

23. The matrix is an incidence matrix.

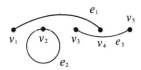

Vertex v_2 has degree 2; the others have degree 1.

25. The matrix is an adjacency matrix.

$v_1 \quad v_2 \quad v_3 \quad v_4$ Each vertex has degree zero.

27. The matrix is an incidence matrix.

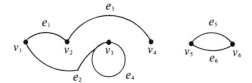

Vertices v_1, v_2, v_5, and v_6 have degree 2; vertex v_3 has degree 3; vertex v_4 has degree 1. The matrix is also an adjacency matrix.

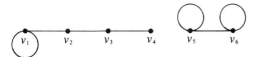

Vertex v_1 has degree 3; v_2 and v_3 have degree 2; v_4 has degree 1; the other vertices have degree 3.

29. The matrix is not an incidence matrix since its last column contains three 1's. It is not an adjacency matrix since it is not square.

31. The matrix is an adjacency matrix. It is also an incidence matrix.

Vertices v_1 and v_6 have degree 1; the other vertices have degree 2.

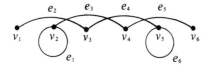

Vertices v_1 and v_6 have degree 1. Vertices v_3 and v_4 have degree 2. Vertices v_2 and v_5 have degree 3.

33. The matrix is an incidence matrix.

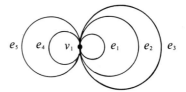

The degree of v_1 is 10.

35. $e_1e_2e_3e_4e_5e_6$; $e_1e_2e_3e_7$; $e_1e_2e_8e_5e_4e_7$; $e_1e_2e_8e_6$; $e_7e_3e_8e_6$; $e_7e_4e_5e_6$

37.
$$\begin{bmatrix} 1 & 0 & 0 \\ 0 & 1 & 0 \\ 0 & 0 & 1 \end{bmatrix} \begin{bmatrix} 1 & 0 & 0 \\ 0 & 0 & 1 \\ 0 & 1 & 0 \end{bmatrix} \begin{bmatrix} 1 & 0 & 0 \\ 0 & 1 & 1 \\ 0 & 1 & 0 \end{bmatrix} \begin{bmatrix} 1 & 0 & 0 \\ 0 & 0 & 1 \\ 0 & 1 & 1 \end{bmatrix}$$

$$\begin{bmatrix} 0 & 1 & 0 \\ 1 & 1 & 0 \\ 0 & 0 & 1 \end{bmatrix} \begin{bmatrix} 0 & 1 & 0 \\ 1 & 0 & 0 \\ 0 & 0 & 1 \end{bmatrix} \begin{bmatrix} 0 & 1 & 0 \\ 1 & 0 & 1 \\ 0 & 1 & 1 \end{bmatrix} \begin{bmatrix} 0 & 1 & 0 \\ 1 & 0 & 1 \\ 0 & 1 & 0 \end{bmatrix}$$

$$\begin{bmatrix} 0 & 0 & 1 \\ 0 & 1 & 0 \\ 1 & 0 & 1 \end{bmatrix} \begin{bmatrix} 0 & 0 & 1 \\ 0 & 0 & 1 \\ 1 & 1 & 0 \end{bmatrix} \begin{bmatrix} 0 & 0 & 1 \\ 0 & 1 & 1 \\ 1 & 1 & 0 \end{bmatrix} \begin{bmatrix} 0 & 0 & 1 \\ 0 & 1 & 0 \\ 1 & 0 & 0 \end{bmatrix}$$

$$\begin{bmatrix} 1 & 1 & 0 \\ 1 & 1 & 0 \\ 0 & 0 & 1 \end{bmatrix} \begin{bmatrix} 1 & 1 & 0 \\ 1 & 0 & 1 \\ 0 & 1 & 0 \end{bmatrix} \begin{bmatrix} 1 & 1 & 0 \\ 1 & 0 & 0 \\ 0 & 0 & 1 \end{bmatrix} \begin{bmatrix} 1 & 1 & 0 \\ 1 & 0 & 1 \\ 0 & 1 & 1 \end{bmatrix}$$

$$\begin{bmatrix} 1 & 0 & 1 \\ 0 & 1 & 1 \\ 1 & 1 & 0 \end{bmatrix} \begin{bmatrix} 1 & 0 & 1 \\ 0 & 0 & 1 \\ 1 & 1 & 0 \end{bmatrix} \begin{bmatrix} 1 & 0 & 1 \\ 0 & 1 & 0 \\ 1 & 0 & 0 \end{bmatrix} \begin{bmatrix} 1 & 0 & 1 \\ 0 & 1 & 0 \\ 1 & 0 & 1 \end{bmatrix}$$

$$\begin{bmatrix} 0 & 1 & 1 \\ 1 & 1 & 0 \\ 1 & 0 & 1 \end{bmatrix} \begin{bmatrix} 0 & 1 & 1 \\ 1 & 1 & 0 \\ 1 & 0 & 0 \end{bmatrix} \begin{bmatrix} 0 & 1 & 1 \\ 1 & 0 & 1 \\ 1 & 1 & 0 \end{bmatrix} \begin{bmatrix} 1 & 0 & 0 \\ 0 & 1 & 1 \\ 0 & 1 & 1 \end{bmatrix}$$

$$\begin{bmatrix} 0 & 1 & 1 \\ 1 & 0 & 0 \\ 1 & 0 & 0 \end{bmatrix} \begin{bmatrix} 0 & 1 & 1 \\ 1 & 0 & 0 \\ 1 & 0 & 1 \end{bmatrix}$$

39. Suppose G is a graph with n vertices and a vertex v of degree $n-1$. Let $e_1, \ldots, e_{n-1}$ be the $n-1$ edges incident with v and let $v_1, \ldots, v_{n-1}$ be at the other ends of the edges $e_1, \ldots, e_{n-1}$. Then the vertices of G are precisely $v, v_1, \ldots, v_{n-1}$ all of which are connected via $e_1, \ldots, e_{n-1}$. Hence, G is connected. Note that

is a disconnected pseudograph with three vertices and a vertex of degree 2.

41. The adjacency matrix:

$$A = \begin{bmatrix} 0 & 2 & 0 \\ 2 & 0 & 2 \\ 0 & 2 & 1 \end{bmatrix} \quad A^3 = \begin{bmatrix} 0 & 16 & 4 \\ 16 & 4 & 18 \\ 4 & 18 & 9 \end{bmatrix}$$

Thus, there are 4 paths of length 3 from v_1 to v_3:

$$e_1, e_3, e_5$$
$$e_1, e_4, e_5$$
$$e_2, e_3, e_5$$
$$e_2, e_4, e_5$$

43. Use a tree diagram:

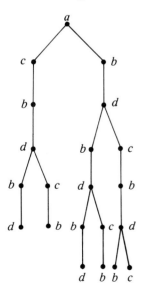

Thus, there are 4 paths starting at vertex a; 3 starting at b; 2 starting at c; and 4 starting at d. Total: 13.

Section 4.2, page 141

1.

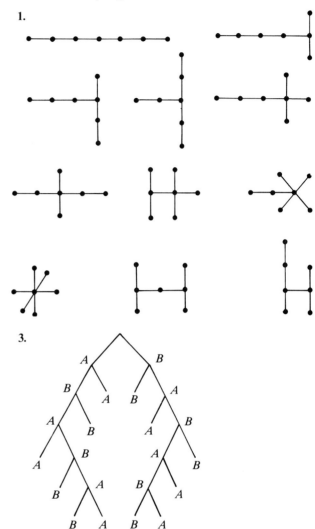

3.

12 ways: A wins 5; B wins 5; 2 draw.

5.

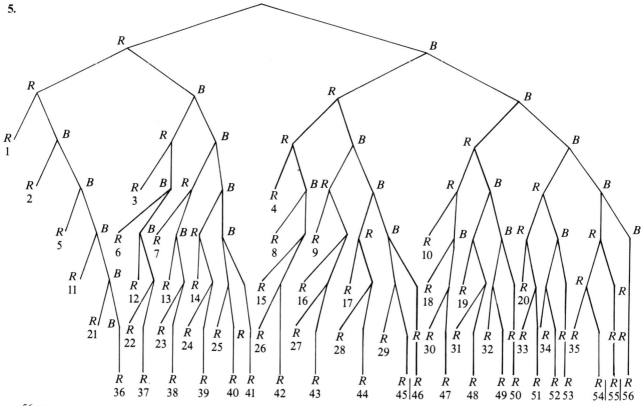

56 ways.

7.

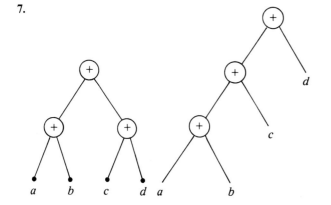

9.

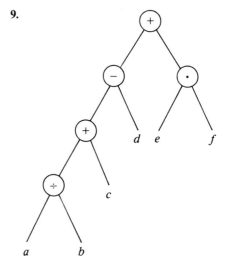

11. $[(a \cdot b + c) - (d \div e)] \cdot f + (g + h) \cdot i$

13. It was a bright cold day in April, and the clocks were striking thirteen.

15.

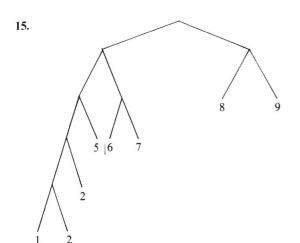

17.

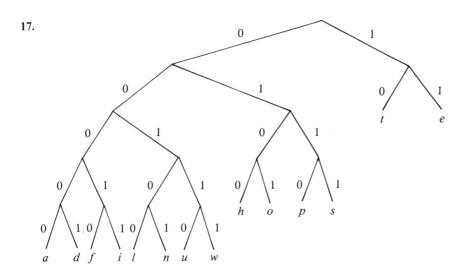

a: 00000; d: 00001; e: 11; f: 00010; h: 0100; i: 00011; l: 00100; n: 00101; o: 0101; p: 0110; s: 0111; t: 10; u: 00110; w: 00111

0011111 10010011 0110110101011000010011 010100010
10010011 0011000101000111011100001
0111100000010110111

19. Depth-first: 1, 2, 6, 8, 9, 7, 10, 11, 5, 3, 12, 13, 4, 14, 15.
Breadth-first: 1, 2, 5, 6, 7, 3, 4, 8, 9, 10, 11, 12, 13, 14, 15.

21. Depth-first: 20, 19, 22, 9, 7, 6, 8, 10, 23, 11, 12, 21, 5, 4, 3, 1, 2, 18, 13, 14, 24, 16, 17, 15.
Breadth-first: 20, 19, 18, 22, 23, 13, 14, 9, 10, 11, 12, 24, 15, 7, 21, 16, 17, 6, 8, 5, 4, 3, 1, 2.

23. Depth-first: Go into the first room; go to the first desk and check all three drawers. Now go to the second desk and check all three drawers. Now go to the second room and repeat the process. Then the third room, etc.
Breadth-first: Go into the first room and check the first drawer in each of the desks. Then check the first drawers in the second room, and so on through all five rooms. Now go back to the first room and check the second drawers, etc.

25.
1. $k \leftarrow 2$.
2. List all possible sequences of vertices: $(c_1, \ldots, c_k)$, where $u = c_1$, c_i is adjacent to c_{i+1} for $1 \le i \le k - 1$, and $c_1, \ldots, c_k$ are distinct.
3. If $c_k = v$, for some sequence with last vertex c_k, STOP.
4. $k \leftarrow k + 1$. Go to 2.

a. $k = 2$. (v_1, v_2), (v_1, v_8). $k = 3$. (v_1, v_2, v_3), (v_1, v_2, v_8), (v_1, v_8, v_3), (v_1, v_8, v_7). STOP. The path is from v_1 to v_8 to v_7.

b. $k = 2$. (v_1, v_2), (v_1, v_8). $k = 3$. (v_1, v_2, v_3), (v_1, v_2, v_8), (v_1, v_8, v_7), (v_1, v_8, v_3). $k = 4$. (v_1, v_2, v_3, v_4), (v_1, v_2, v_3, v_6), (v_1, v_2, v_3, v_8), (v_1, v_2, v_8, v_3), (v_1, v_2, v_8, v_7), (v_1, v_8, v_7, v_3), (v_1, v_8, v_3, v_2), (v_1, v_8, v_3, v_4), (v_1, v_8, v_3, v_6), (v_1, v_8, v_3, v_7). $k = 5$. $(v_1, v_2, v_3, v_4, v_5)$. STOP. The path is from v_1 to v_2 to v_3 to v_4 to v_5.

27. Pre-order: 15, 14, 9, 8, 7, 10, 6, 5, 13, 11, 4, 3, 12, 2, 1.
In-order: 8, 9, 7, 14, 6, 10, 5, 15, 4, 11, 3, 13, 2, 12, 1.
Post-order: 8, 7, 9, 6, 5, 10, 14, 4, 3, 11, 2, 1, 12, 13, 15.

29. Pre-order: 6, 5, 4, 3, 2, 1, 7, 8, 9, 10, 11.
In-order: 1, 2, 7, 3, 8, 4, 9, 5, 10, 6, 11.
Post-order: 1, 7, 2, 8, 3, 9, 4, 10, 5, 11, 6.

31. Polish: $+ \cdot - + \cdot a\,b\,c \div d\,e\,f \cdot + g\,h\,i$
Reverse Polish: $a\,b \cdot c + d\,e \div -f \cdot g\,h + i \cdot +$

33. Polish: $+ - + \div a\,b\,c\,d \cdot e\,f$
Reverse Polish: $a\,b \div c + d - e\,f \cdot +$

Section 4.3, page 155

1. Two of the vertices have odd degree. Thus, it is possible to construct an Eulerian path between them. Here is one:

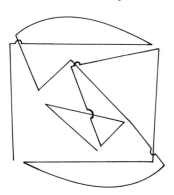

3. Two of the vertices have odd degree. Thus, it is possible to construct an Eulerian path between them. Here is one:

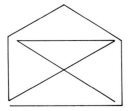

5. Since all the vertices have even degree, the graph contains an Eulerian circuit. Here it is:

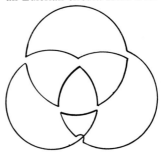

7. In K_5 each vertex has degree 4, which is even. Thus, it contains an Eulerian circuit:

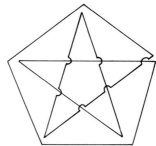

9. Here is one possible route. It is not possible for me to begin and end at home since the vertex there is not one of the two with odd degree.

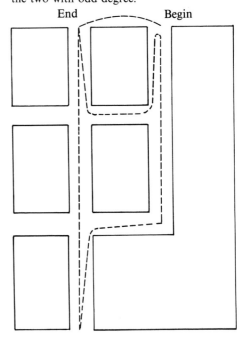

11. The only states in which my trip may begin and end are New York and Vermont.

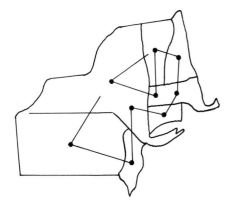

13. The steps are *a*, *ab*, *abc*, *abcd*, *abc*, *ab*, *abd*, *abdc*, and the circuit is *abdca*.

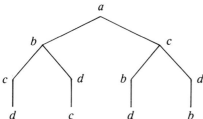

15. The steps are *a*, *ab*, *abc*, *abcd*, *abcde*, *abcd*, *abc*, *ab*, *abd*, *abdc*, *abd*, *ab*, *abe*, *abed*, *abedc*, and the circuit is *abedca*.

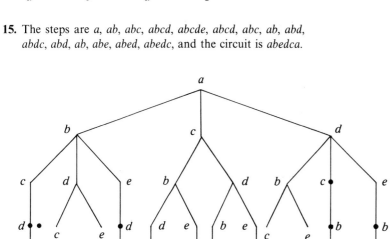

17. Label the graph as follows:
The steps are *a*, *ab*, *abc*, *abce*, *abced*, *abd*, *abde*, *abdec*, *ae*, *aec*, *aecb*, *aecbd*, *aed*, *aedb*, *aedbc*; thus, there is no circuit.

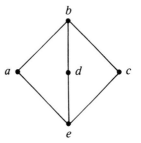

19.

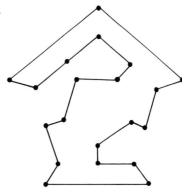

21. $A: (1, 0, 1)$ $E: (1, 0, 0)$
    $B: (1, 1, 1)$ $F: (1, 1, 0)$
    $C: (0, 1, 1)$ $G: (0, 1, 0)$
    $D: (0, 0, 1)$ $H: (0, 0, 0)$

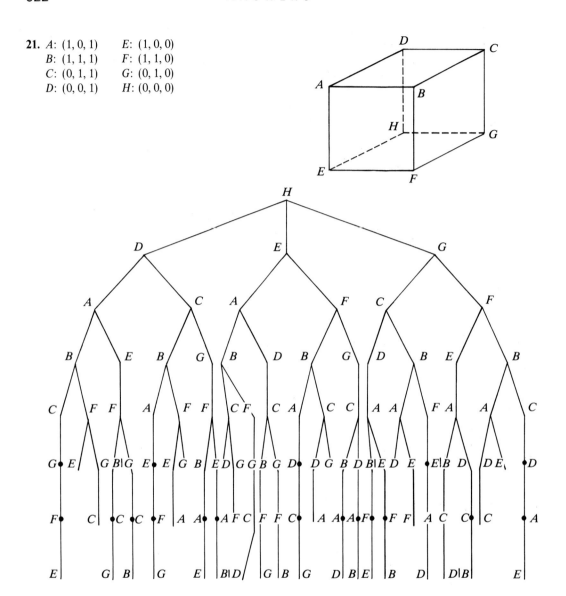

Since $(1, 1, 1)$ is not adjacent to $(0, 0, 0)$, there are only twelve Gray codes:

$(0, 0, 0)$	$(0, 0, 0)$	$(0, 0, 0)$	$(0, 0, 0)$	$(0, 0, 0)$	$(0, 0, 0)$
$(0, 0, 1)$	$(0, 0, 1)$	$(0, 0, 1)$	$(0, 0, 1)$	$(1, 0, 0)$	$(1, 0, 0)$
$(1, 0, 1)$	$(1, 0, 1)$	$(0, 1, 1)$	$(0, 1, 1)$	$(1, 0, 1)$	$(1, 0, 1)$
$(1, 1, 1)$	$(1, 0, 0)$	$(1, 1, 1)$	$(0, 1, 0)$	$(1, 1, 1)$	$(0, 0, 1)$
$(0, 1, 1)$	$(1, 1, 0)$	$(1, 0, 1)$	$(1, 1, 0)$	$(1, 1, 0)$	$(0, 1, 1)$
$(0, 1, 0)$	$(1, 1, 1)$	$(1, 0, 0)$	$(1, 1, 1)$	$(0, 1, 0)$	$(1, 1, 1)$
$(1, 1, 0)$	$(0, 1, 1)$	$(1, 1, 0)$	$(1, 0, 1)$	$(0, 1, 1)$	$(1, 1, 0)$
$(1, 0, 0)$	$(0, 1, 0)$	$(0, 1, 0)$	$(1, 0, 0)$	$(0, 0, 1)$	$(0, 1, 0)$

$(0, 0, 0)$	$(0, 0, 0)$	$(0, 0, 0)$	$(0, 0, 0)$	$(0, 0, 0)$	$(0, 0, 0)$
$(1, 0, 0)$	$(1, 0, 0)$	$(0, 1, 0)$	$(0, 1, 0)$	$(0, 1, 0)$	$(0, 1, 0)$
$(1, 1, 0)$	$(1, 1, 0)$	$(0, 1, 1)$	$(0, 1, 1)$	$(1, 1, 0)$	$(1, 1, 0)$
$(1, 1, 1)$	$(0, 1, 0)$	$(0, 0, 1)$	$(1, 1, 1)$	$(1, 0, 0)$	$(1, 1, 1)$
$(1, 0, 1)$	$(0, 1, 1)$	$(1, 0, 1)$	$(1, 1, 0)$	$(1, 0, 1)$	$(0, 1, 1)$
$(0, 0, 1)$	$(1, 1, 1)$	$(1, 1, 1)$	$(1, 0, 0)$	$(1, 1, 1)$	$(0, 0, 1)$
$(0, 1, 1)$	$(1, 0, 1)$	$(1, 1, 0)$	$(1, 0, 1)$	$(0, 1, 1)$	$(1, 0, 1)$
$(0, 1, 0)$	$(0, 0, 1)$	$(1, 0, 0)$	$(0, 0, 1)$	$(0, 0, 1)$	$(1, 0, 0)$

Section 4.4, page 164

1.

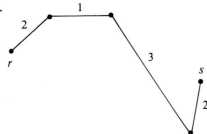

Total weight: 8.

3.

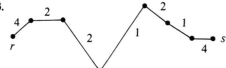

Total weight: 16.

5.

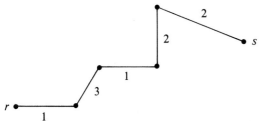

Total weight: 9.

7.

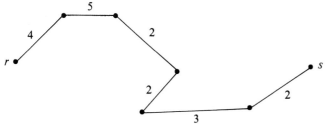

Total weight: 18.

9.

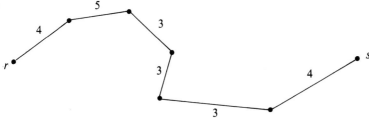

Total weight: 22.

11.

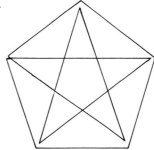

Total weight: 20.

13. Vertices b, d, f, and h have odd degree.
bd: 8; df: 4; bf: 6; dh: 3; bh: 5; fh: 3.

$$bd + fh = 11$$
$$bf + dh = 9$$
$$bh + df = 9$$

There are two minimal choices. We duplicate the edges bf and dh to obtain the circuit:

$$a\ b\ f\ b\ c\ d\ h\ d\ e\ f\ g\ h\ a\ c\ e\ g\ a$$

Total weight: 48.

Section 4.5, page 178

1. Step 1: There are no vertices of degree zero.
Step 6: Delete degree-one vertices:

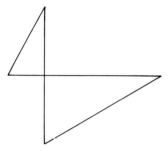

Step 1: There are no degree-zero vertices.
Step 4: There are no degree-one vertices.
Step 5: *G* has a circuit.

3.

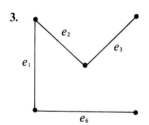

5. ●

7.

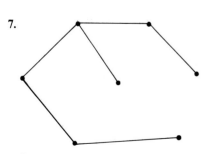

Total weight: 10.

9.

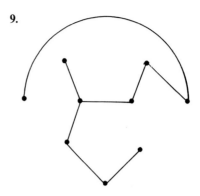

Total weight: 12.

11. Notation and subroutines: For a graph, n = number of vertices, E = set of edges. For $S \subset E$, $W(S)$ = set of all weights of edges of S, $V(S)$ = set of all vertices on edges of S, and for $w \in W(S)$, $e(w, S)$ = the first (really, *any*) edge in S of weight w. For any finite set A, $|A|$ = number of elements of A.

1. $S \leftarrow E$, $T \leftarrow \varnothing$, $i \leftarrow 0$
2. $w \leftarrow \min W(S)$
3. $e \leftarrow e(w, S)$
4. $S \leftarrow S \sim \{e\}$, $T \leftarrow T \cup \{e\}$, $i \leftarrow i + 1$
5. If $i = n - 1$, then STOP
6. $w \leftarrow \min W(S)$
7. $e \leftarrow e(w, S)$
8. If $|V(\{e\}) \cap V(S)| = 1$, then go to 4; otherwise, $S \leftarrow S \sim \{e\}$ and go to 6

13.

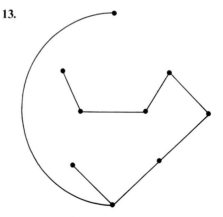

Total weight: 12.

15. 6　　**17.** −72　　**19.** 1　　**21.** 9

23. $4^2 = 16$

$$\det \begin{vmatrix} 3 & -1 & -1 \\ -1 & 3 & -1 \\ -1 & -1 & 3 \end{vmatrix} = \det \begin{vmatrix} 3 & -1 & -1 \\ -4 & 4 & 0 \\ -4 & 0 & 4 \end{vmatrix} = \det \begin{vmatrix} 2 & -1 & -1 \\ 0 & 4 & 0 \\ -4 & 0 & 4 \end{vmatrix} = \det \begin{vmatrix} 1 & -1 & -1 \\ 0 & 4 & 0 \\ 0 & 0 & 4 \end{vmatrix} = 1 \cdot 4 \cdot 4 = 16$$

25. 4:

27. $1157\frac{11}{27}$ days. 333 feet 4 inches high.

CHAPTER FIVE

Section 5.1, page 198

1. $V = 7$; $E = 8$; $F = 3$.   **3.** $V = 5$; $E = 8$; $F = 5$.

5. See Program 4.2 of Section 4.5.

7. Here is $K_{4,4}$:

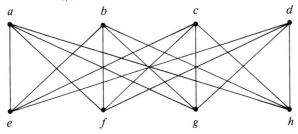

Draw the circuit *aebfcgdh*. There is one bridge. Proceed until you get stuck—for example, with this figure:

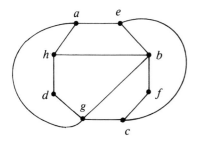

9. Label the graph:

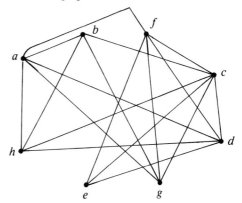

Then the graph can be drawn in the plane as follows:

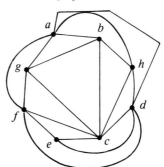

11. The graph is not planar, since it has a subgraph which is $K_{3,3}$ on the vertex sets $\{a, b, c\}$ and $\{A, B, C\}$:

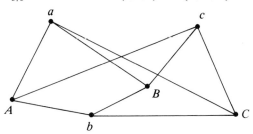

Section 5.2, page 204

1. Color the vertices:

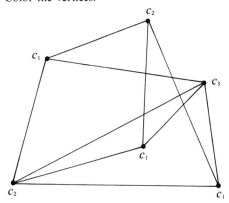

3. Color the vertices:

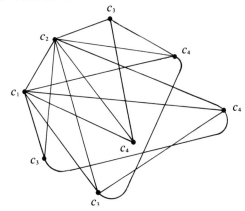

5. Color the vertices: $\begin{bmatrix} v_1 & v_2 & v_3 & v_4 & v_5 & v_6 & v_7 & v_8 \\ c_1 & c_2 & c_3 & c_1 & c_4 & c_2 & c_3 & c_5 \end{bmatrix}$

7.

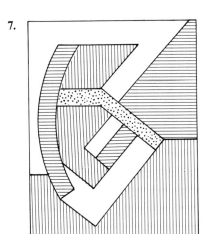

9.

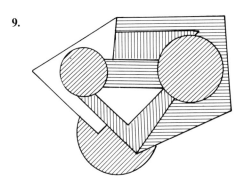

11. n

Section 5.3, page 221

1. 82 wagonloads

3. A maximal flow is 130; a minimal cut consists of the edges from (s) to (1), (s) to (2), and (s) to (3).

5. A maximal flow is 125; a minimal cut consists of all the edges into (t).

7. A maximal flow is 95; a minimal cut consists of the edges from (3) to (11), (7) to (12), (8) to (12), (10) to (13), and (9) to (14).

9. A maximal flow is 400; a minimal cut consists of the edges from (5) to (11), (15) to (t), and (16) to (17).

11. A maximal flow is 600; a minimal cut consists of all the edges out of (s_1), (s_2), and (s_3).

13. A maximal flow is 190; a minimal cut consists of the edges from (1) to (4), (2) to (5), and (7) to (10).

15. The maximal flow is 190. A minimal cut consists of the edges from (8) to (t), (7) to (9), and (10) to (t).

17. a. 190

   b. Build a pipeline from ⑤ to ④ with capacity 130.

Section 5.4, page 244

1. $\lfloor 10(10^{n-1}x - \lfloor 10^{n-1}x \rfloor) \rfloor$ **3.** $.001 \lfloor 1000(x + .005) \rfloor$

5. $.001100110011 \cdots$ **7. a.** 3.718   **b.** 3.719

9. $e(x) = -.004, r(x) \doteq -.00011$

11. $x = 1.3273, r(x) \doteq .00023$

13. $a(x) = 7.128, r(x) \doteq .00006$

15. $e(x) = .062, x = 3.162$

17. $a(x) = -.1, x = -.1012$

19. $3.78261 \times 10^2 + 7.0917 \times 10^{-4}$

21. $3.14020 \times 10^{-2} + .7812 \times 10^{-8}$

23. $-t + 1 = -5. \ a + 10^{-5} = 3.78261 + .00001 = 3.78262$

25. $r(x) = -.00029083/378.262 \doteq -7.68858 \times 10^{-7}$
    $|r(x)| \doteq 7.68858 \times 10^{-7} \leqslant 5 \times 10^{-6}$

27. $e(x) = .1, \ e(y) = .03, \ r(x) = .05, \ r(y) = .005, \ a(x + y) = 8,$
    $e(x + y) = .13$
    $r(x + y) = .13/8$. The right-hand side equals

$$\frac{2}{8}(.05) + \frac{6}{8}(.005) = \frac{.1}{8} + \frac{.03}{8} = \frac{.13}{8}$$

29. We add the inequalities:

$$\frac{\begin{array}{c} -|x_1| \leqslant x_1 \leqslant |x_1| \\ -|x_2| \leqslant x_2 \leqslant |x_2| \end{array}}{-(|x_1| + |x_2|) \leqslant x_1 + x_2 \leqslant |x_1| + |x_2|}$$

so $|x_1 + x_2| \leqslant |x_1| + |x_2|$

31. 16.76, 16.75

33.

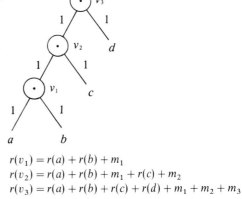

35.

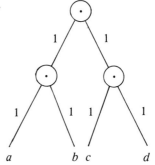

37.

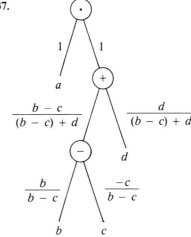

39.

$r(v_1) = r(a) + r(b) + m_1$
$r(v_2) = r(a) + r(b) + m_1 + r(c) + m_2$
$r(v_3) = r(a) + r(b) + r(c) + r(d) + m_1 + m_2 + m_3$

40. $r(v_1) = r(a) + r(b) + m_1$
$r(v_2) = r(c) + r(d) + m_2$
$r(v_3) = r(a) + r(b) + r(c) + r(d) + m_1 + m_2 + m_3$

Conclusion: The order of multiplication is irrelevant.

41. Let $y = ax^2 + bx + c$.

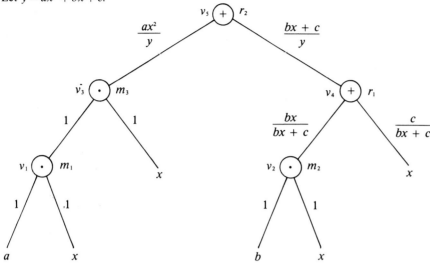

$$r(v_1) = r(a) + r(x) + m_1$$
$$r(v_2) = r(b) + r(x) + m_2$$
$$r(v_3) = r(a) + r(x) + m_1 + r(x) + m_3$$
$$= r(a) + 2r(x) + m_1 + m_3$$

$$r(v_4) = (r(b) + r(x) + m_2)\left[\frac{bx}{bx+c}\right] + \left[\frac{c}{bx+c}\right]r(c) + r_1$$

$$r(v_5) = r(v_3)\frac{ax^2}{y} + r(v_4)\frac{bx+c}{y} + r_2$$

$$e(y) = yr(v_5) = ax^2(r(a) + 2r(x) + m_1 + m_3 + r_2)$$
$$+ bx(r(b) + r(x) + m_2 + r_1 + r_2)$$
$$+ c(r(c) + r_1 + r_2)$$
$$|e(y)| \leqslant (6|a| + 5|b| + 3|c|) \times 5 \times 10^{-t}$$

Let $E1$ be the error bound found in the text for the process graph of Figure 5.36(a), and let $E2$ be the error bound just found. Then $E1 - E2 = (|a| - |c|) \times 5 \times 10^{-t}$. Thus, if $|a| \geqslant |c|$, it is better to use the process graph in Figure 5.36(b). That process is called Horner's rule after the English schoolmaster William George Horner (1786–1837).

CHAPTER SIX

Section 6.1, page 256

1. $\begin{bmatrix} 1 & 1 & 1 & 1 \\ 0 & 0 & 1 & 1 \\ 0 & 0 & 0 & 1 \\ 0 & 0 & 0 & 1 \end{bmatrix}$

3. $\begin{bmatrix} 0 & 1 & 1 & 1 \\ 1 & 0 & 1 & 1 \\ 1 & 1 & 0 & 1 \\ 1 & 1 & 1 & 0 \end{bmatrix}$

13. $\begin{bmatrix} 1 & 0 & 1 & 0 \\ 0 & 1 & 1 & 1 \\ 1 & 0 & 1 & 0 \\ 1 & 1 & 0 & 1 \end{bmatrix}$

15. $\begin{bmatrix} 1 & 0 & 1 & 1 \\ 0 & 0 & 1 & 1 \\ 1 & 1 & 0 & 0 \\ 1 & 1 & 0 & 1 \end{bmatrix}$

5. "Is exactly one less than," for example.

7. "Is exactly one more than or exactly one less than," for example.

9. $a\,\mathsf{R}\,b$ if $ab \neq 0$, for example.

11. $a\,\mathsf{R}\,b$ if $|a - b| \leqslant 1$, for example.

17. $\begin{bmatrix} 1 & 0 & 1 & 0 \\ 1 & 1 & 1 & 1 \\ 1 & 0 & 1 & 0 \\ 1 & 1 & 1 & 1 \end{bmatrix}$

19. $k = 1$: no new pairs.
   $k = 2$: include $(1, 4), (3, 3), (3, 4)$.
   $k = 3$: include $(2, 2), (4, 2), (4, 4)$.
   $k = 4$: include $(2, 1), (3, 1)$.
   $k = 5$: no new pairs.

21. $k = 1$: include $(2, 2), (3, 3), (4, 4), (5, 5)$.
   $k = 2$: include $(1, 1)$.
   Now $R = A \times A$, so no new pairs will be included.

23. Same as 13.

25. Both are $\begin{bmatrix} 1 & 0 & 1 & 1 \\ 0 & 1 & 1 & 1 \\ 1 & 1 & 1 & 0 \\ 1 & 1 & 0 & 1 \end{bmatrix}$

27. In terms of the characteristic matrix, the symmetric closure affects only elements *off* the main diagonal, and the reflexive closure affects only elements *on* the main diagonal. Thus, it does not matter which is done first.

29. Let $R = \{(1, 2)\}$, for example. Then $R^s = \{(1, 2), (2, 1)\}$, so $R^{st} = \{(1, 2), (2, 1), (1, 1), (2, 2)\}$. But $R^t = R$, so $R^{ts} = \{(1, 2), (2, 1)\}$.

31. 3; 4; 7

33. 4; 6; cannot be done; 3

35.

$\otimes$	0	1	2	3
0	0	0	0	0
1	0	1	2	3
2	0	2	0	2
3	0	3	2	0

Z_4

$\otimes$	0	1	2	3	4	5	6
0	0	0	0	0	0	0	0
1	0	1	2	3	4	5	6
2	0	2	4	6	1	3	5
3	0	3	6	2	5	1	4
4	0	4	1	5	2	6	3
5	0	5	3	1	6	4	2
6	0	6	5	4	3	2	1

Z_7

$\otimes$	0	1	2	3	4	5	6	7
0	0	0	0	0	0	0	0	0
1	0	1	2	3	4	5	6	7
2	0	2	4	6	0	2	4	6
3	0	3	6	1	4	7	2	5
4	0	4	0	4	0	4	0	4
5	0	5	2	7	4	1	6	3
6	0	6	4	2	0	6	4	2
7	0	7	6	5	4	3	2	1

Z_8

37. Recall from algebra that $a^k - b^k = (a - b)(a^{k-1} + a^{k-2}b + \cdots + ab^{k-2} + b^{k-1})$. If $a \equiv b \pmod{n}$, then $b - a$ is divisible by n. If $b - a$ is divisible by n, then so is $a^k - b^k$, so $a^k \equiv b^k \pmod{n}$.

39. a. $0 \mid m$ means $m = 0 \cdot n$ for some number n, so m itself must be 0.
   b. If $a \equiv b \pmod 0$, then $0 \mid a - b$, so $a - b = 0$, so $a = b$.

41. "English name has same number of letters as."

43. $(n - 1) + (n - 2) + \cdots + 3 + 2 + 1 = \dfrac{(n-1)n}{2}$

Section 6.2, page 263

1. poset   **3.** poset   **5.** poset

7. In a linear poset each pair of elements is comparable. In the set $\{a, b\}$ suppose $a \leqslant b$. Then $\operatorname{lub}\{a, b\} = b$ and $\operatorname{glb}\{a, b\} = a$.

9. $\{\{1\}, \{1, 2\}, \{1, 2, 3\}, \ldots, \{1, 2, 3, \ldots, n\}, \ldots\}$

11. Suppose $g = \operatorname{glb} B$ and $h = \operatorname{glb} B$. Then $h \leqslant g$ since h and g are lower bounds and g is the greatest lower bound. Also, $g \leqslant h$ since g and h are lower bounds and h is the greatest lower bound. Then by antisymmetry $g = h$.

13. Suppose $a \leqslant b$. Then a is a lower bound of $\{a, b\}$; in fact, it is the greatest lower bound. Thus, $a \wedge b = a$. Suppose $a \wedge b = a$. Then the greatest lower bound of $\{a, b\}$ is a. Thus, $a \leqslant a$ and $a \leqslant b$.

15.

17.

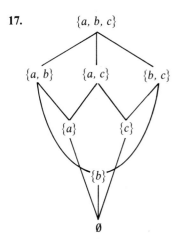

19. $a \wedge a = a$ since clearly $a \leqslant a$ and there is no other element b such that $b \leqslant a$ and $a \leqslant b$.

$a \vee a = a$ since clearly $a \leqslant a$ and there is no other element b such that $a \leqslant b$ and $b \leqslant a$.

Suppose $a \wedge b = c$. Then $c \leqslant a$, $c \leqslant b$, and if $d \leqslant a$ and $d \leqslant b$, then $d \leqslant c$. Thus, $c \leqslant b$, $c \leqslant a$, and if $d \leqslant b$ and $d \leqslant a$, then $d \leqslant c$. That is, $c = b \wedge a$.

Suppose $a \vee b = c$. Then $a \leqslant c$, $b \leqslant c$, and if $a \leqslant d$ and $b \leqslant d$, then $c \leqslant d$. Thus, $b \leqslant c$, $a \leqslant c$, and if $b \leqslant d$ and $a \leqslant d$, then $c \leqslant d$. That is, $c = b \vee a$.

21. First, consider the absorption law $a \wedge (a \vee b) = a$. That is, $\mathrm{glb}(a, \mathrm{lub}(a, b)) = a$. To prove this, let $c = \mathrm{lub}(a, b)$. Then $a \leqslant c$, $b \leqslant c$. Now a is a lower bound of a and c, since $a \leqslant a$ and $a \leqslant c$. Suppose d is also a lower bound. Then $d \leqslant a$ and $d \leqslant c$. In particular, $d \leqslant a$, so a is the greatest lower bound.

Now consider the absorption law $a \vee (a \wedge b) = a$. That is, $\mathrm{lub}(a, \mathrm{glb}(a, b)) = a$. Again $a \leqslant a$ and $\mathrm{glb}(a, b) \leqslant a$. Any other upper bound of a and $\mathrm{glb}(a, b)$ is necessarily larger than a, so a is the least upper bound.

23. To show that $(a \vee b)' = a' \wedge b'$, we need to verify that $a' \wedge b'$ is the complement of $a \vee b$. Thus, we must check that

$$(a \vee b) \wedge (a' \wedge b') = 0$$

and

$$(a \vee b) \vee (a' \wedge b') = 1$$

$(a \vee b) \wedge (a' \wedge b')$
$= [(a \vee b) \wedge a'] \wedge b'$ (associativity)
$= [(a \wedge a') \vee (a' \wedge b)] \wedge b'$ (distributivity)
$= [0 \vee (a' \wedge b)] \wedge b'$ (complement)
$= (a' \wedge b) \wedge b'$ (identity)
$= a' \wedge (b \wedge b')$ (associativity)
$= a' \wedge 0$
$= 0$

$(a \vee b) \vee (a' \wedge b') = [(a \vee b) \vee a'] \wedge [(a \vee b) \vee b']$
$= [(a \vee a') \vee b] \wedge [a \vee (b \vee b')]$
$= (1 \vee b) \wedge (a \vee 1)$
$= 1 \wedge 1$
$= 1$

The other DeMorgan law can be proved in exactly the same way. Or it can be obtained from the first one as follows:

$$(a \wedge b)' = (a'' \wedge b'')'$$
$$= (a' \vee b')''$$
$$= a' \vee b'$$

25.
$$a = a + 0$$
$$= a + aa^*$$
$$= (a + a)(a + a^*)$$
$$= (a + a) \cdot 1$$
$$= a + a$$

$$a = a \cdot 1$$
$$= a(a + a^*)$$
$$= aa + aa^*$$
$$= aa + 0$$
$$= aa$$

27.
$$a + ab = a \cdot 1 + ab$$
$$= a(1 + b)$$
$$= a \cdot 1 \ (\text{Exercise 26})$$
$$= a$$

$$a(a + b) = aa + ab$$
$$= a + ab$$
$$= a$$

29.
$$b = b \cdot 1$$
$$= b(a + a^*)$$
$$= ab + a^*b$$
$$= 0 + a^*b$$
$$= a^*a + a^*b$$
$$= a^*(a + b)$$
$$= a^* \cdot 1$$
$$= a^*$$

31. By Exercise 29 to show $(a + b)^* = a^*b^*$, we need only verify that

$$(a + b) + (a^*b^*) = 1 \text{ and } (a + b)(a^*b^*) = 0$$
$$(a + b) + (a^*b^*) = (a + b + a^*)(a + b + b^*)$$
$$= (1 + b)(1 + a)$$
$$= 1 \cdot 1$$
$$= 1$$

$$(a+b)(a*b*) = (aa*)b + a*bb*$$
$$= 0 \cdot b + 0 \cdot a*$$
$$= 0 + 0$$
$$= 0$$

On the other hand,

$$(ab)* = ((a*)*(b*)*)*$$
$$= (a* + b*)**$$
$$= a* + b*$$

33. By Exercise 32, $(B, \leqslant)$ is a poset. Thus, we need only prove that

$$a + b = \text{lub}\,\{a, b\} \quad \text{and} \quad ab = \text{glb}\,\{a, b\}$$

We first show that $a + b = \text{lub}\,\{a, b\}$.
By Exercise 27, $a(a + b) = a$ and $b(a + b) = b$. Thus, $a \leqslant a + b$ and $b \leqslant a + b$. So $a + b$ is an upper bound for $\{a, b\}$.
Suppose $a \leqslant c$ and $b \leqslant c$. Then $ac = a$ and $bc = b$. Thus, $(a + b)c = ac + bc = a + b$ so $a + b \leqslant c$. Thus, $a + b = \text{lub}\,\{a, b\}$.
We next verify that $ab = \text{glb}\,\{a, b\}$. $ab \leqslant a$ since $aba = aab = ab$. $ab \leqslant b$ since $abb = ab$. Thus, ab is a lower bound of $\{a, b\}$.
Now suppose $c \leqslant a$ and $c \leqslant b$. Then, $ca = c$ and $cb = c$. Thus, $c(ab) = (ca)b = cb = c$. So $c \leqslant ab$ and we are done.

35. $a \vee a* = a + a* = 1$
$a \wedge a* = aa* = 0$
Thus, $a* = a'$.

Section 6.3, page 276

1. $a \circ (b \circ c) = a + (b \circ c) - a(b \circ c)$
$ = a + b + c - bc - a(b + c - bc)$
$ = a + b + c - bc - ab - ac + abc$

$(a \circ b) \circ c = a \circ b + c - (a \circ b)c$
$ = a + b - ab + c - (a + b - ab)c$
$ = a + b + c - ab - ac - bc + abc$

Thus, the operation is associative.

3. $a \circ (b \circ c) = \min(a, \min(b, c)) = \min(a, b, c)$
$(a \circ b) \circ c = \min(\min(a, b), c) = \min(a, b, c)$
Thus, the operation is associative.

5. $a \circ (b \circ c) = \gcd(a, \gcd(b, c)) = \gcd(a, b, c)$
$(a \circ b) \circ c = \gcd(\gcd(a, b), c) = \gcd(a, b, c)$
Thus, the operation is associative.

7. Let a be an element of X.
Then $\{a\} \sim (\varnothing \sim \{a\}) = \{a\} \sim \varnothing = \{a\}$.

$(\{a\} \sim \varnothing) \sim \{a\} = \{a\} \sim \{a\} = \varnothing$
Thus, the operation is not associative.

9. Suppose p, q, and r are all true. Then $(p - q) - r = (p \wedge q') \wedge r'$ is false, but $p - (q - r) = p \wedge (q \wedge r')'$ is true.
Thus, the operation is not associative.

11. If $a \circ e = a$, then $a + e - ae = a$ or $e - ae = 0$ or $e(1 - a) = 0$. Since $a \neq 1$, it follows that the identity is 0.

13. Let e be an identity. Then $e \circ (e + 1) = \min(e, e + 1) = e \neq e + 1$. Thus, the operation has no identity.

15. The identity is 24 since $\gcd(1, 24) = 1$; $\gcd(2, 24) = 2$; $\gcd(4, 24) = 4$; $\gcd(8, 24) = 8$; $\gcd(12, 24) = 12$; and $\gcd(24, 24) = 24$.

17. Suppose E is the identity; then $\varnothing = E \sim E = E$. Thus, the only possible identity is $\varnothing$. The empty set is a "right" identity since $A \sim \varnothing = A$ for any set A. However, if $A \neq \varnothing$, $\varnothing \sim A = \varnothing \neq A$. Thus, there is no identity.

19. We need a proposition e such that $p - e \equiv p \wedge e' \equiv p$ for all propositions p. Thus, $0 \equiv e \wedge e' \equiv e$, so e must be a contradiction. But if e is a contradiction, $p \wedge e \equiv 0$ for all p. It follows that there is no identity.

21. The inverse of a is $a/(a - 1)$ since

$$a \circ (a/(a - 1)) = a + a/(a - 1) - a(a/(a - 1))$$
$$= (a(a - 1) + a - a^2)/(a - 1) = 0$$

Note that $a/(a - 1)$ is defined since $a \neq 1$.

23. Since the operation has no identity, it can have no inverses.

25. The identity is 1, but $\text{lcm}(a, b)$ is at least as large as $\min(a, b)$, so, for example, 2 has no inverse since $\text{lcm}(2, a) \geqslant 2$ for all a.

27. The identity is $\varnothing$. Each set is its own inverse since $A \triangle A = (A - A) \cup (A - A) = \varnothing$ for all A.

29. The identity is $\varnothing$. There can be no inverses (unless $\mathscr{U} = \varnothing$) since if $A \neq \varnothing$, then $A \cup B \neq \varnothing$ for any set B.

31.

$\circ$	a	b
a	a	a
b	a	a

$\circ$	a	b
a	a	a
b	a	b

$\circ$	a	b
a	a	a
b	b	a

$\circ$	a	b
a	a	a
b	b	b

	a	b
a	a	b
b	a	a

	a	b
a	a	b
b	a	b

	a	b
a	a	b
b	b	a

	a	b
a	a	b
b	b	b

	a	b
a	b	a
b	a	a

	a	b
a	b	a
b	a	b

	a	b
a	b	a
b	b	a

	a	b
a	b	a
b	b	b

	a	b
a	b	b
b	a	a

	a	b
a	b	b
b	a	b

	a	b
a	b	b
b	b	a

	a	b
a	b	b
b	b	b

33. n^{n^2}

35. In Exercise 1 you showed that ∘ was associative. In Exercise 11 you found its identity. In Exercise 21 you found that each element had an inverse. The operation is commutative:

$$a \circ b = a + b - ab = b + a - ba = b \circ a$$

The only thing you might have forgotten is closure, especially since in the directions for Exercise 1 we said it was a binary operation. The only reason it would not be closed would be if $a \circ b = 1$ for some a and b. Suppose

$$1 = a \circ b = a + b - ab$$

Then

$$0 = a + b - ab - 1 = (a-1)(b-1)$$

Thus, the only way $a \circ b = 1$ is if $a = 1$ or $b = 1$, which was specifically ruled out.

37. Proceed by induction on n. The formula is trivially true for $n = 1$: $a_1^{-1} = a_1^{-1}$. Suppose the formula is true for $n = k - 1$. Then

$$(a_k a_{k-1} \cdots a_2 a_1)(a_1^{-1} a_2^{-1} \cdots a_k^{-1})$$

is equal to

$$(a_k a_{k-1} \cdots a_2)(a_1 a_1^{-1})(a_2^{-1} \cdots a_k^{-1})$$

is equal to

$$(a_k a_{k-1} \cdots a_2)(a_2^{-1} \cdots a_k^{-1})$$

which equals e by the inductive assumption.

39. For example, $(ht)^{-1} = d^{-1} = d$, but $h^{-1} t^{-1} = hr = f$.

Section 6.4, page 282

1.

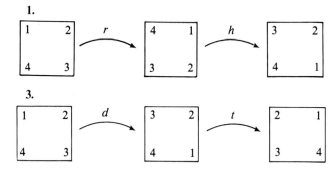

3.

5. $r(1) = 4$, $r(2) = 1$, $r(3) = 2$, $r(4) = 3$

7. $p(1) = 1$, $p(2) = 2$, $p(3) = 4$, $p(4) = 3$, for example. This is not a symmetry of the square since it pins down 1 and 2 but switches 3 and 4.

9. Write $f \circ g$ as fg. Then the table is

	e	f	g	fg	gf	ff
e	e	f	g	fg	gf	ff
f	f	ff	fg	gf	g	e
g	g	gf	e	ff	f	fg
fg	fg	g	f	e	ff	gf
gf	gf	fg	ff	f	e	g
ff	ff	e	gf	g	fg	f

11. Define $f(1) = 2$, $f(2) = 3$, $f(3) = 1$ and $f(k) = k$ for $k > 3$. Define $g(1) = 3$, $g(2) = 2$, $g(3) = 1$ and $g(k) = k$ for $f > 3$. Then $f \circ g(1) = 1$, but $g \circ f(1) = 2$.

13. The rotations form a subgroup. Let $H = \{e, r, s, t\}$. We already know that the composition is associative and that e is the identity. As for closure, it is obvious that the composition of rotations is also a rotation. Explicitly, $r \circ r = s$, $r \circ s = t$, $r \circ t = e$; $s \circ r = t$, $s \circ s = e$, $s \circ t = r$; $t \circ r = e$, $t \circ s = r$, $t \circ t = s$. Thus, H is commutative, as is any four-element group. (H is actually Z_4.) Our calculations also show that $r^{-1} = t$, $s^{-1} = s$, and $t^{-1} = r$.

15. Let e_G and e_H be the respective identities of G and H. First, the binary operation is closed since $*$ and $\circ$ are closed. (e_G, e_H) is the identity. The element (g^{-1}, h^{-1}) is the inverse of (g, h). Associativity is very easy to check, but a bit tedious to write out.

17. $F \times Z_2$ is a group by Exercise 15. It has the eight elements:

$$(e, 0), (a, 0), (b, 0), (c, 0)$$
$$(e, 1), (a, 1), (b, 1), (c, 1)$$

19. In Exercise 36 of Section 6.3 you showed that the set of all subsets of a given set is a commutative group under the operation $\triangle$. Intersection is associative since $A \cap (B \cap C)$ and $(A \cap B) \cap C$ are each the set of elements common to all three of A, B, and C. Intersection is also commutative with identity $\varnothing$. The only ring property left to verify is distributivity:

$$A \cap (B \triangle C) = (A \cap B) \triangle (A \cap C)$$

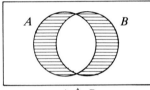

$$A \triangle B$$

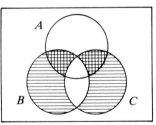

$$A \cap (B \triangle C)$$

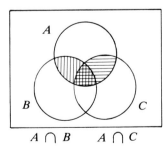

$$A \cap B \qquad A \cap C$$

$$(A \cap B) \triangle (A \cap C)$$

21. In Z_8, $1^{-1} = 1, 3^{-1} = 3, 5^{-1} = 5, 7^{-1} = 7$. In Z_{11}, $1^{-1} = 1$, $2^{-1} = 6, \ 3^{-1} = 4, \ 4^{-1} = 4, \ 5^{-1} = 9, \ 6^{-1} = 2, \ 7^{-1} = 8$, $8^{-1} = 7, 9^{-1} = 5, 10^{-1} = 10$.

23.
$$
\begin{aligned}
x \oplus (y \oplus z) &= x(y \oplus z)^* + x^*(y * z) \\
&= x(yz^* + y^*z)^* + x^*(yz^* + y^*z) \\
&= x[(yz^*)^*(y^*z)^*] + x^*yz^* + x^*y^*z \\
&= x[(y^* + z)(y + z^*)] + x^*yz^* + x^*y^*z \\
&= xy^*z^* + xyz + x^*yz^* + x^*y^*z
\end{aligned}
$$

$$
\begin{aligned}
(x \oplus y) \oplus z &= (x \oplus y)z^* + (x \oplus y)^*z \\
&= (xy^* + x^*y)z^* + (xy^* + x^*y)^*z \\
&= xy^{**}z^* + x^*yz^* + [(xy^*)^*(x^*y)^*]z \\
&= xy^*z^* + x^*yz^* + [(x^* + y)(x + y^*)]z \\
&= xy^*z^* + x^*yz^* + x^*y^*z + xyz
\end{aligned}
$$

That $\otimes$ is associative is Exercise 28 in Section 6.2.

25.
$$x \oplus 0 = (x0^*) + (x^*0) = x \cdot 1 = x$$
$$x \otimes 1 = x \cdot 1 = x$$

Section 6.5, page 296

1.

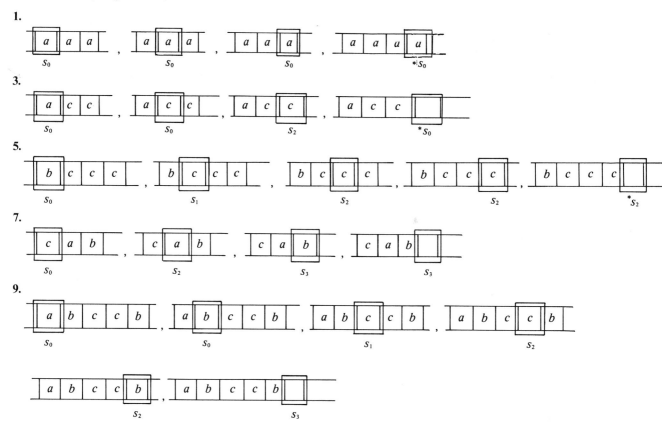

3.

5.

7.

9.

11. All strings that begin do re or re do.

13. All nonempty strings with no consecutive hi or lo.

15. Sam and Janet evening.

17. Begin with p and no other p's or begin with q and no other q's.

19. $(ba)^n, n \geqslant 1$

21.

	0	1
∘*s_0	s_0	s_1
s_1	s_1	s_0

23.

	0	1
∘*s_0	s_0	s_1
s_1	s_1	s_2
s_2	s_2	s_0

25.

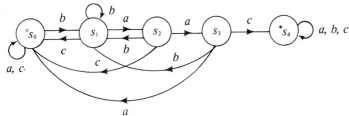

	a	b	c
$\circ s_0$	s_0	s_1	s_0
s_1	s_2	s_1	s_0
s_2	s_3	s_1	s_0
s_3	s_0	s_1	s_4
$*s_4$	s_4	s_4	s_4

27. Any path from an initial state to a terminal state in M will still be there in DM.

29.

RM	a	b
$*s_0$	—	—
$\circ s_1$	$s_1 s_3$	—
s_2	$s_2 s_4$	$s_0 s_4$
$\circ s_3$	s_0	$s_1 s_3$
s_4	—	s_2

DRM		a	b
t_0	$\circ s_1 s_3$	$s_0 s_1 s_3$	$s_1 s_3$
t_1	$s_0 s_1 s_3$	$s_0 s_1 s_3$	$s_1 s_3$

DRM	a	b
$\circ t_0$	t_1	t_0
$*t_1$	t_1	t_0

$RDRM$	a	b
$*t_0$	—	$t_0 t_1$
$\circ t_1$	$t_0 t_1$	—

$DRDRM$		a	b
u_0	$\circ t_1$	$t_0 t_1$	$\varnothing$
u_1	$t_0 t_1$	$t_0 t_1$	$t_0 t_1$
u_2	$\varnothing$	$\varnothing$	$\varnothing$

M'	a	b
$\circ u_0$	u_1	u_2
$*u_1$	u_1	u_1
u_2	u_2	u_2

31.

RM	0	1
$*s_0$	s_3	—
$\circ s_1$	—	$s_0 s_1 s_3$
s_2	$s_0 s_4$	—
$\circ s_3$	—	$s_2 s_4$
s_4	$s_1 s_2 s_5$	—
$\circ s_5$	—	s_5

DRM		0	1
t_0	$\circ s_1 s_3 s_5$	$\varnothing$	S
t_1	$\varnothing$	$\varnothing$	$\varnothing$
t_2	$*S$	S	S

$=$

	0	1
$\circ t_0$	t_1	t_2
t_1	t_1	t_1
$*t_2$	t_2	t_2

$RDRM$	0	1
$*t_0$	—	—
t_1	$t_0 t_1$	t_1
$\circ t_2$	t_2	$t_0 t_2$

$DRDRM$		0	1
u_0	$\circ t_2$	t_2	$t_0 t_2$
u_1	$*t_0 t_2$	t_2	$t_0 t_2$

M'	0	1
$\circ u_0$	u_0	u_1
$*u_1$	u_0	u_1

33.

RM	u	v	w
$*s_0$	—	—	—
s_1	—	—	s_0
$\circ s_2$	—	s_2	$s_1 s_2$
$\circ s_3$	$s_2 s_3$	s_3	s_3
s_4	$s_0 s_1$	—	—
s_5	—	$s_0 s_1 s_5$	s_5
s_6	$s_5 s_6$	s_6	s_6
s_7	$s_4 s_7$	s_4	s_7
$\circ s_8$	—	$s_7 s_8 s_9$	—
s_9	$s_8 s_9$	—	$s_4 s_8 s_9$

DRM	u	v	w
t_0	$\circ s_2 s_3 s_8$	$s_2 s_3$	$s_2 s_3 s_7 s_8 s_9$	$s_1 s_2 s_3$
t_1	$s_2 s_3$	$s_2 s_3$	$s_2 s_3$	$s_1 s_2 s_3$
t_2	$s_2 s_3 s_7 s_8 s_9$	$s_2 s_3 s_4 s_7 s_8 s_9$	$s_2 s_3 s_4 s_7 s_8 s_9$	$s_1 s_2 s_3 s_4 s_7 s_8 s_9$
t_3	$s_1 s_2 s_3$	$s_2 s_3$	$s_2 s_3$	$s_0 s_1 s_2 s_3$
t_4	$s_2 s_3 s_4 s_7 s_8 s_9$	$s_0 s_1 s_2 s_3 s_4 s_7 s_8 s_9$	$s_2 s_3 s_4 s_7 s_8 s_9$	$s_1 s_2 s_3 s_4 s_7 s_8 s_9$
t_5	$s_1 s_2 s_3 s_4 s_7 s_8 s_9$	$s_0 s_1 s_2 s_3 s_4 s_7 s_8 s_9$	$s_2 s_3 s_4 s_7 s_8 s_9$	$s_0 s_1 s_2 s_3 s_4 s_7 s_8 s_9$
t_6	$*s_0 s_1 s_2 s_3$	$s_2 s_3$	$s_2 s_3$	$s_0 s_1 s_2 s_3$
t_7	$*s_0 s_1 s_2 s_3 s_4 s_7 s_8 s_9$	$s_0 s_1 s_2 s_3 s_4 s_7 s_8 s_9$	$s_2 s_3 s_4 s_7 s_8 s_9$	$s_0 s_1 s_2 s_3 s_4 s_7 s_8 s_9$

which equals

DRM	u	v	w
$\circ t_0$	t_1	t_2	t_3
t_1	t_1	t_1	t_3
t_2	t_4	t_4	t_5
t_3	t_1	t_1	t_6
t_4	t_7	t_4	t_5
t_5	t_7	t_4	t_7
$*t_6$	t_1	t_1	t_6
$*t_7$	t_7	t_4	t_7

RDRM	u	v	w
$*t_0$	—	—	—
t_1	$t_0 t_1 t_3 t_6$	$t_1 t_3 t_6$	—
t_2	—	t_0	—
t_3	—	—	$t_0 t_1$
t_4	t_2	$t_2 t_4 t_5 t_7$	—
t_5	—	—	$t_2 t_4$
$\circ t_6$	—	—	$t_3 t_6$
$\circ t_7$	$t_4 t_5 t_7$	—	$t_5 t_7$

that is,

M'	u	v	w
$\circ u_0$	u_1	u_2	u_3
u_1	u_4	u_4	u_4
u_2	u_2	u_2	u_2
u_3	u_1	u_2	u_5
u_4	u_4	u_6	u_4
u_5	u_5	u_5	u_5
$*u_6$	u_4	u_6	u_4

35. Replace each $*s_{1i}$ by $\circ s_{20}$.

37. ((

39. Changes every letter of a string.

41. Writes a in front of the string and b in back.

43.

	p	q	$\#$
$\circ s_0$	$s_0 L$	$s_0 L$	$s_1 L$
s_1	$s_2 \# R$	$s_3 \# R$	—
s_2	—	—	$s_4 p L$
s_3	—	—	$s_4 q L$
s_4	—	—	$s_1 L$

45. $x = \#$ or any letter except ha or ho.

	x	ha	ho
$\circ s_0$	$s_1 ho L$	$s_1 ho L$	$s_1 L$
s_1	$s_2 ha L$	$s_2 L$	$s_2 ha L$
s_2	$s_3 ho R$	$s_3 ho R$	$s_3 R$
s_3	—	$s_4 R$	$s_4 ha R$
s_4	$s_5 ho L$	$s_5 ho L$	$s_5 L$
s_5	—	$s_5 L$	$s_2 ha L$

It never halts. (But *we* do.)

DRDRM	u	v	w
u_0	$\circ t_6 t_7$	$t_4 t_5 t_7$	$\varnothing$	$t_3 t_5 t_6 t_7$
u_1	$t_4 t_5 t_7$	$t_2 t_4 t_5 t_7$	$t_2 t_4 t_5 t_7$	$t_2 t_4 t_5 t_7$
u_2	$\varnothing$	$\varnothing$	$\varnothing$	$\varnothing$
u_3	$t_3 t_5 t_6 t_7$	$t_4 t_5 t_7$	$\varnothing$	S
u_4	$t_2 t_4 t_5 t_7$	$t_2 t_4 t_5 t_7$	$t_0 t_2 t_4 t_5 t_7$	$t_2 t_4 t_5 t_7$
u_5	S	S	S	S
u_6	$*t_0 t_2 t_4 t_5 t_7$	$t_2 t_4 t_5 t_7$	$t_0 t_2 t_4 t_5 t_7$	$t_2 t_4 t_5 t_7$

Symbol Index*

∗ (accepting state), 288
$+_n$ (addition modulo n), 254
⫐ (AND gate), 79
∧ (and; cap; meet), 80, 260, 6
≐ (approximately equal), 59
$a(x)$ (approximation), 232
← (assignment), 2
$[U|I]$ (augmented matrix), 39
∼ (asymptotic; complement), 69, 21

O (big oh), 69–70
lg (binary logarithm), 58
$\binom{n}{j}$ (binomial coefficient), 52
(blank frame; empty string), 284

∧ (cap; and; meet) 260, 80, 6
× (Cartesian product), 23
$\lceil x \rceil$ (ceiling of x), 58
$c(x)$ (chopping error), 235
∼ (complement; asymptotic) 21, 69
∘ (composition; initial state), 265, 288
≡ (congruent), 253
⊂ (contained in; subset), 20
⊃ (contains; superset), 20
0 (contradiction; least element), 91, 259
◁ (covered by), 260
▷ (covers), 260
∨ (cup; join; or), 260, 6, 80

det A (determinant of A), 75, 174
$|A|$ (determinant of A; number of elements in A), 75
| (divides), 248
a_{ij} (double subscript), 28

E (efficiency), 69
∈ (element of), 18
∅ (empty set), 20
(empty string; blank frame), 284
= (equality of sets), 19
[ ] (equivalence class), 255
≡ (equivalent), 89
$e(x)$ (error), 233

! (factorial), 52
$\lfloor x \rfloor$ (floor of x), 58
$f(x)$ (function of x), 24

gcd (greatest common divisor), 260
1 (greatest element; tautology), 257, 91
glb (greatest lower bound), 259

I (identity matrix), 33
⇔ (if and only if), 98
IMCOM (IMaginary COMputer), 2
⇒ (implies), 97
inf (infimum), 259
∞ (infinity), 158
∘ (initial state; composition), 288, 265
Z (integers), 25
Z_n (integers modulo n), 254
∩ (intersection), 20
a^{-1} (inverse of an element), 270
f^{-1} (inverse of a function), 26
A^{-1} (inverse of a matrix), 39

∨ (join; cup; or), 6, 260, 80

$K_{m,n}$ (complete bipartite graph on m and n points), 115

K_n (complete graph on n points), 115

lg (binary logarithm), 58
lcm (least common multiple), 260
≪ (lower order of magnitude), 70
lub (least upper bound), 259
0 (least element; contradiction), 259, 91

$[a_{ij}]$ (matrix), 28
max (maximum), 8
∧ (meet; and; cap), 6, 80, 260
min (minimum), 7
$\times_n$ (multiplication modulo n), 254

⫐∘ NAND gate, 88
$\mathbf{N}$ (natural numbers), 61
$\binom{n}{j}$ (n choose j; binomial coefficient), 52
$x^{[n]}$ (n-fold prime), 93
⫑∘ (NOR gate), 88
▷∘ (NOT gate), 79
a' (not a), 79
∉ (not an element of), 18
$|A|$ (number of elements in A; determinant of A), 75

O (big oh), 69–70
⫐ (OR gate), 80
∨ (or; cup; join), 80, 260, 6
(x, y) (ordered pair), 27
(x, y, z) (ordered triple), 27

Π (product; Petrick proposition), 56, 105

*When a symbol has more than one meaning, the page numbers are listed in the order of the definitions given in parentheses.

$\bar{R}^r$ (reflexive closure), 249
R (relation), 23
$\bar{R}$ (relational closure), 249, 250, 251
$r(x)$ (relative error), 233

$(a_1, ..., a_n)$ (sequence), 7
$\{x:S\}$ (set of all x such that S), 18
sgn (sign of a permutation), 75

$\subset$ (subset; contained in), 20
$\sum$ (sum), 56
$\supset$ (superset; contains), 20
sup (supremum), 259
$\leftrightarrow$ (switch), 10
$\bar{R}^s$ (symmetric closure), 250
$\triangle$ (symmetric difference), 276
$S(A)$ (symmetric group on A), 279
S_n (symmetric group of degree n), 279

1 (tautology; greatest element), 91, 257
$\bar{R}^t$ (transitive closure), 251

$\cup$ (union), 20
$\mathcal{U}$ (universc), 21

$\times$ (Cartesian product), 23

Z (*Zahlen* = integers), 25
$\mathbf{Z}_n$ (integers modulo n), 254

Subject Index

Abel, Niels H. (1802–1829), 275
abelian, 275
absorption law of Boolean algebra, 91
accept, 288
accepting state, 288
addition
  of matrices, 29
  modulo n, 254
  nonassociativity of, 231–232
  principle of, 47
  relative error in, 238
address
  in an array, 7
  of a cell, 16
  in a planar array, 16
adjacency matrix, 113
algebra
  Boolean, 90–99, 262
  origin of word, 2
algebraic expressions and trees,
    128–129
ALGOL (computer language), 3
algorithm (whole book)
  defined, 2
  efficiency of, 68, Section 2.4
  origin of word, 2
Algorithms. *See also* Programs
  Bubblesort, 11
  To color a graph, 202
  For consensus expansion of a
    proposition, 102
  Dijkstra's Algorithm for minimal
    path, 159
  To draw a graph in the plane, 192
  Gauss-Jordan reduction, 37
  To find the inverse of a matrix, 39
  Kruskal's Algorithm for minimal
    spanning tree, 172
  For maximal flow through a

    network (outline), 209
  For minimal
    forms from the consensus
      expansion, 105
    forms of a proposition, 107–108
    weight circuit, 161
    weight path, 159
    weight rooted tree, 131
    weight spanning tree, 172, 180
  Planarity algorithm, 192
  Prim's Algorithm for minimal
    spanning tree, 180
  Selection sort, 11
  To solve a recurrence, 64
  vertex labeling
    for coloring, 201–202
    for flows (outline), 211
  To write a Boolean expression in
    short disjunctive form, 94
  To write the disjunctive form for a
    circuit, 85
Algoritmi (fl. 825), 2
alphabet, 284
alternating group, 75
ancestor, 126
AND gate, 79
antisymmetry law, 258
Appel, Kenneth, 200
approximation, 232
arc, 119
arithmetic, matrix, 29–43
array
  linear, 7
  planar, 15–16
  two-column, 13–15
  two-dimensional, 15–16
The Art of Computer Programming, 17
assignment instruction, 3
associative

binary operation, 266
  general law, 268
  law, 91
    false for computers, 231
asymptotic expressions, 69
attachment, vertices of, 191
augmented matrix, 35
automaton
  deterministic, 285
  nondeterministic, 290
average-case efficiency, 68

back substitution, 72
base sixteen notation, 6–7
BASIC (computer language), 2
Batcher, K. E., 17
Batcher's parallel sorting method,
    17–18
best-case efficiency, 68
bijection, 26
binary
  logarithm, 58–59
  notation, 4–5
  numbers
    join, 6
    meet, 6
  operation, 264
    associative, 266
  relation, 248
  tree, 126
    weighted, 130
Binet, J. P. M., 64
  formula of, 64
binomial, 54
binomial theorem, 54–55
bipartite graph, 117
bit string, 54
Bondy, J. A., 188
Boole, George (1815–1864), 90

Boolean algebra, 90–99, 262
bound
    greatest lower, 259
    law of Boolean algebra, 91
    least upper, 259
    lower, 259
    upper, 258
Boyer, Carl B. (1906–   ), 62
breadth-first search, 136–137
bridge, 190
Brown, J. Randall, 201
bubblesort, 11, 74

cancellation law in groups, 272
Cantor, Georg (1845–1918), 46
cap, 260
capacity, cut, 219
Carroll, Lewis (1832–1898), 21
Cartesian product, 23
Cayley, Arthur (1821–1895), 178
Cayley's formula, 178
ceiling of a number, 58
characteristic
    equation of a recurrence relation, 63
    matrix, 248
    roots, 63
child, 126
chopping error, 235
circle of implications, 124
circuits
    in a graph, 116
    simple, 116, 123
    switching, 78, Section 3.1
class, equivalence, 255
clearing a column, 34
closed path, 116
closure
    reflexive, 249
    symmetric, 250
    transitive, 251
codes, Gray, 152–155
collection of sets, 19
coloring, graph, Section 5.2
column, clearing, 34
column, matrix, 29
combination, 52
combinatorics, Chapter 2
    definition, 46
commutative
    group, 275

law of Boolean algebra, 91
comparable, 258
complement
    of a graph, 189
    in a lattice, 262
    law of Boolean algebra, 91
    of a set, 21
complemented lattice, 262
complete
    bipartite graph on m and n points, 115
    graph on n vertices, 114
    induction, 60
composition, 265
computer program, 2
concatenate, 299
condition, initial, 62
conditional instruction, 3
congruence modulo n, 253
conjunction, 83
    gate, 79
connection, multiple, 111
connected (pseudo)graph, 116
consensus, 100
    expansion and selection, 100–108
    law of Boolean algebra, 100
    literal, 101
    term, 101
contained
    in, 20
    strongly, 297
    weakly, 297
contains, 20
contradiction, 96
contraposition law of Boolean
        algebra, 98
contrapositive, 25
correspondence, one-to-one, 26
counterexample, 25
counting with trees, 126–128
covers, 260
cup, 260
cut, 219
cut, capacity, 219

d.f. (disjunctive form), 85–88
data structure, 7
decimal notation, 3
decomposition, prime, 60
degree, 279

degree of a vertex, 118
derangement, 52–53
DeMorgan, Augustus, (1806–1871), 92, 199
DeMorgan's law of Boolean algebra, 92
Demoucron, G., 188
depth-first search, 135–136
Descartes, Réne (1596–1650), 23
descendants, 126
determinant, 75, 173–175
deterministic automation, 285
determinization, 291
diagonal, main, 33
diagram
    Hasse, 261
    wiring, 83
difference, symmetric, 276
digit, 4
digraph, 119, 288
    of a machine, 288
Dijkstra's algorithm, 159
dimension of a matrix, 28
disjunction, 83
    gate, 80
disjunctive form, 85–88
    short, 94
distributive
    lattice, 261
    law, 280
    law of Boolean algebra, 91
divides, 248
division
    modulo n, 257
    principle of, 51
    relative error in, 238
divisor, proper, 250
Dodgson, Charles L. (1832–1898), 21
domain, 24
Dorn, William S., 228
double subscript notation, 28
dual, 92
duality, principle of, 92

edge, 110
    incident, 111
efficiency, 68, Section 2.4
elementary row operations, 33–34
element (of a set), 18
elimination, Gaussian, 71–72

empty
    set, 20
    string, 284
equality of matrices, 28
equations
    characteristic, 63
    system of linear, 35–38
equivalence
    class, 255
        connection with partitions, 255
    relation, 253
equivalent
    logically, 25
    propositions, 89
error, 232–233
    chopping, 235
    propagation, Section 5.4
    relative, 233
essential term, 105
Euler, Leonhard (1707–1783), 21, 144
Euler's
    formula, 186
    theorem, 147
Eulerian
    graph, 144
    path, 144
    pseudograph, 144
exclusive or, 81, 88
expansion
    of a binomial, 54–55
    consensus, 100–108
    of a determinant, 75

face, 186
factorial, 52
family of sets, 19
Fibonacci (circa 1180–1250), 62
    sequence, 62
field, 281
final state, 287
finite
    sequence, 7
    set, 18
    state machine, 285
floor of a number, 58
Flores, B. See Roberts, S. M.
flow through a network, 208
Ford, L. R. (1886–   ), 206
Ford-Fulkerson labeling method, 211,
        Section 5.3

form
    disjunctive, 85–88
    minimal, 99, Section 3.4
    short disjunctive, 94
four-color problem, 199–200
four-group, 274
frame, 284
Fulkerson, D. R. (1927–   ), 206. See
        also Ford, L. R.
function, 24–27
    bijection, 26
    composition, 265
    domain, 24
    identity, 26
    image, 24
    injective, 25
    inverse, 26
    isomorphism, 273–274
    next state, 285
    one-to-one, 25, 273
    onto, 24
    range, 24
    relabeling, 273
    surjective, 24
    value, 24

gas, water, light problem, 185
gate, 78
    AND, 79
    conjunction, 79
    disjunction, 80
    exclusive OR, 88
    inclusive OR, 81
    inversion, 79
    NAND, 88
    NOR, 88
    NOT, 79
    OR, 80
        exclusive, 88
        inclusive, 81
Gauss, Carl (1777–1855), 36, 71
Gaussian elimination, 71–72
    efficiency of, 73
Gauss-Jordan reduction, 36–43
    efficiency of, 71
general
    associative law, 268
    recurrence relation, 62
Genoa, Giovanni di (fl. 1286), 17
graph. See also Pseudograph, 110
    bipartite, 117

coloring, Section 5.2
complete bipartite on m and n
        points, 115
complete on n vertices, 114
component, 117
connected, 116
definition, 110
importance of, 110
process, 129, 228
pseudo, 110
Gray codes, 152–154
greatest
    element, 259
    integer, 58
    lower bound, 259
group
    abelian, 275
    alternating, 75
    commutative, 275
    cancellation law, 272
    definition, 270–271
    four-group, 274
    isomorphic, 274
    Klein's 4-group, 274
    nonabelian, 275
    symmetric, 75, 279
        of degree n, 279
    theory, 271–272
    trivial, 273
Guthrie
    Francis (c. 1850), 199
    Frederick (c. 1850), 199

Haken, Wolfgang, 200
halt, 285
Hamilton, William Rowan
        (1805–1865), 144
Hamiltonian
    path, 145
    pseudograph, 145
Harris, T. E., 206
Hasse, Helmut (1898–   ), 261
Hasse diagram, 261
hatcheck problem, 52
height of a vertex, 126
hexidecimal notation, 6
Hodges, Andrew, 294
Horner, William George (1786–1837),
        328
Horner's Rule, 328
Huffman codes, 129–134

hypercube, 154

idempotent law of Boolean algebra, 91
identity
　element, 268
　function, 26
　matrix, 33, 122
　ring, 280
if and only if, 98
image
　of an element, 24
　of a function, 24
IMCOM (IMaginary COMputer)
　defined, 2
　program, 3
implicant, 98
implication(s), 97
　circle of, 124
in-order traversal, 139–140
incidence matrix, 111
incident, 111
inclusion-exclusion, 49
inclusive or, 81
inconsistent, 38
index of summation, 56
induction, mathematical, 55–61
　complete, 60
　definition, 55
　strong, 60
　weak, 60
inductive step, 55
inequality, triangle, 235, 245
infinity, 158
initial
　condition, 62
　state, 285
　vertex, 119, 190
injection, 25
instruction, 3
　assignment, 3
　conditional, 3
INT, 58
integers modulo n, 254
intersection (of sets), 20
inverse
　element, 270
　function, 26
　matrix, 39
　ring, 280
inversion gate, 79

involution law of Boolean algebra, 91
isolated vertex, 113
isomorphism, 273–274
isomorphic, 274

Johnson, Samuel (1709–1784), 206
join (of binary numbers), 6
Jordan, Wilhelm (1842–1899), 36

Karnaugh maps, 100
Kirchhoff, G. B. (1824–1887), 173
Kirchhoff's laws, 173
Klein, Felix (1849–1925), 274
Klein's 4-group, 274
$K_{m,n}$ (complete bipartite graph on m
　　and n points), 116
　nonplanarity of $K_{3,3}$, 188, 196–197
K_n (complete graph on n vertices), 115
　nonplanarity of K_5, 188
Knuth, Donald, 17
Königsberg bridge problem, 144
Kruskal's algorithm for minimal
　　spanning tree, 172
Kuratowski, Kasimir (1896–　　　),
　　188
　Theorem, 188

labeling
　graph, 201–202
　method, 211, Section 5.3
　a process graph, 238–239
language, 288
lattice, 260–263
　complemented, 262
　distributive, 261
law
　cancellation, 272
　distributive, 280
laws of Boolean algebra
　absorption, 91
　associative, 91
　bound, 91
　commutative, 91
　complement, 91
　consensus, 100
　contraposition, 98
　DeMorgan's, 92
　distributive, 91
　idempotent, 91
　involution, 91

transitivity of implication, 99
laws for posets
　antisymmetry, 258
　comparability, 258
　reflexive, 258
　transitive, 258
　trichotomy, 258
Laws of Thought, 263
least
　element, 259
　upper bound, 259
leaves, 126
length
　of a path, 116
　of a string, 284
Leonardo of Pisa (circa 1180–1250),
　　62
letters, 284
lexicographic order, 17
linear
　array, 7
　homogeneous constant-coefficient
　　recurrence relation, 63
　order, 258
　poset, 258
　system, 35–38
linked list, 13–15
literal, 83
　consensus, 101
load a tape, 285
logarithm, binary, 58–59
logically equivalent, 25
loop, 111
lower
　bound, 259
　　greatest, 259
　triangular matrix, 174

McCracken, Daniel D., 228
machine, 284, Section 6.5
　digraph representation, 288
　finite state, 285
　Turing, 294–296
magnitude, order of, 69–70
main diagonal, 33, 249
Malgrange, Y., 188
mathematical induction, 55–61
　complete, 60
　definition, 55
　strong, 60

weak, 60
matrix (plural: matrices), 28–43
  addition, 29
  adjacency, 113
  arithmetic, 29–43
  augmented, 35
  characteristic, 248
  clearing a column, 34
  column, 29
  definition, 28
  dimension, 28
  equality, 28
  identity, 33, 122
  incidence, 111
  inversion, 39–43
  lower triangular, 174
  main diagonal, 33, 249
  multiplication, 30–33
  multiplication by a number, 29
  row, 29
  row operations, 33–34
  size, 28
  square, 33
  subtraction, 29
  symmetric, 113
  of a system, 35
  transpose, 75
  triangular form, 71
  upper triangular, 173–174
max, 8
maximum, 8
meet (of binary numbers), 6
MERGE, 66
MERGESORT, 65–67, 74
microsecond, 70
min, 7
minimal
  form, 99, Section 3.4
  pairing problem, 161
  weight spanning tree, 171–173
minimum, 7
minterm, 103
  expansion, 103
modulo n, 253
  addition, 254
  division, 257
  integers, 254
  multiplication, 254
monoid, 269
multiple

connection, 111
  sink, 221
  source, 221
multiplication
  of matrices, 30–33
  of a matrix by a number, 29
  modulo n, 254
  nonassociativity of, 231–232
  principle of, 50
  relative error in, 238
Murty, U.S.R., 188

n-cube, 153
NAND gate, 88
natural numbers, 46
negation, 83
network, 206
von Neumann, John (1903–1957), ix
next-action table, 294
next-state
  function, 285
  table, 285–286
nonabelian group, 275
nondeterministic automaton, 290
NOR gate, 88
NOT gate, 79
notation
  base sixteen (hexidecimal), 6–7
  binary, 4
  decimal, 4
  hexidecimal, 6–7
  octal, 6
  Polish, 89
  product, 55–56
  reverse Polish, 89
  scientific, 231
  summation, 55–56
  ternary, 6
numbers
  natural, 46
  prime, 60
  rational, 46
  real, 46
O (big oh), 69–70
octal notation, 6
one-to-one, 25, 273
one-to-one correspondence, 26
onto, 24
operation
  associative, 266

binary, 264
OR gate, 80
order
  lexicographic, 17
  linear, 258
  of magnitude, 69
ordered
  pair, 27
  triple, 27

pair, ordered, 27
parallel sorting, 17–18
parent, 125
parentheses checking, 293–294
parity checker, 297
partially ordered set. See Poset
partition, 255
  connection with equivalence
    relations, 255
PASCAL (computer language), 3
path, 115
  circuit, 116
  closed, 116
  length, 116
  simple, 124
permutation, 53, 75, 279
  sign of, 75
Pertuiset, R., 188
Petrick proposition, 105
Pinza, Ezio (1892–1957), 297
place a tape, 285
planar
  array, 15–16
  pseudograph, 184, Section 5.1
pointer, 14–15
Polish notation, 89
poset (partially ordered set), 258–260
  linear, 258
post-order traversal, 140
power, 4
pre-order traversal, 139–140
Prim's algorithm for minimal
    spanning tree, 180
prime
  decomposition, 60
  number, 60
principle of
  addition, 47
  division, 51
  duality, 91

inclusion-exclusion, 49
mathematical induction, 55
multiplication, 50
substitution, 90
subtraction, 47
process graph (tree), 126, 228
 labeling, 238–239
product
 Cartesian, 23
 group, 283
 notation, 55–56
program
 computer, 3
 instruction, 3
 pseudo-, 3
 run, 3
 step, 3
Programs. *See also* Algorithms
 bubblesort, 12
 For circuits in a pseudograph, 168
 To evaluate
  $A = B$, 20
  $A \subset B$, 20
  $b \in \{a_1, \ldots, a_n\}$, 19
 To find
  the address of a new number in a
   given sequence, 13
  min $(a_1, \ldots, a_n)$, 8
  a spanning tree, 170
 graph coloring, 202
 graph labeling, 201–202
 matrix multiplication, 31
 MERGE, 66
 MERGESORT, 65–67, 74
 QUICKSORT, 68
 reflexive closure, 249
 To remove repetitions from a set, 19
 Roberts and Flores for Hamiltonian
  paths and circuits, 149–150
 To switch entries, 10
 For symmetric closure, 250
 For transitive closure, 252
 Warshall's algorithm, 252
 To write n in binary notation, 5
proof, 21
 by induction, 55
 by pictures, 21
 by Venn diagrams, 21–22
propagation of errors, Section 5.4
proper divisor, 250

proposition, 83
 dual, 92
 equivalent, 89
 Petrick, 105
 rewrite, 90
pseudograph. *See also* Graph, 110
 bridge, 190
 complement, 189
 component, 116
 connected, 116
 definition, 110
 directed, 119
  of a relation, 119
 Eulerian, 144
 face, 186
 Hamiltonian, 145
 planar, 184
 sub-, 116
pseudo-program, 3

quadratic formula, 63
quicksort, 68
Quine-McClusky method, 100

range, 24
rational numbers, 46
real numbers, 46
recurrence relations, Section 2.3
 general, 62
 general solution, 64
 initial condition, 62
 linear, 63
recursion, Section 2.3
redundant, 38
reflexive, 248
 closure, 249
 law, 258
relabeling, 273
relation, 23–24, Section 6.1
 antisymmetric, 258
 binary, 248
 directed pseudograph of, 119
 equivalence, 253
 partial order, 258
 reflexive, 248
 symmetric, 249
 transitive, 251
relative
 complement, 21
 error, 233

in arithmetic, 238
 chopping, 235
reverse, 290
reverse Polish notation, 89
rewrite, 90
ring, 280
 identity, 280
Roberts, Fred, 46
Roberts, S. M., and Flores, B.,
 algorithm (1966), 149–150
root of a tree, 125
rooted tree, 125
roots, characteristic, 63
Ross, F. S., 206
rounding, symmetric, 233
row
 matrix, 29
 operations, 33–34
run
 a program, 3
 a tape, 285

s.d.f. (short disjunctive form), 94
scientific notation, 231
searching, 134–140
 breadth-first, 136–137
 depth-first, 135–136
 in-order, 139–140
 post-order, 140
 pre-order, 137–139
selection sort, 11
semigroup, 267
sensor, 284
sentence, 83
sequence
 Fibonacci, 62
 finite, 7
set(s), 18
 Cartesian product, 23
 complement, 21
 empty, 20
 family of, 19
 finite, 18
 intersection, 20
 partially ordered. *See* Poset
 relation, 23–24
 relative complement, 21
 union, 20
set theory, 18–28
sgn, 75

Sheffer stroke, 88
short disjunctive form, 94
sign of a permutation, 75
simple
   circuit, 116, 123
   path, 124
sink, multiple, 221
size of a matrix, 28
solvable, 296
sorting
   Batcher's Method, 17–18
   bubble, 11, 74
   merge, 65–66, 74
   selection, 11
   quick, 68
source, multiple, 221
spanning tree, 167, Section 4.5
   minimal weight, 171–173
   number of, 175, 173–178
square
   matrix, 33
   symmetries of, 279
state, 285
   accepting, 288
   final, 287
   initial, 285
   of a machine, 285
   trap, 288
step
   inductive, 55
   in a program, 3
stored string, 284
string, 54, 284
   empty, 284
   length, 284
   strongly contain, 297
   weakly contain, 297
strong induction, 60
strongly contain, 297
structure, data, 7
subgroup, 283
subpseudograph, 116
   bridge, 190
subset, 20
substitution
   back, 72
   principle of, 90
subtraction
   of matrices, 29
   principle of, 47

relative error in, 238
substring, 297
summation
   index of, 56
   notation, 55–56
superset, 20
surjection, 24
switch, 10, 78
switching circuit, 78, Section 3.1
symmetric
   closure, 250
   difference, 276
   group, 75
      on A, 279
      of degree n, 279
   matrix, 113
   rounding, 233
symmetries
   of the square, 277–279
   of a triangle, 283
system of linear equations, 35–38
   inconsistent, 38
   redundant, 38

table
   next action, 294
   next state, 285–286
tape, 284
tautology, 96
term, 83
   consensus, 101
   essential, 105
   min-, 103
terminal vertex, 119, 126, 190
ternary notation, 6
tesseract, 154
transitive, 251
   closure, 251
   law, 258
transitivity of implication law of
      Boolean algebra, 99
transpose, 75
trap, 288
traversal, 134–140
   breadth-first, 136–137
   depth-first, 135–136
   in-order, 139–140
   post-order, 140
   pre-order, 137–139

tree, Section 4.2
   algebraic expression, 128–129
   binary, 126
   for counting, 126–128
   definition, 123
   Huffman code, 129–134
   rooted, 125
   searching, 134–140
   spanning, 167, Section 4.5
   traversal, 134–140
   weighted, 130
triangle
   inequality, 235, 245
   symmetries of a, 283
triangular
   form, 71
   matrix, 173–174
trichotomy law, 258
triple, ordered, 27
trivial group, 273
truth
   table, 96
   value, 95
Turing, Alan (1912–1954), 294
Turing machine, 294–296
two-column array, 13–15
two-dimensional array, 15–16

union of sets, 20
unit, 280
unit n-cube, 153
$\mathcal{U}$: universe, 21
upper
   bound, 258
      least, 259
   triangular matrix, 173–174

value
   of a function, 24
   truth, 95
variable, 83
Venn, John (1834–1923), 21
Venn diagrams, 21–22
vertex (plural: vertices), 110
   adjacent, 113
   ancestor, 126
   of attachment, 191
   children, 126
   degree, 118

height, 126
incident, 111
initial, 119, 190
isolated, 113
leaves, 126
parent, 125

terminal, 119, 126, 190

Warshall, S., 251
Warshall's algorithm, 252
weak induction, 60

weakly contained, 297
weight, 130
weighted binary tree, 130
wiring diagram, 84
word, 288
worst-case efficiency, 68